Randal Schwartz's Perls of Wisdom

RANDAL L. SCHWARTZ

Apress®

Randal Schwartz's Perls of Wisdom

Copyright © 2005 by Randal L. Schwartz

ISBN (pbk): 1-59059-323-5

Printed and bound in the United States of America 9 8 7 6 5 4 3 2 1

Lead Editor: Chris Mills
Technical Reviewer: Mike Schilli
Editorial Board: Steve Anglin, Dan Appleman, Ewan Buckingham, Gary Cornell, Tony Davis,
    Jason Gilmore, Chris Mills, Dominic Shakeshaft, Jim Sumser
Project Manager: Kylie Johnston
Copy Edit Manager: Nicole LeClerc
Copy Editors: Ami Knox, Nicole LeClerc
Production Manager: Kari Brooks-Copony
Production Editor: Ellie Fountain
Compositor: Dina Quan
Indexer: Kevin Broccoli
Cover Designer: Kurt Krames
Manufacturing Manager: Tom Debolski

Distributed to the book trade in the United States by Springer-Verlag New York, Inc., 233 Spring Street, 6th Floor, New York, NY 10013, and outside the United States by Springer-Verlag GmbH & Co. KG, Tiergartenstr. 17, 69112 Heidelberg, Germany.

In the United States: phone 1-800-SPRINGER, fax 201-348-4505, e-mail orders@springer-ny.com, or visit http://www.springer-ny.com. Outside the United States: fax +49 6221 345229, e-mail orders@springer.de, or visit http://www.springer.de.

For information on translations, please contact Apress directly at 2560 Ninth Street, Suite 219, Berkeley, CA 94710. Phone 510-549-5930, fax 510-549-5939, e-mail info@apress.com, or visit http://www.apress.com.

The source code for the complete listings contained in this book is available to readers at http://www.apress.com in the Downloads section.

Contents at a Glance

Contents

v

Preface

Over three decades ago, I wrote my first working computer program. It had been my intention (even as a young boy growing up in a suburb of Portland, Oregon) to be a "computer programmer," whatever that meant. Of course, 30 years ago, that meant that I could look forward to working for a bank or a government research group somewhere, but it's still what I wanted to do.

So, in school I studied hard and learned the art and craft of programming, and entered the real world looking for a job. Somewhat serendipitously, my first full-time employment was as a *technical writer*, not a programmer. I summoned my engineering skills, and learned the art and craft of writing for the next four years on the job. The result was rather useful in the marketplace: I was a trained engineer *and* a technical writer, in every sense of the word. Some half-dozen years later, through a typical random outburst on Usenet, I was invited to design and produce the first-ever book on the then-emerging Perl programming language, called *Programming Perl*, affectionately known as "The Camel Book." With Larry Wall (creator of Perl) as a co-author, I was able to gain legitimacy both as a published author *and* as a leader of the Perl community. I parlayed that into an opportunity to create and present a Perl training course, which eventually led to the best-selling *Learning Perl*, and an entire business of developing and presenting on-site and open-enrollment trainings through my fledgling Stonehenge Consulting Services company.

After *Learning Perl*, I was approached to produce a bimonthly column in *Unix Review* magazine. The only suggested topic range was "intermediate Perl," which left me both the burden and the freedom to choose something interesting every other month. I saw the column as an opportunity to get paid and get publicity for what I was doing for free on my longer Usenet articles, and the column was a gradual success. But even before I wrote my first article, I suggested that I would want to publish my articles on the then infant "web," and obtained the rights to do so, as long as I let the magazine have right of first publication. It didn't occur to me at the time, but this was an amazing and as-yet unheard-of promotional win, because I was able to draw traffic to my site over time, promoting both my company and the magazine.

A few months later, the same company producing *Unix Review* had wanted to spin off a web-related magazine, eventually titled *Web Techniques*. I was asked to be in the premiere issue, to which I replied "But I've never even been a webmaster!" With the understanding that we could part friends after a few monthly issues if it didn't work out, I started on a journey that lasted 70 issues, until the magazine itself ended shortly after the dot-com bubble burst.

As if writing a bimonthly column for *Unix Review* and a monthly column for *Web Techniques* wasn't already confusing enough, I was approached by the publishers of the new *Linux Magazine*, again asking if I'd contribute something monthly to their endeavor. I started after their first issue, continuing to this day, writing again about whatever I want, ignoring the editorial schedule as I often do.

My associate, brian d foy, had a column in the newly revived *Perl Journal* at the beginning of 2003, but was called up for active duty, fighting in Iraq as an MP. When he took off, I took over, and produced a series of articles for that magazine, again ensuring that I could reproduce those on my website for cross-promotional purposes. As I write this, I recently yielded that column back to brian, so I'm back to 1.5 articles a month, instead of the grueling 2.5 a month that I faced for many years. All in all, I've written over 200 magazine articles and contributed to a half-dozen best selling books on Perl.

This makes me the world's busiest Perl print author, of which I'm rather proud. Knowing this, Apress approached me about taking the best and most frequently referenced of my already legendary column articles, and turning them into a smart-to-read book. I let them pick the best 70-or-so columns (with a bit of nudging here and there), and insisted that they be published in a manner that was historically accurate. I did this mostly out of self-preservation: you can always rewrite an article, and spend almost as much time in the second pass, but we didn't have that much time in the schedule. However, adjacent to most articles, I've added a note (as appropriate) to indicate my contemporary thoughts about the topic and solution contained within the article. For example, in a few cases a module has appeared on the CPAN, making most of my code redundant except as a learning exercise. In others, I lament not having some module available to me at the time, or some bug fixed that was later corrected. In any case, the columns here all have great learning value, and teach the very best techniques used by the masters in solving Perl problems each and every day, at hundreds of Internet Web sites and thousands of companies and organizations.

I hope you find this collection useful, and fun to read. Enjoy!

—Randal L. Schwartz,
Stonehenge Consulting Services, Inc.,
Portland, Oregon

■ ■ ■

## CHAPTER 1

Advanced Perl Tutorials

It's All About Context

Unix Review, Column 38 (June 2001)

■**Randal's Note** I really enjoyed writing the following article as a way of sneaking in a crossover between the two ways in which large numbers of people know me, as a Perl trainer and author, and as a convicted felon for a controversial criminal case. Most of the inspiration comes from the material we teach in Stonehenge's "llama" class.

Just recently, an article on the Slashdot site (`www.slashdot.org`) discussed the surprising story of a high-school student who had made a small Perl programming mistake that got him into a big amount of trouble. On his dynamically generated web page, he had used the code

```
my($f) = `fortune`;
```

when what he should have done was

```
my $f = `fortune`;
```

Now, both of these invoke the `fortune` program, capturing its random quip of text. In this particular case, when the school administrators had visited the boy's page, `fortune` had selected a quote from a William Gibson novel:

```
I put the shotgun in an Adidas bag and padded it out with four pairs of tennis
socks, not my style at all, but that was what I was aiming for:  If they think
you're crude, go technical; if they think you're technical, go crude.  I'm a
very technical boy.  So I decided to get as crude as possible.  These days,
though, you have to be pretty technical before you can even aspire to
crudeness.
- Johnny Mnemonic, by William Gibson
```

Now, if you can't tell what would be in $f for both of the preceding code fragments, read on, and you'll see how an unwitting mistake can leave someone with an unexpected police file.

The problem is a matter of context (in more ways than one). Perl's operators are "context sensitive," in that the operator can detect whether it is being used in a place looking for a scalar rather than looking for a list, and return an appropriate result. In this case, the backtick operator returns a differing result, depending on whether it was invoked in a scalar context or a list context.

To understand this, let's first look at how to detect context. Starting with the basics, the right-hand side of an assignment to a scalar variable must be a scalar value:

```
$a = ...
```

Whatever's over there on the right, it's got to be a scalar value, because that's the only thing that'll fit into a scalar variable. Similarly, the right side of an assignment to an array can be any list value:

```
@b = ...
```

Let's put some things in both places and see how it differs. One that you are almost certainly familiar with is the readline operator, spelled "less-than filehandle greater-than":

```
$a = <STDIN>
```

In this "scalar context," the readline operator returns the next line to be read, or undef if an I/O error occurs (such as at end-of-file).

However, the very same operator and punctuation in a "list context" yields all the remaining lines until end-of-file is reached, or an empty list if already at end of file:

```
@b = <STDIN>
```

Now, Larry Wall could have come up with two different operators for these two similar operations, but by making the operator "context sensitive," we get the savings of brainspace and keyboardspace. Apparently, we humans are fairly good at grokking context, so why not leverage off that a bit in the language?

Similarly, the matching operator in a scalar context returns a success value:

```
$a = /(\w+) (\d+)/
```

which is true if the regular expression matches $_ and false otherwise. If the result was true, we'd look in $1 for the word, and $2 for the digit string. A shorter way to do the same thing though is to use the same regular expression in a list context:

```
@b = /(\w+) (\d+)/
```

And now, the regular expression match operator is not returning true/false, but rather a list of two items (the two memories) or an empty list if the match was not successful. So $b[0] ends up with the word, and $b[1] gets the digit string.

In both of these operators, the scalar interpretation and the list interpretation are related, but not by any predictable formula. That's the way it is in general. You can't apply a general rule, except that there are no rules. It's whatever Larry thought would be the most practical and useful, and least surprising (well, least surprising to Larry).

A few more examples to keep getting our feet progressively more wet, and then we'll look some more at detecting context.

In a scalar context, gmtime returns a human-readable string of the GMT time (defaulting to the current time, but optionally converting any Unix-epoch integer timestamp). But in a list context, a nine-element list contains the various second, minute, hour (and so on) pieces of the time for easy manipulation.

The readdir operator acts similarly to the readline operator, returning the "next" name from a directory in a scalar context, but all the remaining names in a list context.

And finally, a very common operation is to use the name of an array in both contexts. The "operator" of @x in a list context yields the current elements of the @x array. However, in a scalar context, the same "operator" yields the *number* of elements in that same array (sometimes called the "length of the array," but that can be confusing, so I'd rather not use that here).

Please note on that last example that at no time does Perl first extract all the elements in the scalar context, only to then somehow "convert" it to a count. From the very beginning, Perl knows that the @x operation is in a scalar context and performs the "scalar" version of that operation.

Put another way, there is no way to "coerce" or "convert" a list to a scalar, because *it can never happen*, in spite of what some of the so-called commercial Perl documentation incorrectly implies.

So, where does context occur? Everywhere! Let's introduce a convention for a moment, to make it easy to talk. If a portion of the expression is evaluated in scalar context, let's use SCALAR to represent that:

```
$a = SCALAR;
```

And similarly, we'll show list context with LIST:

```
@x = LIST;
```

So, let's look at some other common ones. Assigning to the element of an array looks like this:

```
$w[SCALAR] = SCALAR;
```

Note that the subscripting expression is evaluated in a scalar context. That means if we had an array name on the left, and a readline operation on the right, we'll use scalar meanings for both:

```
$w[@x] = <STDIN>;
```

and assign a single line (or undef) to the element of @w indexed by the *number* of elements currently in @x. As an aside, that's always evaluated before the assignment starts to happen, so

```
$w[@w] = <STDIN>;
```

adds the next line to the end of @w, although you'll probably scare people doing that. Slices are in list context, even with only a single value for an index:

```
@w[LIST] = LIST;
@w[3] = LIST;
```

Even hash slices work that way:

```
@h{LIST} = LIST;
```

Lists of scalars are always lists, even with only a single value (or no values) on the left:

```
($a, $b, $c) = LIST;
($a) = LIST;
() = LIST;
```

And then we have the context provided by some common operations:

```
foreach (LIST) { ... }
if (SCALAR) { ... }
while (SCALAR) { ... }
@w = map { LIST } LIST;
@x = grep { SCALAR } LIST;
```

One useful rule is that anything being evaluated for a true/false value is always a scalar, as shown in the if, while, and grep items previously.

Subroutines act "at a distance." The return value of a subroutine is always evaluated in the context of the invocation of the subroutine. Here's the basic form:

```
$a = &fred(LIST); sub fred { ....; return SCALAR; }
@b = &barney(LIST); sub barney { ....; return LIST; }
```

But what if I had used fred for both of those? Yes, the context would pass through, and be different for different invocations! If that makes your head spin, try not to do that for a while until you fully understand it.

Speaking of subroutines: a common thing to do is to create a lexical variable (often called a my variable) to hold incoming subroutine arguments or temporary values, as in

```
sub marine {
  my ($a) = @_;
  ...
}
```

In this case, if the parentheses are included, we get list context (imagine the my is not there). The many elements of @_ get returned, but only the first of which is stored into $a (the remainder are ignored).

However, the same expression without parentheses provides scalar context to the right side:

```
my $a = @_;
```

which gets the *number of elements* in $@ (the argument list). There's not one that's "more right"; you need to learn the difference, and use the appropriate one.

And that brings us full circle to the question I posted at the beginning. What *is* the difference? Backquotes in a scalar context generate the entire value as one string:

```
my $f = `fortune`;
```

but the same expression in a list context generates a list of items (one line per item, just like reading from a file), only the first of which can fit into the scalar on the left:

```
my ($f) = `fortune`;
```

So $f gets just the first line of the fortune, harmless for those one-liners, but pretty devastating when a school official sees that a student has apparently written

```
I put the shotgun in an Adidas bag
and padded it out with four pairs of tennis
```

on this schoolboy's page, in light of the tragic schoolyard shootings we seem to be hearing more about these days. Nevermind that a simple reload of the page had shown something different each time, or that this is really just a random quote.

The police were called, the boy was questioned, and now has a police file simply because he added some erroneous parentheses. No charges resulted, but the embarrassment here is certainly unwelcome. (I say this from personal experience: my own ongoing saga about misplaced understandings and resulting criminal charges can be found at the archive located at www.lightlink.com/fors/.)

And the embarrassment was also avoidable with a little more care in programming and quality-assurance testing. So when you hack Perl, and you wonder about context, get the text right or you may end up a con. Until next time, enjoy!

Subroutines

Unix Review, Column 5 (November 1995)

Like most algorithmic languages, Perl provides a mechanism to place portions of the code into a "subroutine." Subroutines can be used to provide easy reuse of algorithms, especially when someone else has written the code. Subroutines can also make it easier to follow the logic of a program, because the details of a subroutine are hidden away from its use. In this column, I'm going to talk about the basics of subroutine invocation and linkage, from parameters to recursion.

Let's take a simple problem. You have a bunch of numbers in @data, and you want to know the sum total of those numbers. You could write code that looks like this:

```
... code ...
$sum = 0;
foreach (@data) {
        $sum += $_;
}
# now use $sum
```

This initializes the value $sum to zero, and then adds each element of @data into the current value of $sum. We can wrap this up into a subroutine like so:

```
sub sum_data {
        $sum = 0;
        foreach (@data) {
                $sum += $_;
        }
}
```

and when we want to set $sum equal to the current value of @data, simply invoke the subroutine:

```
&sum_data();
```

This works. I can type the code to add @data into $sum once, somewhere in the program (often towards the end), and then reuse the code repeatedly by invoking the subroutine from different places in the main part of the code.

The result is left in the variable $sum. However, every subroutine invocation also returns a value, because technically the invocation is always within some expression. (In this case, the expression's value is thrown away.) This "return value" of a subroutine is whatever expression is evaluated last within the subroutine. As it turns out, the last thing evaluated in this subroutine is always the $sum += $_ line, which will result in the return value being the same as $sum!

So, we can write the subroutine invocation like this:

```
$total = &sum_data();
```

and $total will also be the same value as $sum. Or even

```
$two_total = &sum_data() + &sum_data();
```

which evaluates the sum twice, ending up in $two_total. This is wasteful, of course, and would probably be reduced to

```
$two_total = 2 * &sum_data();
```

in a real program.

If you can't tell that $sum is the return value of &sum_data(), you can also put $sum explicitly as the last expression evaluated like so:

```
sub sum_data {
        $sum = 0;
        foreach (@data) {
                $sum += $_;
        }
        $sum; # return value
}
```

Note that $sum as an expression on its own is enough to make it the last expression evaluated within the subroutine, and therefore the return value of the subroutine.

This subroutine is interesting, but it is limited to computing the sum of values in the @data array. What if we had @data_one and @data_two? We'd have to write a different version of &sum_data() for each array. Well, no, that's not necessary. Just as a subroutine can return back a value, it can also take a list of values as arguments or parameters:

```
$total = &sum_this(@data);
```

In this case, the values of @data are collected up into a new array called @_ within the subroutine like so:

```
sub sum_this {
        $sum = 0;
        foreach (@_) {
```

```
                    $sum += $_;
            }
            $sum;
    }
```

Note that all I've done is change @data to @_, which holds the values of the passed-in parameters. The values passed to the subroutine are constructed from any list. For example, I can also say

```
    $more_total = &sum_this(5,@data);
```

which will prepend 5 to @data, yielding an array in @_ that is one element larger than @data.

The routine &sum_this is pretty useful now. However, what if I'm using the $sum variable in some other part of my program? By default, all variables within a subroutine refer to the global use of those variables, so the &sum_this routine will clobber whatever value was previously in $sum. To fix this, I can (and should) make the $sum variable local to the subroutine:

```
    sub sum_this {
            my $sum = 0;
            foreach (@_) {
                    $sum += $_;
            }
            $sum;
    }
```

Now, for the duration of this routine, the variable $sum refers not to a global $sum, but to a new local variable that is thrown away as soon as the subroutine returns.

If you are not yet up to Perl version 5 (released roughly a year ago, but surprisingly, some have not gotten with the program yet), you can use Perl version 4's construct called local, which performs a similar function:

```
    sub sum_this {
            local($sum) = 0;
            foreach (@_) {
                    $sum += $_;
            }
            $sum;
    }
```

However, had this subroutine (with local instead of my) called another subroutine, any reference in that subroutine to $sum would have accessed this subroutine's $sum, rather than the global $sum, and that can get quite confusing to say the least.

If you had a program with &sum_data, and also added &sum_this, you could rewrite &sum_data in terms of &sum_this like so:

```
    sub sum_data { &sum_this(@data); }
```

I have done this from time to time as I rewrite specific subroutines into general ones.

A subroutine can return a list of values rather than just a single value (a scalar). Let's hack on this subroutine a bit to get it to return all the intermediate sums instead of just the final sum:

```perl
sub sum_this {
        my $sum = 0;
        my @sums;
        for (@_) {
                $sum += $_;
                push(@sums,$sum);
        }
        @sums;
}
```

Now, what's going on here? I'm creating a new array called @sums that will hold the incremental results of adding each new element to the sum. As each sum is calculated, it is pushed onto the end of the list. When the loop is complete, the value of @sums is returned. This means I can call this subroutine like so:

```perl
@result = &sum_this(1,2,3);
print "@result\n"; # prints "1 3 6\n"
```

What happens when I call this subroutine in a scalar context (such as assigning the result to a scalar)? Well, the scalar context gets passed down into the last expression evaluated—in this case, the name of @sums. The name of an array in a scalar context is the number of elements in the array, so we'll get

```perl
$what = &sum_this(1,2,3);
print $what;
```

which will print "3", the number of elements in the return value. With a little bit of trickery, we can combine the two kinds of subroutines into one:

```perl
sub sum_this {
        my $sum = 0;
        my @sums;
        for (@_) {
                $sum += $_;
                push(@sums,$sum);
        }
        if (wantarray) {
                @sums;
        } else {
                $sum;
        }
}
```

In this case, if the subroutine is being invoked in an array context (assigned to an array, for example), the built-in value wantarray is true, and the @sums array is returned. If not, the built-in value wantarray is false, so $sum gets returned instead.

Now, we get results like this:

```
$total = &sum_this(1,2,3); # gets 6
@totals = &sum_this(1,2,3); # gets 1,3,6
```

Obviously, a subroutine designer has a lot of flexibility. If you implement a general-purpose subroutine for others, be sure to consider what it does in a scalar and array context, and if sense, use the wantarray construct to make sure that it returns an appropriate value.

Like most algorithmic languages, Perl supports recursive subroutines. This means that a subroutine can call itself to perform a part of the task. A classic example of this is a subroutine to calculate a Fibonacci number, F(n), defined as follows:

```
F(0) = 0;
F(1) = 1;
F(n) = F(n-1)+F(n-2) for n > 1;
```

Now, this definition can be translated directly into a Perl subroutine as follows:

```
sub F {
        my ($n) = @_;
        if ($n == 0) {
                0;
        } elsif ($n == 1) {
                1;
        } else {
                &F($n - 1) + &F($n - 2);
        }
}
```

This will indeed generate the correct result. However, for a large value of $n, the subroutine will be called repeatedly with the exact same values of numbers smaller than $n. For example, the call to compute F(10) will compute F(9) and F(8). However, the call to compute F(9) will also call F(8) again, and so on.

A quick solution to this is to maintain a cache of the previous return values. Let's call the cache @F_cache, and use it as follows:

```
sub F {
        my ($n) = @_;
        if ($n == 0) {
                0;
        } elsif ($n == 1) {
                1;
        } elsif ($F_cache[$n]) {
                $F_cache[$n];
        } else {
                $F_cache[$n] =
                        &F($n - 1) + &F($n - 2);
        }
}
```

Now, if a number greater than 1 is passed into this function, one of two things can happen: if the number has been computed already, we simply return the computed value; if the number hasn't been computed, we compute the value, and remember it for a possible future invocation. Note that the assignment to @F_cache is also the return value.

I've used this technique on many subroutines that have an expensive value to calculate. For example, mapping the IP number to a name via DNS can take a little while, so I wrote a routine that remembers the previous return values that it has seen, thereby saving the second and subsequent lookups (at least in this particular invocation of the program). The subroutine looked like this:

```
sub ip_to_name {
        if ($ip_to_name{$_[0]}) {
                $ip_to_name{$_[0]};
        } else {
                $ip_to_name{$_[0]} =
                        ... calculations ...
        }
}
```

Here, the first parameter $_[0] is looked up as the key of an associative array. If the entry is found, that value is returned immediately, otherwise a new value is calculated and remembered for future invocations. This kind of cache is a speed-up only when the subroutine is likely to be called with multiple instances of the same argument—otherwise, you're just wasting time.

I hope you've enjoyed this little excursion into subroutines. Next time, I'll probably talk about something different.

Getting Some Directory Assistance

Linux Magazine, Column 21 (February 2001)

■**Randal's Note**   I try to vary my articles completely up and down the spectrum, from beginning to expert. This article is about the basics: getting filenames from directories. But like many "basics," it's amazing to me just how buried the details are within the Perl docs, and thus an article on the simplest things often gets great feedback and acknowledgement. This article was written before my own C<File::Finder> module in the CPAN, or I would have included it as well.

Most Perl scripts aren't doing anything glamorous. They're the workhorse of your system, moving things around while you aren't necessarily looking, and handling those mundane repetitive tasks.

Those tasks are often on a series of filenames, perhaps not known in advance, but obtained by looking at the contents of a directory. Perl has a few primary different means of getting lists of names, so let's take a look at them.

The simplest to use and understand is "globbing." Globbing is what the shell does when you use `echo *.c` to get a list of all the C source files in a directory. The term globbing comes from the use of the old `/etc/glob` program in early versions of Unix, with a name derived from something like "global expansion."

Now, most programs running from the shell don't have to know how to do globbing for themselves. For example, the `rm` command in

```
$ rm *.c
```

never sees the `*.c`. Instead, the shell expands (globs) the filename pattern, comes up with a list of names, and then hands those names to the arguments of `rm`. This is why the `rm` command cannot help you when you've accidentally typed a space between the asterisk and the period: it never sees the asterisk, but rather a list of explicit names, just as if you'd laboriously typed all of them directly.

Similarly, if you invoke your Perl program with a glob pattern on the command line:

```
$ my_perl_prog *.c
```

then your Perl program already has the expanded values, and nothing further needs to be done to process the elements of `@ARGV`.

But sometimes, you don't have the luxury in your Perl program of having the files already all be passed on the command line. What to do then? Use the `glob` operator from within Perl!

```
my @c_source = glob "*.c";
```

Here, `@list` will be loaded up with all the names in the current directory that don't begin with a dot but do end in `.c`, just as if I had handed that to the shell for expansion. To get all the C source files *and* object files, I can use either

```
my @c_source_and_object = glob "*.c *.o";
```

or

```
my @c_source_and_object = glob "*.[co]";
```

Notice that multiple patterns can be specified in one `glob` by separating them with whitespace, similar to the shell, or we can use a character-class-like entry.

Another way to write the `glob` operator is to put angle brackets around the glob pattern:

```
my @c_source_and_object = <*.c *.o>;
```

The value between the angle brackets is interpreted as if it were a double-quoted string, so Perl variables become their current Perl values before the glob is evaluated. This lets us vary the patterns at runtime:

```
for my $suffix (qw(.c .o .out)) {
    $files_with{$suffix} = [<*$suffix>];
}
```

Here, I'm creating a hash of arrayrefs, so `$files_with{".o"}` will be an arrayref of all matching files.

Either syntax is fine: the glob named operator is a fairly recent invention (and takes five more characters of typing), so legacy programs tend to use the angle bracket version as well.

One word of caution about the angle bracket syntax: if the only thing inside the angle brackets is just a simple scalar variable, then angle brackets take on their more familiar meaning of "read a line from a filehandle." But here, the filehandle is an "indirect" filehandle, meaning that the variable contains the name of or a reference to a filehandle. If you're not sure whether you'll be getting a glob or not, always use the glob named operator.

Globbing can perform anything the shell normally does. For example, get all the files in the current directory or any first-level nested subdirectory that end in .c:

```perl
my @many_c_files = <*.c */*.c>;
```

Here, we're reading many subdirectories potentially. Directories that are two levels down are still ignored, however. The normal Perl globbing syntax doesn't have an entry for "recursively descend," in spite of many modern shell extended globbing forms that can indeed handle that.

Also, just as in the shell, files that begin with a dot will not have their dot matched by a wildcard character. Instead, the dot must be matched explicitly, giving us the easy equivalent of the "hidden file." To get all the files, we need two separate glob patterns, perhaps both invoked in the same expression:

```perl
my @everything = <.* *>;
```

The resulting list includes all files, with or without dots. The separate lists are sorted individually, but not merged. If you want the entire list sorted together, you've got to manage that on your own:

```perl
my @sorted_everything = sort <* .*>;
```

Of course, the output of glob can easily be used as the input to other operations. Here's the equivalent of rm -i *:

```perl
for my $filename (<*>) {
  print "remove $filename? ";
  next unless <STDIN> =~ /^y/i;
  unlink $filename or warn "Cannot unlink $filename: $!";
}
```

As simple as globbing is to use and understand, it doesn't come without its drawbacks. Prior to the 5.6 release of Perl (and dating all the way back to Perl 1.0 in 1987), globbing was implemented by literally forking off a C-shell behind the scenes (or a Bourne-style shell if C-shell was not available) and asking that shell to expand the globs. This had several consequences.

For one thing, the globbing syntax was actually slightly dependent on the particular shell being used behind the scenes. As long as you stayed with the simple star, question mark, square brackets stuff, you'd be fine, but if perchance you took advantage of curly-brace alternations, and then moved to a box without that, your program would blow up.

Second, the syntax was sensitive to shell special characters. For example, one of my "Just another Perl hacker" signatures reads something like this:

```perl
print <;echo Just another Perl hacker,>;
```

which works because the child shell's glob operation was terminated by the semicolon, and then we began a new operation, which would show up as a single filename to the shell-to-Perl interface, which then became the return value from the globbing operation, and dumped out to STDOUT via print. Scary, when you then consider the full security implications of passing an arbitrary string as part of a glob pattern.

Third, because the shell was a separate process, each glob incurred the expense of a fork and exec operation. Fine if you do it once or twice in a program, but prohibitively expensive to get, say, every file of every directory below a given large directory.

And finally, and perhaps most significantly, the classic C-shell had a fixed-size buffer for globbing expansion (roughly 10K if my memory serves me right). If you've ever gone into a "fat" directory (with lots of long names) and typed rm * only to be greeted with "NCARGMAX exceeded" or some equally obscure error message, you've seen this in action. So, the C-shell can expand only so many names, but since Perl is counting on the C-shell for a complete expansion, Perl also loses.

And this leads most people who were wanting to write robust, efficient, and secure directory lookups to avoid glob entirely, and jump directly to a lower-level mechanism for directory access: the directory handle.

A directory handle is like a filehandle; you open it (with opendir), read from it (with readdir), and perhaps close it when you are done (with closedir). I say perhaps because directory handles, like filehandles, close automatically at the end of the program, or whenever the handle is successfully reopened.

In a scalar context, readdir returns one item at a time. In a list context, readdir returns all items, again, just like a filehandle. But what items?

Well, we'll get back the contents of the directory as a list of names. This list of names is not sorted in any particular order, and consists of the basenames only (everything after the final slash of a pathname) of the entries within that directory. These entries include everything, such as plain files, directories, and even Unix-domain sockets. But it also includes files that begin with a dot, and especially the mandatory entries of "." and "..". The entries are also unsorted (for speed).

So, to dump everything in the current directory, we could use this:

```
opendir HERE, "." or die "Cannot opendir .: $!";
foreach my $name (readdir HERE) {
  print "one name in the current directory is $name\n";
}
closedir HERE;
```

The closedir isn't necessary here, but does free up a few resources that would otherwise be tied up until program's end. The names of this listing will be the same order and contents as an ls -f command or a find . -print if there were no subdirectories. To get just the same thing as ls with no options, we'll need to toss the entries that begin with dot, and sort them alphabetically:

```
opendir HERE, "." or die "opendir: $!";
foreach my $name (sort grep !/^\./, readdir HERE) {
  print "$name\n";
}
closedir HERE;
```

Because the names are simply the names *within* the directory, and not the full path-names, they aren't directly usable or testable. For example, consider this incorrect code to pick out all the directories of a given directory:

```
opendir THERE, "/usr" or die "opendir: $!";
foreach my $name (readdir THERE) {
  next unless -d $name; # THIS IS WRONG
  print "one directory in /usr is $name\n";
}
```

This is wrong because one of the names returned by readdir will be, say, lib, which we are then testing for directory-ness as if it were in the *current* directory! One solution is to patch up the name to include the full path before we use it with file tests or further access. Here's a refined solution that skips over dot files as well, making all directories immediately under /usr to be mode 755 (read/write/execute for root, and read/execute for group and others):

```
opendir THERE, "/usr" or die "opendir: $!";
foreach my $name (readdir THERE) {
  next if /^\./; # skip over dot files
  my $fullname = "/usr/$name"; # get full name
  next unless -d $fullname;
  chmod 0755, $fullname or warn "Cannot chmod $fullname: $!";
}
closedir THERE;
```

What about subdirectories? What if we wanted to examine every directory recursively below /usr looking for world-writable entries? Well, we could certainly use find for that, but in Perl, it's not much harder to write this:

```
use File::Find;
find sub {
  return unless -d; # is it a directory?
  return unless (stat)[2] & 2; # and world writeable?
  print "$File::Find::name is world writable!\n";
}, "/usr";
```

The first use defines the find subroutine. This subroutine expects a "coderef" as its first argument, which we're providing by using an anonymous subroutine. The remaining arguments to find are a list of top-level starting points for which find will locate all names recursively. For each found entry, find calls the subroutine, passing the basename of the entry in $_ and the full name in $File::Find::name. In addition, the working directory has been changed to that of the entry (for speed on further file tests).

So in this example, I tested $_ to see if it was a directory, and if so, then further tested its "stat 2" element (the tricky one with the type encoded along with the permissions values) to see if the second bit from the right was set. That's the world-writable bit. If both of those were successful tests, we sail on to print out the full name. (Printing $_ there would be not very helpful, since that's just the basename).

Note that this subroutine in its simplicity will actually print each name twice. Once while we are looking at the directory "from above," and once when the name is passed as "dot" in the "current directory." To reject that, you could add:

```
    return if $_ eq "." or $_ eq "..";
```

near the beginning of the subroutine. Now we'll get just the names, although we'd never find /usr as a world-writable directory. For that, it'd take a little more sophisticated juggling.

The File::Find module is included with Perl (from all the way back to Perl 5.000), so there's no excuse not to use it whenever you think of anything to do with recursing down directories. There's a version that does "depth first" recursion (giving you the names before the containing directory) and a mechanism for pruning the tree if you head into areas of noninterest. The version included with Perl 5.6 also has the ability to follow symlinks and provide sorted names, so check the documentation to stay up to date.

I hope this directory assistance has got your number now. Until next time, enjoy!

Launching Processes

Linux Magazine, Column 5 (October 1999)

■**Randal's Note** Like the previous section on getting a list of filenames, this article covered the basics on creating child processes. Perl is amazingly flexible, and sometimes it's hard to know exactly which way to flex! Please note that this article was written before the modern multi-arg pipe-open, and thus omits an important member of the arsenal.

Perl has many ways of launching and managing child processes. That's good, because a lot of Perl's role as the "duct tape of the Internet" is to glue programs together. So, let's look at some of the most common ways, including the limitations and potential security considerations.

The easiest way to launch a child process is with system:

```
    system "date";
```

The child process here is the date command. Anything that can be invoked from a shell command prompt can be used in this string.

The child process inherits Perl's standard input, output, and error output, so the output of this date command will show up wherever Perl's STDOUT is going.

The command can be arbitrarily complex, including everything that /bin/sh (or its nearby equivalent) can handle:

```
    system "for i in *; do echo == \$i ==; cat \$i; done";
```

Here, we're dumping out the contents of a directory, one file at a time. The $i vars are backslashed here, because Perl would have expanded them to their current Perl values, and we want the shell to see its own $i instead. A quick solution here is to use single quotes instead of double quotes:

```
    system 'for i in *; do echo == $i ==; cat $i; done';
```

Or, you can just set the value of Perl's $i to '$i', but that's pretty twisted, and will probably drive the maintenance programmer who inherits your code crazy.

This might look better spaced over multiple lines, so we can use a here-string to fix it:

```
system <<'END';
for i in *
do
        echo == $i ==
        cat $i
done
END
```

Yeah, that cleans it up a bit.

If the argument is simple enough, Perl avoids the shell, finding the program directly. You may wish to adjust $ENV{PATH} before calling system so that the program is found in the right place. Anything complicated forces a shell though.

That shell can get in the way a bit. Imagine invoking grep on a few files based on a string in a scalar variable:

```
system "grep $look_for brief1 brief2 brief3";
```

Now if $look_for is a nice easy string like "Monica", no big deal. But if it's complicated like "White House", we now have a problem, because that'll interpolate like this:

```
system "grep White House brief1 brief2 brief3";
```

which is looking for White in the other four names, including a file named House. That's broken. Badly. So, perhaps we can fix it by including some quotes:

```
system "grep '$look_for' brief1 brief2 brief3";
```

This works for White House, but fails on Don't lie!. And if we change the shell single quotes to double quotes, that will just mess up when $look_for contains double quotes!

Luckily, we can avoid the shell entirely, using the multiple argument version of system:

```
system "grep", $look_for, "brief1", "brief2", "brief3";
```

When system is given more than one argument, the first argument must be a program found along the PATH. The remaining arguments are handed, uninterpreted by any shell, directly to the program. That is, if it were another Perl script, the elements of @ARGV in the called program would be exactly one-for-one the same elements as this list.

Because we now no longer call a shell, things like I/O redirection no longer work. So there are tradeoffs to this method, but it sure comes in handy. It's also a bit more secure—no chance that a nefarious user will come along and sneak a newline or semicolon in there. Some very popular CGI scripts didn't get this matter right, and ended up triggering a CERT notification as a security hole.

While the child process is executing, Perl is stopped. So if a command takes 35 seconds to run, Perl is stopped for 35 seconds. You can fork a child process in the background in the same way you'd do it in the shell:

```
system "long_running_command and the parameters &";
```

Beware, however, that you'll have no easy way to interact with this command, nor even know its PID to kill it or see if it's still alive.

The return value of the system operator is the value from the wait (or waitpid) system call. That is, if the child process exited with a zero value (everything went OK), so too will the return value from system be zero. A nonzero value is shifted left 8 bits (or multiplied by 256, if you prefer). If a signal killed the process, that's bitwise-or'ed into the number, and a 128 is added if there's a core file cluttering up the directory now.

If you don't grab the result from system, the same number is available in the special $? variable—that is, until another process is waited for, because $? records only the most recently waited-for process status. So, to get the specs on the most recent exit, it's something like

```
$status = ($? >> 8);
$core_dumped = ($? & 128) > 0;
$signal = ($? & 127);
```

Because the "zero if everything is OK" is backwards from most of the rest of Perl, you shouldn't use or die directly. Instead, the easiest fix is to invert the output of system with a logical "not" operation:

```
!system "some_maybe_failing_command"
        or die "we broke it";
```

The exec operator works like system, with respect to everything previously. However, instead of creating a child process to run the selected command, the Perl process *becomes* the selected command. Think of this as a *goto* instead of a subroutine call. For example:

```
exec "date";
```

Once this date command begins executing, there's no Perl to come back to. The only reason to put Perl code after an exec is to explain that date was not found along the command path:

```
exec "date";
die "date not found in $ENV{PATH}";
```

In fact, if you turn on compile-time warnings and have anything but a die after exec, you'll get notified.

One use of exec is to use Perl to set up the operating environment for a long-running command:

```
$ENV{DATABASE} = "MyDataBase";
$ENV{PATH} = "/usr/bin:/bin:/opt/DataBase";
chdir "/usr/lib/my.data" or die "Cannot chdir: $!";
exec "data_mangler";
die "data_mangler not found";
```

Replacing exec with system here would have still invoked data_mangler, but then we'd have a mostly useless Perl program sitting around just waiting for data_mangler to exit.

The processes started with system and exec can be interactive, since they've inherited Perl's input and output. And, to aid in the interaction with complicated programs like vi, Perl ignores SIGINT during the system invocation, so that hitting Control-C doesn't abort Perl early.

Sometimes, you'll be invoking commands to capture their output value as a string in the program. The simplest way to do this is with backquotes, which function similarly to the shell's use of backquotes:

```
$now = `date`;
```

Here, the standard output of date is a 30-ish character string followed by a newline. Everything sent to standard output is captured as a string value, returned by the backquotes, and here saved into $now. If the value contains multiple lines, we may want to split it on a newline to get each line. But it's probably easier to use backquotes in a list context, which does this for us:

```
@logins = `who`;
```

Here, @logins will have one element for each line of who's output. We can parse that in a loop like this:

```
for (`who`) {
        ($user, $tty, $when_where) =
                /^(\S+)\s+(\S+)\s+(.*)/;
        $logins{$user}{$tty} = $when_where;
}
```

Each iteration through the loop gathers a different user's login, shoving it into a two-level hash keyed by user name and then terminal. When we're all done, we can dump it out ordered by user:

```
for $user (sort keys %logins) {
        for $tty (sort keys %{$logins{$user}}) {
                print "$user is on $tty from $logins{$user}{$tty}\n";
        }
}
```

Standard input for a backquoted command is inherited from Perl's standard input, making it possible to have an external command suck down all of STDIN returning a modified version:

```
@sorted_input = `sort`;
```

Here, the sort command (not the built-in Perl operator) is reading all of standard input, sorting it, and then returning that to Perl as a very large string value.

The backquoted command is double-quote interpolated, meaning that we can use escapes like \n and \t, but also include Perl variables to build parts of the command:

```
$checksum = `sum $file`;
```

However, everything that I warned you earlier about the single-argument system operator applies here as well—what if $file has embedded whitespace or other shell-significant characters?

One solution is to use yet another way of invoking a child process: the process-as-filehandle. Let's start with the easy form of that first, and return to this whitespace problem after getting the basics down.

If the second argument to open ends in a vertical bar (pipe symbol), Perl treats that as a command to launch rather than a filename:

```
open DATE, "date|";
```

At this point, a date command is launched, with its standard output connected to the DATE filehandle open for reading. The rest of the program doesn't know, doesn't care, and would have to work pretty hard to figure out, that this is not a file but just another program. So, we'll read from the output using the normal filehandle operations:

```
$now = <DATE>;
```

The process is running in parallel with Perl, with all the coordination provided for standard pipe read/writes. So if the date command sent its output before Perl was ready, it would just wait there, and if Perl read before date was ready to write, the Perl process would simply block until output was available, consuming no CPU.

So how does this solve our whitespace problem of earlier? Well, there's a special kind of command opening like this:

```
my $pid = open CHILD, "-|";
```

which is a combination of a pipe open and a fork. You may recall that a fork splits the current process into two processes: a parent process and a child process. Initially, both processes are running identical code, but we distinguish them by the return value from the fork call. The parent gets back the child's process ID number (PID), and the child gets a zero value.

This fork-and-pipe opening operates similarly: the Perl process forks, and the parent and child see differing results from the open just like a fork. However, the child's STDOUT is attached to the parent's CHILD filehandle automatically. This means that the child can act like the date command earlier, sending stuff to its standard output, and we can read from that in the parent process.

So, to finish out the date example, we could do it all within Perl like so:

```
if ($pid) { # I'm the parent
        $now = <CHILD>; # read child
} else { # I'm the child
        print scalar localtime, "\n";
        exit 0;
}
```

And now $now is set to the output of the child process. We can also exec in the child like so:

```
if ($pid) {
        $checksum = <CHILD>;
} else {
        exec 'sum', $myfile;
        die "sum not found: $!";
}
```

And now we have used the two-argument form of exec so there's never any shell-character worries!

Perl also offers arbitrary invocations of fork, waitpid, pipe, and file-descriptor shuffling, permitting full access to the underlying Unix system calls, but I've run out of space to talk about them. Until next time, have fun launching processes!

Extending Unix Utilities with Perl (grep)

Unix Review, Column 9 (July 1996)

■**Randal's Note**   I like writing articles where an opaque Unix utility gets emulated in a few mere lines of Perl, partly to take the magic out of the existing utilities, and partly to help figure out how to write something similar when a Unix utility falls short. Of course, this also shows off how powerful Perl can be.

Perl's text processing capabilities provide direct access to a number of high-level facilities for manipulating text. However, sometimes the problem is not what to do with the text once you've got it, but eliminating stuff that doesn't look like text. Let's take a look at how to use Perl's facility for recognizing text files (as opposed to binary files) to ease a typical processing task.

First, let's reconstruct the simplest form of program that emulates the standard Unix grep command.

```
#!/usr/bin/perl
$search = shift;
$showname = @ARGV > 1;
while (<>) {
        next unless /$search/o;
        print "$ARGV: " if $showname;
        print;
}
```

The first executable line after the #! header takes the first command-line parameter (found in @ARGV) and shifts it off into the $search variable. Here, I take advantage of the fact that the shift operator defaults to @ARGV.

Next, if there is more than one argument remaining, I'll need to remember that in the $showname variable, so that I can print the filename along with the found lines, just like the grep command does. $showname will be true when the number of arguments is greater than one, and false otherwise.

Then comes an ordinary "diamond loop": each line from each file specified on the command line is read into the $_ variable, and the body of the loops gets to take a whack at it.

The first line in the loop looks for $search (interpreted as a Perl regular expression) within the contents of $_. If it isn't found, we go on to the "next" line. The o modifier on the regular expression match is a speed optimization—without it, the regular expression would have to be "compiled" on each turn through the loop, slowing us down needlessly because the regular expression is not changing each time.

The $showname variable is then consulted: if it is true, we need to prefix the output line with the filename in which the line was found. Luckily, Perl provides the filename for us in the $ARGV scalar variable (only coincidentally named like the ARGV filehandle and the @ARGV array).

Finally, whether or not the filename was printed, the current line is printed (from $_, because the print operator defaults to printing $_).

So, this little program emulates the simplest form of the Unix grep command: namely, the invocation like

```
grep regex [file ... ]
```

I've also been told that this program actually executes faster than the corresponding Vendor-supplied grep invocation for certain regular expressions: the regular expression stuff inside Perl is supposed to be some of the fastest around.

So, why have I rewritten grep? So that I can give it additional functionality! The system-supplied grep command groks through both text files and binary files. Many times, it'd be nice for me to simply say something like

```
textgrep regex *
```

and have this magical textgrep look only in the text files, ignoring the binary files that match *. In particular, my personal "binary" directory ($HOME/.bin) has a number of binary programs, but many more executable scripts (mostly in Perl :-), and I'd like to be able to

```
cd $HOME/.bin
textgrep "somestring" *
```

to grep just the scripts, for example. Another use might be inside a "build" directory with a lot of program source and objects. If you're looking for a particular literal string in a source file, you don't also want to hit the binary from which the source was compiled!

So, let's see if we can make our "grep-in-perl" become a textgrep. The first step is distinguishing text files from binary files. Perl makes this easy, with its built-in -T operator. This operator returns true if the argument string (a filename) or filehandle represents a "text file." Now, Unix doesn't have a simple bit to test if something is "text" or "binary," so instead, the Perl process grabs a chunk of bytes from the file, and guesses whether it's more likely to be a text file or binary file. It usually guesses right, but occasionally can get fooled.

Because @ARGV contains a series of filenames, it seems natural then to test each one with -T to see if is text-like or binary-ish. We can even do this in a compact way with the grep operator (not to be confused with the Unix grep command although the name was chosen for its similarity).

The grep operator evaluates a block for each element of a list, setting each element into $_ temporarily. For those elements where the block returns true, the elements are retained in the return value, so at first glance, we can just write

```
@ARGV = grep { -T } @ARGV;
```

However, this fails in the face of the possibility of having "-" somewhere in the @ARGV list. The "-" is supposed to mean "read from standard input here" which hopefully is a text file. However, -T will reject this as a nonexisting file, so we have to special-case it to ensure that it survives the preening. Not too difficult, but it now looks like

```
@ARGV = grep { -T or $_ eq "-" } @ARGV;
```

Nice! @ARGV now contains only text files! Only one other weird case to deal with now. If the original list contains only binaries, the new @ARGV is now empty. We can't have that, because that would mean that the program reads from standard input, even though the user originally supplied a series of names on the command line. Take a look at how I handled it in the finished program:

```perl
#!/usr/bin/perl
$search = shift;
$showname = @ARGV > 1;
@ARGV = "-" unless @ARGV;
@ARGV = grep { -T or $_ eq "-" } @ARGV;
exit 0 unless @ARGV;
while (<>) {
        next unless /$search/o;
        print "$ARGV: " if $showname;
        print;
}
```

Notice that the fourth line replaces an empty @ARGV with an @ARGV consisting solely of a list containing "-". This doesn't change its meaning at all, but it does allow me to test later whether we've reduced an original list to nothingness.

The following line is the "text file only" reduction as described previously. The line after that terminates the program if the list is now empty, because there's nothing to scan! The remainder of the program is identical to the previous version.

We now have a program that could be called textgrep. It has no arguments, although it understands "-" in the list of files to mean "standard input," and presumes that standard input is always a text file.

Let's take it further. The standard Unix grep command has a -l (lowercase L, not capital I) option which says to simply list the matching filenames one at a time, rather than the lines that match. This is useful to perform further operations. For example, to edit all the files in the current directory that match "fred", I could say

```
vi `grep -l fred *`
```

Or to move them all to the ../freds directory:

```
mv `grep -l fred *` ../freds
```

So, let's give textgrep this same functionality. Here's the code:

```perl
#!/usr/bin/perl
$names++, shift if $ARGV[0] eq "-l";
$search = shift;
$showname = @ARGV > 1;
@ARGV = "-" unless @ARGV;
@ARGV = grep { -T or $_ eq "-" } @ARGV;
exit 0 unless @ARGV;
while (<>) {
        next unless /$search/o;
        if ($names) {
```

```
                print "$ARGV\n";
                close ARGV;
        } else {
                print "$ARGV: " if $showname;
                print;
        }
   }
```

Only half a dozen additional lines. Let's see: the first line after the comment examines $ARGV[0] (the first argument). If this is equal to "-l", I want to invoke "names-only" mode, so I set $names, and shift away the "-l". Hopefully, anything else is a regular expression, captured in the following line.

The other change is within the body of the diamond loop. Note that when a line is found, $names is checked again. If true, the program prints the name of the file followed by a newline, and then closes ARGV. The point of closing ARGV is that the diamond operator will automatically advance to the next file when we get to the top of the loop. Once a matching line is found, there's no point in checking the rest of the file. This also ensures that a given filename will be shown only once, no matter how many potential matches there are in the file.

If $names is false, the -l option wasn't seen, so the behavior from the previous textgrep program is selected in the else block.

With this program, I can then examine just the text files. For example, edit only the text files that contain fred:

```
    vi `textgrep -l fred *`
```

Or even send all text files (but just text files) to the line printer:

```
    pr `textgrep -l '^' *` | lpr -Pslatewriter
```

Note here that "^" matches the beginning of the line, which is normally true for every file that grep sees, but remember that textgrep rejects nontext files!

As you can see, with about a dozen lines of Perl code, I've re-created a very common Unix utility, and even given it additional functionality. I hope you've enjoyed this little bit of text (manipulation). See ya next time!

Set Operations

Unix Review, Column 11 (November 1996)

■**Randal's Note** Most of the idioms described in this article can also be performed with a Set::Object (from the CPAN) or even with a Quantum::Superpositions object. However, for pure simplicity and portability, the described idioms are still the best way.

One of the things that Perl excels at is manipulating lists of data. In fact, with the addition of references to Perl 5.0, list manipulation became even easier. In this column, I will show you some simple list manipulation techniques that you may find handy. After all, there is no reason to reinvent the wheel—someone else has probably already done the hard work. (And often when you reinvent the wheel, you end up with casters.)

One of the most common tasks to perform on a list is to remove duplicates. This question comes up a lot on the `comp.lang.perl.misc` newsgroup. The most efficient way (and even the simplest to write, go figure!) is to use a hash (formerly called "associative array") to keep track of the list elements seen so far, and reject additional copies of those elements. That'd look something like this:

```
%temp = ();
@list = grep ++$temp{$_} < 2, @list;
```

Here, I clear out a hash called `%temp` by assigning it the empty list. The next statement does all the hard work, and there's a lot going on here, so let's take it apart bit by bit.

First, I'm presuming the data I want to reduce to unique elements is in the `@list` array. I next perform a `grep` operation on the current value of this list. Similar to its Unix command counterpart, the `grep` operator selects and rejects various elements of this list based on a true/false expression. Here, the expression is an evaluation of a hash element access, using `$_` as the key. The `grep` operator gives each value in `@list` one at a time to `$_`, and the evaluations are sequential. So, the first time `$_` is, say, the string `"fred"`, the value of `++$temp{"fred"}` is an increment from `undef` (because the element cannot be found in the hash) to 1. Now, since this value is less than 2, the full expression returns true, and the element is included at that point.

On second and subsequent occurrences of `"fred"`, the value returned by `++$temp{"fred"}` is 2 or more. Because the expression then evaluates to false, those elements are thus rejected. The result of the `grep` operator is then assigned to the `@list` variable, and we have accomplished the task at hand.

Someone asked recently on the `comp.unix.shell` newsgroup about how to remove the duplicate names from a list of mailing addresses. Now, while a simple sort command with a `-u` switch would have performed this operation, I decided to tackle this problem with a Perl script, to give an added value solution. Namely, the mailing addresses uniqueness check should be "case insensitive," since `fred@BIG.COM` is the same address as `fred@big.com`. With just a little more programming than the previous example, we can accomplish this rather easily. Here's a sample of that:

```
@list = split /\n/, <<END;
fred@big.com
barney@little.com
fred@BIG.COM
barney@ivy.edu
END
# ... later in the program ...
{
        my %temp;
        foreach (@list) {
                $temp{lc} = $_;
        }
        @list = sort values %temp;
}
```

Now, the first few lines set up the @list variable. The block of the last seven lines form a temporary area where I can create a new %temp variable. This variable is guaranteed to start as empty, similar to the previous code snippet. However, by wrapping the variable definition in a block, the variable will automatically go away at the end of the block, thus reclaiming the memory used by the variable, *and* if the name conflicts with an existing variable, our newly created local variable takes precedence. Neat trick for temporary variables.

After the empty local variable %temp is created, I then loop through the @list variable. Each iteration through the loop sets a local $_ to a different value. Within the loop is a simple hash element setting, where I'm putting the key as the lowercased contents of $_ (using the lc function), and $_ (the original email address) becomes the value. By doing it this way, I force two email addresses that are identical except for a change in case (upper vs. lower) to both try to occupy the same hash element. Since this is impossible, the second email address over-writes the first, and I get one value instead.

After the loop is completed, I pull out the values, sorted "ascii-betically." Why not the keys? Well, the keys have all been lowercased, but the values will preserve at least *one* of the preferred capitalizations of the email address. Pretty cool, eh?

Now, for something slightly different. Another task that comes up frequently is removing a list of things from another list of things. This might be called "set subtraction" or "set differ-ence" if you are into those sorts of words. Well, once again, the hash comes to the rescue. In fact, generally whenever you think of set "somethings," you can almost immediately think "the set is the keys of a hash" and be pretty close. So, here's some code to perform a set sub-traction between @list and @stoplist:

```
%temp = ();
@temp{@list} = ();
foreach (@stoplist) {
        delete $temp{$_};
}
@list = sort keys %temp;
```

Once again, I have the temporary %temp hash variable, clearing it out so that I can work from a clean slate. The next step creates elements within %temp for all the keys of @list, using a hash slice operation. The values will all be undef (the undefined value), but that's irrelevant for this particular solution. The foreach loop causes every element present in @stoplist to be deleted from the %temp hash. It's OK if some of these elements aren't present—the delete oper-ator just ignores them.

At one time, the syntax of

```
delete @temp{@stoplist};
```

was being discussed amongst the Perl developers, which would eliminate the loop, but this hasn't been implemented to my knowledge. Maybe in Perl 6.0, perhaps?

Finally, the new list is gathered by taking the remaining keys from %temp, sorting them "ascii-betically." This will be the result of @list, without the elements of @stoplist. As a side effect, any duplicate elements of @list will be removed as well.

We can wrap up this routine into a subroutine like so:

```
sub remove {
        my($listref,$stopref) = @_;
        my(%temp);

        @temp{@$listref} = ();
        foreach (@$stopref) {
                delete $temp{$_};
        }
        sort keys %temp;
}
```

Notice here that the first two parameters are *references* to lists, not lists themselves. This allows for rather efficient passing of the list into the subroutine. The first parameter is stored into $listref, and the second into $stopref, and %temp is created as an empty, local hash.

The $listref is dereferenced in the next statement, using a notation of @$listref, which asks for the list denoted by $listref. Similarly, the $stopref is dereferenced with @$stopref. The last expression evaluated in this subroutine (sort keys %temp) becomes the return value for the subroutine.

Here's a sample invocation of this subroutine:

```
@input = qw(fred barney betty);
@guys = remove(
        \@input,
        [qw(betty wilma pebbles)]
);
```

We have @input being a few different names, and we're invoking the remove routine, passing it a reference (made with backslash) to the @input variable, and an anonymous list created from the three names. The result in @guys will be the set difference between the @input and the literal list.

How about set intersection, where an element has to be in both lists to make it through? That'd be something like this:

```
%temp = ();
@temp{@list_one} = (1) x @list_one;
@result = grep $temp{$_}, @list_two;
```

The first step clears our now-famous %temp hash. (Or, if this were truly a temporary variable, you wouldn't need this.) The next step creates a hash slice into %temp, with an interesting property. The left side is a list belonging to @list_one—the right side is a list of 1's, replicated (with the x operator) to be long enough to exactly equal the list on the left side. This has the effect that all elements of %temp with keys of the elements of @list_one are now set to a value of 1.

The result is then computed by noting which elements of @list_two have corresponding elements in @list_one, using those elements in %temp that have been set in the previous step.

I hope this gives you some sets of ideas to manipulate lists. Enjoy!

Getting Better References Through Perl

Linux Magazine, Column 8 (January 2000)

To start off the New Year, I'm going to begin with one of the Perl basics: references. References permit complex data types to be cleanly represented in Perl, and provide ways to pass and return large amounts of data into and out of subroutines.

Let's look at a reference, first by example. Suppose I wanted to have a "reverse chomp" operator that would add a newline to every element of an array. I could write the code as follows:

```
for $element (@array) {
  $element .= "\n";
}
```

And while this would certainly work, it locks me in to a specific variable named @array. If I wanted to make a general subroutine, I'd be out of luck, without references (unless I wanted to do something evil and nonscalable like alter @_ directly). A reference permits the selected variable to be changed at will, using an additional level of indirection. Consider the following code:

```
$this_reference = \@named_array;
```

Here, the \ operator "takes a reference to" the named @named_array variable. The value is called an "array reference," or arrayref for short (occasionally incorrectly called "listref"). The reference fits nearly anywhere a scalar value fits, and so we've shoved it into $this_reference. This arrayref "points at" @named_array.

To use the reference, we must dereference it. Let's set @named_array to the values of 1 through 10, but using the reference:

```
# @named_array      = (1..10);
  @{$this_reference} = (1..10);
```

The syntax for dereferencing is to write the operation as we would without the reference, but then replace the *name* of the variable with a block of code (enclosed in braces) returning a reference to the variable. So, we've now got a piece of code that affects @named_array, at least this time. However, with a different array reference stored in $this_reference, the same code affects a different variable:

```
$this_reference = \@another_array;
@{$this_reference) = (1..10);
```

Now we've set @another_array to those 10 values. We can even use the reference syntax to access individual elements:

```
# $another_array   [2] = "three";
  ${$this_reference}[2] = "three";
```

Again, replace the name with a block returning the thing holding the reference, and we get the dereferencing form.

So, we can start to see how to make our unchomp work. We'll write the code so that it uses a reference, and pass that reference as a parameter:

```
sub unchomp {
  my $ref = shift;
  for $element (@{$ref}) {
    $element .= "\n";
  }
}
```

And then call it with a reference to the array we want unchomped:

```
unchomp(\@named_array);
unchomp(\@another_array);
```

The reference passes as a single parameter, which is then shifted into $ref, and dereferenced into the foreach loop. Bingo.

Since the reference fits into a scalar variable, can we have a list element be a reference? Certainly:

```
for $aref (\@named_array, \@another_array) {
  unchomp($aref);
}
```

In fact, we can even store this list into another array:

```
@do_these = (\@named_array, \@another_array);
for $aref (@do_these) {
  unchomp($aref);
}
```

But what have we done? We now have an array, each element of which is an arrayref, which can in turn be dereferenced to access the individual elements. So, what does it look like to access each layer?

```
@do_these # two elements, each an arrayref
@{$do_these[0]} # @named_array
${$do_these[0]}[3] # $named_array[3]
@{$do_these[1]}[4,5] # @another_array[4,5]
$#{$do_these[0]} # $#named_array
```

Some people call this structure a "list of lists," but that's pretty loose, since really it's an array of arrayrefs. Perl doesn't have "lists of lists."

Now, let's simplify the syntax a bit. The preceding rules always work for dereferencing (replace the name with a block), but can start looking pretty ugly for common things. First, if the expression inside the block is *only* a simple scalar variable, we can lose the curly braces. Thus, we can change @{$aref} to @$aref, but we have to leave @{$do_these[0]} alone.

There's another optimization available for accessing array elements through a reference. In place of

```
${WHATEVER}[WHEREVER]
```

we can always write

```
WHATEVER->[WHEREVER]
```

The `->` operator followed by square brackets means to treat the previous value as an arrayref, dereference it, and then select the requested element. Thus, we can rewrite

```
${$aref}[2]
```

to just

```
$aref->[2]
```

and

```
${$do_these[0]}[3]
```

to simply

```
$do_these[0]->[3]
```

There's one more optimization available for that last one. If the arrow ends up between subscripts, we can drop the arrow safely:

```
$do_these[0][3]
```

which looks vaguely C-like. Cool. We *cannot* remove the arrow between $aref and [2] on the previous example though, because that would be looking at an element of @aref, not at all what we want.

Did we need the named arrays here, to set up @do_these? Nope. We can also use an "anonymous array constructor":

```
$do_these[0] = [1..10];
```

Here, the value 1..10 is computed in a list context, then placed into an array structure. A reference to this array is returned as the value of the square brackets, and placed into $do_these[0]. Except for the fact that we don't have a named array any more, the rest of the code would run identically. We could even initialize the entire array as

```
@do_these = ([1..10], [11..20]);
```

And we get two different 10-element arrays, held as arrayrefs in @do_these. Note that the placement of square brackets and parens here is essential; swapping them would have gotten us into a mess.

Adding elements to an array has always been a "self-extend" operation in Perl. Assigning to elements that don't yet exist causes the array to be autoextended:

```
@a = ();
$a[3] = "barney";
$a[7] = "dino";
```

And we end up with

```
@a = (undef, undef, undef,
      "barney", undef, undef,
      undef, "dino");
```

Notice that the intermediate elements are automatically undef. Similarly, any variable when used as if it was an arrayref, but not yet containing anything (or just undef), is automatically stuffed with an arrayref to an empty anonymous array. This process is called "autovivification," and makes populating so-called "multidimensional" arrays trivial:

```perl
@a = ();
$a[3]->[2] = "hello";
# same as:
# $a[3] = [];
# $a[3]->[2] = "hello";
```

This even works on multiple levels:

```perl
@a = ();
$a[2]->[4]->[5]->[3] = "foo";
# or $a[2][4][5][3] = "foo";
```

Very nice.

Arrays aren't the only things that can be referenced. Hashes are another popular target:

```perl
%last_name = (
    "fred" => "flintstone",
    "wilma" => "flintstone",
    "barney" => "rubble",
);
$hashref = \%last_name;
@firsts = keys %{$hashref};
```

That last line can be written as keys %$hashref as well, using the same abbreviations given earlier. Accessing an element can also be abbreviated:

```perl
# looking at $last_name{"fred"}:
${$hashref}{"fred"}
# removing optional {}'s:
$$hashref{"fred"}
# or switching to arrow form:
$hashref->{"fred"}
```

We can put an arrayref as a hash value:

```perl
$score{"fred"} = [180, 150, 165];
$score{"barney"} = [172, 190, 158];
```

and then access that with everything we've seen:

```perl
@fred_scores = @{$score{"fred"}};
${$score{"fred"}}[2] = 168; # fix 165 to 168
$score{"fred"}->[2] = 168; # same thing
$score{"fred"}[2] = 168; # same thing
```

Note that we can drop an arrow between either kind of subscript.

Like arrayrefs, hashrefs can also appear from nowhere using the autovivification:

```
%bytes = ();
# ...
$bytes{$src}{$dest} += $count;
```

This creates a hash of hashrefs, with each hashref being added only when a new $src shows up, and each second-level hash element being added for a new $dst for that $src.

Hashrefs can also come from anonymous hash constructors:

```
$hashref = {
  "fred" => "flintstone",
  "barney" => "rubble",
  "betty" => "rubble",
};
```

The value inside the braces is evaluated like the right side of a hash assignment (list context, alternating key/value pairs). A hash is built, and a reference to that hash is returned. So, to build a reference to the previous scores, we could do this:

```
$game = {
  "fred" => [180, 150, 165],
  "barney" => [172, 190, 158],
};
```

which could have been part of the league scores:

```
$week[0] = $game;
$week[1] = {
  "fred" => [201, 188, 65],
  "barney" => [189, 252, 99],
};
# or more directly:
@week = ({
  "fred" => [180, 150, 165],
  "barney" => [172, 190, 158],
},{
  "fred" => [201, 188, 65],
  "barney" => [189, 252, 99],
});
```

Now we get the score for game $i of week $j for fred with $week[$j-1]{"fred"}[$i-1], subtracting 1 because Perl counts starting at 0, not 1.

Less frequently used, but still just as cool, are scalar references (scalarrefs):

```
$that = \$scalar_var;
$$that = 17; # $scalar_var = 17
```

Scalarrefs autovivify as well, although that's not very impressive:

```
$that = undef;
$$that = 3; # anonymous var becomes 3
```

Anonymous data structures can also occur when a variable goes out of scope:

```
my $x;
{
  my $prince = "van gogh";
  $x = \$prince;
}
```

Here, $x is pointing to what is now an anonymous string, the artist formerly known as $prince. This frequently happens when returning a data structure reference from a subroutine:

```
sub marine {
  my %things;
  # ...
  return \%things;
}
```

The return value here will be a hashref, now pointing into the anonymous value. New invocations of the subroutine create new instances of %things. Memory for the previous return values is reclaimed only when the last reference is removed.

So, that should give you a start into references. For further information, check the documentation that comes with Perl, especially perlref and perllol and perldsc, as well as Chapter 4 of my book *Programming Perl, Second Edition* from O'Reilly and Associates (co-authored by Larry Wall and Tom Christiansen). Enjoy!

References to Subroutines and Aliases (glob References)

Unix Review, Column 8 (May 1996)

■**Randal's Note** This article was written before the $coderef->(@args) syntax was available, which would have simplified the syntax in many places. That feature was introduced on a bet for a glass of my favorite adult beverage (I won), and if you see me, you can buy me another glass of said beverage for the whole story.

In my last column, I introduced the notion of a Perl "reference," like a pointer in C. I talked about references to scalars, arrays, and associative arrays. In this column, I'm going to talk about references to subroutines, and using references to mess with the Perl runtime symbol table to create aliases.

A reference to a subroutine can be created with the "make-a-reference-to" operator, a backslash (one of the probably 17 meanings for backslash):

```
sub wilma {
        print "Hello, @_!";
}
$ref_to_wilma = \&wilma;
```

Here, the subroutine &wilma is defined, and then a reference to that subroutine is created and stored into $ref_to_wilma. It is not necessary to define a subroutine before taking a reference to it however.

This $ref_to_wilma can be used wherever the invocation of wilma is also used, although we have to "dereference" it in the same way we dereference other references. The syntactic rules are similar—replace the name "wilma" in an invocation of &wilma with {$ref_to_wilma} (or $ref_to_wilma, because it is a scalar variable), as in

```perl
&wilma("fred"); # say hello to fred
&{ $ref_to_wilma }("fred"); # same thing
&$ref_to_wilma("fred"); # also same thing
```

Now, these refs can be used to select different operations on the same data. Consider a series of subroutines to perform the basic four math operations on their arguments, returning the result:

```perl
sub add { $_[0]+$_[1]; }
sub subtract { $_[0]-$_[1]; }
sub multiply { $_[0]*$_[1]; }
sub divide { $_[0]/$_[1]; }
```

Now, let's allow the user to enter one of the operators, followed by the two operands (prefix notation), and then select one of the four subroutines, using conventional code (no references):

```perl
print "enter operator op1 op2\n";
$_ = <STDIN>;
## break the result on whitespace:
($op,$op1,$op2) = split;
if ($op eq "+") {
        $res = &add($op1,$op2);
} elsif ($op eq "-") {
        $res = &subtract($op1,$op2);
} elsif ($op eq "*") {
        $res = &multiply($op1,$op2);
} else { # divide, we hope
        $res = &divide($op1,$op2);
}
print "result is $res\n";
```

Boy, think of how much harder this would be if I had 15 operators. The regularity of the pattern of code makes me think that I can factor that out somehow, and in fact, I can, using references.

```perl
## initialize op table
%op_table = (
        "+" => \&add,
        "-" => \&subtract,
        "*" => \&multiply,
        "/" => \&divide,
```

```
     );
     print "enter operator op1 op2\n";
     $_ = <STDIN>;
     ## break the result on whitespace:
     ($op,$op1,$op2) = split;
     ## get reference:
     $sub_ref = $op_table{$op};
     ## and now evaluate
     $res = &{$sub_ref}($op1,$op2);
     print "result is $res\n";
```

First, $op is used as a key into the %op_table associative array, selecting one of the four subroutine references into $sub_ref. That reference is then dereferenced, passing the two operands. This is possible only because all four subroutines take the same style of arguments. Had there been some irregularity, we would have been in trouble.

However, we can shorten the lookup-execute steps even further, as in

```
     $res = &{$op_table{$op}}($op1,$op2);
```

which simply does the lookup and dereference all in one fell swoop. Slick, eh?

Like anonymous lists and anonymous associative arrays, I can create an anonymous subroutine. For example, back to something like the &wilma subroutine:

```
     $greet_ref = sub {
             print "hello, @_!\n";
     };
```

What we now have in $say_ref is a reference to a subroutine, but the subroutine has no name. This subroutine is invoked by dereferencing the subroutine reference, in the same way as other subroutine references:

```
     &$greet_ref("barney"); # hello, barney!
```

One advantage of the anonymous subroutine is that it can be used in places where coming up with names might seem a little silly. For example, the names of &add, &subtract, &multiply, and &divide were rather arbitrary in the previous examples. As I add operators, I'd have to keep naming the subroutines, even though the name was used in only one other place—the %op_table. So, using anonymous subroutines, I can eliminate the names entirely:

```
     ## initialize op table
     %op_table = (
             "+" => sub { $_[0]+$_[1] },
             "-" => sub { $_[0]-$_[1] },
             "*" => sub { $_[0]*$_[1] },
             "/" => sub { $_[0]/$_[1] },
     );
```

and in fact, this %op_table functions identically to the previous one, except that I didn't have to hurt myself coming up with names for the four subroutines. This is really a help for maintenance—to add exponentiation (using **) for example, all I have to do is add an entry to the %op_table:

```
"**" => sub { $_[0]**$_[1] },
```

rather than first coming up with a named subroutine, and then adding a reference to that subroutine in the %op_table.

Subroutine references are also handy to pass into subroutines. For example, suppose I wrote a routine to throw away blank lines until it got something useful, and then return the useful thing. As its first arg, it could take a subroutine that defines how to "get the next thing." Sometimes, this might be "read from a filehandle," and other times it might be "shift from an array." Here's how it would look:

```
$next = &non_blank(
        sub { <STDIN>; }
); # read from stdin
$next = &non_blank(
        sub { shift @cache; }
}; # grab from list @cache
```

Within the &non_blank subroutine, the first parameter is then a reference to a subroutine that will "fetch the next value." Here's one possible implementation of that subroutine:

```
sub non_blank {
        my($scanner) = @_;
        my($return);
        {
                $return = &{$scanner}();
                redo until $return =~ /\S/;
        }
        $return;
}
```

Here, the subroutine referenced by $scanner is invoked repeatedly until its return value (stuffed into $return) has a nonblank value in it. When it is invoked with the subroutine containing <STDIN>, a line at a time is read. When it is invoked with shift @cache, we get a line from @cache each time instead.

Unfortunately, while testing this, I discovered a problem. Sometimes, there are no more further things in the stream being scanned by &non_blank that contain a nonblank character, and this subroutine then runs indefinitely. Ouch! So, a simple patch in the logic as well as a modification to the definition fixes it. I'm going to return undef if no further element fits the needs, as in

```
sub non_blank {
        my($scanner) = @_;
        my($return);
        {
                $return = &{$scanner}();
                last unless defined $return;
                redo until $return =~ /\S/;
        }
        $return;
}
```

There. That handles it. Now, if my program required scanning <STDIN>, @cache, or even calling another subroutine to fetch the next nonblank line, it doesn't matter. And this same bug fix is handled once, rather than having to patch all the similar-looking code in the program.

By the way, I got carried away with punctuation there—let's simplify that middle one for the record to

```
$return = &$scanner();
```

Enough on subroutines for the moment. Let's turn to another use for references—as a way of modifying the symbol table of Perl. Why would you want to do this? One reason is to create an alias for another symbol:

```
*fred = *barney;
```

Here, we've said that the "fred" symbol is to be aliased to the "barney" symbol. We call this a "glob" reference, because it is hacking the global symbol table.

Once this is done, every use of barney in a variable can be replaced by fred:

```
$barney = 3;
$fred = 3; # same thing
@barney = (1,2,4);
print "@fred"; # prints "1 2 4"
%fred = ("a" => 1);
print $barney{"a"}; # prints 1
```

Even subroutines get aliased in this way, as well as filehandles, directory handles, and format names.

We can be more selective by giving the glob assignment a specific reference type:

```
*fred = \&wilma;
```

Now here, $fred is still $barney, @fred is still @barney, %fred is still %barney, but &fred is &wilma. You can often find this inside a block with a local glob:

```
*fred = *barney;
{
        local(*fred) = \&wilma;
        &fred(3,4,5); # &wilma(3,4,5)
}
&fred(6,7,8); # &barney(6,7,8)
```

The localized glob assignment is effective only within the block. When we exit the block, the previous glob assignment appears again, as if by magic.

We can rewrite &non_blank shown previously to use a local glob alias rather than an explicit dereferencing:

```
sub non_blank {
        local(*scanner) = @_;
        my($return);
        {
                $return = &scanner();
                last unless defined $return;
```

```
                    redo until $return =~ /\S/;
            }
            $return;
    }
```

Notice that we can now invoke &scanner, rather than the clumsier &&$scanner.

We can also use glob references to tidy up the &brack_it subroutine from the last column. Rather than explicitly dereferencing the value $list_ref in

```
sub brack_it {
        my($list_ref) = @_;
        foreach (@$list_ref) {
                print "[$_]"; # print element in brackets
        }
        print "\n";
}
```

we can replace it with a glob assignment:

```
sub brack_it {
        local(*list) = @_; # list ref we hope
        foreach (@list) {
                print "[$_]"; # print element in brackets
        }
        print "\n";
}
```

Another use of glob assignments is to make a sort subroutine a little more generic. For example, the classic "sort by value" for a particular associative array is written as

```
sub by_numeric_value {
        $hash{$a} <=> $hash{$b}
}
```

which works fine as a sort subroutine provided the data is in the %hash associative array like so:

```
sub sort_hash_by_value {
        sort by_numeric_value keys %hash;
}
@them = &sort_hash_by_value;
```

Here, the value in @them is the keys of %hash sorted by their corresponding numeric value. We can now make this routine more generic:

```
sub sort_by_value {
        local(*hash) = @_; # ref to hash
        sort by_numeric_value keys %hash;
}
@them_hash = &sort_by_value(\%hash);
```

So far, this does the same thing as the previous one, but I've passed in the name of %hash as the first argument. This then gets aliased to (gasp) itself, and the subroutine functions as before. Where it gets fun is when I can pass other associative arrays:

```
@them_there = &sort_by_value(\%there);
```

which now does exactly the same thing on the %there associative array! In this case, the sort subroutine &sort_hash_by_value thinks it is accessing %hash, when in fact because of the alias, it is accessing %there. Very cool.

Once again, I hope this excursion into the features of Perl (especially the more powerful features of references) has been useful for you. Enjoy!

Finding Old Things

Unix Review, Column 43 (September 2002)

■**Randal's Note**   This is one of many articles where I bring up how to use File::Find, and the evils of hand-coding such code. Of course, today, I'd also include a reference to my own File::Finder from the CPAN, which provides a greatly simplified interface.

One of the great things about the relatively large size of the Perl community is the many ways in which information can be obtained about Perl to solve typical tasks, or get past those sticky little frustrating points. Besides the professional documentation that others and I have written, there's also the myriad of manpages that come with the Perl distribution itself, and the CPAN modules.

And with a little searching on the net, we also quickly find very active support for Perl in the way of Usenet newsgroups, mailing lists, and a few web communities. The most active Perl web community that I participate in is known as the Perl Monastery, at http://perlmonks.org. Each day, a few hundred active users and a few thousand visitors post and answer questions, and chat in the "chatterbox." Activity at the Monastery gives you "experience points," which gives you access to more functions and acknowledges the additional responsibility and track record.

In my past roles as a system administrator, it seems like I was always under pressure to keep trying to solve problems in annoyingly brief amounts of time. The Monastery is a welcome resource, because questions often get answered within minutes, so help is just a browser-reload or two away.

Recently, a relatively new Monk (as we call the participants) who goes by the name "Aquilo" asked for help with a script that recurses through a directory structure and checks if more than half of the files in that directory have been used in the past 180 days. The path of directories that are predominately unused is appended to a list of directories that will be used to archive them.

Aquilo gave some sample code that performed directory recursion in the traditional beginner way. I say traditional, because it appears that one of Perl's "rites of passage" seems to be to "write a directory recursion routine." Generally, these solutions are not as flexible or efficient or portable as Perl's built-in File::Find module, but the beginners generally aren't aware of this module.

A typical hand-rolled directory recursion starts like so:

```
sub do_this {
  my ($dir) = shift;
  if (opendir DIR, $dir) { # it's a directory
    for my $entry (sort readdir DIR) {
      do_this("$dir/$entry"); # recurse
    }
  } else { # it's a file
    # operate on $dir (not shown)
  }
}
do_this("fred"); # our top-level directory
```

And when that gets typed in, and it runs forever, the beginner will start to scratch their head wondering why. Well, the basic structure is correct, except that the readdir call in the fourth line returns not only the files contained within the directory, but also the directories contained within the directory. That's good for the most part, but we also get the always-present "dot" and "dot-dot" entries pointing at the current directory and the parent directory.

This means that while we are processing our first directory (say fred), we'll also recurse to process that directory followed by slash-dot (fred/.), which processes the same directory again, which then recurses to process that new name followed by slash-dot (fred/./.), forever. Ooops! Similarly, we'll also process the parent directory, which then contains this directory as an entry. Even the fastest supercomputer cannot process an infinite loop in less than infinite time.

So, the next move the beginner usually takes is to strip out the dot files, or maybe just dot and dot-dot. Something like this:

```
sub do_this {
  my ($dir) = shift;
  if (opendir DIR, $dir) { # it's a directory
    for my $entry (sort readdir DIR) {
      next if $entry eq "." or $entry eq "..";
      do_this("$dir/$entry"); # recurse
    }
  } else { # it's a file
    # operate on $dir (not shown)
  }
}
do_this("fred"); # our top-level directory
```

And this is a bit better. For the most part, everything runs fine, but we still run into trouble when we hit a symbolic link (or "symlink"). If the symlink points to a directory in a parallel part of the tree, that's usually OK. But if it points to a directory deeper in the current tree, we'll process that portion twice: once as a result of following the symlink, and once when we actually get there by normal directory recursion.

And then there's the possibility of a symlink pointing to a directory *above* our current directory. It's just as bad as following dot-dot: we'll process the new directory recursively, coming right back down to where we've already gone. Infinite loop time again.

So, the next necessary refinement is often "ignore symbolic links":

```perl
sub do_this {
  my ($dir) = shift;
  if (opendir DIR, $dir) { # it's a directory
    for my $entry (sort readdir DIR) {
      next if $entry eq "." or $entry eq "..";
      next if -l "$dir/$entry";
      do_this("$dir/$entry"); # recurse
    }
  } else { # it's a file
    # operate on $dir (not shown)
  }
}
do_this("fred"); # our top-level directory
```

And there you have a perfectly fine directory recursion routine. As long as you're running on Unix, and not MacOS, VMS, OS/2, or Windows, because the step that creates $dir/$entry is wrong for those others. And, there are some speed optimization steps to keep from recursing into directories that have no subdirectories that we haven't even begun to consider here. Luckily, that's all done for us in the File::Find module, so let's get back to solving the issue raised by Aquilo.

First, we'll pull in the module:

```perl
use File::Find;
```

Next, let's set up a hash: actually, a nested hash.

```perl
my %ages;
```

We'll use this to keep track of the number of items in the directory that are both newer and older than 180-days old. We'll make each key in %ages be the full directory pathname. The corresponding value will be a hashref pointing to a hash with two keys in it: old and new. The values of those two entries will be a running count of the number of files of that category in that directory.

Now the easy and fun part: calling File::Find::find.

```perl
find \&wanted, "fred";
```

The find routine expects a reference to a subroutine ("coderef") as its first parameter. It then descends down into all of the directories listed as the remaining arguments: in this case, just fred. The subroutine gets called for every entry below the listed directories, with a few parameters set. Let's take a look at wanted now:

```
sub wanted {
  return unless -f $_;
  my $old_flag = -M $_ > 180 ? 'old' : 'new';
  $ages{$File::Find::dir}{$old_flag}++;
}
```

There's a lot going on in these few lines. First, the subroutine returns quickly if we're not looking at a file. The value of $_ is the basename of the current entry (like $entry in the hand-rolled version earlier), and our current directory is the directory being examined. Next, $old_flag is set to either old or new, based on looking at the file modification time. Finally, the hash referenced by the value of $ages{$File::Find::dir} has one of its two entries incremented, based on this $old_flag. The value of $File::Find::dir is the full pathname to our current directory. So, if a file in fred/a named dino was newer than 180 days, then ${"fred/a"}{new} would be incremented, showing that we have a new file.

After the directory recursion pass is complete, we merely have to walk the data to see what's old enough now:

```
for my $dir (sort keys %ages) {
  if ($ages{$dir}{old} > $ages{$dir}{new}) {
    print "$dir has more old than new\n";
  }
}
```

And there you have it! For all directories that have more old entries than new entries, we'll report it.

On that last comparison, we'll get warnings if -w or use warnings is enabled, because some directories have new items but not old, or old items but not new. For a small program like this, I probably wouldn't bother enabling warnings, but if you're a stickler for that, then you might also want to clean it up a bit before comparing:

```
for my $dir (sort keys %ages) {
  my $old = $ages{$dir}{old} || 0;
  my $new = $ages{$dir}{new} || 0;
  if ($old > $new and $old > 50) {
    print "$dir has more old than new\n";
  }
}
```

And notice, while I was cleaning up, I couldn't resist tinkering a bit, making it so that directories with less than 50 old items aren't reported. Just one more thing that was made slightly easier.

And there you have it. A typical system administration task hacked out in a few lines of code, and a reference to a great resource. Until next time, enjoy!

Finding Things

Linux Magazine, Column 45 (February 2003)

■**Randal's Note** Another article on `File::Find`, this time mostly talking about why `finddepth` and `$prune` are needed, which I don't think I discussed anywhere else.

"Where do we start?"

This is the phrase I often utter as I'm beginning a new magazine article, a response to a PerlMonks or Usenet posting, or even a new book. It's also a phrase I use when writing a new program. Where is the data coming from? How do I find the data?

Often, the tasks I tackle with Perl involve taking data from one or more files, performing some sort of data reduction or reporting task against the data, then generating one or more files or actions. The files are often all within a single directory, but just as often, it seems the files are in a hierarchy of directories.

The canonical Unix command-line tool for dealing with files in a hierarchy of directories is the `find` command. For example, getting a listing of all files in `/tmp` that have not been accessed in the past 14 days is as simple as typing

```
find /tmp -type f -atime +14 -print
```

And finding all files or directories below the current directory is again as simple as

```
find . -print
```

When faced with similar tasks within a Perl program, you could simply call the `find` command. Or, you could stare at the documentation for the `readdir` operator for a while, and write your own recursive directory descent routine.

But it's usually simpler to use the `File::Find` module, included with the core of the Perl distribution for many recent releases. Let's see how this works, by starting with that simple `find` command.

To list the names of all files and directories below the current directory, use this code:

```
use File::Find;
find \&wanted, ".";
sub wanted {
  print "$File::Find::name\n";
}
```

The first line brings in the `File::Find` module, defining the `find` routine. The second line invokes the `find` routine, passing it two parameters. The first parameter is a "callback": a reference to a subroutine that will be called for each name (such as a file or directory) found below the directory given as the second parameter. (You can include more than one starting point if you wish, but none of these examples uses that feature.)

For every entry below the starting directory (here "."), `find` will call `wanted`, passing it the full path in `$File::Find::name`, which we're printing. The current directory is set to the directory containing the name, and $_ is set to just the basename (the path without the directory part) of the file. This strategy permits maximum flexibility and speed, as we'll see in the later examples.

The wanted subroutine is being used only by the find invocation. Rather than coming up with a subroutine name just to use it in one other place, we can use an anonymous subroutine instead, saving a bit of brainpower trying to come up with a name:

```
use File::Find;
find sub {
  print "$File::Find::name\n";
}, ".";
```

Because the filename is placed in $_, we can use file tests with the default argument to narrow our display. For example, suppose we wanted only the directories in our display:

```
use File::Find;
find sub {
  return unless -d;
  print "$File::Find::name\n";
}, ".";
```

If the callback routine is handed a directory, the -d is true, so the return exits the subroutine early. Note that the callback subroutine is always called for every entry, and it's up to the callback subroutine to reject the entries that do not meet the desired conditions.

The /tmp example earlier can also be processed in a similar way:

```
use File::Find;
find sub {
  return unless -f;
  return unless -A > 14;
  print "$File::Find::name\n";
}, "/tmp";
```

The -A operator here returns the age in days as a floating-point value, perfect for our test.

As the find routine recurses through directories, the callback routine for a given directory will be called before any of the directory contents are examined. So, if subdir contained file1 and file2, we'd get them in that order: subdir, subdir/file1, and subdir/file2. For some tasks, we need to see the directory name *after* the contents of the directory. For this, we replace find with finddepth. (This is similar to the -depth switch of the Unix find command.)

One example of this is when you're renaming things. Let's say you're fixing up a hierarchy of Unix files so that it can be placed onto a Joliet filesystem on a CD. While Unix restricts only NUL and slash within a filename, the Windows operating system has a much narrower view of valid filenames and filename lengths. Let's do a cheap "rename everything illegal to an underscore" fixup, as follows:

```
use File::Find;
finddepth sub {
  (my $new = $_) =~ tr{\x00-\x1f\x80-\xFF*/:;?\\}{_};
  substr($new, 128) = "" if length $new > 128;
  if ($new ne $_) { # needs renaming
```

```
      if (-e $new) { # oops, already a file by that name!
        warn "Cannot rename $File::Find::name to $new: file exists!\n";
      } else {
        warn "renaming $File::Find::name to $new\n";
        rename $_, $new or warn "Cannot rename $File::Find::name to $new: $!\n";
      }
    }
}, ".";
```

For every name below dot, first compute $new, which is the name $_ but with all illegal characters translated to underscore. The substr trims the name to 128 characters or less. If the new name is not the same as the original name, we'll check first to make sure we're not renaming over the top of an existing file, and then attempt to rename the file to the fixed name. We needed finddepth here, because if we had renamed the directory name before the contents, we wouldn't be able to find the contents any more!

The callback subroutine's return value is ignored. How do we accumulate any results then, like total blocks used? We simply let the callback subroutine see an outer lexical variable, modifying it as needed. For example, suppose we want total disk blocks used, broken down by owner ID. We'll define a %blocks hash keyed by user ID number, like so:

```
my %blocks;
use File::Find;
find sub {
  return unless -f;
  return unless my @stat = stat;
  $blocks{$stat[4]} += $stat[12];
}, ".";
```

At the end of this recursion, %blocks has the total blocks broken down by user, and a simple display loop shows the results:

```
for (sort {$blocks{$b} <=> $blocks{$a}} keys %blocks) {
  printf "%16s %8d\n", scalar getpwuid($_), $blocks{$_};
}
```

The recursion can be corralled by using the "prune" feature. If the variable $File::Find::prune is set to any true value during the callback routine when looking at a directory, that directory will not be examined further. (Of course, this works only when finddepth is not used, because by then it's too late.)

For example, let's look at the count and size of all files in a CVS repository, organized by MIME type (text/plain, image/gif, and so on). We'll use File::MMagic to determine the MIME type, and we'll need to ignore the contents of any CVS directory:

```
use File::MMagic;
use File::Find;
my $mm = File::MMagic->new;
my %total;
```

```
find sub {
  return $File::Find::prune = 1 if $_ eq "CVS";
  return if -d;
  my $type = $mm->checktype_filename($_);
  $total{$type}{count}++;
  $total{$type}{size} += (stat($_))[12];
  ## push @{$total{$type}{names}}, $File::Find::name;
}, "/cvs/bigproject1";
```

At the beginning of the callback routine, if the name is exactly CVS, we'll set the prune variable to 1 and return from the subroutine. This prevents the processing not only of this entry, but also any entry below it. Next, we'll figure out the MIME type, then compute a count and blocksize summation. The commented line can be uncommented to track the exact filenames belonging to that MIME type.

Once the hash is created, we'll dump the data as follows:

```
for (sort keys %total) {
  print "$_ has $total{$_}{count} items with $total{$_}{size} blocks\n";
  ## print map "  $_\n", sort @{$total{$_}{names}};
}
```

If we added the filenames, we can uncomment the corresponding line in this loop to dump the filenames as well. This is useful if you get a MIME type of foo/bar, and you didn't think you had any foobar objects in your tree.

When I need to look at the contents of each file, and I don't need to decide pruning based on that, I find it's faster to push all the relevant filenames into @ARGV, and then use a <> loop to examine the contents. For example, suppose I want to dump out all the text files in the repository:

```
use File::Find;
@ARGV = ();
find sub {
  return $File::Find::prune = 1 if $_ eq "CVS";
  return if -d;
  push @ARGV, $File::Find::name if -T;
}, "/cvs/bigproject1";
```

Here, we'll start by clearing out the @ARGV array, then wandering down through the repository, ignoring any CVS directories and contents, and any other directories. For those that pass the -T test, we'll add the names to @ARGV. When this is done, it's as simple as

```
@ARGV = sort @ARGV;
while (<>) {
  print "$ARGV\t$_";
}
```

As each file is processed, the name of the file is placed into $ARGV, which I'm prefixing in front of each content line. What if I wanted line numbers? I just need to steal a bit more code from the perlfunc manpage, near the eof function description:

```
@ARGV = sort @ARGV;
while (<>) {
  print "$ARGV\t$.\t$_";
} continue {
  close ARGV if eof;
}
```

And now I get the filename, the line number, and the contents of the line for all the text files in my CVS tree.

Well, hopefully I've shown you some of the power of using File::Find. I've recently discovered in the CPAN a simple wrapper around this module called File::Find::Rule that makes it easier to specify some of the more common filters, but alas, have run out of space in this article. Perhaps I'll cover that in a future article. Until then, enjoy!

Introduction to Objects, Part 1

Linux Magazine, Column 11 (April 2000)

■**Randal's Note** Ah yes, the famous text which eventually became the perlboot manpage, or at least the first half of it. The program snippets for this text were written at a karaoke bar in San Francisco the night before I needed to present them to my client in Marin County. Yes, I was sitting with my laptop at a bar, madly scribbling down better ways to teach objects. Unlike most approaches, which attempted to teach bless, the method arrow, and hashes-as-data-structures all at once, I believe the success of this approach is the simplicity of learning one thing at a time.

In earlier columns, I looked at using "references" in Perl. References are an important part of capturing and reflecting the structure of real-world data—a table of employees, each of which has various attributes, can be represented as an array of hashrefs, pointing at attribute hashes for each employee.

Now, let's turn to capturing and reflecting the real-world processes, in the form of "objects." Objects provide encapsulation (to control access to data), abstract data types (to let the data more closely model the real world), and inheritance (to reuse operations that are similar but have some variation).

The Perl distribution includes perlobj, a basic reference in using objects, and perltoot, which introduces readers to the peculiarities of Perl's object system in a tutorial way. However, I found that both of these documentation sections tend to be opaque to those of us with less experience with objects. And that seems to be the majority of users coming from the system administration or CGI web development background (Perl's core audience).

So I created some courseware for Stonehenge's Perl training classes that took a different approach to objects, presuming no prior exposure to objects. It goes something like this . . .

If We Could Talk to the Animals . . .

Let's let the animals talk for a moment:

```
sub Cow::speak {
  print "a Cow goes moooo!\n";
}
sub Horse::speak {
  print "a Horse goes neigh!\n";
}
sub Sheep::speak {
  print "a Sheep goes baaaah!\n"
}
Cow::speak;
Horse::speak;
Sheep::speak;
```

This results in

```
a Cow goes moooo!
a Horse goes neigh!
a Sheep goes baaaah!
```

Nothing spectacular here. Simple subroutines, albeit from separate packages, and called using the full package name. So let's create an entire pasture:

```
# Cow::speak, Horse::speak, Sheep::speak as before
@pasture = qw(Cow Cow Horse Sheep Sheep);
foreach $animal (@pasture) {
  &{$animal."::speak"};
}
```

This results in

```
a Cow goes moooo!
a Cow goes moooo!
a Horse goes neigh!
a Sheep goes baaaah!
a Sheep goes baaaah!
```

Wow. That symbolic coderef dereferencing there is pretty nasty. We're counting on no strict subs mode, certainly not recommended for larger programs. And why was that necessary? Because the name of the package seems to be inseparable from the name of the subroutine we want to invoke within that package.

Or is it?

Introducing the Method Invocation Arrow

For now, let's say that `Class->method` invokes subroutine `method` in package `Class`. That's not completely accurate, but we'll do this one step at a time. Now let's use it like so:

```
# Cow::speak, Horse::speak, Sheep::speak as before
Cow->speak;
Horse->speak;
Sheep->speak;
```

And once again, this results in

```
a Cow goes moooo!
a Horse goes neigh!
a Sheep goes baaaah!
```

That's not fun yet. Same number of characters, all constant, no variables. But yet, the parts are separable now. Watch:

```
$a = "Cow";
$a->speak; # invokes Cow->speak
```

Ahh! Now that the package name has been parted from the subroutine name, we can use a variable package name. And this time, we've got something that works even when `use strict refs` is enabled.

Invoking a Barnyard

Let's take that new arrow invocation and put it back in the barnyard example:

```
sub Cow::speak {
  print "a Cow goes moooo!\n";
}
sub Horse::speak {
  print "a Horse goes neigh!\n";
}
sub Sheep::speak {
  print "a Sheep goes baaaah!\n"
}
@pasture = qw(Cow Cow Horse Sheep Sheep);
foreach $animal (@pasture) {
  $animal->speak;
}
```

There! Now we have the animals all talking, and safely at that, without the use of symbolic coderefs.

But look at all that common code. Each of the `speak` routines has a similar structure: a `print` operator and a string that contains common text, except for two of the words. It'd be nice if we could factor out the commonality, in case we decide later to change it all to `says` instead of `goes`.

And we actually have a way of doing that without much fuss, but we have to hear a bit more about what the method invocation arrow is actually doing for us.

The Extra Parameter of Method Invocation

The invocation of

```
Class->method(@args)
```

attempts to invoke subroutine `Class::method` as

```
Class::method("Class", @args);
```

(If the subroutine can't be found, "inheritance" kicks in, but we'll get to that later.) This means that we get the class name as the first parameter. So we can rewrite the Sheep speaking subroutine as

```
sub Sheep::speak {
  my $class = shift;
  print "a $class goes baaaah!\n";
}
```

And the other two animals come out similarly:

```
sub Cow::speak {
  my $class = shift;
  print "a $class goes moooo!\n";
}
sub Horse::speak {
  my $class = shift;
  print "a $class goes neigh!\n";
}
```

In each case, `$class` will get the value appropriate for that subroutine. But once again, we have a lot of similar structure. Can we factor that out even further? Yes, by calling another method in the same class.

Calling a Second Method to Simplify Things

Let's call out from speak to a helper method called sound. This method provides the constant text for the sound itself.

```
{ package Cow;
  sub sound { "moooo" }
  sub speak {
    my $class = shift;
    print "a $class goes ", $class->sound, "!\n"
  }
}
```

Now, when we call Cow->speak, we get a $class of Cow in speak. This in turn selects the Cow->sound method, which returns moooo. But how different would this be for the Horse?

```
{ package Horse;
  sub sound { "neigh" }
  sub speak {
    my $class = shift;
    print "a $class goes ", $class->sound, "!\n"
  }
}
```

Only the name of the package and the specific sound change. So can we somehow share the definition for speak between the Cow and the Horse? Yes, with inheritance!

Inheriting the Windpipes

We'll define a common subroutine package called Animal, with the definition for speak:

```
{ package Animal;
  sub speak {
    my $class = shift;
    print "a $class goes ", $class->sound, "!\n"
  }
}
```

Then, for each animal, we say it "inherits" from Animal, along with the animal-specific sound:

```
{ package Cow;
  @ISA = qw(Animal);
  sub sound { "moooo" }
}
```

Note the added @ISA array. We'll get to that in a minute.

But what happens when we invoke Cow->speak now?

First, Perl constructs the argument list. In this case, it's just Cow. Then Perl looks for Cow::speak. But that's not there, so Perl checks for the inheritance array @Cow::ISA. It's there, and contains the single name Animal.

Perl next checks for speak inside Animal instead, as in Animal::speak. And that's found, so Perl invokes that subroutine with the already frozen argument list.

Inside the Animal::speak subroutine, $class becomes Cow (the first argument). So when we get to the step of invoking $class->sound, it'll be looking for Cow->sound, which gets it on the first try without looking at @ISA. Success!

A Few Notes About @ISA

This magical @ISA variable (pronounced "is a" not "ice-uh") has declared that Cow "is a" Animal. Note that it's an array, not a simple single value, because on rare occasions, it makes sense to have more than one parent class search for the missing methods.

If Animal also had an @ISA, then we'd check there too. The search is recursive, depth-first, left-to-right in each @ISA.

When we turn on use strict, we'll get complaints on @ISA, since it's not a variable containing an explicit package name, nor is it a lexical (my) variable. We can't make it a lexical variable though, so there's a couple of straightforward ways to handle that.

The easiest is to just spell the package name out:

```perl
@Cow::ISA = qw(Animal);
```

Or allow it as an implicitly named package variable:

```perl
package Cow;
use vars qw(@ISA);
@ISA = qw(Animal);
```

If you're bringing in the class from outside, via an object-oriented module, you change

```perl
package Cow;
use Animal;
use vars qw(@ISA);
@ISA = qw(Animal);
```

into just

```perl
package Cow;
use base qw(Animal);
```

And that's pretty darn compact.

Overriding the Methods

Let's add a mouse, which can barely be heard:

```perl
# Animal package from before
{ package Mouse;
  @ISA = qw(Animal);
  sub sound { "squeak" }
  sub speak {
    my $class = shift;
    print "a $class goes ", $class->sound, "!\n";
    print "[but you can barely hear it!]\n";
  }
}
Mouse->speak;
```

which results in

```
a Mouse goes squeak!
[but you can barely hear it!]
```

Here, Mouse has its own speaking routine, so Mouse->speak doesn't immediately invoke Animal->speak. This is known as "overriding." In fact, we didn't even need to say that a Mouse was an Animal at all, since all of the methods needed for speak are completely defined with Mouse.

But we've now duplicated some of the code from Animal->speak, and this can once again be a maintenance headache. So, can we avoid that? Can we say somehow that a Mouse does everything any other Animal does, but add in the extra comment? Sure!

First, we can invoke the Animal::speak method directly:

```
# Animal package from before
{ package Mouse;
  @ISA = qw(Animal);
  sub sound { "squeak" }
  sub speak {
    my $class = shift;
    Animal::speak($class);
    print "[but you can barely hear it!]\n";
  }
}
```

Note that we have to include the $class parameter (almost surely the value of Mouse) as the first parameter to Animal::speak, since we've stopped using the method arrow. Why did we stop? Well, if we invoke Animal->speak there, the first parameter to the method will be Animal not Mouse, and when time comes for it to call for the sound, it won't have the right class to come back to this package.

Invoking Animal::speak directly is a mess, however. What if Animal::speak didn't exist before, and was being inherited from a class mentioned in @Animal::ISA? Because we are no longer using the method arrow, we get one and only one chance to hit the right subroutine.

Also note that the Animal class name is now hardwired into the subroutine selection. This is a mess if someone maintaining the code changes @ISA for Mouse and doesn't notice Animal there in speak. So, this is probably not the right way to go.

Starting the Search from a Different Place

A better solution is to tell Perl to search from a higher place in the inheritance chain:

```
# same Animal as before
{ package Mouse;
  @ISA = qw(Animal);
  sub sound { "squeak" }
  sub speak {
    my $class = shift;
    $class->Animal::speak;
    print "[but you can barely hear it!]\n";
  }
}
```

Ahh. This works. Using this syntax, we start with Animal to find speak, and use all of Animal's inheritance chain if not found immediately. And yet the first parameter will be $class, so the found speak method will get Mouse as its first entry, and eventually work its way back to Mouse::sound for the details.

But this isn't the best solution. We still have to keep the @ISA and the initial search package coordinated. Worse, if Mouse had multiple entries in @ISA, we wouldn't necessarily know which one had actually defined speak. So, is there an even better way?

The SUPER Way of Doing Things

By changing the Animal class to the SUPER class in that invocation, we get a search of all of our superclasses automatically:

```
# same Animal as before
{ package Mouse;
  @ISA = qw(Animal);
  sub sound { "squeak" }
  sub speak {
    my $class = shift;
    $class->SUPER::speak;
    print "[but you can barely hear it!]\n";
  }
}
```

So, SUPER::speak means look in the current package's @ISA for speak, invoking the first one found.

In Summary

So far, I've introduced a method arrow syntax:

```
Class->method(@args);
```

or the equivalent:

```
$a = "Class";
$a->method(@args);
```

which constructs an argument list of

```
("Class", @args)
```

and attempts to invoke

```
Class::method("Class", @Args);
```

However, if Class::method is not found, then @Class::ISA is examined (recursively) to locate a package that does indeed contain method, and that subroutine is invoked instead.

Using this simple syntax, we have class methods, (multiple) inheritance, overriding, and extending. Using just what we've seen so far, we've been able to factor out common code, and provide a nice way to reuse implementations with variations. This is at the core of what objects provide, but objects also provide instance data, which we haven't even begun to cover.

But I've run out of space for this time, so see Part 2 next month. Until then, enjoy.

Introduction to Objects, Part 2

Linux Magazine, Column 12 (May 2000)

■**Randal's Note** This article, together with the previous article, forms the core of the `perlboot` man-page, and the initial object portion of my book, *Learning Perl Objects, References and Modules*. When you've got something that works, you use it a lot.

Last month, I started talking about Perl objects, introducing the method arrow syntax, as follows:

```
Class->method(@args);
```

or the equivalent:

```
$a = "Class";
$a->method(@args);
```

which constructs an argument list of

```
("Class", @args)
```

and attempts to invoke

```
Class::method("Class", @args);
```

However, if `Class::method` is not found, then `@Class::ISA` is examined (recursively) to locate a package that does indeed contain `method`, and that subroutine is invoked instead.

Using this simple syntax, we have class methods, (multiple) inheritance, overriding, and extending. Using just what we've seen so far, we've been able to factor out common code, and provide a nice way to reuse implementations with variations. This is at the core of what objects provide, but objects also provide instance data, which we haven't even begun to cover. Until now.

A Horse Is a Horse, of Course, of Course—OR IS IT?

Let's start with the code from last month for the `Animal` class and the `Horse` class:

```
{ package Animal;
  sub speak {
    my $class = shift;
    print "a $class goes ", $class->sound, "!\n"
  }
}
{ package Horse;
  @ISA = qw(Animal);
  sub sound { "neigh" }
}
```

This lets us invoke Horse->speak to ripple upward to Animal::speak, calling back to Horse::sound to get the specific sound, and the output of

```
a Horse goes neigh!
```

But all of our Horse objects would have to be absolutely identical. If I add a subroutine, all horses automatically share it. That's great for making horses the same, but how do we capture the distinctions about an individual horse? For example, suppose I want to give my first horse a name. There's got to be a way to keep its name separate from the other horses.

We can do that by drawing a new distinction, called an "instance." An instance is generally created by a class. In Perl, any reference can be an instance, so let's start with the simplest reference that can hold a horse's name: a scalar reference.

```
my $name = "Mr. Ed";
my $talking = \$name;
```

So now $talking is a reference to what will be the instance-specific data (the name). The final step in turning this into a real instance is with a special operator called bless:

```
bless $talking, Horse;
```

This operator stores information about the package named Horse into the thing pointed at by the reference. At this point, we say $talking is an instance of Horse. That is, it's a specific horse. The reference is otherwise unchanged, and can still be used with traditional dereferencing operators.

Invoking an Instance Method

The method arrow can be used on instances, as well as names of packages (classes). So, let's get the sound that $talking makes:

```
my $noise = $talking->sound;
```

To invoke sound, Perl first notes that $talking is a blessed reference (and thus an instance). It then constructs an argument list, in this case from just ($talking). (Later we'll see that arguments will take their place following the instance variable, just like with classes.)

Now for the fun part: Perl takes the class in which the instance was blessed, in this case Horse, and uses that to locate the subroutine to invoke the method. In this case, Horse::sound is found directly (without using inheritance), yielding the final subroutine invocation:

```
Horse::sound($talking)
```

Note that the first parameter here is still the instance, not the name of the class as before. We'll get neigh as the return value, and that'll end up as the preceding $noise variable.

If Horse::sound had not been found, we'd be wandering up the @Horse::ISA list to try to find the method in one of the superclasses, just as for a class method. The only difference between a class method and an instance method is whether the first parameter is a instance (a blessed reference) or a class name (a string).

Accessing the Instance Data

Because we get the instance as the first parameter, we can now access the instance-specific data. In this case, let's add a way to get at the name:

```
{ package Horse;
  @ISA = qw(Animal);
  sub sound { "neigh" }
  sub name {
    my $self = shift;
    $$self;
  }
}
```

Now we call for the name:

```
print $talking->name, " says ", $talking->sound, "\n";
```

Inside Horse::name, the @_ array contains just $talking, which the shift stores into $self. (It's traditional to shift the first parameter off into a variable named $self for instance methods, so stay with that unless you have strong reasons otherwise.) Then, $self gets dereferenced as a scalar ref, yielding Mr. Ed, and we're done with that. The result is

```
Mr. Ed says neigh.
```

How to Build a Horse

Of course, if we constructed all of our horses by hand, we'd most likely make mistakes from time to time. We're also violating one of the properties of object-oriented programming, in that the "inside guts" of a Horse are visible. That's good if you're a veterinarian, but not if you just like to own horses. So, let's let the Horse class build a new horse:

```
{ package Horse;
  @ISA = qw(Animal);
  sub sound { "neigh" }
  sub name {
    my $self = shift;
    $$self;
  }
  sub named {
    my $class = shift;
    my $name = shift;
    bless \$name, $class;
  }
}
```

Now with the new named method, we can build a horse:

```
my $talking = Horse->named("Mr. Ed");
```

Notice we're back to a class method, so the two arguments to Horse::named are Horse and Mr. Ed. The bless operator not only blesses $name, it also returns the reference to $name, so that's fine as a return value. And that's how to build a horse.

Inheriting the Constructor

But was there anything specific to Horse in that method? No. Therefore, it's also the same recipe for building anything else that inherited from Animal, so let's put it there:

```
{ package Animal;
  sub speak {
    my $class = shift;
    print "a $class goes ", $class->sound, "!\n"
  }
  sub name {
    my $self = shift;
    $$self;
  }
  sub named {
    my $class = shift;
    my $name = shift;
    bless \$name, $class;
  }
}
{ package Horse;
  @ISA = qw(Animal);
  sub sound { "neigh" }
}
```

Ah, but what happens if we invoke speak on an instance?

```
my $talking = Horse->named("Mr. Ed");
$talking->speak;
```

We get a debugging value:

```
a Horse=SCALAR(0xaca42ac) goes neigh!
```

Why? Because the Animal::speak routine is expecting a class name as its first parameter, not an instance. When the instance is passed in, we'll end up using a blessed scalar reference as a string, and that shows up as we saw it just now.

Making a Method Work with Either Classes or Instances

All we need is for a method to detect if it is being called on a class or called on an instance. The most straightforward way is with the ref operator. This returns a string (the class name) when used on a blessed reference, and undef when used on a string (like a class name). Let's modify the name method first to notice the change:

```perl
sub name {
  my $either = shift;
  ref $either
    ? $$either # it's an instance, return name
    : "an unnamed $either"; # it's a class, return generic
}
```

Here, the ?: operator comes in handy to select either the dereference or a derived string. Now we can use this with either an instance or a class. Note that I've changed the first parameter holder to $either to show that this is intended:

```perl
my $talking = Horse->named("Mr. Ed");
print Horse->name, "\n"; # prints "an unnamed Horse\n"
print $talking->name, "\n"; # prints "Mr Ed.\n"
```

and now we'll fix speak to use this:

```perl
sub speak {
  my $either = shift;
  print $either->name, " goes ", $either->sound, "\n";
}
```

And since sound already worked with either a class or an instance, we're done!

Adding Parameters to a Method

Let's train our animals to eat:

```perl
{ package Animal;
  sub named {
    my $class = shift;
    my $name = shift;
    bless \$name, $class;
  }
  sub name {
    my $either = shift;
    ref $either
      ? $$either # it's an instance, return name
      : "an unnamed $either"; # it's a class, return generic
  }
  sub speak {
    my $either = shift;
    print $either->name, " goes ", $either->sound, "\n";
  }
  sub eat {
    my $either = shift;
    my $food = shift;
    print $either->name, " eats $food.\n";
  }
}
```

```
{ package Horse;
  @ISA = qw(Animal);
  sub sound { "neigh" }
}
{ package Sheep;
  @ISA = qw(Animal);
  sub sound { "baaaah" }
}
```

And now try it out:

```
my $talking = Horse->named("Mr. Ed");
$talking->eat("hay");
Sheep->eat("grass");
```

which prints

```
Mr. Ed eats hay.
an unnamed Sheep eats grass.
```

An instance method with parameters gets invoked with the instance, and then the list of parameters. So that first invocation is like

```
Animal::eat($talking, "hay");
```

More Interesting Instances

What if an instance needs more data? Most interesting instances are made of many items, each of which can in turn be a reference or even another object. The easiest way to store these is often in a hash. The keys of the hash serve as the names of parts of the object (often called "instance variables" or "member variables"), and the corresponding values are, well, the values.

But how do we turn the horse into a hash? Recall that an object was any blessed reference. We can just as easily make it a blessed hash reference as a blessed scalar reference, as long as everything that looks at the reference is changed accordingly.

Let's make a sheep that has a name and a color:

```
my $bad = bless { Name => "Evil", Color => "black" }, Sheep;
```

so $bad->{Name} has Evil, and $bad->{Color} has black. But we want to make $bad->name access the name, and that's now messed up because it's expecting a scalar reference. Not to worry, because that's pretty easy to fix up:

```
## in Animal
sub name {
  my $either = shift;
  ref $either ?
    $either->{Name} :
    "an unnamed $either";
}
```

And of course named still builds a scalar sheep, so let's fix that as well:

```
## in Animal
sub named {
  my $class = shift;
  my $name = shift;
  my $self = { Name => $name, Color => $class->default_color };
  bless $self, $class;
}
```

What's this default_color? Well, if named has only the name, we still need to set a color, so we'll have a class-specific initial color. For a sheep, we might define it as white:

```
## in Sheep
sub default_color { "white" }
```

And then to keep from having to define one for each additional class, we'll define a "backstop" method that serves as the "default default" directly in Animal:

```
## in Animal
sub default_color { "brown" }
```

Now, because name and named were the only methods that referenced the "structure" of the object, the rest of the methods can remain the same, so speak still works as before.

A Horse of a Different Color

But having all our horses be brown would be boring. So let's add a method or two to get and set the color.

```
## in Animal
sub color {
  $_[0]->{Color}
}
sub set_color {
  $_[0]->{Color} = $_[1];
}
```

Note the alternate way of accessing the arguments: $_[0] is used in-place, rather than with a shift. (This saves us a bit of time for something that may be invoked frequently.) And now we can fix that color for Mr. Ed:

```
my $talking = Horse->named("Mr. Ed");
$talking->set_color("black-and-white");
print $talking->name, " is colored ", $talking->color, "\n";
```

which results in

```
Mr. Ed is colored black-and-white
```

Summary

So, now we have class methods, constructors, instance methods, instance data, and even accessors. But that's still just the beginning of what Perl has to offer. We haven't even begun to talk about accessors that double as getters and setters, destructors, indirect object notation, subclasses that add instance data, per-class data, overloading, "isa" and "can" tests, UNIVERSAL class, and so on. Perhaps in a future column, eh?

For more information, see the Perl documentation for perlobj (the reference information about objects), perltoot (the tutorial for those who already know objects), perlbot (for some more tricks), and books such as Damian Conway's excellent *Object Oriented Perl*. And as always, enjoy!

Constructing Objects

Unix Review, Column 52 (May 2004)

To construct an object in Perl, you need to select a valid package name for the object's class, populate that package with subroutines to define the methods, set the value of @ISA within that package to define the base (parent) classes for that class, and then create a blessed reference.

For example, we can make widgets that know how to say their name and take on a new name with the following code (I'll describe $self in a moment here):

```perl
package Widget;
sub display {
  my $self = shift;
  print $self->{name}, "\n";
}
sub rename {
  my $self = shift;
  $self->{name} = shift;
  $self;
}
```

A constructed object compatible with this definition has to be a hashref with at least a key of name holding the name of the object. We can construct such a hashref like so:

```perl
my $dog = { name => 'Spot' };
bless $dog, 'Widget';
```

The bless operation puts a little Post-it note on the hash data structure (not the reference!) that says "I belong to Widget." Now, we can invoke the methods like so:

```perl
$dog->display; # prints "Spot\n"
$dog->rename("Fido");
$dog->display; # prints "Fido\n"
```

How does this work? To execute the `rename` call, for example, Perl constructs an argument list consisting of the object variable ($dog) plus any arguments given to the method, resulting in

```
($dog, "Fido")
```

Next, Perl looks for a subroutine in the package given by the Post-it note (the object's class) named the same as the method. The subroutine `Widget::rename` gets invoked, and the first argument ends up in $self. The second argument gets assigned as an element of the hash, and finally the subroutine returns $self (not a requirement, but handy for other operations).

Normally, we wouldn't hand-construct the object. The lines to create the hash and bless the object will be found in a constructor within the class. We'll invoke the constructor as

```
my $dog = Widget->named("Spot");
```

To execute this class method invocation, Perl again constructs an argument list, but this time puts the name of the package as the first element:

```
("Widget", "Spot")
```

And upon finding the `Widget::named` subroutine, invokes it:

```perl
package Widget;
sub named {
  my $class = shift; # gets Widget (usually)
  my $self = { name => shift };
  bless $self, $class;
  $self;
}
```

Comparing this code to the preceding code, we see that we'll be returning $self, which is just like the $dog from earlier. (One common optimization is to know that `bless` also returns $self in this case, so we can leave that last line out with no change in result.)

For a more detailed explanation of this process, please see my most recent tutorial book, *Learning Perl Objects, References and Modules*, from O'Reilly and Associates.

Now, why didn't we just hardcode the `Widget` value into the `bless`, and what's up with that "usually" in the comment? The complication arises when we get to inheritance. Suppose we have a subclass called `ColoredWidget` that inherits from `Widget` and adds two methods to manage the color of the widget:

```perl
package ColoredWidget;
use base qw(Widget); # sets @ISA
sub color {
  my $self = shift;
  $self->{color};
}
sub recolor {
  my $self = shift;
  $self->{color} = shift;
  $self;
}
```

Calling color or recolor on a ColoredWidget uses the subroutines found in the ColoredWidget package, but calling named on ColoredWidget uses the @ISA to find the named routine from the base class, Widget. In this case, the argument list will look like

```
("ColoredWidget", "Spot")
```

Because the first argument to named is shifted off into $class, and then used in the bless, we get an object of class ColoredWidget instead of Widget.

Our display method for ColoredWidget needs a bit more work now though, if we want the color as well. We can use *overriding* to handle that:

```
package ColoredWidget;
sub display {
  my $self = shift;
  print $self->name, ", colored ", $self->color, "\n";
}
```

Now, for ColoredWidget objects, this version of display is used in preference to the previous version. We can also *extend* rather than override by reusing the base class version of display:

```
package ColoredWidget;
sub display {
  my $self = shift;
  $self->SUPER::display;
  print "[color: ", $self->color, "]\n";
}
```

Now when we invoke display on a ColoredWidget, we first invoke the first display found in the base class (as if there was no definition in this class). That invocation produces the name by itself. Then control returns to this method, and we add the color in brackets below.

The constructor here is named named because it reads like what it does: give me a Widget named Spot. But for tradition's sake, I could also call the constructor new. In fact, I might make a constructor new that returns an unnamed Widget (the name left as undef if referenced). This'd look like

```
package Widget;
sub new {
  my $class = shift;
  bless {}, $class;
}
```

Here, a simple reference to an empty hash is generated, blessed into the right class, and returned. To make Spot, I can now say

```
my $dog = Widget->new;
$dog->rename("Spot");
```

That's a little more clumsy, but at least it gets the job done.

Another advantage to always naming your constructor as new is that you can easily create an object that is "like" another object. For example, if we have an unknown object $object, we can call ref $object to get its class, then create another object of the same class by calling new:

```
my $similar = (ref $object)->new;
```

But this works only if all of our possible classes of $object understand the same new method. Fortunately, for the times we're likely to do this, we've also made the classes work this way.

Another common operation is *cloning*: making an object that is a copy of the current object. It's not enough to simply copy the reference:

```
my $puppy = $dog;
```

This action copies the reference to the data, but not the data itself. So if I rename the $puppy, the $dog changes its name as well! Cloning is best handled by copying all of the data. A naive clone could be executed as

```
package Widget;
sub clone {
  my $self = shift;
  my $clone = { %$self }; # copy keys/values one level deep
  bless $clone, ref $self; # copy the object class, returning $clone
}
```

This will work properly for objects that do not have a deep structure, such as we've seen here so far. But what if one of the object attributes is a reference to yet another data structure? Again, we're copying the reference, and not the data, so the data will be shared amongst the clones (See *Unix Review, Column 30*, later on in this chapter, for more details on deep copying.)

An alternative method of cloning is a more piecemeal approach. Teach each class in the hierarchy to clone the attributes added by that class.

```
package Widget;
sub clone {
  my $self = shift;
  my $clone = (ref $self)->new; # empty object of same class
  $clone->rename($self->name); # copy name attribute
  $clone;
}
package SubWidget;
sub clone {
  my $self = shift;
  my $clone = $self->SUPER::clone; # clone base class stuff
  $clone->recolor($self->color); # copy color attribute
  $clone;
}
```

Note the similarity of design. If a class knows that it adds a complex attribute (a reference to a deeper data structure), then it can add special copying instructions for that attribute to the new clone. This is a good OO design, because the information contained within each base and derived class is maintained closely with the logic it depends on.

And now, before I run out of space, let me touch on a hot-button for me. The `perltoot` manpage contains an archetypal `new` routine that looks like

```
sub new {
  my $proto = shift;
  my $class = ref($proto) || $proto;
  my $self  = {};
  ...
}
```

The purpose of these few lines of extra code is to permit

```
my $other = $dog->new;
```

to act like

```
my $other = (ref $dog)->new;
```

But here's the problem. When I survey experienced object-oriented programmers, and ask them what they expect `new` means when called on an instance (without looking at the implementation), the result usually divides rather equally into three camps: those who go "Huh, why would you do that?" and think it should throw an error, those who say that it would *clone* the object, and those who say it would *copy* the object's class but not the contents.

So, no matter what you intend, if you make your `new` do one of those three things, two thirds of the people who look at it will be wrong. It's not intuitive. So, don't write code like that, and especially don't just cargo-cult that from the manpage into your code. If you want an object *like* another object, use `ref` explicitly, as shown previously. If you want a clone, put cloning code into your package, and call `clone`, as we saw earlier.

Hopefully, you've learned at least one or two things about objects that you might not have considered before. Until next time, enjoy!

Wrappers Utilizing exec

Unix Review, Column 10 (September 1996)

▩**Randal's Note**   This article is again inspired by materials I wrote for Stonehenge's "llama" class. Whenever I'm stuck for an article topic, I think about what I taught or answered the previous week (or earlier that day), and turn it into a magazine article.

In *Unix Review, Column 9*, shown earlier, I re-created a portion of the common Unix utility, grep, while giving it additional functionality—the ability to ignore nontext files. This time, I'm going to illustrate how to use a Perl "wrapper" to use the existing grep command for the actual search, but still retaining the "text-only" nature of the function.

A wrapper generally replaces the invocation of a particular program: I'd invoke textgrep instead of grep in my scripts, for example. If I wanted to be particularly clever, I could call the wrapper grep, and then put the real grep into a place not normally found in my path, known only to the wrapper.

In this case, the wrapper is invoked with the same arguments as the standard grep command. The wrapper will examine only the filename arguments (ignoring the others), and remove any filename argument that corresponds to a binary file. Any remaining filename arguments, along with the previously ignored arguments, are then passed to the real grep command transparently.

The first part of the program is to recognize the difference between the filename arguments and the other arguments. Let's look at this part of the program:

```
while ($ARGV[0] =~ /^-[a-z]$/) {
        push @OPTS, shift;
}
```

Here, we're looking at the first entry of @ARGV (as designated by $ARGV[0]), and if it looks like an option (a minus followed by a single letter), we transfer it from @ARGV to @OPTS. Here, the shift operator is removing the first element of @ARGV by default.

But this strategy fails on the -e and -f options, which take a following parameter. This parameter would not likely look like an option, so we need to add an additional step:

```
while ($ARGV[0] =~ /^-[a-z]$/) {
        if ($ARGV[0] =~ /^-[ef]$/) {
                push @OPTS, shift;
        }
        push @OPTS, shift;
}
```

There. Now, if it's -e or -f, two args get moved over instead of one. As you can see, writing a wrapper requires a fairly complete understanding of the arguments to the wrapped program.

Next, we need to process whatever's left in @ARGV, ripping out the nontext filenames. This is pretty much the same code as in the last column:

```
@ARGV = "-" unless @ARGV;
@ARGV = grep { -T or $_ eq "-" } @ARGV;
exit 0 unless @ARGV;
```

The first step inserts "-" if there's no remaining arguments. This won't change the meaning of @ARGV, but gives us something to work with later. The second step removes from @ARGV any filename that is neither a "text" file (as determined by the -T operator) or the "-" (meaning standard input). Standard input is always considered to be a text file. The third step causes us to exit with a zero exit status if there are no text files to process.

Finally, we need to invoke grep with this thus-modified command line:

```
exec "grep", @OPTS, @ARGV;
```

The exec operator invokes the grep command (found according to the current PATH environment variable), passing it the options (in @OPTS) if any, and then the list of filenames to process (in @ARGV).

This gets us most of the way there. I could stick this program into textgrep, and it'd work. However, let's look at the wrapper like I mentioned earlier: something to replace the grep command that I would still invoke as grep. First, I'll need to move the grep command out of the way (say, to /usr/bin/realgrep), and tell this program where it is:

```perl
$real_grep = "/usr/bin/realgrep";
```

Next, I'll want to invoke this realgrep, but convince it that it is being invoked as grep (in case it cares.) This is done by lying to it about its name and location. I'll want the real grep to believe it is named the same as my textgrep script (which will now be called grep). Fortunately, this path is available in the $0 variable, and can be passed as the argv[0] to the new program using a funky feature of exec:

```perl
exec $0 $real_grep, @OPTS, @ARGV;
```

Notice the $0 in the slot between the exec operator and the program name to execute and the list of arguments to pass.

There's now not much the real grep command can do to find out that it wasn't really located in the old location. Putting it all together:

```perl
#!/usr/bin/perl
$real_grep = "/usr/bin/realgrep";
while ($ARGV[0] =~ /^-[a-z]$/) {
        if ($ARGV[0] =~ /^-[ef]$/) {
                push @OPTS, shift;
        }
        push @OPTS, shift;
}
@ARGV = "-" unless @ARGV;
@ARGV = grep { -T or $_ eq "-" } @ARGV;
exit 0 unless @ARGV;
exec $0 $real_grep, @OPTS, @ARGV;
die "cannot exec $real_grep: $!";
```

I've added a die here to capture the problems of not being able to find the $real_grep program.

Now, why exec instead of system? Using exec causes the Perl script to exec the grep program, rather than launching grep as a child process. If this step is successful (as it mostly will be if we got the pathnames correct), then the Perl interpreter is gone, having become the grep command. The only code after an exec should be to handle a failed exec (such as the die here).

There are other uses for wrapper scripts. For example, suppose you had a database accounting package that needed to have a certain umask and current directory established, as well as a few important environment variables. While you could create a shell script to do all of this, let's see how it's done in Perl:

```perl
#!/usr/bin/perl
my $DB_HOME = "/home/merlyn/database";
chdir $DB_HOME
        or die "cannot get to db dir: $!";
umask 2;
$ENV{'DB_HOME'} = $DB_HOME;
$ENV{'PATH'} .= ":$DB_HOME";
exec "accounting", @ARGV;
die "Cannot exec accounting: $!";
```

Here, I've established a Perl variable $DB_HOME, representing the directory of this accounting package. Then, I cd there in the Perl process, and set my umask to 002 (making newly created files or directories with only the "other-write" permission off). Next, I set the environment variable DB_HOME to the value of the Perl variable of the same name. Note that Perl variables are not automatically exported, so this is the equivalent of

```
setenv DB_HOME $DB_HOME
```

in the C-shell, or

```
export DB_HOME
```

in the Bourne shell. Also, I've updated the PATH environment variable to attach the DB_HOME directory as one of the directories containing programs. Note that I am appending the new directory to the end of the list, and not the beginning. If I wanted to do the beginning, I'd have to write it as

```
$ENV{'PATH'} = "$DB_HOME:$ENV{'PATH'}";
```

And finally, the invocation of the accounting program, followed by a diagnostic if the exec fails. Note that I'm passing the @ARGV list through to the accounting package, essentially uninterpreted. If there were some common arguments to pass, say -d and $DB_HOME, it'd look like this:

```
exec "accounting", "-d",
     $DB_HOME, @ARGV;
```

(This is probably a pretty stupid accounting package that requires so many things to be set to DB_HOME, but hopefully you can see where I'm going here.)

Another kind of a wrapper is one that messes with the standard file descriptors to alter the behavior slightly. For example, the standard find command has the mostly useful feature of reporting unscannable directories via a message to standard error. However, when we aren't interested in what find cannot do, these messages are just an annoyance.

Certainly, with the proper command-line I/O redirection, I can cause STDERR to be tossed away. However, let's create a wrapper instead that completely eliminates the messages for STDERR:

```
#!/usr/bin/perl
open STDERR, ">/dev/null";
exec "find", @ARGV;
die "Cannot exec find: $!";
```

There. Pretty simple. I could stick this into a file named qfind (for "quiet find"), and then invoke it with

```
qfind / -name '*perl*' -ls
```

and now I won't get all those messages telling me about directories I cannot enter.

I could also do the same on the accounting database wrapper to log all STDERR messages into a log file (just before I invoke exec):

```
open STDERR, ">>log";
```

Well, this about wraps up my discussion of wrappers. Hope you enjoyed it.

Taint So Easy, Is It?

Unix Review, Column 33 (August 2000)

■Randal's Note The `Scalar::Util` module (in the core in recent versions of Perl) lets us test whether a value is tainted, but that module hadn't been written when I wrote this article. Otherwise, this is all good sound advice on how to use one of the unique Perl features to increase relative security.

If you've been reading my columns for any length of time, you've probably seen me mention "taint mode," usually briefly while I'm describing a "hash-bang" line of something like

```
#!/usr/bin/perl -Tw
```

which turns on warnings (the `-w`) and taint mode (the `-T`). But what *is* taint mode?

Taint mode is a security feature of Perl, and includes two levels of operation. First, while taint mode is in effect, some operations are forbidden. One of these is that `$ENV{PATH}` cannot contain any world-writable directories when firing off a child process (like with backticks or `system`). Should your program attempt an unsafe action, the program aborts (via `die`) immediately, before the action has a chance to create a potential security violation. You could have included code to check this yourself, but having Perl perform the checks ensures a consistency and a "best practices" level of competence that you may not have the capability or resources to include explicitly.

The second level of operation is much more interesting and unique to Perl (amongst all the popular languages I know of), in which Perl keeps track of a "distrust" of each scalar value in the program. Every item of data coming from input sources (command-line arguments, environment variables, locale information, some system calls, and all file input) is marked "tainted."

For example, the following operations all generate tainted data:

```
$t1 = <STDIN>;
$t2 = $ENV{USER};
$t3 = $ARGV[2];
@t4 = <*.txt>;
```

In each of these examples, the data has come "from the outside world," and is therefore treated as potentially dangerous. Once data is tainted, the taint propagates to any data *derived* from the tainted data:

```
$t5 = $t4[0];
$t6 = "/home/$t2";
chomp($t1);
@x = ("help", "me", $t3, "please");
```

Note that tainting is on a per-scalar basis. So `$x[2]` is tainted, not the entire array `@x`.

Once data is marked tainted, nearly any attempt to use the data to affect the outside world will be blocked, causing an immediate die with a taint violation. For example, invoking rename where either the source name or destination name is tainted is considered dangerous. This permits normal operations:

```
rename $x[0], $x[1];
```

But not operations that involve tainted data (recall that $x[2] is tainted from earlier):

```
rename $x[0], $x[2];
```

What this means is that data that comes in from the outside world cannot trivially affect the outside world as well. Why is this important?

Well, the typical use of taint mode is to enable programs that act on behalf of other users to operate in a safer manner. For example, a setuid or setgid program borrows the privileges of its owner for the duration of execution, allowing an ordinary user to act as root (or some other user) for a selected set of operations. Or a CGI program, executing as the web server ID (typically nobody), is acting with that user's privileges on behalf of a request from any web client, generally without direct access to the server except through the web server.

In both of these cases, it's important that input data be checked so as not to permit the user who invokes the program from borrowing the privileges of the executing user ID to perform unintended actions.

For example, it'd be pretty dangerous to rename a file based on the input from a CGI form:

```
use CGI qw(param);
...
my $source = param('source');
my $dest = param('destination');
rename $source, $dest;
```

Now perhaps the author of this CGI script believed that since the form contained only radio buttons or pop-up menus that were clearly defined this would be a safe program. But in reality, a person with intent to damage or break in could just as easily invoke this script passing arbitrary data in source and destination, and potentially rename any file to which the web userid has access!

With taint mode enabled, the CGI parameters (having been derived from either reading STDIN or an environment variable) are marked tainted, and therefore the rename operation would fail before it has committed potential damage. (To enable taint mode on a CGI script, just include -T in the #! line, as shown earlier.) And that's exactly the safest thing to do here.

But obviously, there are times when input data must in fact legitimately affect the outside world. Here's where the next feature of taint mode comes in. As a sole exception, the results of a regular expression memory reference (usually accessed as the numeric variables like $1 and $2 and so on) are never tainted, even though the match may have been performed on tainted data. This gives us the "carefully guarded gate in the fence," when used properly. For example:

```
my $source = param('source');
unless ($source =~ /^(gilligan|skipper|professor)$/) {
  die "unexpected source $source\n";
}
$safe_source = $1;
```

Here, $source is expected to be one of gilligan, skipper, or professor. If not, we'll die before executing the next statement, which copies the captured memory into $safe_source. (Note the parens in the regular expression match are performing double duty, needed for both proper precedence regarding the vertical bar and the beginning and ending of string anchors, as well as having the side effect of setting up the first back-reference memory. Sometimes, you get lucky.)

The value of $safe_source is now legitimate to be used in the rename operation earlier, as it came from a regular expression memory, and not directly from input data. In fact, we could even have assigned it back over $source (a common thing to do):

```
$source = $1; # source now untainted
```

Of course, we'd have to perform a similar operation on $destination to complete the operation.

So, if someone attempts to give us an incorrect value for the source parameter, like ginger, the program aborts. Certainly, this program would have aborted with or without taint mode, but in taint mode it works only because we *added* the extra code to perform a regular expression match, during which we needed to think about what the possible legal values for the string might have been.

And that brings up the next point: we typically can't perform an explicit match against a known list of values. More often, the data is a user-specified value that needs to fit a general description, but again, regular expressions are pretty good at matching many things.

So, let's say the $source there came from a text field box, rather than a pop-up menu, permitting an arbitrary string. How do we pass that along to the rename operator? Well, first we have to decide what a legitimate string might be. For example, let's restrict to filenames that contain only \w-matching characters, including a dot (as long as the dot is not the first character). That'd be like this:

```
$source = param('source');
$source =~ /^(\w[\w.]*)$/ or die;
$source = $1;
```

Once again, if the string is not as expected, we die. And only if we haven't died will we continue on to use $1, which has now been verified to be a name of the form that we expect.

Note that it's *very* important to test the result of the regular expression match, because $1 (and the other memory variables) is set only when you have a successful regular expression match. Otherwise, you get an earlier match, and that's definitely bad news:

```
## bad code do not use ##
$param('source') =~ /^(\w[\w.]*)$/;
$source = $1;
## bad code do not use ##
```

A slightly more compact way of writing this correctly might be

```
my ($source) = param('source') =~ /^(\w[\w.]*)$/
    or die "bad source";
```

Here, I'm using $1 implicitly as the list context result of the regular expression match, and declaring the variable that will hold it, and checking for errors, all in one compact statement.

The regular expression pattern should be as restrictive as you can get. For example, if you use something like /(.*)/s, you've effectively removed any of the benefits of taint mode for that particular data, making it potentially possible for someone to hijack your program in unintended ways.

So, I hope this gives you a bit of insight into how to use taint mode, and why it is useful. If this column "taint" enough for you, I suggest you check out the perlsec manpage (perhaps using the command perldoc perlsec at a prompt). Until next time, enjoy your new security knowledge.

Discovering Incomprehensible Documentation

Linux Magazine, Column 18 (November 2000)

■Randal's Note The Perl Power Tools project was abandoned, and restarted as an updated project by Casey West (at http://ppt.caseywest.com), so the URLs listed in the article are now wrong. Also, had I written this today, I'd probably again use my File::Finder instead of the awkward File::Find there.

Ahh, manpages. Some of them are great. But a few of them are just, well, incomprehensible.

So I was sitting back a few days ago, wondering if there was a way to locate the ugly ones for some sort of award, and then I remembered that I had seen a neat module called Lingua::EN::Fathom that could compute various statistics about a chunk of text or a file, including the relative readability indices, such as the "Fog" index. The "Fog" index is interesting in particular because it was originally calibrated to be an indication of the "grade level," with 1.0 being "first grade text" and 12.0 as "high school senior." At least, that's the way I remember it.

While I don't believe in the irrational religion applied to these indices sometimes ("We shall have no documentation with a Fog factor of higher than 10.0"), I do think they are an indicator that something is amiss.

So, in an hour or so, I hacked out a program that wanders through all of the manpages in my MANPATH, extracts the text information (discarding the troff markup), and sorts them by Fog index for my amusement. Since I brought together a lot of different technologies and CPAN modules to do it, I thought I'd share this program with you, found in Listing 1-1, later.

Line 1 gives the path to Perl, along with turning on warnings. I usually don't trigger any warnings, but it's nice to run with the safetys on occasionally.

Line 2 enables the normal compiler restrictions, requiring me to declare all variables, quote all quoted strings (rather than using barewords), and prevents me from using those hard-to-debug symbolic references.

Line 3 ensures that each print operation on STDOUT results in an immediate I/O operation. Normally, we'd like STDOUT to be buffered to minimize the number of system calls, but since this program produces a trace of what's happening, I would kinda like to know that it's happening *while* it is happening, not after we got 8000 bytes to throw from a buffer. As an aside, some people would prefer that I use $| = 1; here because it would be clearer. But I find the $|++ form easier to type, and I saw Larry do it once, so it must be blessed.

Line 6 provides the only configuration variable for this program: the location of the memory to be used between invocations. Running the text analysis on the data each time is expensive (especially while I was testing the report generator at the bottom of the program), so I'm keeping a file in my home directory to hold the results. The filename will have an extension appended to it, depending on the chosen DBM library.

Line 9 is what got me started on this program: a module from the CPAN to compute readability scores. As this is not part of the standard distribution, you'll need to install this yourself.

Line 10 provides the two constants I needed for the later DBM association.

Line 11 pulls in the "multilevel database" adaptor. MLDBM wraps the fetch and store routines for a DBM-tied hash so that any reference (meaning a data structure) is first "serialized." The result is that a complex data structure is turned into a simple byte string during storage, and when retrieved, the reverse occurs, so that we get a similar data structure again. There are interesting limitations, but none of them got in my way for this program.

The args to the use indicate that we want to use DB_File as our DBM, and Storable as our serializer. DB_File is found in the Perl distribution, but you must have installed "Berkeley DB" before building Perl for this to be useful. Replace that with SDBM if you can't find DB_File. Storable is also found in the CPAN, and is my preferred serializer for its robustness and speed. Data::Dumper can also be used here, with the advantage that it's the default.

Line 12 selects the ever-popular File::Find module (included in the distribution) to recurse downward through the man directories to scout out the manpage files.

Line 13 enables simple trapping of signals with a trivial die operation. I found that without this, if I pressed Control-C too early in the process, none of my database would be updated, which makes sense after I thought about it. (An interrupt stops everything, not even giving Perl a chance to write the data to the file by closing the database cleanly.)

Line 15 associates %DB with the multilevel database named in $DATAFILE. The remaining parameters are passed to the underlying DB_File tie operation, and select the creation as needed of the database, and the permissions to give to the file if needed.

Line 17 sets up a global @manpages variable to hold the manpages found by the subroutine in lines 20 through 23.

Lines 19 through 24 walk through the directories named in my MANPATH, looking for manpages. First, the MANPATH is split on colons, then each element is suffixed with slash-period-slash. As far as File::Find is concerned, this doesn't change the starting directories, but the presence of this marker is needed later to distinguish the prefix directory from the location within that directory, as we'll see in line 29.

The anonymous subroutine starting in line 19 is called repeatedly by File::Find's find routine. The full name of each file can be found in $File::Find::name, while $_ is set up properly together with the current directory to perform file stat tests. The conditions I'm using here declare that we're looking for a plain file (not symbolic link) that isn't named whatis, and that it not be too big or too small. If it's a go, the name gets stuffed at the end of @manpages.

Line 26 creates the text analyzer object. I humored myself at the time by calling it $fat, which originally was a shortened form of "fathom." As I write this text the next day, I can't remember why I found that funny. I guess it's meta-funny.

And now for the first big loop, in lines 28 to 48. This is where we've got the list of manpages, and it's time to go see just how awful they are.

Line 29 pulls apart the $dir, which is the original element of my MANPATH, from the $file, which is the path below that directory. This is possible because we included the slash-dot-slash marker in the middle of the path during the filename searching, and necessary because the troff commands of the manpages presume that the current directory is at the top of the manpage tree during processing, particularly for the `.so` command, which can bring in another manpage like an include file.

Line 30 refixes the name to avoid the marker, and line 31 shows us our progress with that updated name.

Lines 32 through 36 keep us from rescanning the same file. First, the modification time-stamp is grabbed into `$mtime`. Next, we check the existing database entry (if any) to see if the recorded modification time from a previous run is the same as the modification time we've just seen. If they're the same, we've already done this file on some prior run, and we can skip this one altogether. If not, we gotta get our hands dirty on it instead.

Line 38 is where this program spends most of its time. We have a `deroff` command that reads a troff file, and removes most of the troff embedded control sequences and commands. While it's not perfect, it's fairly useful, and close enough for this demonstration. And we need to be in that parent directory so that relative filenames work; that's handled with the simple one-liner shell command inside the backquotes.

"But wait," you may ask, "I don't have a `deroff`!" Never fear. I ran into the same problem myself. A quick search on the net (thank you, `www.google.com`!) revealed that this had been one of the already completed commands in the *Perl Power Tools* project, archived at `http://language.perl.com/ppt/`. So, I downloaded the `.tar.gz` file from that page, extracted the pure Perl implementation of `deroff`, and installed it quite nicely. Yes, there's a few open-source C versions out there, but I didn't want to futz around.

Line 39 detects a failure in the attempt to deroff the text, and moves along if something broke. Nothing went wrong in the hundreds of files I analyzed, but ya never know.

Line 40 is where this program does some heavy CPU on its own. The text of the deroff'ed manpage is crunched, looking for the various statistics, including our readability scores. There didn't appear to be any error return possible from this call, so I didn't try to detect one.

Line 42 creates the `%info` data structure to hold the attributes of this particular file that we want to store into the database. We'll start with the modification time that we fetched earlier, to ensure that later passes will go "Hey, I've already seen this version."

Lines 43 through 45 use the `$fat` object to access the three scores, via the `fog`, `flesch`, and `kincaid` methods. I've used a nice trick here: an "indirect method call," where the name of the method comes from a variable. The result is as if I had said

```
$info{"fog"} = $fat->fog();
$info{"flesch"} = $fat->flesch();
$info{"kincaid"} = $fat->kincaid();
```

but with a lot less typing. (That is, until just now, to illustrate the point.)

Line 46 stores the information into the database. The value is a reference to the hash, but the `MLDBM` triggers a serialization, so that the actual DBM value stored is just a byte string that can be reconverted into a similar data structure upon access. And in fact, an access already potentially occurred up in line 33. The access to `$DB{$name}` fetched a byte string from the disk database, which was then reconverted into a hashref so that the subsequent access to the hashref element with a key of `mtime` would succeed.

Line 47 lets us know we did the deed for this file, and are moving on.

And that completes the data gathering phase, so it's now time to do the report, as indicated in line 50.

Line 54 is a quick trick with interesting performance consequences. The hash of %DB acts like a normal hash, but actually involves two levels of tied data structures. This can be quite slow, especially when performing repeated accesses for sorting. So, we *copy* the entire database as an in-memory hash in one brief operation, to the %db hash. Now we can use %db in the same way we would have used %DB, but without the same access expense. Of course, since it's a copy, we can't change the real database, but that's not needed here.

Lines 55 to 57 sort the database by the key specified in $kind, defined in line 52. We've got a descending numeric sort, to put the worst offenders first. A simple printf makes the columns line up nicely.

And my output from running this program looks something like Listing 1-2, shown later. Yeah, that first file ranked in at a whopping "grade 167" education to read it. In theory. And about 5th grade or 6th grade for the simplest few. As a comparison, the text of this column (before editing) came out at around 13.3 on the Fog index. Hmm. I hope you all made it through high school! Until next time, keep your sentences short, and to the point. Enjoy!

Listing 1-1

```
=0=     ##### LISTING ONE #####
=1=     #!/usr/bin/perl -w
=2=     use strict;
=3=     $|++;
=4=
=5=     ## config
=6=     my $DATAFILE = "/home/merlyn/.manfog";
=7=     ## end config
=8=
=9=     use Lingua::EN::Fathom;
=10=    use Fcntl qw(O_CREAT O_RDWR);
=11=    use MLDBM qw(DB_File Storable);
=12=    use File::Find;
=13=    use sigtrap qw(die normal-signals);
=14=
=15=    tie my %DB, 'MLDBM', $DATAFILE, O_CREAT|O_RDWR, 0644 or die ⏎
          "Cannot tie: $!";
=16=
=17=    my @manpages;
=18=
=19=    find sub {
=20=      return unless -f and not -l and $_ ne "whatis";
=21=      my $size = -s;
=22=      return if $size < 80 or $size > 16384;
=23=      push @manpages, $File::Find::name;
=24=    }, map "$_/./", split /:/, $ENV{MANPATH};
=25=
=26=    my $fat = Lingua::EN::Fathom->new;
=27=
=28=    for my $name (@manpages) {
```

```
=29=        next unless my ($dir, $file) = $name =~ m{(.*?)/\./(.*)}s;
=30=        $name = "$dir/$file";
=31=        print "$name ==> ";
=32=        my $mtime = (stat $name)[9];
=33=        if (exists $DB{$name} and $DB{$name}{mtime} == $mtime) {
=34=          print "... already computed\n";
=35=          next;
=36=        }
=37=
=38=        my $text = `cd $dir && deroff $file`;
=39=        (print "cannot deroff: exit status $?"), next if $?;
=40=        $fat->analyse_block($text);
=41=
=42=        my %info = ( mtime => $mtime );
=43=        for my $meth (qw(fog flesch kincaid)) {
=44=          $info{$meth} = $fat->$meth();
=45=        }
=46=        $DB{$name} = \%info;
=47=        print "... done\n";
=48=      }
=49=
=50=    print "final report:\n\n";
=51=
=52=    my $kind = "fog";
=53=
=54=    my %db = %DB;                    # speed up the cache
=55=    for my $page (sort { $db{$b}{$kind} <=> $db{$a}{$kind} } keys %db) {
=56=      printf "%10.3f %s\n", $db{$page}{$kind}, $page;
=57=    }
```

Listing 1-2

```
=0=    ##### LISTING 1-2 #####
=1=    final report:
=2=
=3=      167.341 /usr/lib/perl5/5.00503/man/man3/WWW::Search::Euroseek.3
=4=      154.020 /usr/lib/perl5/5.00503/man/man3/GTop.3
=5=       65.528 /usr/lib/perl5/5.00503/man/man3/Tk::X.3
=6=       56.616 /usr/man/man1/mh-chart.1
=7=       45.591 /usr/man/man1/tar.1
=8=       40.133 /usr/lib/perl5/5.00503/man/man3/Bio::SeqFeatureI.3
=9=       39.012 /usr/lib/perl5/5.00503/man/man3/XML::BMEcat.3
=10=      37.714 /usr/lib/perl5/5.00503/man/man3/less.3
=11=      37.200 /usr/lib/perl5/5.00503/man/man3/Business::UPC.3
=12=      36.809 /usr/lib/perl5/5.00503/man/man3/Number::Spell.3
=13=    [...many lines omitted...]
=14=       7.179 /usr/man/man1/tiffsplit.1
```

```
=15=        7.174 /usr/lib/perl5/5.00503/man/man3/Tie::NetAddr::IP.3
=16=        7.018 /usr/lib/perl5/5.00503/man/man3/DaCart.3
=17=        6.957 /usr/man/man3/form_driver.3x
=18=        6.899 /usr/man/man7/samba.7
=19=        6.814 /usr/lib/perl5/5.00503/man/man3/Array::Reform.3
=20=        6.740 /usr/lib/perl5/5.00503/man/man3/Net::GrpNetworks.3
=21=        6.314 /usr/man/man5/rcsfile.5
=22=        6.210 /usr/lib/perl5/5.00503/man/man3/Network::IPv4Addr.3
=23=        6.002 /usr/lib/perl5/5.00503/man/man3/Net::IPv4Addr.3
=24=        5.881 /usr/man/man8/kbdrate.8
=25=        5.130 /usr/lib/perl5/5.00503/man/man3/Net::Netmask.3
```

What Is That, Anyway?

Unix Review, Column 36 (February 2001)

■**Randal's Note** Another article on `File::Find`, and identifying things, first with the built-in type switches, and then with `File::MMagic`, which knows enough to peer inside the contents of files to pick out things of interest.

So, you've got a directory full of mixed stuff, or maybe an entire tree of directories. Just what's behind each of those names? Are they directories, symbolic links, or just plain files? And if they're files, are they text files or binary files? And if they're binary files, are they images, executables, or some random garbage?

Perl has many built-in operators to make getting lists of names easy, and also for figuring out what you really have once you have a name.

For example, let's find all the subdirectories within the current directory:

```
for my $name (glob '*') {
  next unless -d $name;
  print "one directory is $name\n";
}
```

Here, the `glob` operator expands to all the non-dot-prefixed names within the current directory, and the `-d` operator returns true for all those names that are directories.

What if we wanted to do this recursively? We need to step outside of the core Perl, but not very far away. A core-included module called `File::Find` takes care of nearly all of our recursive directory processing problems. Let's find all directories below the current directory:

```
use File::Find;
find sub {
  return unless -d $_;
  print "one directory is $File::Find::name\n";
}, ".";
```

The `find` subroutine takes a subroutine reference (called a "coderef"), here provided with the anonymous subroutine constructor. Each name found below . (specified on the last line of this snippet) will trigger an invocation of this subroutine, with `$File::Find::name` set to the full name, and `$_` set to the basename (with the working directory already selected to the directory in which the name is located).

If you run this, you'll see that each directory is typically shown two or more times! Once as a name within its parent directory, once as the name of . when we're in the directory, and perhaps one or more times for each of the subdirectories contained within the directory. So how do we eliminate that? Well, just rejecting "dot" and "dot-dot" in the subroutine will do nicely:

```perl
use File::Find;
find sub {
  return if $_ eq "." or $_ eq "..";
  return unless -d $_;
  print "one directory is $File::Find::name\n";
}, ".";
```

There. We'll keep moving forward from this as our base, because rejecting the meta-links of dot and dot-dot is generally a useful thing.

What about all the symbolic links? Can we find those? Sure! That's the -l operator:

```perl
use File::Find;
find sub {
  return if $_ eq "." or $_ eq "..";
  return unless -l $_;
  print "one symlink is $File::Find::name\n";
}, ".";
```

Cool! But where do they point? That's the `readlink` operator, as in

```perl
use File::Find;
find sub {
  return if $_ eq "." or $_ eq "..";
  return unless -l $_;
  my $dest = readlink($_);
  print "one symlink is $File::Find::name, pointing to $dest\n";
}, ".";
```

We can skip the -l test by knowing that any non-symlink will automatically return `undef` on the `readlink`, as in

```perl
use File::Find;
my @search = @ARGV;
@search = qw(.) unless @search;
find sub {
  return if $_ eq "." or $_ eq "..";
  return unless defined (my $dest = readlink($_));
  print "one symlink is $File::Find::name, pointing to $dest\n";
}, @search;
```

I've also made it simpler to run this on different directories by passing them on the command line.

So, what do we have left? We can notice and skip over directories and symbolic links. How about files? Files are where the real action is located. And some of them are text-like, and some of them are binary-like. Although even those lines are blurry: you could argue that XML is really just a text-like binary format, and a Microsoft Word document is clearly text inside a binary-like format.

But back to what Perl can help with, first. Let's add the -T operator to distinguish those text files:

```
use File::Find;
my @search = @ARGV;
@search = qw(.) unless @search;
find sub {
  return if -d $_ or -l $_;
  return unless -T $_;
  print "One text file is $File::Find::name\n";
}, @search;
```

And that's pretty cool. Just a list of text files. But this actually doesn't tell us too much. What we might really want is a list of all the Perl scripts. What can tell us that? Well, the Unix command called file can peer inside the contents of a file to figure out what it is. Let's invoke that on each file:

```
use File::Find;
my @search = @ARGV;
@search = qw(.) unless @search;
find sub {
  return if -d $_ or -l $_;
  my $file_said = `file $_`;
  if ($file_said =~ /perl/) {
    print "$File::Find::name: $file_said";
  }
}, @search;
```

Hey, look at that. Now we're pulling out just the names that file insists are possibly Perl programs. But this program will slow to a crawl on a large tree. We're reinvoking the file command individually on every file in the tree.

There's a couple of ways to go from here to speed it up. I could save all the filenames to invoke file once at the end of the program:

```
use File::Find;
my @search = @ARGV;
@search = qw(.) unless @search;
my @list;
find sub {
  return if -d $_ or -l $_;
  push @list, $File::Find::name;
```

```
    }, @search;
    for (`file @list`) {
      if (/perl/) {
        print;
      }
    }
```

And yes, that sped it up considerably faster, but now we don't get the results until the end of the tree walk, and we'll run into problems if the number of arguments exceeds a comfortable limit for `file`.

But there's another way. Out in the CPAN (at places such as `http://search.cpan.org`), we can find the `File::MMagic` module, which apparently is a Perl module derived from the `file` command created for the PPT project originally based on code written for Apache to implement the `mod_mime` module, to emulate the standard `file` command. Wow. And now I'm going to write a recursive controllable `file`-like program on top of that. Will the reuse ever stop? (I hope not!)

So, what we need from this module is the method called `checktype_filename`, which returns back a MIME type (like `text/plain` or `image/jpeg`), and perhaps a semicolon and some additional information. So let's find all the Perl scripts quickly. First, after a little playing around, I see that the string I'm looking for has "executable" followed by a space, then something ending in "perl" followed by a space and then "script". That's a simple regular expression, so I'll add that at the right place:

```
use File::Find;
use File::MMagic;
my $mm = File::MMagic->new;
my @search = @ARGV;
@search = qw(.) unless @search;
my @list;
find sub {
  return if -d $_ or -l $_;
  my $type = $mm->checktype_filename($_);
  next unless $type =~ /executable \S+\/perl script/;
  print "$File::Find::name: $type\n";
}, @search;
```

Now I know what programs to look at when I upgrade, to see which modules they all use. (Hmm. Sounds like an idea for another column. I'll note that.)

And one last fun one. Let's find all the images in the tree, and then call `Image::Size` (also found in the CPAN) on them to see their respective sizes. Just a few more tweaks:

```
use File::Find;
use File::MMagic;
use Image::Size;
my $mm = File::MMagic->new;
my @search = @ARGV;
@search = qw(.) unless @search;
my @list;
find sub {
```

```
    return if -d $_ or -l $_;
    my $type = $mm->checktype_filename($_);
    next unless $type =~ /^image\//;
    print "$File::Find::name: $type: ";
    my ($x, $y, $imgtype) = imgsize($_);
    if (defined $x) {
      print "$imgtype: $x x $y\n";
    } else {
      print "error: $imgtype\n";
    }
  }, @search;
```

And as it turns out, I could have left the File::MMagic out of this program, since Image::Size can cheerfully inform me when it wasn't called on an image, but you know the old Perl motto: There's More Than One Way To Do It!

So, next time someone asks you "What do you have?," I hope you can answer them with a nice short Perl program now. Until next time, enjoy!

Speeding Up Your Perl Programs

Unix Review, Column 49 (November 2003)

How fast does your Perl run? Hopefully, most of the time, the answer is "fast enough." But sometimes it isn't. How do we speed up a Perl program? How do we know what's making it unacceptably slow?

The first rule of speed optimization is "don't." Certainly, don't write things that waste time, but first aim for clarity and maintainability. With today's processor speeds far exceeding the "supercomputers" of yesterday, sometimes that's "fast enough."

But how do we know if something is "fast enough"? The first easy cut is to just check total runtime. That's usually as simple as putting "time" in front of your program invocation, and looking at the result (which may vary depending on your operating system and choice of shell). For example, here's a run of one of my frequently invoked programs, preceding the command get.mini with time:

```
[localhost:~] merlyn% time get.mini
authors/01mailrc.txt.gz ... up to date
modules/02packages.details.txt.gz ... up to date
modules/03modlist.data.gz ... up to date
67.540u 3.290s 1:40.62 70.3%        0+0k 1585+566io 0pf+0w
```

So, this tells me that this program took about 70 CPU seconds over a 100-second timespan, essentially doing nothing useful for me except verifying that my local mirror of the CPAN is up to date. (Generally, to get sensible numbers, I have to do this on an otherwise idle system.)

Hmm. I wonder where it's actually spending all of its time? We can get the next level of information by invoking the built-in Perl profiler on the script. Simply include -d:DProf as a Perl command switch, and Perl will automatically record where the program is spending its time into a file called tmon.out in the current directory:

```
[localhost:~] merlyn% perl -d:DProf `which get.mini`
authors/01mailrc.txt.gz ... up to date
modules/02packages.details.txt.gz ... up to date
modules/03modlist.data.gz ... up to date
[localhost:~] merlyn% ls -l tmon.out
-rw-r-r-   1 merlyn   staff    44991232 Sep  8 08:46 tmon.out
[localhost:~] merlyn%
```

(I have to use which here because perl won't look in my shell's search path for the script.) The
execution under the profiler slows the program down a bit, but otherwise doesn't affect any
functionality. We now need to summarize the raw data of tmon.out with the dprofpp (also
included with Perl):

```
[localhost:~] merlyn% dprofpp
Total Elapsed Time = 99.50810 Seconds
  User+System Time = 70.79810 Seconds
Exclusive Times
%Time ExclSec CumulS #Calls sec/call Csec/c  Name
 14.9  10.60 12.739 545807  0.0000 0.0000  URI::_generic::authority
 14.8  10.54 12.002 461833  0.0000 0.0000  URI::_generic::path
 13.1   9.296 19.853 293900  0.0000 0.0001  URI::new
 12.8   9.108 39.082  83971  0.0001 0.0005  URI::_generic::abs
 9.82   6.953 12.677 461842  0.0000 0.0000  URI::_scheme
 8.16   5.778  6.024 293900  0.0000 0.0000  URI::_init
 7.58   5.368 91.054  41987  0.0001 0.0022  main::my_mirror
 6.39   4.522  4.521 293900  0.0000 0.0000  URI::implementor
 5.78   4.093 32.267  41984  0.0001 0.0008  URI::_generic::rel
 5.07   3.588  3.588 251910  0.0000 0.0000  URI::_generic::_check_path
 4.26   3.016  3.016  83976  0.0000 0.0000  File::Spec::Unix::canonpath
 3.92   2.775 15.390  83968  0.0000 0.0002  URI::http::canonical
 3.48   2.465 14.186 377874  0.0000 0.0000  URI::scheme
 3.09   2.185  9.973  83968  0.0000 0.0001  URI::_server::canonical
 2.25   1.596  3.419  41988  0.0000 0.0001  File::Spec::Unix::catdir
[localhost:~] merlyn%
```

Now, this is some interesting information that we can use. We took 70 CPU seconds. This
is just like the previous run, so the profiling didn't significantly alter our execution. The first
routine listed, URI::_generic::authority, was called half a million times, contributing about
10 CPU seconds to the total. (There are other switches to dprofpp, but the default options
seem to be the most useful most of the time.)

If we could make URI::_generic::authority twice as fast, we'd save about 5 seconds on
the run. Even making URI::new run twice as fast would save us 5 seconds on the run as well,
even though it's called half as frequently. Generally, the important thing here is to note total
CPU for a routine, not the number of times it is invoked, or the CPU spent on an individual
invocation. Although, I do find it interesting that I had to create 293,000 URI objects: perhaps
there's some redesign of my algorithm to avoid that. Good algorithm design is important, and
is both a science and an art.

The other thing to note is that most of the routines that are burning CPU are in libraries, not in my code. So, without changing the code of a library, I need to call library routines more efficiently or less frequently if I want to speed this up.

Then we have the bigger picture to consider. I invoke this program maybe a dozen times a day. If I worked hard to reduce this program to 35 CPU seconds instead of 70 CPU seconds, I'll save about 5 CPU minutes a day. How long would I have to work to optimize it to that level? And how many times would I have to invoke the program before the money I spent on the (usually otherwise idle) CPU being saved is equal to my billing rate for the time I spent?

This is why we usually don't worry about speed. CPUs are cheap. Programmer time is expensive.

But let's push it the other way for a minute. Suppose this program had to be invoked once a minute continuously. At 70 CPU seconds per run, we've just run out of processor (not to mention that the real-time speed was even longer). So we're forced to optimize the program, or buy a bigger machine, or run the program on multiple machines (if possible).

Armed with the data from the profiling run, we might want to tackle the URI::new routine. But rather than tweaking the code a bit, and rerunning the program overall, it's generally more effective to benchmark various versions of the code for given inputs, in isolation from the rest of the program.

For example, suppose we wanted to speed up the part of the routine that determines the URI's scheme separate from the rest of the URL. Three possible strategies come to mind for me initially: a regular expression match, a split, or an index/substr, implemented roughly as follows:

```perl
sub re_match {
  my $str = "http://www.stonehenge.com/perltraining/";;
  my ($scheme, $rest) = $str =~ /(.*?):(.*)/;
}
sub split_it {
  my $str = "http://www.stonehenge.com/perltraining/";;
  my ($scheme, $rest) = split /:/, $str, 2;
}
sub index_substr {
  my $str = "http://www.stonehenge.com/perltraining/";;
  my $pos = index($str, ":");
  my $scheme = substr($str, 0, $pos-1);
  my $rest = substr($str, $pos+1);
}
```

We now have three candidates. Which one is faster? For that, we can use the built-in Benchmark module, as follows:

```perl
use Benchmark qw(cmpthese);
my $URI = "http://www.stonehenge.com/perltraining/";;
sub re_match {
  my $str = $URI;
  my ($scheme, $rest) = $str =~ /(.*?):(.*)/;
}
sub split_it {
```

```perl
  my $str = $URI;
  my ($scheme, $rest) = split /:/, $str, 2;
}
sub index_substr {
  my $str = $URI;
  my $pos = index($str, ":");
  my $scheme = substr($str, 0, $pos-1);
  my $rest = substr($str, $pos+1);
}
cmpthese(-1, {
  re_match => \&re_match,
  split_it => \&split_it,
  index_substr => \&index_substr,
});
```

which when run results in

	Rate	re_match	split_it	index_substr
re_match	131022/s	–	-37%	-46%
split_it	208777/s	59%	–	-14%
index_substr	242811/s	85%	16%	–

The -1 on the cmpthese call says "run each of these for roughly 1 CPU second." Note that index_substr seems to be the clear winner here, even though there are more things for me to type and get correct.

One thing to watch out for in benchmarking is optimizing for atypical data. For example, the URI I picked is probably typical, but what happens if the URL is longer instead?

```perl
my $URI = "http://www.stonehenge.com/merlyn/"; .
  "Pictures/Trips/2003/03-06-PerlWhirlMacMania/" .
  "Day-0-Pearl-Harbor/?show=14";
```

Now our results show that index_substr is even better!

	Rate	re_match	split_it	index_substr
re_match	117108/s	–	-41%	-49%
split_it	199110/s	70%	–	-13%
index_substr	229682/s	96%	15%	–

Given those two extremes, I'd say that index_substr is probably the right tool for this particular task, all other things being equal.

Armed with Perl's built-in profiler and the Benchmark module, I can usually fine-tune my routines, and get the speed I want out of my Perl programs. If that's not enough, I could take those frequently called expensive routines and code them in a lower-level language instead. But usually that won't be needed. Until next time, enjoy!

Deep Copying, Not Deep Secrets

Unix Review, Column 30 (February 2000)

One of the modules I encountered in the CPAN had a problem with creating multiple objects. Each object got created fine, but on further use simultaneously in the program, some of the data from one object mysteriously shows up in the second one, even if the first one is freed!

Upon inspection, I found that the object was being initialized from a *shallow copy* of a template, and I told the author that he needed to *deep copy* the template instead. He was puzzled by the suggestion, and if you aren't familiar with these two terms, I bet you are a little confused now as well.

What is deep copying and why do we need it? Let's start with a simple example, and work back to the problem I posed a moment ago.

For example, let's grab all the password information into a simple hash, with the key being the username, and the value being an arrayref pointing to the nine-element value returned by getpwent(). On a first cut, we quickly hack out something like this:

```
while (@x = getpwent()) {
  $info{$x[0]} = \@x;
}
for (sort keys %info) {
  print "$_ => @{$info{$_}}\n"
}
```

What? Where did all the data go? We stored a reference to the data into the hash value. Well, maybe this will make it clearer:

```
while (@x = getpwent()) {
  $info{$x[0]} = \@x;
  print "$info{$x[0]}\n";
}
```

On my machine, this printed ARRAY(0x80ce7fc) dozens of times, once for every user on the system. So what does that mean? It means that we are reusing the same array repeatedly, and therefore we don't have dozens of arrayrefs pointing to distinct arrays, we have a single array with many pointers to the same data. So on the last pass through the gathering loop, @x is emptied, and therefore all the array references are pointing to the identical empty data.

This is because we made a *shallow copy* of the reference to @x into the hash value, which is a copy of only the top-level pointer, but not the contents. What we really needed was not only a copy of the reference, but a copy of to what the reference pointed. That's simple enough here:

```
while (@x = getpwent()) {
  $info{$x[0]} = [@x];
}
for (sort keys %info) {
  print "$_ => $info{$_} => @{$info{$_}}\n"
}
```

And now notice, we've got a distinct arrayref for each hash element, pointing to an independent copy of the nine elements of the array originally contained in @x. This worked because we created a new anonymous arrayref with the expression [@x], which also gives this anonymous array an initial value made of copies of the elements of @x.

So that's a basic *deep copy*: copying not only the top-level pointer, but also all the things within the data structure to maintain complete independence.

Actually there was one other way to ensure unique subelements in this example, and I'll show it for completeness lest my Perl hacking friends get irritated. You don't need to copy anything if you just generate the data in a distinct array in the first place:

```
while (my @x = getpwent()) {
  $info{$x[0]} = \@x;
}
for (sort keys %info) {
  print "$_ => $info{$_} => @{$info{$_}}\n"
}
```

Here, each pass through the loop starts with a brand-new completely distinct lexical @x rather than reusing the old existing variable. So when a reference is taken to it, and it falls out of scope at the bottom of the loop, the variable automatically remains behind as an anonymous variable.

But let's get back to deep copying. Here's another example. Let's suppose Fred and Barney are sharing a house:

```
$place = {
  Street => "123 Shady Lane",
  City => "Granite Junction",
};
$fred = {
  First_name => "Fred",
  Last_name => "Flintstone",
  Address => $place,
};
$barney = {
  First_name => "Barney",
  Last_name => "Rubble",
  Address => $place,
};
```

Now note that $fred->{Address}{City} is "Granite Junction" just as we might expect it, as is $barney->{Address}{City}. But we've done a shallow copy from $place into both of the Address element values. This means that there's not two copies of the data, but just one. We can see this when we change one of the values. Let's let Fred move to his own place:

```
$fred->{Address}{Street} = "456 Palm Drive";
$fred->{Address}{City} = "Bedrock";
```

Looks safe enough. But what happened to Barney? He moved along with Fred!

```
print "@{$barney->{Address}}{qw(Street City)}\n";
```

This prints Fred's new address! Why did that happen? Once again, the assignment of $place as the address in both cases made a shallow copy: both data structures shared a common pointer to the common street and city data. Again, a deep copy would have helped:

```perl
$place = {
  Street => "123 Shady Lane",
  City => "Granite Junction",
};
$fred = {
  First_name => "Fred",
  Last_name => "Flintstone",
  Address => {%$place},
};
$barney = {
  First_name => "Barney",
  Last_name => "Rubble",
  Address => {%$place},
};
$fred->{Address}{Street} = "456 Palm Drive";
$fred->{Address}{City} = "Bedrock";
print "@{$barney->{Address}}{qw(Street City)}\n";
```

There . . . now each Address field is a completely disconnected copy, so when we update one, the other stays pure. This works because just like the [@x] construct, we are creating a new independent anonymous hash and taking a reference to it.

But what if $place was itself a deeper structure? That is, suppose the street address was made up of a number and a name:

```perl
$place = {
  Street => {
    Number => 123,
    Name => "Shady Lane",
  },
  City => "Granite Junction",
};
$fred = {
  First_name => "Fred",
  Last_name => "Flintstone",
  Address => {%$place},
};
$barney = {
  First_name => "Barney",
  Last_name => "Rubble",
  Address => {%$place},
};
```

We've now done something that's not quite a deep copy, but also not a shallow copy. Certainly, the hash at $fred->{Address} is different from $barney->{Address}. But they both contain a value that is identical to the $place->{Street} hashref! So if we move Fred just down the street:

```
$fred->{Address}{Street}{Number} = 456;
```

then Barney moves along with him again! Now, we could fix this problem by applying the logic for copying the address one more time to the street structure:

```
$fred = {
  First_name => "Fred",
  Last_name => "Flintstone",
  Address => {
    Street => {%{$place->{Street}}},
    City => $place->{City},
  },
};
```

But as you can see, it's getting more and more convoluted. And what if we change City to be another structure, or added another level to Street? Bleh.

Fortunately, we can write a simple general-purpose deep copier with a recursive subroutine. Here's a simple little deep copy routine:

```
sub deep_copy {
  my $this = shift;
  if (not ref $this) {
    $this;
  } elsif (ref $this eq "ARRAY") {
    [map deep_copy($_), @$this];
  } elsif (ref $this eq "HASH") {
    +{map { $_ => deep_copy($this->{$_}) } keys %$this};
  } else { die "what type is $_?" }
}
```

This subroutine expects a single item: the top of a tree of hashrefs and listrefs and scalars. If the item is a scalar, it is simply returned, since a shallow copy of a scalar is also a deep copy. If it's an arrayref, we create a new anonymous array from the data. However, each element of this array could itself be a data structure, so we need a deep copy of it. The solution is straightforward: simply call deep_copy on each item. Similarly, a new hashref is constructed by copying each element, including a deep copy of its value. (The hash key is always a simple scalar, so it needs no copy, although that would have been easy enough to add.) To see it work, let's give some data:

```
$place = {
  Street => {
    Number => 123,
    Name => [qw(Shady Lane)],
  },
```

```
  City => "Granite Junction",
  Zip => [97007, 4456],
};
$place2 = $place;
$place3 = {%$place};
$place4 = deep_copy($place);
```

Hmm. How do we see what we've done, and what's being shared? Let's add a call to the standard library module, Data::Dumper:

```
use Data::Dumper;
$Data::Dumper::Indent = 1;
print Data::Dumper->Dump(
  [$place, $place2, $place3, $place4],
  [qw(place place2 place3 place4)]
);
```

And that generates on my system

```
$place = {
  'City' => 'Granite Junction',
  'Zip' => [
    97007,
    4456
  ],
  'Street' => {
    'Name' => [
      'Shady',
      'Lane'
    ],
    'Number' => 123
  }
};
$place2 = $place;
$place3 = {
  'City' => 'Granite Junction',
  'Zip' => $place->{'Zip'},
  'Street' => $place->{'Street'}
};
$place4 = {
  'City' => 'Granite Junction',
  'Zip' => [
    97007,
    4456
  ],
  'Street' => {
    'Number' => 123,
    'Name' => [
```

```
          'Shady',
          'Lane'
      ]
    }
  };
```

Hey, look at that. `Data::Dumper` let me know that `$place2` is a shallow copy of `$place`, while `$place3` is an intermediately copied value. Notice the elements of `$place` inside `$place3`. And since `$place4` contains no previously seen references, we know it's a completely independent deep copy. Success! (The ordering of the hash elements is inconsistent, but that's immaterial and undetectable in normal use.)

Now, this simple `deep_copy` routine will break if there are recursive data pointers (references that point to already seen data higher in the tree). For that, you might look at the `dclone` method of the `Storable` module, found in the CPAN.

So, when you use = with a structure, be sure you know what you are doing. You may need a deep copy instead of that shallow copy. For further information, check out your online documentation with `perldoc perldsc` and `perldoc perllol` and even `perldoc perlref` and `perldoc perlreftut` for the basics. Until next time, enjoy!

Mirroring Your Own Mini-CPAN

Linux Magazine, Column 42 (November 2002)

The Comprehensive Perl Archive Network, known as "the CPAN," is the "one-stop shopping center" for all things Perl. This 1.2 GB archive contains over 13,000 modules for inclusion in your programs, as well as scripts, documentation, many non-Unix Perl binaries, and other interesting things.

Although there's nearly always a good, fast CPAN archive nearby when you are connected to the net, sometimes you're connected to the net at different speeds (like quickly at work, but slowly at home, or vice versa), or not at all. And what do you do then when you're like me, at 30,000 feet jetting off to yet another conference or customer site, and you realize you need a module that you haven't yet installed on your laptop? (This is especially an issue when a deadline for a magazine column looms close.)

Well, for the past year or so, I've been mirroring the entire CPAN to my laptop, thanks to the permission and cooperation of the owner of one of the major archive sites (and a few carefully constructed `rsync` commands). But at a recent conference, someone said, "Hey, can you just burn that onto a CD for me?," and I was stuck. The current CPAN exceeds the size of a CD-ROM, even though only a small portion of the files are needed for module installation!

So that got me thinking. If I brought down only the files that were needed by `CPAN.pm` to perform the installation of the latest release of a module, how big would that be? And the answer was wonderfully surprising: a bit more than 200 MB, which easily fits on a CD-ROM.

Unfortunately, I didn't see any clean, easy-to-use, efficient "mirror only the latest modules of the CPAN" program out there, so I wrote my own, which I present in Listing 1-3 later.

Lines 1 through 3 start nearly every long program that I write, enabling warnings, compiler restrictions, and disabling buffering on `STDOUT`.

Lines 5 through 17 form the configuration section of this program. There's really only three things to set here.

$REMOTE is the URL prefix leading to the nearest CPAN archive. The uncommented value is the main United States CPAN archive. The next value is the Finland archive, which also happens to be the master archive. If you want the most up-to-date sources, they're here. And because I was initially developing this program at the annual SAGE-AU conference in Australia, the value following that is the Australian CPAN archive. Finally, I have a *complete* CPAN archive on my laptop's disk already, so I can point to that with a file: URL as well, as shown by the fourth value.

That's the source, and we need to define a destination, and that's in $LOCAL. This is a simple Unix path. If you're on a non-Unix system, you can specify this in the local directory syntax, since we'll be using the cross-platform File::Spec library to manipulate this path. And, as the comment warns, this program owns the contents of that directory, and is free to delete anything it sees fit, so keep that in mind as you are specifying the path.

Finally, a simple true/false $TRACE flag decides whether this program is noisy by default or quiet by default. The noise is limited to actual activity, and reassures me during execution that something is happening.

Next, from lines 20 to 30, we'll pull in the necessary modules. The standard Perl bundle gives us the dirname, catfile, and find routines. The optional CPAN-installable LWP library gives us the URI object module and the mirror routine (and some associated status values). And Compress::Zlib lets us expand the gzip-compressed index file so we know what distributions are needed for the mirror.

Once we've got everything set up, it's time to transfer everything needed for a typical operation of the core CPAN module (described by perldoc CPAN in a typical Perl installation). First, we need the index files, defined in lines 34 to 36. We'll call my_mirror on each of those, defined later. For now, we'll presume that this creates or refreshes each of those files below the $LOCAL-identified directory.

The 02packages.details.txt.gz file is a flat text file with a short header that contains the path to each distribution for each module in the CPAN. However, this file is gzip-compressed, so we need to expand the file to process the contents. Stealing the example out of the Compress::Zlib manpage nearly directly, lines 40 to 52 expand this file and extract the necessary information.

Line 40 constructs the filename in a platform-independent way by using the catfile routine. Note that we're actually passing three parameters. The first parameter is the value of $LOCAL, which serves as the starting point, from which we descend further to the subdirectory called modules, and thence finally to a file within that directory called 02packages.details.txt.gz. I've tested this only on Unix, but I'll presume that the program is portable, because I've used the portable functions.

Line 41 takes this constructed path, and creates a Compress::Zlib object, which can be asked to deliver the uncompressed file line-by-line. If that fails, we're in an unrecoverable state, and we'll abort.

The data contains a header, delimited by a blank line, so we need to skip over all the data up to and including that blank line. We'll do this by setting a flag to an initial 1 value in line 42. Line 43 reads a line at a time into $_, stopping when there is no more data (or there's an I/O error). Lines 44 to 47 look for the end of the header as long as we're still in the header. A header ends on a line that doesn't contain a nonblank character, hence the unless.

If we make it to line 49, we're staring at a standard line from the index, which looks something like

```
Parse::RecDescent 1.80 D/DC/DCONWAY/Parse-RecDescent-1.80.tar.gz
```

The first column is the module name (here `Parse::RecDescent`), and is not very interesting to us. Neither is the second column, which is the current version number. But the third column contains (the unique part of) the path to the distribution for this module, and that's what the `CPAN` module will be looking for, and what we need to mirror.

Note that many module names will share the same common distribution file, so we'll need logic to avoid downloading duplicates. We'll defer that problem to the `my_mirror` subroutine.

A few of the modules are listed as belonging to a core Perl distribution. To avoid mirroring the various Perl distributions (and wasting space in our mirror), we'll skip over them in line 50. The regular expression is somewhat ad-hoc, but seems to do the right thing.

Line 51 mirrors the requested distribution into our local mirror. The 1 parameter says "If it already exists, it's up to date," and is an optimization based on external knowledge that a given distribution will never be updated in place. Rather, a new file will be created with a new version number. Of course, like any optimization, we do this with some hesitation and a bit of caution.

Once we've passed through the entire module list, we need to delete any outdated modules. A CPAN contributor has the option of leaving older versions of modules in the CPAN, or deleting them. We need to keep track of everything that is current, and delete anything not mentioned, in order to keep in sync with the master archive.

And that's it, as line 57 confirms.

But of course, that's not the whole story. We need to manage the mirroring. There are two steps to mirroring: fetching the files, and throwing away anything left over. These need to share a common hash, which we'll define as a closure variable inside a `BEGIN` block starting in line 59. The `%mirrored` hash in line 62 is keyed by the filename, and has a value of 1 to indicate that the file has been at least checked for existence, and 2 to indicate that it has been mirrored from the remote site and brought up to date. At the end of the run, any files that aren't either 1 or 2 for values are deleted files or temp files, and should be deleted from our mirror.

The `my_mirror` routine starting in line 64 does the hard work. The two parameters are the partial URL path and the "skip if present" flag.

In line 68, we use the `URI` module to construct the full URL, based on the `$REMOTE` value and the partial path. Line 69 constructs the local file path, based on `$LOCAL` and the partial path as well. The task for the remainder of the subroutine is to make the local file be up to date with respect to the remote URL.

Line 70 manages the checksum file. Each distribution is checksummed to ensure proper complete transfer. We'll first pretend that the checksum file doesn't need updating, but later remove that assumption if we end up transferring the distribution file.

Starting in line 72, we look at what to do to bring this file up to date. If `$skip_if_present` is true, then we'll never worry about the remote timestamp being out of sync. If the file is present, it's good enough, noted by the `-f` flag in line 72. Line 74 records that the file was at least checked for existence, so we don't delete it during the cleanup phase.

If `$skip_if_present` is not true, or the file doesn't exist, then it's time to do a full mirror on this distribution. We'll note that in line 77. Line 79 creates the directory to receive the file. (I would argue that `LWP` should do this for me, but that's not the way it works.) The `$TRACE` value causes a series of `mkdir` command lines to be traced to the output; otherwise, this operation is silent. Line 80 also puts out some noise if `$TRACE` is set: note the absence of a newline, because we're going to follow on with a result status.

Line 81 is where the real work happens. We'll call `mirror` to bring the remote URL to the local file. This is done in such a way that the existing modification timestamp (if any) is noted and respected, minimizing the load on the remote server. And the file is actually written into a temp file, and then renamed only when the transfer is complete, thus ensuring that other users of this directory will not see partially transferred files at normal locations. (If one of these transfers aborts midway, the cleanup phase at the end of this program will delete the partial transfer.) The modification time is also updated to that of the remote data, so that a later mirror will again note that the file is up to date.

The result of mirror is an HTTP status value. If it's RC_OK, then we've got a new version of the remote file. In this case, the checksum file may now be out of date: we can't merely check for its existence, so we'll flag that by setting the variable to 0 in line 84.

If the response is RC_NOT_MODIFIED, then we already had an up-to-date version of the file, and the remote server has informed us of such without even sending us a new version. In that case, we end up in line 90, finishing out the tracing message if needed.

However, if the status is neither of these, then something wrong has happened, and we'll generate a warn noting the status, and abort any further operation on this path by returning from the subroutine.

Once the distribution has been transferred, it's time to grab the checksum file. If the path is a distribution (checked in line 94), we'll compute the path to the CHECKSUMS file in lines 95 and 96. We must be careful to perform URL calculations here, not native path calculations. And, to keep the algorithm easy, we need to compute the path relative to the original CPAN mirror base, not a full path. Thankfully, this is also trivial with the URI module.

In line 97, if we're not already looking at a CHECKSUMS file, we need to call back to ourselves to transfer the file. This is a clean tail recursion, so I could have simply used a goto or a loop, but the subroutine call seemed easier and clearer at the time. If the checksum might already be up to date, it will merely be checked for its presence. If a transfer has taken place, a full mirror call will be issued instead.

Finally, we have the cleanup phase routine. We'll start at $LOCAL using the File::Find recursion. If a file exists, and it's not noted as such in the %mirrored hash (line 105), then we remove it (line 107).

And there you have it. Set up the configuration, and let it rip. On the first execution, you will want to be on a fast link (or a relatively unloaded time of day), because it downloads about 200 megabytes of data. After that, it's about 2–5 minutes per (average) day on a 28.8 link, which is completely tolerable for me from my hotel room when I'm on the road. And don't forget: you're downloading only installable modules, not the rest of the CPAN.

To use this mini-CPAN mirror with CPAN.pm, you'll need to enter at the CPAN prompt

```
o conf urllist unshift file://$LOCAL
o conf commit
reload index
```

Here, $LOCAL is replaced by the value you've set in $LOCAL but specified as a URL path (forward slashes for directory delimiters, and percent-escaped unusual characters). That's because CPAN.pm is expecting a URL, not a file path.

At the risk of repeating myself: this won't make CPAN installations any faster, unless you happen to be a road warrior like me, needing to do CPAN installations when you are on a very slow net link (or no link at all). Of course, you could burn a daily CD for your friends, and "hand them a CPAN archive on a disk," providing a gateway between your bandwidth and the sneakernet. At least you won't be worrying trying to figure out how to fit the full 1.2+ GB CPAN on a CD-ROM! Until next time, enjoy!

Listing 1-3

```
=1=     #!/usr/bin/perl -w
=2=     use strict;
=3=     $|++;
=4=
=5=     ### CONFIG
=6=
=7=     my $REMOTE = "http://www.cpan.org/";;
=8=     # my $REMOTE = "http://fi.cpan.org/";;
=9=     # my $REMOTE = "http://au.cpan.org/";;
=10=    # my $REMOTE = "file://Users/merlyn/MIRROR/CPAN/";;
=11=
=12=    ## warning: unknown files below this dir are deleted!
=13=    my $LOCAL = "/Users/merlyn/MIRROR/MINICPAN/";
=14=
=15=    my $TRACE = 1;
=16=
=17=    ### END CONFIG
=18=
=19=    ## core -
=20=    use File::Path qw(mkpath);
=21=    use File::Basename qw(dirname);
=22=    use File::Spec::Functions qw(catfile);
=23=    use File::Find qw(find);
=24=
=25=    ## LWP -
=26=    use URI ();
=27=    use LWP::Simple qw(mirror RC_OK RC_NOT_MODIFIED);
=28=
=29=    ## Compress::Zlib -
=30=    use Compress::Zlib qw(gzopen $gzerrno);
=31=
=32=    ## first, get index files
=33=    my_mirror($_) for qw(
=34=                    authors/01mailrc.txt.gz
=35=                    modules/02packages.details.txt.gz
=36=                    modules/03modlist.data.gz
=37=                    );
=38=
=39=    ## now walk the packages list
=40=    my $details = catfile($LOCAL, qw(modules ⏎
        02packages.details.txt.gz));
=41=    my $gz = gzopen($details, "rb") or die "Cannot open details: ⏎
        $gzerrno";
=42=    my $inheader = 1;
=43=    while ($gz->gzreadline($_) > 0) {
```

```
=44=       if ($inheader) {
=45=         $inheader = 0 unless /\S/;
=46=         next;
=47=       }
=48=
=49=       my ($module, $version, $path) = split;
=50=       next if $path =~ m{/perl-5};  # skip Perl distributions
=51=       my_mirror("authors/id/$path", 1);
=52=     }
=53=
=54=     ## finally, clean the files we didn't stick there
=55=     clean_unmirrored();
=56=
=57=     exit 0;
=58=
=59=     BEGIN {
=60=       ## %mirrored tracks the already done, keyed by filename
=61=       ## 1 = local-checked, 2 = remote-mirrored
=62=       my %mirrored;
=63=
=64=       sub my_mirror {
=65=         my $path = shift;            # partial URL
=66=         my $skip_if_present = shift; # true/false
=67=
=68=         my $remote_uri = URI->new_abs($path, $REMOTE)->as_string; ↵
                 # full URL
=69=         my $local_file = catfile($LOCAL, split "/", $path); ↵
                 # native absolute file
=70=         my $checksum_might_be_up_to_date = 1;
=71=
=72=         if ($skip_if_present and -f $local_file) {
=73=           ## upgrade to checked if not already
=74=           $mirrored{$local_file} = 1 unless $mirrored{$local_file};
=75=         } elsif (($mirrored{$local_file} || 0) < 2) {
=76=           ## upgrade to full mirror
=77=           $mirrored{$local_file} = 2;
=78=
=79=           mkpath(dirname($local_file), $TRACE, 0711);
=80=           print $path if $TRACE;
=81=           my $status = mirror($remote_uri, $local_file);
=82=
=83=           if ($status == RC_OK) {
=84=             $checksum_might_be_up_to_date = 0;
=85=             print " ... updated\n" if $TRACE;
=86=           } elsif ($status != RC_NOT_MODIFIED) {
=87=             warn "\n$remote_uri: $status\n";
=88=             return;
```

```
=89=           } else {
=90=              print " ... up to date\n" if $TRACE;
=91=           }
=92=        }
=93=
=94=        if ($path =~ m{^authors/id}) { # maybe fetch CHECKSUMS
=95=          my $checksum_path =
=96=             URI->new_abs("CHECKSUMS", $remote_uri)->rel($REMOTE);
=97=          if ($path ne $checksum_path) {
=98=             my_mirror($checksum_path, $checksum_might_be_up_to_date);
=99=          }
=100=       }
=101=    }
=102=
=103=    sub clean_unmirrored {
=104=      find sub {
=105=        return unless -f and not $mirrored{$File::Find::name};
=106=        print "$File::Find::name ... removed\n" if $TRACE;
=107=        unlink $_ or warn "Cannot remove $File::Find::name: $!";
=108=      }, $LOCAL;
=109=    }
=110=  }
```

CHAPTER 2

■ ■ ■

Text Searching and Editing

Little Acts of Magic

Unix Review, Column 34 (October 2000)

■**Randal's Note** Another of my fundamentals columns. In retrospect, I probably would have replaced that &&-as-control-structure with a "backwards if," but the code still works.

So, let's start with some text manipulation. I have a poem written by a good friend of mine, Peg Edera, in a file named peg_poem, as follows:

```
The Little Acts

Maybe there is no magic.
Maybe it is only faith.
The lonely girl stuffs a letter
In a bottle, casts it in the sea.
It floats, it sinks.
What counts is that it's cast.
Those little intentions,
The petals placed on the altar,
The prayer whispered into air,
The deep breath.
The little acts,
The candles lit,
The incense burning
And we remember what counts
And we know what we need
In the little acts.
Then is when to listen.
What is it that brought you
To this?
There's the magic.
```

Right in hearing what
Sends you to
Hope.

    Peg Edera
    February 8, 2000

The title of her poem inspired the theme of this column, so it's only appropriate that we use the text as grist for the mill. Let's start with the basics of opening the file and reading. That'd be something like

```
open POEM, "peg_poem" or die "Cannot open: $!";
while (<POEM>) {
    ... do something here with each line
}
```

Within the body of this while loop, $_ contains each line from the poem. So on the first iteration, we get "The Little Acts" and a newline, and so on.

If we just want to copy the data to STDOUT, a simple print will do:

```
# open...
while (<POEM>) {
  print;
}
```

Here, the print defaults to STDOUT, so we'll end up copying the input to the output. What if we wanted line numbers? The variable $. contains the line number of the most recently read file:

```
# open...
while (<POEM>) {
  print "$.: $_";
}
```

And now we get a nice display labeled by line numbers. Let's optimize this a bit . . . there's too much typing for such a small thing happening in the middle of the loop:

```
# open...
print "$.: $_" while <POEM>;
```

Ahh yes, the while modifier form. Each line is still read into $_, and thus the print gets the right info.

Even the open can be optimized out of there, by using the cool "diamond" operator. The operator looks at the current value of @ARGV for a list of filenames, so let's give it one:

```
@ARGV = qw(peg_poem);
while (<>) {
  print;
}
```

Notice we don't have to explicitly open now, because that's handled by the diamond. Of course, copying files is best done by a special-purpose module for copying:

```
use File::Copy;
copy "peg_poem", \*STDOUT;
```

But that's just another way of doing it.

Let's go the other direction: processing the information before sending it out. As an artist, I'm sure Peg appreciates the ability to include blank lines between the paragraphs of the poem. But how would we strip those blank lines on the output? Simple enough: use a regular expression:

```
while (<>) {
  print if /\S/;
}
```

Here, the regular expression is looking for any single non-whitespace character. If there aren't any of those, the line is at least blank looking, and not worth printing.

Besides printing things as quickly as we read them, we can also read the entire file into memory for more interesting operations:

```
while (<>) {
  push @data, $_;
}
```

Each new line is added to the end of @data, which initially starts empty. Now we can print them out in the reverse order:

```
for ($i = $#data; $i >= 0; $i-) {
  print $data[$i];
}
```

And while this works (it's a normal for loop), it's actually much less work for the programmer (and slightly more for Perl) to write this simply as

```
print reverse @data;
```

which takes the @data value and reverses a copy of it end-for-end before handing this new list off to print.

What if we wanted to reverse each string? Hmm. Well, the reverse operator in a scalar context turns the string around. But then the newline is at the wrong end. So, it's a multiple-step procedure:

```
foreach $line (@data) {
  chomp($copy = $line);
  print reverse($copy)."\n";
}
```

Here, I take the string, copy it into a separate variable (so that the chomp doesn't affect the original @data element), then reverse that variable's contents in a scalar context (because it's the operand of the string concatenation operator), and then dump that out.

Another way to grab the part of the string up to but not including the newline is with a regular expression:

```
foreach (@data) {
  print reverse($1)."\n" if /(.*)/;
}
```

In this case, I'm using the implicit $_ variable together with a regular-expression match to find all the characters that don't include newline (because dot doesn't match a newline), and then using that as the argument to reverse. Magic!

We could also drift this towards a mapping operation, now that I look at it. Let's make a little assembly line:

```
@reversed = map {
  /(.*)/ && reverse($1)."\n";
} @data;
print @reversed;
```

The map operation takes every element of @data and temporarily places it into $_. The regular expression match always succeeds, and when it does, $1 contains the string up to but not including the newline, which then gets reversed and a newline is tacked on the end. Of course, we don't need that intermediate variable:

```
print map {
  /(.*)/ && reverse($1)."\n";
} @data;
```

I think Peg would probably laugh at the output of that program applied to her work, so let's look at some other small magic items.

If we wanted to break the lines into a series of words, the easiest way is to apply a regular expression match with a "global" modifier to each line, like so:

```
while (<>) {
  push @words, /(\S+)/g;
}
```

Here, the regular expression of \S+ matches every contiguous chunk of non-whitespace characters. So, after the first line has been processed, we'll have

```
@words = ("The", "Little", "Acts");
```

And the second line contributes nothing to the array, because there are no matches. We can shorten this slightly, using that map operator again:

```
@words = map /(\S+)/g, <>;
```

And this is pretty powerful, so let me go through it slowly. First, the diamond operator on the right is being used in a list context, meaning that all the lines from all the files of @ARGV are being sucked in at once. Next, the map operator takes each element (line) from the list, and shoves it into $_. The regular expression is evaluated in a list context, and since the match can occur multiple times on a given string, each match contributes 0 or more elements to the result list. That result list then becomes the value for @words. Wow, all in one line of code.

The problem with this particular rendering is that we're sucking in the punctuation as well. So `magic` is in the array as `magic.`, and that's not the same word, especially if we want to count the words.

So, we can alter this a bit:

```
@words = map /(\w+)/g, <>;
```

And now we're grabbing all contiguous alphanumerics and underscores, selected by the things that `\w+` matches.

But that breaks the word <`There's`> into two pieces. Bleh. There are many long hacking sessions when I've wished that the definition for `\w` had included apostrophes but excluded underscores. So, it's a slightly more precise and explicit regex for me:

```
@words = map /([a-zA-Z']+)/g, <>;
```

There. That works for this poem. And leaves out those nasty date numbers as well.

Now, as a final bit of magic, let's see what the most frequent word is. Wait, some of them are initial caps, so we need to do one more hop:

```
@words = map lc, map /([a-zA-Z']+)/g, <>;
```

That fixes it so they're all lowercase. Better! Now let's count them:

```
$count{$_}++ for @words;
```

No . . . it can't be that simple? But it is. Each of the words ends up in `$_`. We use that as a key to a hash. The value initially is `undef`, and incremented as we see each word.

Now it's time to dump them out:

```
@by_order = sort { $count{$b} <=> $count{$a} } keys %count;
for (@by_order) {
  print "$_ => $count{$_}\n";
}
```

And that dumps them out in the sorted order. We're using a sort block to control the ordering of the keys, then dumping them in that order.

Well, I hope you see that Perl can be a little magic at times. It's the little things that count. Until next time, enjoy!

The Sort Operator

Unix Review, Column 6 (January 1996)

■**Randal's Note** This is the column that introduced the world to my explanation of the Schwartzian Transform, which was named *for* me, but not *by* me.

One of the most important tasks in managing data is getting it into some sort of sensible order. Perl provides a fairly powerful sort operator, which has a tremendous amount of flexibility.

I'm going to talk about some sorts of sorts, and hopefully you'll sort everything out by the time you're finished reading. (And no, despite the similarity to my name, I will not talk about "random sorts.")

Let's take a simple case. I have the words in a list somewhere in the Perl program, and I want to sort them into alphabetical (technically, ascending ASCII) order. Easy enough:

```perl
@somelist = ("Fred","Barney","Betty","Wilma");
@sortedlist = sort @somelist;
```

This puts the value of ("Barney", "Betty","Fred","Wilma") into @sortedlist. If I had had these names in a file, I could have read them from the file:

```perl
#!/usr/bin/perl
@somelist = <>; # read everything
@sortedlist = sort @somelist;
print @sortedlist;
```

In this case, @somelist (and thus @sortedlist) will also have newlines at the end of each name. That's OK here, because it won't affect the sort order, and it makes printing them out that much easier.

Of course, I can shorten this a bit:

```perl
#!/usr/bin/perl
@somelist = <>;
print sort @somelist;
```

Or even further:

```perl
#!/usr/bin/perl
print sort <>;
```

(I suppose this is what gives Perl its reputation for being cryptic.) Here, I've used no variables at all. However, it does indeed sort everything being read, and print the result.

These sorts of sorts are fine if the data is textual. However, if the data is numeric, we'll get a bad order. That's because comparing 15 with 3 as strings will place 15 before 3, not after it. Because the default sort is textual, we need some other way to tell sort to sort numerically, not textually.

Anything besides a textual sort of the values of the element of the list has to be handled with a "sort subroutine." The way this works is simple—at some point, when Perl is looking at two elements from the larger list, trying to figure out how to order those two elements, it has to perform a comparison of some sort (heh). By default, this is an ASCII string comparison. However, you can give your own comparison function using a sort subroutine, with the following interface rules:

1. Your sort subroutine will be called repeatedly with two elements of the larger list.

2. The two elements will appear in the scalar variables $a and $b. (No need to make them local or look at @_.)

3. You need to "compare" $a and $b in the sort subroutine, and decide which is bigger.

4. You need to return -1, 0, or +1, depending on whether $a is "less than," "equal to," or "greater than" $b, using your comparison operation.

Those of you familiar with the qsort() library function from C should recognize this stuff. In fact, Perl uses the qsort() function, so it's no surprise.

So, here's a sort subroutine that does the job in comparing $a and $b numerically, rather than as text:

```
sub numerically {
    if ($a < $b) { -1; }
    elsif ($a == $b) { 0; }
    else { +1; }
}
```

Now, all we have to do is tell Perl to use this sort subroutine as the comparison function, rather than the built-in ASCII ascending sort. That's done by placing the name of the subroutine (without any leading ampersand) between the keyword sort and the list of things to be sorted. For example:

```
@newlist = sort numerically 32,1,4,8,16,2;
```

And now, instead of the list coming out in ASCII order (as it would if I had left out the "numerically" word), I get the powers of two in proper numeric sequence in @newlist.

The comparison of $a and $b numerically to generate one of -1, 0, or +1 is performed often enough that Larry Wall believed it warranted its own operator, <=>, which has come to be known as the "spaceship operator" for reasons I would rather not discuss. So, I can shorten "numerically" down to this:

```
sub numerically {
    $a <=> $b;
}
```

Now this is short enough that it seems a waste to have to define a separate subroutine, and in fact Perl allows an even more compact notation: the inline sort block, which looks like this:

```
@newlist = sort { $a <=> $b; } @oldlist;
```

The interface to this inline sort block is exactly as I've described for the subroutine earlier. It's just a little more compact. Personally, I use this style whenever the sort subroutine is under 40 characters or so, and break down to create a real subroutine above that.

Let's look at reading a list of numbers from the input again:

```
#!/usr/bin/perl
print sort numerically <>;
sub numerically { $a <=> $b; }
```

Now, if I present this program with a list of numbers, I'll get the sorted list of numbers. This is functionally equivalent to a Unix sort command with an -n switch.

Let's get a little crazier. Suppose I have a file that has people's names in the first column, and bowling scores in the second column:

```
Fred 210
Barney 195
Betty 200
Wilma 170
Dino 30
```

and that I want to sort this file based on bowling scores. Well, getting the data into the program is pretty simple:

```
#!/usr/bin/perl
@data = <>;
```

but each element of @data looks like Fred 210\n, and so on. How do I sort this list @data, but look only at the number and not the name?

Well, I'd need to pull the number out of the string. How do I do that? One way is with split:

```
$a = "Fred 210\n";
($name,$score) = split /\s+/, $a;
```

Here, I split $a by whitespace, yielding a two-element list. The first element goes into $name (which I really don't care about) and the second element goes into $score. There. Now all I have to do is tell Perl to look at just the score:

```
sub scores {
    ($name_a,$score_a) = split /\s+/, $a;
    ($name_b,$score_b) = split /\s+/, $b;
    $score_a <=> $score_b;
}
```

and in fact, this will do it!

```
#!/usr/bin/perl
sub scores { ... } # as above
print sort scores <>;
```

So, what's wrong with this picture? Well, it'd be just fine if we only looked at each entry in the list once. However, after we're done comparing Fred's score to Barney (and decide Fred is better), we also have to compare Fred's score to Betty's score. That means that we've had to split Fred's data twice so far. In fact, for a huge list, it'll have to perform the very same split over and over and over again.

There's a few ways out of this. One is to compute a separate array that has only the scores, and then sort that array. Let's look at that first.

The goal is to first read the data, and then compute an associative array whose keys represent a particular element of the array, and values represent the precomputed scores. Then, we are reducing the problem to one of an associative array lookup instead of a (perhaps) expensive split.

```
@data = <>; # read data
foreach (@data) {
    ($name,$score) = split; # get score
    $score{$_} = $score; # record it
}
```

Now, $score{''Fred 210\n''} will be just 210, and so on, for each of the original elements of @data.

Next, we have to use the information. We need a subroutine that, given two elements of @data in $a and $b, looks up the corresponding scores in %score, and compares those numerically:

```
sub score {
    $score{$a} <=> $score{$b};
}
```

and this indeed does it. Let's put it all together:

```
#!/usr/bin/perl
@data = <>; # read data
foreach (@data) {
    ($name,$score) = split; # get score
    $score{$_} = $score; # record it
}
print sort {
    $score{$a} <=> $score{$b};
} @data;
```

Note that in this version, I recoded the sort subroutine as an inline block instead. (I'm just trying to give you a lot of alternative notations to play with.)

Another way to tackle the problem is to massage the list into a list of pairs of things. The second element of each pair (actually, an anonymous list of two elements) will be the computed sort determinant, and the first element will be the original data value (so we can get back to the original data). This is best handled with the map operator (not available in older Perl versions).

```
@pairs = map {
    ($name, $score) = split;
    [ $_, $score ];
} @data;
```

Here, the block of code is executed for each element of @data, with $_ set to the element. This causes each element to be split into $name and $score, and then I build a two-element anonymous list from the $score and the original value $_. These are collected into a new list. If @data had five elements, then @pairs has five elements, each of which is a reference to a two-element anonymous list. Ouch!

The next step is to sort the @pairs list. Within the sort subroutine, $a and $b will be references to two-element lists. The second element of each list is the sort key, and is addressed like $a->[1]. So, we get a sort subroutine like this:

```
sub mangle {
    $a->[1] <=> $b->[1];
}
```

and the sort looks like this:

```
@sorted = sort mangle @pairs;
```

Now, @sorted is still the same pairs of data, but sorted according to the scores (did you forget we were still working with the scores?). I have to peel away the anonymous lists to get back the original data, while still preserving the order. Easy—map to the rescue again:

```
@finally = map {
    $_->[0];
} @sorted;
```

This is because $_ will be each element of @sorted—a reference to an anonymous list, and therefore $->[0] will fetch the first element of the anonymous list pointed to by $_, which is the original data. Whew!

Of course, in the Perl tradition, I can shove all this stuff together in a very lisp-like way. You've got to read this back to front to see what is happening:

```
#!/usr/bin/perl
print
    map { $_->[0] }
    sort { $a->[1] <=> $b->[1] }
    map {
        ($name,$score) = split;
        [$_,$score];
    } <>;
```

Eeek. But hey, it works!

One last optimization: I can put the split directly inside the anonymous list creation:

```
#!/usr/bin/perl
print
    map { $_->[0] }
    sort { $a->[1] <=> $b->[1] }
    map { [$_, (split)[1] ] }
    <>;
```

which works because the split here is being pulled apart by a "literal slice"—only the second element of the list remains after we slice it up.

Perl provides some powerful sorting techniques, which can really be a boon once mastered. I hope I have inspired you more than I've confused you. Next time, something entirely different.

Getting It to Look the Way You Want

Unix Review, Column 32 (June 2000)

For the most part, Perl programmers tend to use the nice standby print operator for output, or drift occasionally into the realm of formats to quickly lay out a look for a customized report. However, the often overlooked printf operator provides a nice amount of custom control to get those output strings to look exactly the way you want.

The printf operator takes a format string, and zero or more values. The format string drives the whole process. With a few exceptions, each percent % field in the format string matches up with one of the additional values, defining how the value will appear in the output. For example:

```
printf "my string %s has %d characters.\n", $str, length($str);
```

Here, the %s field calls for a string value, provided by $str. Similarly, the %d field calls for a decimal integer, provided by the length($str) computation. The parameters are evaluated in a list context, so we could have also used the following code to accomplish the same output:

```
@output = ($str, length($str));
printf "my string %s has %d characters.\n", @output;
```

This gets interesting if we don't know the length of @output, because we need a %-field for each element of @output, but since we set it up ourselves here, that's not a problem.

Besides %s for string, and %d for decimal integer, another common format is %f for floating point:

```
printf "he has $%f in his account\n", 3.50;
```

Here, the value 3.5 is printed as a floating point number, 3.500000. But why all the extra zeroes? Well, the default precision for floating point output appears to be six places after the decimal point. To narrow that down, we can add a precision control between the % and the f in the format:

```
printf "he has $%.2f in his account\n", 3.50;
```

And that'll generate 3.50 as we expect. The 2 here means two digits after the decimal point, and that makes cents, er, uh, sense. The value is rounded to fit, so 3.509 would show up as 3.51, whereas 3.502 shows up as 3.50. As an extreme, we can use %.0f to round to the nearest whole number, and no decimal point will be used.

Another common format is scientific notation, %e. This is handy when the number would be normally too large to represent in a few digits:

```
printf "2 to the 100 power is approximately %e\n", 2 ** 100;
```

And this shows up as 1.267651e+30, again defaulting to 6 digits after the decimal point unless we use a precision control like %.10e.

But %e is used rarely (that I've seen). Generally, when a number of unknown magnitude or precision is displayed, most programmers fall back to the %g "general number" format. In this case, the number is formatted using whatever of %d, %f, or %e gives "better" results. If it's a nice integer, we get a nice integer format. If it's a reasonably sized floating point number, that format is used, and otherwise, we fall back on to the scientific notation.

```
printf "Your number is %g\n", $number;
```

The precision can again be used, but in this case specifies the maximum number of significant digits, defaulting to 6 again. So, for %.15g, we get the best possible display for the 15 most significant digits.

For strings, we get a similar "precision" control. If we include a precision on a string, and the string is longer, it's automatically truncated:

```
printf "I said %.5s!\n", "hello world";
```

which prints I said hello!, truncating the string.

Another feature of printf is the field width padding. After the value for a particular field is determined, a specified minimum width can be respected, indicated by decimal integer after the percent:

```
printf "=%10s=\n", "hello";
```

Here, the six-character string is not a full ten characters, so four spaces are added on the left. This is a minimum width, not a maximum, so if the string were longer, it'd still be included in its entirely. We can combine the precision field with the width field to get a string that is space-padded up to a size, or truncated if it exceeds the size. Take the sample code:

```
printf "=%5.5s=\n", substr("1234567890", 0, $_) for 0..10;
```

which displays a nice pattern of

```
=     =
=    1=
=   12=
=  123=
= 1234=
=12345=
=12345=
=12345=
=12345=
=12345=
=12345=
```

The space padding can appear on the right instead of the left by using a negative number for the minimum width:

```
printf "=%-5.5s=\n", substr("1234567890", 0, $_) for 0..10;
```

which displays a nice pattern of

```
=      =
=1     =
=12    =
=123   =
=1234 =
=12345=
=12345=
=12345=
=12345=
=12345=
=12345=
```

Additionally, numbers can be zero padded rather than space padded, using a leading 0 in front of the width:

```
printf "%02d:%02d:%02d %s", $h, $m, $s, $ampm;
```

If the number for $m is less than 10 (like 7), we get a leading 0 in the output (as in 07), very handy for time displays like this one.

A literal % can be obtained by doubling it up, as in

```
printf "He scored %.0f%% of the goals", 100 * $him / $total;
```

Note that the often-attempted backslashing of % won't do. This isn't a string-interpolation escaping problem: it's a printf-interpretation problem.

One of the less-frequently used formats is the "character" format:

```
printf "the letter A is %c\n", 65;
```

Here, the value of 65 is treated as an ASCII code, and turned into the uppercase "A." It's not as frequently used in Perl as in C, because Perl deals with strings as first-class datatypes, rarely exposing the numeric values of the individual characters to the programmer.

And then there's the "programmer-type" formats . . . %h for hexadecimal, %o for octal, and new in Perl 5.6, %b for binary. For example, here's one way to look at the permission bits of a file:

```
printf "%s is mode %o\n", $_, 07777 & (stat)[2] for @ARGV;
```

But looking at the output, the values juggle all around. Ahh, time to use the minimum field width:

```
printf "%30s is mode %04o\n", $_, 07777 & (stat)[2] for @ARGV;
```

So, that's the basics, but let's look at some practical code as well. Suppose I have a series of values in @numbers that I want to print in a vertical column, all with a format of %15g. You might think that I could simply do this:

```
printf "%15g\n", @numbers; # bad
```

but this won't work, because there needs to be a % field for each value used from the list (as we saw earlier). Well, a simple way to fix that is to use a loop:

```
printf "%15g\n", $_ for @numbers;
```

But another way to do this is to replicate the format string. If we need to print three entries, we need a string like %15g\n%15g\n%15g\n, which we can get with "%15g\n" x 3. So, we need the number of elements in @numbers on the right of that x. Easy enough: just use the array name in a scalar context (which it is!):

```
printf "%15g\n" x @numbers, @numbers;
```

Here, @numbers is used in both a scalar context and a list context in the same expression: same text, different meaning. Just like when you wind up with no wind for your kite.

Occasionally, you may need to have a variable width for a column. Let's say you needed that 15 from the previous example to be configurable:

```
$width = 15;
printf "%$widthg\n", $_ for @numbers; # bad
```

This won't work, because Perl is looking for a variable named $widthg, even though you intended that as $width followed by g. But you also can't put a space in there, because the printf format is picky and can't understand a space. One solution is to delimit the variable name:

```
$width = 15;
printf "%${width}g\n", $_ for @numbers;
```

Another is to use the * indirection in the list to define the number. Each * in a format field calls for an element to be used from the values for the numeric value that the * stands in for:

```
$width = 15;
printf "%*g\n", $width, $_ for @numbers;
```

And there you have it. Many ways to print your numbers, strings, and anything else you come up with in your evaluations. Until next time, enjoy!

Understanding Regular Expressions

Linux Magazine, Column 27 (August 2001)

■**Randal's Note** The PCRE library tries to track whatever is currently being matched by Perl's regular expressions. Of course, it cannot be exactly the same, because that would require an embedded Perl interpreter, thanks to the fact that modern versions of Perl allow the C<(?{...})> code blocks embedded into a pattern string.

Also, modern versions of Perl actually fare a bit better on that first benchmark. If there's only one variable regex, the result is now cached, so the one-variable version and the constant version are now identical. Ahh, progress!

One of the things that distinguishes Perl as a powerful, practical tool in the Linux toolbox is Perl's ability to wrangle text in interesting ways that makes it seem effortless. And a majority of that ability can be attributed to Perl's very powerful regular expressions.

Regular expressions are nothing new. I was using Unix tools in 1977 with regular expressions, and I suspect they go back even further than that. But Perl continues to push the edge of how regular expressions work; so much so that the GNU project includes a perl compatible regular expressions library (PCRE) so that other tools can catch up to Perl!

But before we get to the advanced stuff, let's quickly review the basics. A regular expression defines a template to match against a string. We say the string either matches, or doesn't match, the given regular expression, based on whether the string has properties that the regular expression demands.

For example, the regular expression /a/ demands that there be the letter "a" somewhere in the string. If there's a choice, and it matters, it matches the leftmost "a" (this is called the "leftmost rule"). (We typically write the regular expression enclosed in forward slashes, because that's the most common use in Perl, although there are others.)

Of the "atoms" in a regular expression (from which the regular expression is built), the most common are the ordinary characters (such as the letter "a"), including any special characters preceded by a backslash. And everything that works in a double-quoted string also works in a regular expression, so \n is a newline, and \001 is a Control-A, and so on.

But atoms also include character classes, such as [aeiou], looking for any single vowel, and [^qwertyuiop], looking for any single character not found on the top alphabetic row of the keyboard, and [a-z] indicating any one of the lowercase letters. Some character classes have abbreviations, such as \s for whitespace (and its companion \S for non-whitespace). And the very common . means match any single character except a newline character.

We can follow any of these atoms by a repetition operator, such as * (zero or more) or + (one or more) or ? (zero or one). Given the opportunity, these repetition operators allow the string to match the longest string possible while still letting the rest of the regular expression match. We'll see an example or two of that later.

There's also the generalized repetition range operator, {m,n}, which looks for m through n instances of the atom it follows, and the modified forms of {m,} for "m or more" and {n} for "exactly n."

Atoms, with or without a trailing repetition operator, are frequently connected into sequences. The regular expression /pqr/ means look for a p immediately followed by a q and then an r. So /d[aiou]g/ looks for dag, dig, dog, or dug. And /fre*ed/ will match freeeed or freed or even fred, because the repetition operator will "back off" after first matching the final "e" so that the nonrepeated "e" gets a chance to match. We'd typically write that last one as /fre+d/ though.

A sequence can also contain "assertions." The two most common assertions are "beginning of string" as ^ or "end of string" as $. So /small$/ matches the word "small" only when it appears at the end of the string, failing to match smalltalk.

Sequences can be alternated with the | operator, as in /fred|barney/ matching either of those names, or the names "manfred" or "redbarney", since we can still match any substring and be valid.

And finally, a regular expression enclosed in parentheses (called a "subexpression") can be considered an atom again, starting us over at the top. So to apply a repetition to an alternation of two sequences, we can say /(fred|barney)+/, which means at least one fred or barney, such as fred or barney or barneyfred or fredfredfredbarneyfred.

Parentheses also serve to indicate memory. As the regular expression is being matched against the string, the contents of the string matching a subexpression (enclosed in parentheses) ends up in a memory. First subexpression yields the first memory, second subexpression yields the second memory, and so on.

We have two ways of accessing the memories. First, when the smoke clears, the contents of the first subexpression are in the read-only Perl variable called $1, with the second in $2, and so on. So after we match /abc(.*)def/ against "abcGHIdef", we'll have GHI in $1, until the next successful match.

The other way of accessing the memory (which is used less frequently, but can still come in handy) is the backreference, where \1 is an atom denoting the first memory already saved earlier with the same regular expression. So /(['"])(.*)\1/ matches a single- or double-quoted string, with $2 being the contents between the quotes, and yet the quote marks have to be the same type of quotes. Rare, but cool when you need it.

Occasionally, we'll need a set of parentheses that does not trigger a memory. For that, we can use ?: just inside the open parenthesis. As an example, /([0-9]+(?:\.[0-9]+)?)\s+([a-z]+)/ means an integer or floating point value followed by some whitespace and a lowercase word. The number will be in $1 and the word will be in $2, even though we had to use a third set of parentheses to make the fractional portion of the number optional.

Those are the basics, and will get you through about 90% of what you need for regular expressions. Let's look at how regular expressions are used now.

Perl's regular expression operators include the match, the substitute, and split. (I say "include" because I can't think of any others, but I'm trying to be accurate.) A scalar match is the most common:

```
print "What small integer? ";
chomp($_ = <STDIN>);
if (/^(\d+)$/) {
    print "Good, you said $1!\n";
}
```

Note here that the match is against the contents of $_ by default, but we can refer to any other value with the =~ operator. This code does the same thing as the preceding code:

```
print "What small integer? ";
if (<STDIN> =~ /^(\d+)$/) {
    print "Good, you said $1!\n";
}
```

Note that we didn't even need the chomp here: an often-misunderstood property of the $ assertion is that it matches either right at the end of the string, or just before a newline at the end of the string. As this can lead to security holes, I'm now starting to include \z instead of $ more often in my programs, which says "I absolutely want the end of the string here for this to match."

The substitute operator replaces a portion of a string (by default in $_, but you can change that using =~) with another double-quoted string on a successful match.

```
$_ = "hello, world";
s/hello/Hello/; # "Hello, world"
s/(Hello, )/$1 Perl/; # "Hello, Perl world"
s/(.*), (.*)/$2, $1!/; # "Perl world, Hello!"
```

Both the match and the substitute operator can use alternate delimiters (any other punctuation character) if the forward slash is troublesome: in particular when the regular expression or replacement have forward slashes.

```
my $filename = "/home/merlyn/.newsrc";
my $basename = $filename;
$basename =~ s!.*/!!; # $basename now ".newsrc"
```

Note the use of ! as the delimiter here. We're guaranteed to match down to the final slash, because the .* matches zero or more of (nearly) any character, but the longest possible match that still lets the rest of the regular expression match.

We successfully extracted the basename from that particular filename, but we blew it in the general case. Why? Because a newline character is valid in a Unix pathname. We need to match any possible characters before the final slash. We can do that with a character range:

```
$basename =~ s![\000-\377]*/!!;
```

or more simply by tagging a s modifier onto the substitute:

```
$basename =~ s!.*/!!s;
```

The s modifier changes . so that it matches newlines as well, and we now get any possible character there. Another useful modifier is the case-insensitive modifier of i. For example, /[aeiou]/i finds any vowel in upper- or lowercase. Note that you can also write that as /a|e|i|o|u/i, but the character class version will be considerably faster.

What if we had wanted to find the nearest slash instead of the furthest slash? The easiest way is to tell the * repetition operator to be "lazy" instead of "greedy." Placing a ? immediately after a repetition operator tells it to take as few matches of that atom as possible, instead of the greatest number. For example:

```
my $filename = "/home/bob/summary";
my $one = my $two = $filename;
$one =~ s!/.*/!/etc/!; # "/etc/summary";
$two =~ s!/.*?/!/etc/!; # "/etc/bob/summary";
```

For $one, we grabbed the first slash, as many characters as we could, and then the final (third) slash.

But for $two, we grabbed the first slash, as few characters as we could, and then the next immediate slash (the second slash). Note that this didn't find the "shortest overall match" as some people have claimed incorrectly (which would have been /bob/ rather than /home/). It still starts with the first slash. This is similar to how /([ab]+)/ will match the a's in ___aa___bbb___, rather than the (longer) sequence of b's. It's "leftmost match first" and then the repetitions individually have biases towards "longer matches" (the default) or "shorter matches" from that starting point.

The split operator uses its regular expression to define a "delimiter," which is then found (usually multiple times) in a string. Each match is discarded (leading one of my friends to call it the "deliminator"), leaving us with the pieces of string left as the list return value. So, a typical /etc/passwd-style file is parsed with relative ease:

```
my $line = "merlyn:x:904:100:Randal L. Schwartz:/home/merlyn:/bin/perl\n";
chomp $line;
my @values = split /:/, $line;
```

Now @values has seven elements, corresponding to the seven items between the delimiters. If two colons were in a row, we'd get an empty element in the list:

```
my @values = split /:/, "merlyn2::905:100::/home/merlyn2:/bin/perl";
```

Here, the second and fifth elements of @values are empty. Had we instead used /:+/ for the delimiter expression, those two consecutive colons would have been considered one big fat delimiter, and we'd have gotten five return values instead of seven.

This is typically desired when we are using whitespace as the delimiter: we'll use /\s+/ for the expression, because generally a hunk of whitespace in a row is a big fat delimiter, not many small omitted items.

Sometimes, it's easier to specify what we keep instead of what we throw away. For example, suppose I want to keep any integer or floating point values in a line, discarding anything else that doesn't look like a number. For that, we can use a match with a g modifier (for global) in a list context, which contributes $1 to a list result for each match:

```
$_ = '12.24 dollars for 35 fish?  Are you crazy?!';
my @hits = /([0-9]+(?:\.[0-9]+)?)/g;
```

Now @hits will be 12.24 and 35. We can pick out the following words using the regular expression we presented earlier.

```
my @hits2 = /([0-9]+(?:\.[0-9]+)?)\s+([a-z]+)/g;
```

Now @hits2 is "12.24", "dollars", "35", "fish", because on each match, we contribute the two memories to the result.

So, this is just a start, but I've run out of space. Some other things to look up in the perlre documentation (via perldoc perlre) include other assertions (such as lookahead and lookbehind assertions), scalar use of the match g modifier, creating regular expressions from variables, using whitespace within the regular expression to embed commentary, evaluating code during the match, and so on. And you might check out the perlretut page while you're at it, which covers a lot of the same ground as what you've just read, but in a different way. Hope this helps! Until next time, enjoy!

Compiling Regular Expressions

Unix Review, Column 28 (October 1999)

Perl's regular expressions set Perl apart from most other scripting languages. Some features (like the positive and negative lookahead, and the optional lazy evaluation of multipliers) make matching troublesome strings trivial in Perl. This power has not gone unnoticed by the open-source software community—a package called PCRE available on the net (use your favorite search engine) claims to implement "a regular expression matching engine that's compatible with Perl 5.004's syntax."

Just like the strings they are matching, regular expressions can come from many sources. The most common source is inside the program:

```
@ARGV = qw(/usr/dict/words);
while (<>) {
    print if /foo/ || /bar/;
}
```

This little guy ran in about a quarter of a CPU second for me, and generated a nice list of words that contain foo and bar. Notice that I wrote /foo/ and /bar/ as separate regular expressions, instead of the seemingly identical /foo|bar/. Why did I do that? Experience. As reported by the following program:

```
@ARGV = qw(/usr/dict/words);
@words = <>;
use Benchmark;
timethese (10 => {
    'expression or' =>
        '@x = grep /foo/ || /bar/, @words',
    'regex or' =>
        '@x = grep /foo|bar/, @words',
});
```

we get the following output from Benchmark:

```
Benchmark: timing 10 iterations of expression or, regex or...
expression or:  1 wallclock secs ( 0.97 usr +  0.00 sys =  0.97 CPU)
regex or:  3 wallclock secs ( 2.87 usr +  0.00 sys =  2.87 CPU)
```

This shows for this example that using the regular expression | operator was more than twice as slow. There are certain optimizations that kick in when the text to be matched is a constant string that cannot be done when we have something more complex, or so says the online documentation. The exact list of optimized things varies from release to release of Perl, so Benchmark is your friend.

Often, the regular expression will come from a computed string, such as the value of a web form field or a command-line parameter or the result of a prompted query. The Perl syntax lets us interpolate a variable into a regular expression, permitting the regular expression to be created at runtime:

```
@ARGV = qw(/usr/dict/words);
@words = <>;
$regex1 = "foo";
@result = grep /$regex1/, @words;
```

In order to be useful, a regular expression first has to be "compiled." This is often an expensive step compared to the actual matching of the string to the regular expression.

So, usually, this compilation happens while the Perl program itself is parsed and compiled, before the execution of the program. However, when part of a regular expression is a variable (such as the preceding example), Perl can't do that, and defers the regular expression compilation until execution time.

While this provides a powerful option (creating a regular expression at runtime), it comes with a performance penalty if used incorrectly. Let's test this out:

```
@ARGV = qw(/usr/dict/words);
@words = <>;
push @words, @words;
push @words, @words;
use Benchmark;
$foo = '[f][o][o]';
$bar = '[b][a][r]';
timethese (5 => {
    'constant' =>
        '@x = grep /[f][o][o]/ || /[b][a][r]/, @words',
    'one variable' =>
        '@x = grep /$foo/ || /[b][a][r]/, @words',
    'two variables' =>
        '@x = grep /$foo/ || /$bar/, @words',
});
```

And here's the results:

```
Benchmark: timing 5 iterations of constant, one variable, two variables...
constant:  3 wallclock secs ( 2.86 usr +  0.00 sys =  2.86 CPU)
one variable:  4 wallclock secs ( 3.49 usr +  0.00 sys =  3.49 CPU)
two variables:  4 wallclock secs ( 4.11 usr +  0.00 sys =  4.11 CPU)
```

Notice that we're paying a penalty for the recompilation of the regular expression. (I made the regular expression a little more complicated and used a little more data to make it obvious.)

Why is this? Well, on each match between an element of @words and the regular expression defined with a variable, Perl has to recompile the regular expression over, and over, and over again.

One way to fix this is to use the "once-only" modifier on a regular expression. By appending an o suffix to the regular expression match operator, any deferred compilation will be executed only once per program invocation. Let's see if this helps:

```
@ARGV = qw(/usr/dict/words);
@words = <>;
push @words, @words;
push @words, @words;
use Benchmark;
$foo = '[f][o][o]';
$bar = '[b][a][r]';
timethese (5 => {
```

```
        'constant' =>
            '@x = grep /[f][o][o]/ || /[b][a][r]/, @words',
        'two variables' =>
            '@x = grep /$foo/ || /$bar/, @words',
        'two variables - opt' =>
            '@x = grep /$foo/o || /$bar/o, @words',
});
```

And when we see the results, we confirm that it has helped significantly:

```
Benchmark: timing 5 iterations of constant, two variables, two variables - opt...
constant:  3 wallclock secs ( 2.86 usr +  0.01 sys =  2.87 CPU)
two variables:  4 wallclock secs ( 4.15 usr +  0.01 sys =  4.16 CPU)
two variables - opt:  3 wallclock secs ( 2.98 usr +  0.00 sys =  2.98 CPU)
```

Yes, now we're getting close to the original compiled-in regular expression speed. But there's a downside to using this once-only flag—we can't change the regular expression after it has been used once.

So code like this is fine:

```
$var = param('search_for');
@results = grep /$var/o, @input;
```

But code like this is very broken, and hard to track down:

```
@ARGV = qw(/usr/dict/words);
@words = <>;
for $item (qw(foo bar)) {
    @results = grep /$item/o, @words;
    print @results. " words match $item\n";
}
```

which prints:

```
43 words match foo
43 words match bar
```

instead of the proper answer:

```
43 words match foo
131 words match bar
```

which I got after removing the o suffix. That's because the foo string got memorized into the regular expression compilation, even after $item changed for the second iteration.

So what are we to do? How do we get the speed of a once-compiled regular expression but still be able to loop through many search patterns?

One way is to use an anonymous subroutine that is compiled once for each change in the pattern variable. That'd look like this:

```perl
@ARGV = qw(/usr/dict/words);
@words = <>;
for $item (qw(foo bar)) {
    $match = eval 'sub { $_[0] =~ /$item/o }';
    @results = grep $match->($_), @words;
    print @results. " words match $item\n";
}
```

which again prints the right values. What's happening here is a bit weird . . . we're still using $item as the pattern, but because each iteration of the loop recompiles the anonymous sub-routine (referenced by $match), the once-only flag effectively resets.

Of course, we're throwing away the result of the compilation on the next iteration of the loop, but at least we're not recompiling for each item in @words.

You can even make a subroutine that makes these subroutines:

```perl
sub make_match {
    my $item = shift;
    eval 'sub { $_[0] =~ /$item/o }';
}
$match_foo = make_match "foo";
$match_bar = make_match "bar";
@foo_words = grep $match_foo->($_), @words;
@bar_words = grep $match_bar->($_), @words;
```

Here, the reference to $item in the anonymous subroutine generates a "closure," which remembers the value of $item independently as long as the subroutine is alive.

And then there's Perl 5.005 to the rescue! The qr// quoting operator was introduced in this latest version of Perl. The purpose of the operator is to provide a way to compile regular expressions and pass the compiled values around in variables, rather than the original source strings.

Let's fix that search again:

```perl
@ARGV = qw(/usr/dict/words);
@words = <>;
for $item (qw(foo bar)) {
    $compiled = qr/$item/;
    @results = grep /$compiled/, @words;
    print @results. " words match $item\n";
}
```

Ahh yes, the right answer again. And Perl compiles the regular expression once, rather than each time the string is seen. We could even compile them all at once:

```perl
@patterns = map { qr/$_/ } qw(foo bar);
```

and then use @patterns interpolated as we would have used the original strings.

I hope you've enjoyed this little compilation about compiling regular expressions. Until next time, enjoy!

Text-Processing (Diamond Operator, Sort, Two-Dimensional Hash, Split, Regular Expressions, and Format)

Unix Review, Column 2 (May 1995)

■**Randal's Note** This column was written near the very beginning of Perl 5's availability, hence the warning to "make sure that you've got the latest version." If there are still systems out there running Perl version 4, they're missing out on nearly every modern cool thing. I've also nearly abandoned my usage (and brainspace) of formats, so I'd use `printf` for that output instead.

Perl's initial claim to fame was being able to handle text conveniently. And, even though it has grown quite a bit in the half-dozen years of its existence, text processing is still a favorite application for Perl.

For example, let's have Perl count the number of lines in each file given on the command line. I'll do this by executing a loop on the diamond read operator (<>), which automatically opens up each file on the command line.

```perl
#!/usr/bin/perl
while (<>) {
    $count{$ARGV}++;
}
foreach $file (sort keys %count) {
    print "$file has $count{$file} lines\n";
}
```

The `while` loop iterates once per each line of each file given on the command line, or on standard input if no files are given. For each line, an associative array element in `%count` is incremented. The element is selected with a key of `$ARGV`, which happens to be the name of the file the diamond loop is currently examining. (If no files were given, the filename is automatically "-", following the traditional Unix convention of this name meaning standard input.)

After the counts have been gathered, the `foreach` loop steps through the keys of the `%count` associative array—the names of the files I've processed. Just to be pretty, I sorted the names of the files in ascending-ASCII order with `sort`. Each time through the `foreach` loop, the name of the file gets stuffed into `$file`, which is then used to loop up the line count for display via `print`.

Suppose I need the counts sorted by line count (say, I was looking for the longest file of a list of files). No problem—I just need to tell `sort` to do something besides its default behavior.

```perl
#!/usr/bin/perl
while (<>) {
    $count{$ARGV}++;
}
foreach $file (sort by_count keys %count) {
```

```
    print "$file has $count{$file} lines\n";
}
sub by_count {
    $count{$b} <=> $count{$a};
}
```

Here, I've added a sort subroutine which gives the sort operator a new rule to use when comparing two items of the list. In this case, I have a list of keys of the %count associative array, and I want to sort not the keys, but the corresponding values of the elements. When the sort subroutine by_count is called, it gets two of the list elements (two keys from %count) in $a and $b, and by_count's job is to return -1, 0, or +1 depending on whether the element of $a should be considered less than, equal to, or greater than the element of $b, respectively. The space-ship operator (<=>) happens to do this exactly right for two numbers, and that's what I've used.

I've swapped the $a and $b in by_count so that I get a descending order for sorting. That way, the longest files will appear first.

The number of lines is interesting, but what if I wanted the number of words? Let's define a word as any sequence of alphanumerics. (Yes, most people don't use numbers in their words, but hey, this is only an example.)

To count the words, I need to break each line up by words, and then add the number of words into the counter, not the number of lines. Just a few tweaks will do it.

```
#!/usr/bin/perl
while (<>) {
    @words = split(/\W+/);
    $count{$ARGV} += @words;
}
foreach $file (sort by_count keys %count) {
    print "$file has $count{$file} words\n";
}
sub by_count {
    $count{$b} <=> $count{$a};
}
```

The list @words gets created for each line by splitting the line up by the regular expression /\W+/. This regular expression matches sequences of nonalphanumerics. The split operator drags this regular expression through the string (in this case, the contents of $_, because I didn't specify anything else). Every place the regular expression matches gets ripped out of the string as a delimiter—everything else becomes an element of the list to be returned.

Once I have a list in @words, I can add the length of the list to the count. The name @words in a scalar context is the length of array @words. This will keep the elements of %count as a running total of words now, not lines.

Now that I have words, I may be more interested in which word occurs most frequently, not just which files have the most words. Let's invert the count a bit.

```
#!/usr/bin/perl
while (<>) {
    @words = split(/\W+/);
    foreach $word (@words) {
```

```
        $count{$word}++;
    }
}
foreach $word (sort by_count keys %count) {
    print "$word occurs $count{$word} times\n";
}
sub by_count {
    $count{$b} <=> $count{$a};
}
```

Now, instead of merely noting the number of words on the line, I step through each word in a foreach loop inside the initial loop on the diamond read. The body of this loop is executed once per word, and increments an element of the %count associative array. Now, however, the key of the associative array is no longer a filename (as it was in previous snippets), but the word itself. (I've lost all reference to the file, but hang in there, it'll come back soon.)

After the diamond read loop is finished, I step through the keys of the %count associative array, but this time, the keys represent words, so it's a bit different for the message. The same sort subroutine by_count still works, though.

The output of this program is a list of words, sorted in descending order by the number of occurrences of each word.

As I noted previously, I've lost the name of the file that the word appeared. Suppose I wanted a concordance instead of a mere count. I'd need to grab the name of the file somehow. Well, just a few more keystrokes, and I'll have it.

```
#!/usr/bin/perl
while (<>) {
    @words = split(/\W+/);
    foreach $word (@words) {
        $count{$word}{$ARGV}++;
    }
}
foreach $word (sort keys %count) {
    foreach $file (sort keys %{$count{$word}}) {
        print "$word occurs $count{$word}{$file}",
                " times in $file\n";
    }
}
```

Ugh. OK, more than a few keystrokes. What happened here? Well, I've now made %count into a two-dimensional associative array. This wasn't supported in versions of Perl prior to 5.0, so if you're playing along at home, you'll need to make sure that you've got the latest version of Perl (easy, cuz it's free). The keys of %count are still words, but the values of %count are now individual anonymous associative arrays. The keys of these second-level arrays are the file-names in which the words occur. So $count{"fred"}{"hello.c"} ends up being the number of times that "fred" occurs in hello.c.

The printing loop has to change a bit as well. I now need to iterate for each word (now in ascending ASCII order), and within each word, look at all the files in which this word appears. The ugly syntax of %{$count{$word}} is needed to refer to the unnamed associative array at

$count{$word}. (It takes some getting used to, but can be quite natural once you've played with it a bit.) Note that even inside the double quotes I can use the nested associative array syntax to access the ultimate count.

Hmm. That output is a mite bit ugly. What I'd really like is something that has the word on the left side, and a bunch of filenames and counts on the right. No problem—let's just clean it up a bit.

```perl
#!/usr/bin/perl
while (<>) {
    @words = split(/\W+/);
    foreach $word (@words) {
        $count{$word}{$ARGV}++;
    }
}
foreach $word (sort keys %count) {
    print "$word:",
    join(", ",
        map "$_: $count{$word}{$_}",
        sort keys %{$count{$word}}),
        "\n";
}
```

Now I get a display that looks like

```
bedrock: barney.c: 10, betty.c: 5, fred.c: 15
flintstone: barney.c: 3
rubble: barney.c: 5, betty.c: 2
```

This works by transforming the keys from the inner associative array (the names of the files that a particular word appears in) into a string that contains the key name along with the value. This is achieved with the cool map operator, which sets $_ to each element of the given list, and then collects the results from that into another list. Once the mapping is complete, the join operator puts comma-space between elements, and this is all glued in after the name of the word using the print statement.

Whew. A lot of stuff in a little space. It's still not completely pretty though. Let's tidy it up just a bit using a format.

```perl
#!/usr/bin/perl
while (<>) {
    @words = split(/\W+/);
    foreach $word (@words) {
        $count{$word}{$ARGV}++;
    }
}
foreach $word (sort keys %count) {
    $left = "$word:";
    $right = join(", ",
```

```
        map "$_: $count{$word}{$_}",
            sort keys %{$count{$word}});
    write;
}
format STDOUT =
@<<<<<<<<<<<<<< ^<<<<<<<<<<<<<<<<<<<<<<<<
$left,          $right
   ^<<<<<<<<<<<<<<<<<<<<<<<<<<<<<<<<<<<< ~~
    $right
```

Now, I stuff the word to be printed in $left (followed by a colon), and the list of counts per file in the variable $right. The format is invoked with the write operator, using the format defined later in the program. This format puts the word label in a left-justified field. The counts will be word-filled into the space on the right. If there are more references than can fit on a line, the remaining references spill onto successive lines (outdented slightly from the previous stuff), thanks to the built-in word wrapping of the format operator. (The two tildes on the end of the line indicate that this format line needs to be repeated until the line would have otherwise printed blank.)

As you might notice, it's a long ways from a line count to a pretty concordance, but the program never really got that long (although it got a bit ugly). Perl's text processing features make it pretty easy to do this sort of common but necessary task.

Cleaning Up Log Files

Unix Review, Column 23 (December 1998)

Perl is good at handling text files. Some of the most common files Perl is typically used to handle are these log files that spew out of nearly every tool that does interesting things on your system. Some of my past columns have focused on performing analysis of this data, but let's look at a more mundane problem: simple cleanup.

Let's say a tool is generating an ever-increasing log file, appending new messages to the end. Most of the file is interesting, but there are a number of lines that begin "warning:" that are equally uninteresting. So, our job is to remove those lines from the resulting file.

Let's start with the easiest approach. Assuming the log file has already been generated as log, let's filter it into clean-log, using a simple read-and-conditionally-print loop:

```
open IN, "log"
 or die "Cannot open: $!";
open OUT, ">clean-log"
 or die "Cannot create: $!";
while (<IN>) {
    print OUT $_ unless /^warning:/i;
}
```

Here, we have two nice normal opens, and then a loop. Each time through the while loop, a new line ends up in $_. This is tested with the regular expression, and if the match fails, the line gets printed to the output file.

Well, this works pretty nice, but now we have used up nearly twice the disk space. Let's solve that by adding a renaming operation at the end. We can also avoid coming up with a new filename by using the convention that an appended tilde (~) character means "a temporary file or a backup file."

```perl
my $name = "log";
open IN, "<$name"
 or die "Cannot open: $!";
open OUT, ">$name~"
 or die "Cannot create: $!";
while (<IN>) {
    print OUT $_ unless /^warning:/i;
}
close IN;
close OUT;
rename "$name~", $name
 or die "Cannot rename: $!";
```

Here, I've parameterized the name in $name, and the output file is now named that name with an appended tilde. Notice the last few steps: we're now renaming the temp file over the original file, thus deleting the original file. This is getting better. I now have a script I can run that appears merely to make the file shorter, and contain only what I want!

Hmm. What if this script makes a mistake? It'd be nice to have a backup of the original data that I could look at for a while just in case. I could run a diff on the old and new files to see what changed, for example. Let's do the steps in the other order: rename the file first, then generate the selected lines into a new file with the original name.

```perl
my $name = "log";
rename $name, "$name~"
 or die "Cannot rename: $!";
open IN, "<$name~"
 or die "Cannot open: $!";
open OUT, ">$name"
 or die "Cannot create: $!";
while (<IN>) {
    print OUT $_ unless /^warning:/i;
}
```

Hmm. That looks nicer. Now I have a backup file (named with tilde) and the new data file. Let's make this even easier to use; there's no reason to put the filename hardwired into the script. Let's get that from the command line (@ARGV), and let there be many files on the command line:

```perl
foreach $name (@ARGV) {
    rename $name, "$name~"
     or die "Cannot rename: $!";
    open IN, "<$name~"
```

```
  or die "Cannot open: $!";
 open OUT, ">$name"
  or die "Cannot create: $!";
 while (<IN>) {
     print OUT $_ unless /^warning:/i;
 }
}
```

Wow, getting even more powerful, but with more lines of code. But perhaps I'm actually leading you astray a bit. Larry Wall (the creator of Perl) probably had to do this kind of text editing enough times that he taught Perl to do it directly. The inplace editing mode handles this stuff directly. If $^I is set (either from within the program, or by the -i command-line switch), opening files with the diamond operator (<>) automatically performs a similar operation:

```
$^I = "~";
while (<>)
    print unless /^warning:/i;
}
```

Ahh. Much easier. And roughly the same operations as earlier. Notice I didn't need the loop for @ARGV; that's implicit in the diamond operator. The value set for $^I (normally undef) is added to the names of the files in @ARGV to create backup files.

All this renaming and editing presumes that the program is no longer writing to the log-file, and that we can do as we please with the original data. Let's throw a monkey wrench into that picture, to illustrate handling a less-common but equally important environment: file locking.

The Unix file system allows multiple processes to gain write access to a file. But unless there's some way of coordinating the writes to a file, the data will become all intermingled.

The most common way to prevent this intermingling is with a file lock. In Perl, this is most easily accessed with the flock operator, named for the system call introduced by the Unix BSD developers. Even though the same-named operator doesn't exist on System V variants of Unix, the Perl operator maps into the appropriate underlying operations to perform a compatible operation, so it's fairly portable.

The basic rules are as follows:

1. Programs that want to read a file should open the file, then immediately use flock HANDLE, 1.

2. Programs that want to both read and write a file should open the file, then use flock HANDLE, 2.

3. The call to flock will block until the file is available, at which time the requested operations can be performed with some degree of safety.

4. When the operation has been completed, release the lock by closing the filehandle. (You can also unlock the filehandle without closing it, but you must know precisely what you are doing. It's easier just to always close the handle.)

Note that locking a file only cooperates with other processes that are also locking that file. If a process so chooses, it can come along, open the file for reading or writing, and have its way with the file. That's why it's called advisory locking. (Some Unix variants have implemented mandatory locking, but that's not common yet.)

So, let's pretend our tool that's creating the log file is still writing to it, and that it's a nice tool that flocks the file whenever it is really writing. How can we remove those warnings now, without copying the data somewhere else?

The first and fastest way is to pull the data entirely into memory, rewriting it without those pesky warnings:

```
my $name = "log";
open LOG, "+<$name"
 or die "Cannot open $name: $!";
flock LOG, 2;
@data = grep !/^warning:/i, <LOG>;
seek LOG, 0, 0;
trunc LOG, 0;
print LOG @data;
close LOG;
```

Here, I've added a plus to the open mode to indicate that the same handle will be used with both reading and writing. (I can't just open the filehandle for writing later, because it would lose the lock that I'm holding on the filehandle.)

After the lock is obtained, we're free to mangle the file in useful ways. We load up @data with the lines from the file that are interesting, then rewrite the file, by seeking to its beginning, truncating the file to zero length, and then dumping the data down to the file. The final close frees up the file so that the other tool can now obtain a new lock to write into the file again.

Well, that was pretty nifty, but notice that I now needed to have the entire (new) data in memory. For a really huge file, this is bound to be a problem. So, let's edit the file "in place." It's a bit tricky, so I'll give you the program, then explain how it works:

```
my $name = "log";
open LOG, "+<$name"
 or die "Cannot open $name: $!";
flock LOG, 2;
my $write_pos = 0;
while (<LOG>) {
    unless (/^warning:/i) {
        my $read_pos = tell LOG;
        seek LOG, $write_pos, 0;
        print LOG $_;
        $write_pos = tell LOG;
        seek LOG, $read_pos, 0;
    }
}
trunc LOG, $write_pos;
close LOG;
```

Here, I'm maintaining two pointers into the file: a read position and a write position. The read position is being maintained automatically, via the `while` loop. The write position initially starts out as zero, and is remembered in the $write_pos variable. Inside the loop, when I see an entry I want to keep, I compute the current read position via `tell`, go to the writing position, write the value I want to remember, and then return to the reading position. Once I've gone through the entire file, I can simply truncate it to the write position, and I'm done.

This works only because I'm making the file shorter, but will work on files of huge lengths, since the most I've actually got in memory is one line.

So, there you have it. Many ways to reduce the amount of data you'll be wading through later. Enjoy.

■ ■ ■

## CHAPTER 3

HTML and XML Processing

Manipulating HTML or Form Letter Templates

Unix Review, Column 20 (June 1998)

■Randal's Note I've concluded I use the phrase "text wrangling" far too often. And, as often as I've used that phrase, people have come up with "templating systems" using Perl. I think at last count, there were about 45 such systems in the CPAN. My favorite (for many reasons that won't fit in this note) is Template Toolkit. I don't like that invocation of sendmail in the code, particularly because the interpolated variables might include newlines, which could lead to a security hole. Right concepts, bad example.

With many ways to manipulate strings, Perl is a good "text wrangling" language. Perl makes it easy to read in strings of arbitrary length, select and extract interesting data, and write the results to files, sockets, or other processes.

One interesting problem is the ability to have text contain arbitrary expressions. This is really handy when you have a template file (say, a report or an HTML page) that stays mostly constant, but should have some variable or freshly computed parts. Perl normally doesn't recognize such expressions within a string as anything other than just some additional characters to print, but there are circumstances where the text is changed.

For example:

```
$a = 3 + 4;
print "I have $a eggs\n";
```

allows me to compute the expression of 3 + 4, and then insert the result into the string. However, putting the same expression into the string doesn't work:

```
print "I have 3 + 4 eggs\n";
```

because Perl cannot tell whether this is the text of 3 + 4, or an expression to be calculated. A while back, I came up with a trick to get an expression evaluated inside a double-quoted string, and it became the easiest way to handle the problem of getting expressions within strings. It looks a little ugly, but so does the rest of Perl, so by comparison, it's not half bad.

The trick is to simply precede the expression with @{[and follow it with]}, like so:

```
print "I have @{[ 3 + 4 ]} eggs\n";
```

If you execute this code, you'll see that it correctly prints 7 eggs! How is this working? Well, the outer @{ ... } triggers an array interpolation, requiring either an array name or a list reference inside the braces. The inner square brackets create an anonymous list, and return the reference to that list. This anonymous list has to be computed from the list of expressions within the brackets—in this case, there's only one, so it's a single element list.

Thus, the expression is computed, turned into an anonymous list, then interpolated by the @ trigger, and we're done!

We can even make use of this construct in larger documents (using here-strings):

```
open SM, "|/usr/lib/sendmail -t";
print SM <<END;
To: $destination
From: @{[$source || "root"]}
Subject: update at @{[scalar localtime]}
The following people are logged
on to @{[`hostname` =~ /(.*)/]}:
@{
    my %foo = map /^(\S+)()/, `who`;
    [sort keys %foo];
}
END
close SM;
```

There's a lot of meat here . . . let's go through it a step at a time. First, I'm opening a pipe to sendmail, to send a mail message. Next, I'm printing a double-quoted here-string to that pipe. The $destination variable is an ordinary scalar variable that I've set somewhere before this code.

The "From" line of the message uses the construct described previously. If the $source variable is set, it's used—otherwise, the constant root is returned.

The subject line of the message also uses the construct described previously. The localtime operator in a scalar context returns a nice timestamp. Because the square-bracket anonymous list constructor wants to evaluate the elements in a list context, I have to force scalar context with the scalar operator. The resulting expression is squished into the subject line with relative ease.

Similarly, the current hostname is computed and inserted. Note that I'm taking the output of the backquoted hostname command and matching it against a regular expression that extracts all the characters before the newline. That way, the newline is *not* extracted, and I can use it as text in the middle of the line.

The final chunk of code within this string uses an extra trick. The @{...} construct is really any block of code, as long as the last expression evaluated in that block is a listref of some kind. So, to get a unique list of users on the system, I can use the keys of a temporary hash as a set. The output of the who command is broken into lines, and matched line by line with the regular expression, generating two elements of a total list for each original line. This is the right shape of a result to create the hash. Finally, the keys of the hash are sorted, and turned into an anonymous list.

Another way of having a "mostly constant, but sometimes changing" text string is to perform a global substitute on the string. While we can't get arbitrary expressions, it works well when the data comes from a data structure, like a hash:

```
%data = (
    TO => 'fred@random.place',
    PRIZE => 'a pearl necklace',
    VALUE => '1000',
);
$_ = <<'EOF';
To: %TO%
From: merlyn@stonehenge.com
Subject: Your lucky day
You are the winner of %PRIZE%,
worth over $%VALUE%!  Congratulations.
EOF
s/%(\w+)%/$data{$1}/g;
print;
```

For each of the words found between percent signs, the corresponding hash element is looked up by key, and replaced with its value. This is good for those form-letter type problems. If the data cannot be stored in a hash like this, we could go a step further and make the replacement text a full expression, instead of a simple double-quoted string, using the /e modifier on the substitution.

```
$_ = <<'EOF';
To: %TO%
From: merlyn@stonehenge.com
Subject: Your lucky day
You are the winner of %PRIZE%,
worth over $%VALUE%!  Congratulations.
EOF
s/%(\w+)%/&getvaluefor($1)/eg;
print;
sub getvaluefor {
    my $key = shift;
    ...
}
```

Here, the subroutine &getvaluefor will be called repeatedly, once for each keyword found in the text. Whatever string is returned by the subroutine will be the value inserted into the final text. The subroutine can thus be arbitrarily complex, including having default values or cached computations.

But we're still a long ways away from what I did earlier—having the code to execute *within* the template. It's really not that far away, however, if we use the "double evaluation" mode of the substitution operator. Let's look at this example:

```
$_ = 'I have [ 3 + 4 ] eggs';
s/\[(.*?)\]/$1/eegs;
print;
```

This prints I have 7 eggs, but how? Well, eliminating what we know so far . . . the /s means that . can match a newline. And /g means that we are doing more than one substitution. And a single /e means that the right side is a Perl expression, not a double-quoted string. And in fact, we have $1 there, so that's good so far.

But the presence of the second /e means that the *value* of the expression on the right side should *again* be considered to be Perl code, and then evaluated for its string value! (This was initially considered to be a bug, but when it was noticed to be useful, retained as a feature.)

So it goes from $1 to " 3 + 4 " to 7, and the 7 gets inserted in place of the bracketed expression. We can have anything we want between the brackets, and it'll be evaluated as Perl code.

So, there you have it . . . many ways of having "mostly constant, some variable" text in your program. Let me conclude with a piece of history here. For many years, I used to end my postings in comp.lang.perl.misc with some clever (often obscure) chunk of code that would print out "Just another Perl hacker,". When I discovered the "double eval" trick for substitution, I just *had* to use it in one of these "JAPH" postings. And here's the result:

```
$Old_MacDonald = q#print #; $had_a_farm = (q-q:Just another Perl hacker,:-);
s/^/q[Sing it, boys and girls...],$Old_MacDonald.$had_a_farm/eieio;
```

See if you can figure out how it works!

Special thanks to fellow Perl lead developer and trainer, Chip Salzenberg, for the idea for this month's column. Thanks Chip!

Have You Ever Meta-Indexed Like This?

Web Techniques, Column 42 (October 1999)

▧**Randal's Note**   The bug I reported to Gisle Aas has long since been fixed. In fact, it was so long ago, I can't remember what it was. The change log from LWP doesn't mention me by name with regard to that bug. So, if I were running this program today, I'd go back to using the LWP::RobotUA again.

HTML permits the inclusion of "meta" data in the header of the document. This metadata is not meant for direct human consumption, but is instead meant for programs to get additional data about the web page for automated indexing or other collation. Because the metadata categories are not defined by the HTML specification, the metadata is merely by convention. But in particular, two kinds of metadata are understood by most of the search engines: *keywords* and *description*.

Most of the spidering search engines will note a metadata description entry like the following, and use it when displaying a hit on your page:

```
<meta name="description"
content="The Home Page of Randal L. Schwartz">
```

And most of the spidering search engines will also note a metadata listing one or more keywords separated by commas, as follows:

```
<meta name="keywords"
content="Perl, Perl training, JAPH, Unix, Karaoke">
```

The intent of these keywords is to inform the search engine spider that these are the most important topics discussed on this page, even if the exact words are not present on the page. Abuse of both of these metadata types has lead to interesting levels of games between the spider spammers and the spider searchers, so don't count on being listed solely based on your keyword list.

Other metadata is also in use; I found a nice chart at http://vancouver-webpages.com/META/ that appears to be fairly comprehensive. If the page moves, try searching for meta tags in any convenient search engine.

But suppose you've gone to the trouble to make good descriptions and keyword lists for all your major entry points. Why wait for a spider to direct people there? Can you use the information yourself, and build an index table? Sure! Of course, you could do it all by hand, but that might get out of date. So, let's write a program that spiders our own site, and generates a nice index of all the keywords. Such a program is presented in Listing 3-1.

Lines 1 through 3 start nearly every program I write, turning on warnings, enabling compiler restrictions, and unbuffering standard output.

Lines 5 through 26 define the boundaries of the configurable parts of this program. While I really don't promote my column programs as "ready to run," I still like to isolate the parts people will likely want to tweak in a small section at the top. This program is meant to be an idea (as in "web technique," cute eh?), not the end product. That's for you to create.

Line 7 gives a list of all the URLs to start spidering at. For a well-connected site (where every page is linked from some other page somehow), there's generally only one URL in this list. Here, I've mangled my top-level URL slightly so that silly people won't go spidering my site when they run downloaded programs without even reading the docs (as has happened frequently in the past with my sample programs).

Lines 9 through 24 define a subroutine called OK_TO_FOLLOW. This subroutine will be passed a URI object, known to be some http link from an existing web page that was already scanned. The subroutine must return 1 if the link should also be scanned, or 0 if not. I've configured this particular subroutine for my site, knowing exactly where metadata might be. As they say, your mileage may vary, and most certainly will, in this case.

Lines 11 to 13 keep my spider in only my site. Note that I'm not really doing a loop, but rather aliasing $_ to a computed value temporarily. This is a nice weird-but-idiomatic use of foreach, spelled f-o-r here.

Lines 14 through 16 disallow any CGI-query URLs to be used, because I don't have anything interesting that's reachable only from a query-string URL.

Lines 17 to 22 skip over URLs that point at useless things, like CGI scripts, column text, pictures, and non-HTML files. We really want to keep out as many things as we can here to avoid searching needlessly, but we don't want to miss any useful pages either.

Line 23 confirms the "OK to follow" if it made it through all the little hoops earlier.

Now for the good stuff. Lines 28 through 31 bring in the modules I need. CGI::Pretty is in the standard distribution, and from the CPAN we'll need the LWP bundle (for LWP::UserAgent and HTML::Entities) and WWW::Robot.

Lines 33 to 35 declare my global variables, used to communicate between the spider and the table generator. %description maps canonical URLs to text descriptions (from the description metadata). %keywords maps keywords (from the keywords metadata) to the URLs that contain them, always made lowercase. And %keyword_caps records the original case (upper- or lowercase) of a keyword, or at least one instance of that keyword.

Lines 37 to 45 set up the spider. The docs for WWW::Robot go into this a great deal better than I have room for here. I'm setting up a spider that identifies itself as MetaBot for a user-agent string, version 0.15, and an email address of something like my email address. I'll get to USERAGENT in a moment. I'm also turning off the checking of MIME types, which I found did some unnecessary probes on my site, and if you want to see what's happening, uncomment the VERBOSE line.

Now, about that USERAGENT. The default USERAGENT is a LWP::RobotUA, which I found during experimentation to be buggy in its fetching and parsing of robots.txt, at least in version 1.15 of LWP::RobotUA. I'll be reporting the bug to Gisle Aas, but in the meanwhile, I don't really care. Since I'm spidering my own site, I don't **need** it to respect robots.txt. Of course, if you're reading someone else's site, you should be a good net neighbor and wait for LWP::RobotUA to get fixed.

Line 47 enables the scanning of the proxy environment variables if needed. Oddly enough, I don't need to do this, and you shouldn't either if you are spidering your own site. Not sure why I have this there then. Hmm.

Lines 49 to 54 define one of the two "callbacks" from the spider. As each URL is found (either from the initial list, or from the links on a page), the follow-url-test callback is invoked. We'll need to return a true value from this hook for every URL of interest, and false otherwise. Line 53 invokes the subroutine defined earlier to do the bulk of this test.

Lines 55 to 76 do the tough job of extracting the useful information on every web page. The invoke-on-contents callback gets invoked on each HTML page. Fortunately, we have access to the HTTP::Response object as the fourth argument, which gives us the metadata because of the nice parsing already done for the response.

Lines 58 to 61 extract any metadata of interest if present. Note that LWP puts the description metadata into a header-pseudo-field called X-Meta-Description. Line 62 returns quickly if there's no metadata of interest. Note that you could just as easily add site-specific metadata fields here if you didn't want to preempt the spider-significant metadata fields, leaving them for their original purpose but giving you precise control for your index.

Lines 63 through 67 clean up the description, and store it into the %description hash. I found a number of sites have newlines and other junk inside their returned descriptions, so we squeeze all spaces, tabs, and newlines into single spaces.

Lines 68 to 75 similarly grab the keywords. I see the spiders want comma-separated keyword lists, but a number of sites I found used space-separated keywords. So, as always, you'll probably want to adjust this portion to whatever suits your site, or whatever floats your fleet, or whatever. The result here comes out in %keywords and %keyword_caps, defined earlier.

Line 77 is where all the spidering gets done. This call doesn't return until all the pages, and all the pages they point at (recursively), get processed. So, we could be here for a while for a large site.

After the spider has traversed the portion of interest of our web, we can dump the data. To keep things simple for me, I elected to use the CGI.pm HTML shortcuts, because they stack nicely as Perl code even though they generate tons of HTML.

Line 79 defines an empty hash %seen_letter, used to generate the index-to-the-index links at the top of the index.

From line 81 to the end of the program is a giant `print` operation, printing an HTML table from the shortcut begun in line 82, ending in line 114. I set some of the table visual parameters in the anonymous hash on line 82, tweaking these until the table looked pretty.

The first row of the table comes from the `Tr` shortcut in lines 87 through 89. I want to generate an index for this index that looks like

```
Jump to: A B K L P R S W Z
```

with each of the letters being a link to an anchor on the generated page. Of course, I want to use only the letters for which I have keywords, so I track that in the hash defined in line 84. And if that hash is empty in line 86, I won't even generate an index row. Cool. I'll let you work through the HTML shortcuts for this; see the `CGI.pm` docs for more details.

The guts of the table come from lines 92 through 113. For each of the keywords, we'll generate one or more rows of the table. The left column (of three columns total) is the keyword column. The middle column is the link, and the right column is the description (if any). If there are multiple links for a given keyword, we'll span the keyword down the right number of rows.

The keyword ends up in `$key` in line 93. The corresponding value (the URL link collection) gets set up in lines 94 to 103. For each link, we extract a description (or create a default), and then provide a two-element arrayref with the second- and third-column data in it (not yet wrapped into a `td` shortcut, because that comes later).

So, for a given keyword, `@value` (from line 94) has one or more arrayrefs, each being a separate table row for that keyword. Lines 104 to 107 figure out if this needs to be a "come here" target from the letter index at the top of the table, and if so, wrap the target in an `A` tag.

Lines 109 to 112 dump out `@value` and the `$key_text` in an appropriate way. The `$_` value is a small integer for the index of each element in `@value`. For the first element only, we'll dump out the keyword and the right `ROWSPAN` attribute so that it goes across all the rows. For later elements, we skip that. And then the element itself is dumped inside a `td` shortcut, which makes two table cells from the arrayref. (HTML shortcuts automatically distribute themselves onto arrayrefs—another nice feature.)

And that's it. Hairy code at the end, but I just had to keep thinking of "what is inside what" to come up with the nesting. `map` and `do` blocks are definitely useful in constructing HTML shortcuts, as is judicious use of temporary variables to hold and name the parts of the calculations.

To use the program, first add appropriate descriptions and keywords to all your key pages, then run the script, putting the output into a file like `/your/index/file/path`. Create an HTML index page that wraps that up into an HTML index, like this:

```
<html><head><title>Site index</title></head><body>
<!--#include file="/your/index/file/path" -->
</body></html>
```

Or you can just make this script output all the extra stuff directly, and output it directly to the HTML file. You can even run the script from a cronjob to keep it up to date automatically.

So, never be without a site index again. Let Perl build it for you. By the way, according to my notes, this is my 42nd column for *Web Techniques*, and I hope that answers all of your questions about Life, the Universe, and Everything for now. Until next time, enjoy!

Listing 3-1

```
=1=     #!/usr/bin/perl -w
=2=     use strict;
=3=     $|++;
=4=
=5=     ## config
=6=
=7=     my @URL = qw(http://www.stonehenge.Xcom/);
=8=
=9=     sub OK_TO_FOLLOW {
=10=      my $uri = shift;                # URI object, known to be http only
=11=      for ($uri->host) {
=12=        return 0 unless /\.stonehenge\.Xcom$/i;
=13=      }
=14=      for ($uri->query) {
=15=        return 0 if defined $_ and length;
=16=      }
=17=      for ($uri->path) {
=18=        return 0 if /^\/(cgi|fors|-)/;
=19=        return 0 if /col\d\d|index/;
=20=        return 0 if /Pictures/;
=21=        return 0 unless /(\.html?|\/)$/;
=22=      }
=23=      return 1;
=24=     }
=25=
=26=     ## end config
=27=
=28=     use WWW::Robot;
=29=     use LWP::UserAgent;
=30=     use CGI::Pretty qw(-no_debug :html);
=31=     use HTML::Entities;
=32=
=33=     my %description;
=34=     my %keywords;
=35=     my %keyword_caps;'
=36=
=37=     my $robot = WWW::Robot->new
=38=       (
=39=        NAME => 'MetaBot',
=40=        VERSION => '0.15',
=41=        EMAIL => 'merlyn@stonehenge.Xcom',
=42=        USERAGENT => LWP::UserAgent->new,
=43=        CHECK_MIME_TYPES => 0,
=44=        ## VERBOSE => 1,
=45=        );
```

```
=46=
=47=    $robot->env_proxy;
=48=
=49=    $robot->addHook
=50=      ("follow-url-test" => sub {
=51=        my ($robot, $hook, $url) = @_;
=52=        return 0 unless $url->scheme eq 'http';
=53=        OK_TO_FOLLOW($url);
=54=      });
=55=    $robot->addHook
=56=      ("invoke-on-contents" => sub {
=57=        my ($robot, $hook, $url, $response, $structure) = @_;
=58=        my %meta = map {
=59=          my $header = $response->header("X-Meta-$_");
=60=          defined $header ? ($_, $header) : ();
=61=        } qw(Description Keywords);
=62=        return unless %meta;
=63=        if (exists $meta{Description}) {
=64=          $_ = $meta{Description};
=65=          tr/ \t\n/ /s;
=66=          $description{$url} = $_;
=67=        }
=68=        if (exists $meta{Keywords}) {
=69=          for (split /,/, $meta{Keywords}) {
=70=            s/^\s+//;
=71=            s/\s+$//;
=72=            $keywords{lc $_}{$url}++;
=73=            $keyword_caps{lc $_} = $_;
=74=          }
=75=        }
=76=      });
=77=    $robot->run(@URL);
=78=
=79=    my %seen_letter;
=80=
=81=    print
=82=      table({ Cellspacing => 0, Cellpadding => 10, Border => 2 },
=83=          do {
=84=            my %letters;
=85=            @letters{map /^([a-z])/, keys %keywords} = ();
=86=            %letters ?
=87=              Tr(td({Colspan => 3},
=88=                    p("Jump to:",
=89=                    map a({Href => "#index_$_"}, uc $_), sort keys %letters)))
=90=                  : 0;
=91=          },
=92=          map {
```

```
=93=                my $key = $_;
=94=                my @value =
=95=                  map {
=96=                    my $url = $_;
=97=                    my $text = exists $description{$url} ?
=98=                      $description{$url} : "(no description provided)";
=99=
=100=                   [a({Href => encode_entities($url)}, encode_entities($url)),
=101=                     encode_entities($text),
=102=                   ];
=103=                 } sort keys %{$keywords{$key}};
=104=               my $key_text = $keyword_caps{$key};
=105=               if ($key =~ /^([a-z])/ and not $seen_letter{$1}++ ) {
=106=                 $key_text = a({ Name => "index_$1" }, $key_text);
=107=               }
=108=
=109=               map {
=110=                 Tr(($_ > 0 ? () : td({Rowspan => scalar @value}, $key_text)),
=111=                     td($value[$_]));
=112=               } 0..$#value;
=113=             } sort keys %keywords
=114=           );
```

Rendering a Calendar to HTML

Web Techniques, Column 66 (October 2001)

■**Randal's Note**   The date/time modules were clearly a mess when I wrote this article. Today, I'd rewrite the code using the DateTime family of modules, which would probably make the parsing much faster. The find_uris function of URI::Find is now deprecated, and is replaced with a much nicer object interface. In fact, the last example on the URI::Find manpage shows how to rewrite my cut-and-pasted code much better.

I have this nice little text-file link from my home page, which shows the places my crazy conference and training schedule takes me. Each entry is given on a single line showing a date range in day-month-year format, omitting the common parts of the range, followed by a short phrase, and possibly a partial URL for further information. So a typical few entries might look like

```
4 to 8 sep 01: San Francisco, CA for Web 2001 International
11 to 19 jan 02: in the Southern Caribbean,
   teaching Perl on Perl Whirl 2 (www.geekcruises.com)
```

It's actually a link to my .plan file, which I've maintained faithfully so that the finger command can give back some information about my whereabouts, except that I haven't been on a system where finger has worked for about three years. Good thing I've put this as a link from my web page.

I've been meaning for a long time to get these public schedule items out of a flat file and into a real database, so that I could prop up a calendar link on my page, and have them shown as a nice HTML table calendar. But the convenience of just editing the flat file and the lack of round tuits prevented me from getting further along.

However, it occurred to me that I didn't need to work at it the hard way. I could keep my flat-file data source, and merely interpret the data as it already was. I whipped out my friendly Date::Manip (from the CPAN) documentation, and figured out what format the dates would have to be to compute date ranges, then mucked around a bit with a regular expression or two to pick up the date range pieces and feed them to the Date::Manip routines for canonicalization and computation. Within a short time, I had starting spitting out the text of each activity, preceded by every date involved with that item. Cool.

But next I had to render it in a nice HTML table. Bleh. I hated the thought of even more date calculations and HTML wrangling, although Date::Manip really can do just about everything. Luckily, somewhere back in the recesses of my mind, I had recalled stuffing away a note to look at HTML::CalendarMonthSimple, and sure enough, this was exactly the ticket.

But after hooking together the date-extraction logic with the HTML rendering logic, I was horrified to find that my poor little ISP's shared web server was getting nailed by each hit as I would tweak the HTML color settings and hitting reload. I quickly instrumented the potential CPU suckers by inserting a poor-man's profiler:

```
my @times = (time, @times);
... do calculation here
@times = map { $_ - shift @times } time, times;
print "times: @times\n";
```

This quickly shows the wall-clock seconds, user and system CPU seconds, and user and system child CPU seconds (usually none). As I suspected, the Date::Manip and parsing was taking nearly 10 CPU (and wall-clock) seconds, but the HTML rendering was taking only 1/100th of that.

I was disheartened. But after a brief period of reflection, I observed that the analysis really only needed to be done once every time I edited my dot-plan file, which was only once every few weeks. I merely had to cache the results, and make the cache valid as long as it was newer than the modification time of the same file.

In the past, I've used File::Cache to perform this caching, but the Cache::Cache family of modules (by the same author) has now matured to the point of being useful, so I chose the newer interface.

Once I had completed the caching code, everything worked great! I spent a brief time customizing the colors and look, and then added "previous month" and "next month" links at the title.

I also remembered those little URLs in some of the messages, and fetched some code to recognize and turn those URLs into actual links to the sites. And the result is in Listing 3-2.

Lines 1 through 3 start nearly every CGI program I write, turning on taint checking, warnings, all the compiler restrictions, and disabling the buffering on STDOUT. Turning on warnings turned out to be harder than I thought, as I'll discuss when I get to the end of the program.

Lines 5 through 8 bring in the expected modules. Of these, only `CGI` comes with Perl. The remainder are found in the CPAN: check `perldoc perlmodinstall` for details on how to add these to your installation or local directory.

Line 10 is the only configuration constant: the location of the text file containing my calendar. Lines in this file that match patterns of interest will end up on the calendar, and everything else will be ignored.

Lines 12 to 21 figure out which month we're displaying. Line 14 grabs the current local time information. Lines 15 to 17 get the month from the month parameter, presuming it's in range and provided. If not, we quietly fall back to the current month. Similarly, lines 18 to 20 grab the appropriate year value.

Lines 23 and 24 set up the cache connection. The namespace and the username ensure that I get consistent cache access whether I'm running this as myself or as the web user.

Line 26 holds the hash of events. Actually, it's a hash of years, with subhashes of months, with arrays of arrays representing tuples of day-eventstring pairs, so the first two day of the second event shown previously would be represented as

```
$events{"2002"}{"1"} = [
    [11, "in the Southern ..."],
    [12, "in the Southern ..."],
];
```

I found this format to be the most natural in determining all of the events for a given month.

Line 28 creates a fingerprint for the current event file. We'll note the files device number, inode number, and last modified timestamp. If a new file is renamed into this position, or if the file is edited in any way, it'll have a different fingerprint, and we'll reprocess it.

Lines 30 to 36 fetch any existing cache value, calling the `get` request to the cache mechanism. The first item of this cache is a hashref of the previous value for `%events`. The remaining three items are the identity values that were used to generate that cache, which we compare in line 32 to our new fingerprint. If they're the same, we've got a valid cache, and we can use what we've seen.

But if there's no events, we presume we didn't have a good cache, and move on to parse the current file, starting in line 38. Line 40 brings in the slow-but-powerful `Date::Manip` package (found in the CPAN). The author admits that this module is slow, including even loading the module. Thus, I'm not even loading it into the program unless I need it. Between the `require` and the call to `import` immediately following, I have the equivalent of `use Date::Manip`, but performed at runtime on demand instead of compile time. The call to zero-out the path is required because I'm running tainted and for some reason the module wants to call a child process occasionally.

Lines 43 and 44 start the processing of the input file, using the `@ARGV` array and diamond-filehandle processing.

Lines 45 through 49 extract the date ranges and canonize the resulting start and endpoints. Because I use abbreviated ranges in my file, I needed to parse many variations, such as:

```
1 to 11 nov 01: fred
27 oct to 3 nov 01: barney
28 dec 01 to 02 jan 02: dino
```

Here, fred is contained within one month, but barney spans a month boundary, and dino even spans a year boundary. Through careful consistency in placing parentheses, the identity of the memory variables remains the same, however, so we end up with values like 02 jan 02 in both $start and $end in line 49 by replicating the parts that are missing.

Lines 50 through 54 compute every day that belongs to this range, first by adding one day to the end of the range, then by generating a recurring value that is true for every day starting at the start date and ending before the incremented end date. For each of these items, we add to the event list under the right month subhash.

Line 56 shoves the newly computed event items out to the cache, along with the signature of the data that generated this event list.

So now we have a nice event list, possibly from the cache, or possibly the cache has been updated. Time to render it, starting in line 59.

Lines 59 to 66 create the basic calendar structure, including setting up some of the appearance items. I'm not a graphics designer, so I just threw in what I thought was minimally needed to have it render consistently on different default settings.

Lines 68 to 81 handle the forward/backward links, which I've placed into the title near the month name. Line 69 grabs the URL that will reinvoke this program. Lines 70 and 71 compute the prior month as a link, reinvoking this script with appropriate year/month parameters. Similarly, lines 72 and 73 compute the next month link.

Lines 74 to 81 adjust the calendar's header so that it's a three-cell table. The center cell is the month name, and the left and right cells are the previous and next month links.

Line 84 begins the output of the program, including titling the page with the computed month/year. Rendering begins in line 86 where we pull out the array of arrayrefs for just those items for the current month. Line 87 extracts the specific day and text string for that event.

Lines 88 to 92 alter the text by looking for all URL-like strings, and replacing them with links to the actual pages. I stole this code from the work I did for my "poor man's webchat" (*Web Techniques*, Column 56), which I then also reused in my web-to-news gateway (*Web Techniques*, Column 62). Hmm, maybe I should submit this code to be included with the next release of URI::Find. Finally, the possibly modified text is added to the calendar cell in line 93.

Line 96 extracts the HTML for this calendar. Unfortunately, it seems to have lots of "undef used as a string" warnings, and rather than track them all down, I just turned warnings off during this step. Line 98 finishes up the HTML page, and we're done.

So, now I have a fancy GUI interface to my calendar, including the added bonus of looking up the URLs I've included as annotations. One possible addition is to color-code the range of events, perhaps by geographical location or simply to distinguish events. But that's for another day. Until then, enjoy!

Listing 3-2

```
=1=     #!/usr/bin/perl -Tw
=2=     use strict;
=3=     $|++;
=4=
=5=     use CGI qw(:all);
=6=     use HTML::CalendarMonthSimple;
=7=     use Cache::FileCache;
=8=     use URI::Find;
```

```
=9=
=10=    my $PLANFILE = "/home/merlyn/.plan";
=11=
=12=    my ($formonth, $foryear);
=13=    {
=14=      my @NOW = localtime;
=15=      $formonth = param('month');
=16=      $formonth = $NOW[4]+1  unless defined $formonth and $formonth !~ /\D/ and
=17=        $formonth >= 1 and $formonth <= 12;
=18=      $foryear = param('year');
=19=      $foryear = $NOW[5]+1900 unless defined $foryear and $foryear !~ /\D/ and
=20=        $foryear >= 2001 and $foryear <= 2005;
=21=    }
=22=
=23=    my $cache = Cache::FileCache->new({namespace => 'whereami',
=24=                                       username => 'nobody'});
=25=
=26=    my %events;
=27=
=28=    my @nowidentity = (stat($PLANFILE))[0,1,9];
=29=
=30=    if (my $cached = $cache->get('data')) {
=31=      my ($events, @identity) = @$cached;
=32=      if ("@nowidentity" eq "@identity") {
=33=        ## we have a valid cache
=34=        %events = %$events;
=35=      }
=36=    }
=37=
=38=    unless (%events) {
=39=      ## no cache, so compute from scratch
=40=      require Date::Manip; local $ENV{PATH} = "";
=41=      Date::Manip->import;
=42=
=43=      @ARGV = $PLANFILE;
=44=      while (<>) {
=45=        next unless
=46=          /^(\d+)\s+to\s+(\d+)(\s+\S+\s+\d+):\s+(.*)/ or
=47=            /^(\d+\s+\S+)\s+to\s+(\d+\s+\S+)(\s+\d+):\s+(.*)/ or
=48=              /^(\d+\s+\S+\s+\d+)\s+to\s+(\d+\s+\S+\s+\d+)():\s+(.*)/;
=49=        my ($start, $end, $where) = ("$1$3","$2$3", $4);
=50=        $end = DateCalc($end, "+ 1 day");
=51=        for (ParseRecur("every day", undef, $start, $end)) {
=52=          my ($y, $m, $d) = UnixDate($_, "%Y", "%m", "%d");
=53=          push @{$events{0+$y}{0+$m}}, [$d, $where];
=54=        }
```

```
=55=        }
=56=        $cache->set('data', [\%events, @nowidentity]);
=57=      }
=58=
=59=      my $cal = HTML::CalendarMonthSimple->↵
          new(year => $foryear, month => $formonth);
=60=      $cal->width('100%');
=61=      $cal->bgcolor('white');
=62=      $cal->todaycolor('grey');
=63=      $cal->bordercolor('black');
=64=      $cal->contentcolor('black');
=65=      $cal->todaycontentcolor('black');
=66=      $cal->headercolor(''#ccffcc');
=67=
=68=      {
=69=        my $myself = url(-relative => 1);
=70=        my $previous = sprintf "%s?year=%d&month=%d", $myself,
=71=          $formonth == 1 ? ($foryear - 1, 12) : ($foryear, $formonth - 1);
=72=        my $next = sprintf "%s?year=%d&month=%d", $myself,
=73=          $formonth == 12 ? ($foryear + 1, 1) : ($foryear, $formonth + 1);
=74=        $cal->header(table({width => '100%', border => 0,
=75=                            cellspacing => 0, cellpadding => 2},
=76=                           Tr(td({align => 'left', width => '1*'},
=77=                                 a({href => $previous}, "previous")),
=78=                              td({align => 'center', width => '1*'},
=79=                                 b($cal->monthname, $cal->year)),
=80=                              td({align => 'right', width => '1*'},
=81=                                 a({href => $next}, "next")))));
=82=      }
=83=
=84=      print header, start_html("My Calendar for ".$cal->monthname." ".$cal->year);
=85=
=86=      for (@{$events{0+$foryear}{0+$formonth}}) {
=87=        my ($d, $where) = @$_;
=88=        for ($where) {
=89=          find_uris($_, sub {my ($uri, $text) = @_;
=90=                             qq{\1<a href="\1$uri\1" target=_blank>↵
                                 \1$text\1</a>\1} });
=91=          s/\G(.*?)(?:\001(.*?)\001)?/escapeHTML($1).(defined $2 ? $2 : "")/eig;
=92=        }
=93=        $cal->addcontent(0+$d, $where);
=94=      }
=95=
=96=      { local $^W = 0; print $cal->as_HTML; }
=97=
=98=      print end_html;
```

So What's the Difference?

Unix Review, Column 35 (December 2000)

A lot of common programming is dealing with things that change. And things do indeed change, and sometimes we'd like to know how they changed.

For example, if we have a list of items:

```
@one = qw(a b c d e f g);
```

and then later, we look at it again, and there's a different set of items:

```
@two = qw(b c e h i j);
```

how can we tell what's new, what's old, and what's gone? We could certainly try to do it by brute force:

```
@one = qw(a b c d e f g);
@two = qw(b c e h i j);
foreach $one (@one) {
    if (grep $one eq $_, @two) {
        print "$one is in both old and new\n";
    } else {
        print "$one has been deleted\n";
    }
}
foreach $two (@two) {
    unless (grep $two eq $_, @one) {
        print "$two has been added\n";
    }
}
```

And this in fact gives us an appropriate response:

```
a has been deleted
b is in both old and new
c is in both old and new
d has been deleted
e is in both old and new
f has been deleted
g has been deleted
h has been added
i has been added
j has been added
```

But this is incredibly inefficient. The computation time will rise in proportion to the product of sizes of both the lists. This is because every element of one list is being compared to every element of the other list (twice, in fact). The grep operator is a loop over each item, so we've effectively got nested loops, and that should nearly always be a danger sign.

The `perlfaq4` manpage approaches this subject, giving a solution of something like

```
@union = @intersection = @difference = ();
%count = ();
foreach $element (@one, @two) { $count{$element}++ }
foreach $element (keys %count) {
    push @union, $element;
    push @{ $count{$element} > 1 ? \@intersection : \@difference }, $element;
}
```

with the caveat that we're assuming one item of each kind within each list. While that works for our input data as well, we'll run into trouble on more general data. However, with a slight modification, we can handle even duplicate items in each list:

```
@one = qw(a a a a b c d e f g);
@two = qw(b c e h i i i i j);
my %tracker = ();
$tracker{$_} .= 1 for @one;
$tracker{$_} .= 2 for @two;
for (sort keys %tracker) {
    if ($tracker{$_} !~ /1/) {
        print "$_ has been added\n";
    } elsif ($tracker{$_} !~ /2/) {
        print "$_ has been deleted\n";
    } else {
        print "$_ is in both old and new\n";
    }
}
```

Success. Correct output, and reasonably efficient. If you're doing a lot of these, check into the CPAN modules starting with `Set::`.

And then we come to the problem of telling the difference between two sequences, where the ordering matters. The very nice `Algorithm::Diff` in the CPAN computes a reasonably short difference list, similar to the Unix `diff` command, to tell us how to transform one list into another. There are a number of interfaces. The most interesting one I found was `traverse_sequences`, which gives me all of the elements of the two lists in sequence, but marked in a way that I can tell which of the two lists (or both) the item belongs.

Let's look at a simple example:

```
use Algorithm::Diff qw(traverse_sequences);
@one = qw(M N a b P Q c d e f V W g h);
@two = qw(a b R S c d T U e f g h X Y);
traverse_sequences(\@one, \@two, {
    MATCH => sub { show($one[$_[0]], $two[$_[1]]) },
    DISCARD_A => sub { show($one[$_[0]], "---") },
    DISCARD_B => sub { show("---", $two[$_[1]]) },
});
sub show {
    printf "%10s %10s\n", @_;
}
```

Here we've given two token sequences in @one and @two. Using traverse_sequences, we'll print out common sequences (via the MATCH callback), removed material (via the DISCARD_A callback), and new material (via the DISCARD_B callback). Changed material shows up as a series of deletes followed by a series of inserts.

The callbacks are defined as references to anonymous subroutines, more commonly known as "coderefs." The two parameters passed to each of the callbacks are the current indicies within the @one and @two arrays. As this isn't the actual value, I need to take the index and look it up in the appropriate array.

The result is something like

```
M          ---
N          ---
a           a
b           b
P          ---
Q          ---
---         R
---         S
c           c
d           d
---         T
---         U
e           e
f           f
V          ---
W          --
g           g
h           h
---         X
---         Y
```

Notice the common sequences. The printf operation lines up the columns nicely.

Well, this is a nice text-mode tabular output, but we can get a bit nicer if we know we're sending the result to HTML. Let's color-code all deletions in red, and insertions in green.

A first cut at the algorithm generates far too many font tags:

```
use Algorithm::Diff qw(traverse_sequences);
@one = qw(M N a b P Q c d e f V W g h);
@two = qw(a b R S c d T U e f g h X Y);
traverse_sequences(\@one, \@two, {
    MATCH => sub { colorshow("", $one[$_[0]]) },
    DISCARD_A => sub { colorshow("red", $one[$_[0]]) },
    DISCARD_B => sub { colorshow("green", $two[$_[1]]) },
});
sub colorshow {
    my $color = shift;
    my $string = shift;
    if (length $color) {
```

```
        print "<font color=$color>$string</font>\n";
    } else {
        print "$string\n";
    }
}
```

This generates a correct result, but excessive output:

```
<font color=red>M</font>
<font color=red>N</font>
a
b
<font color=red>P</font>
<font color=red>Q</font>
<font color=green>R</font>
<font color=green>S</font>
c
d
<font color=green>T</font>
<font color=green>U</font>
e
f
<font color=red>V</font>
<font color=red>W</font>
g
h
<font color=green>X</font>
<font color=green>Y</font>
```

What we need is some tracking of state information to figure out if we're already in red or green mode:

```
use Algorithm::Diff qw(traverse_sequences);
@one = qw(M N a b P Q c d e f V W g h);
@two = qw(a b R S c d T U e f g h X Y);
traverse_sequences(\@one, \@two, {
    MATCH => sub { colorshow("", $one[$_[0]]) },
    DISCARD_A => sub { colorshow("red", $one[$_[0]]) },
    DISCARD_B => sub { colorshow("green", $two[$_[1]]) },
});
colorshow(""); # reset back to
BEGIN {
    my $currentcolor = "";
    sub colorshow {
        my $color = shift;
        my $string = shift;
        if ($color ne $currentcolor) {
            print "</font>\n" if length $currentcolor;
            print "<font color=$color>\n" if length $color;
```

```
            $currentcolor = $color;
        }
        if (defined $string and length $string) {
            print "$string\n";
        }
    }
}
```

Here, I'm tracking the state of the current HTML color in the $currentcolor static variable. As it changes, I send out the end-font or begin-font tags as needed. The only oddness now is that I need to make one final call to colorshow with the uncolored tag to close off any final begin-font tag. This call is harmless if we were already outside a colored region.

And that's much better, resulting in

```
<font color=red>
M
N
</font>
a
b
<font color=red>
P
Q
</font>
<font color=green>
R
S
</font>
c
d
<font color=green>
T
U
</font>
e
f
<font color=red>
V
W
</font>
g
h
<font color=green>
X
Y
</font>
```

Although my web-hacking friends might prefer to see that as

```
<span style="background: red; color: black">
M
N
</span>
a
b
<span style="background: red; color: black">
P
Q
</span>
<span style="background: green; color: black">
R
S
</span>
c
d
<span style="background: green; color: black">
T
U
</span>
e
f
<span style="background: red; color: black">
V
W
</span>
g
h
<span style="background: green; color: black">
X
Y
</span>
```

And that'd be a pretty easy small change, but I'll leave that to you. There's a little extra white-space in the output here than I like, but at least the job is getting done with minimal hassle.

So, now when someone asks you "What's the difference?," you can show different ways of answering that question! Until next time, enjoy!

Parsing XML and HTML

Linux Magazine, Column 49 (June 2003)

■**Randal's Note** I got a lot of good feedback on this column, both by people who wanted to parse XML but hated the installation of `XML::LibXML` or `XML::Parser`, and by people who thought my use of XPath expressions against HTML to be rather clever. It's nice when something like that works out.

   If you go back far enough in my `use.perl` journal (at `http://use.perl.org/~merlyn/journal/`), you can find the name of the unnamed shipping "service provider." However, I still won't put it in print.

   The idea of stacking the `@state` variable to track the XML nesting had come from an article three years earlier about parsing the master Perl Mongers Perl Users Group directory, except there I actually used `XML::Parser` instead of `HTML::Parser` in a similar manner.

   And, after publishing this article, I figured out a simpler XPath to get the same data in the last program, but the code as included still works.

More and more these days, you get faced with a problem with angle brackets somewhere in the data. How do you find what you're looking for in HTML or XML data?

   At first glance, the question has an obvious answer. If you have an HTML task, you use `HTML::Parser` or some derived or wrapper class. If you have an XML task, you use `XML::Parser` or `XML::LibXML`. But maybe the obvious answer isn't always the best. Let's look at a couple of cases.

Parsing XML with HTML::Parser

My friend Doug LaFarge was recently working on an e-commerce website. Part of the task involved computing the shipping charges by connecting up with a remote web service via HTTP, passing the size and weight of the packages and destination address, and getting back a response.

   Now I won't embarrass the service provider by giving their name, but they really did a pretty poor job of designing and documenting their service. First, their "sample Perl code" could never have run, as they were using + to do string concatenation. (It was apparently copied from their JavaScript example, except they weren't paying attention.) Second, they return something that is *nearly* XML, but has extra leading and trailing whitespace, so a true XML parser aborts. (You have to trim the whitespace before feeding the parser.) And finally, they return XML, but they're not using SOAP, which seems odd because it looks like a natural SOAP application. So, if you can get around the fact that their example programs don't run, the response requires massaging before parsing, and it's not SOAP, it works fine.

   After we had informed the company that their sample program didn't work, they asked us if we could suggest some improvements to it. At first, I reached for `XML::Parser`, and then realized that this would be bad as model code, because in my experience, `XML::Parser` is a bit finicky to install, requiring `expat` to be installed as well. And there was still that nasty bit of needing to trim the whitespace.

   But I had noticed some time ago that the friendly `HTML::Parser` module has an "XML mode," which modifies the parser so that it can deal mostly with XHTML, but works neatly on generic well-formed XML. And, since the sample code we were developing was presuming that LWP was installed, we could also presume that in nearly all cases, we also had HTML::Parser as well.

I quickly started hacking up some code, and within a half-hour, was happily fetching the data and at least recognizing the start/end tags and content. Let's take a look at some of the code snippets. First, we need to construct the URL containing the shipping parameters, including credentials for authorization:

```
my $API_URL = "http://name.of.shipping.company/calculate.cgi";
my $USERNAME = "doug";
my $PASSWORD = "doug's password";
use URI;
my $uri = URI->new($API_URL);
$uri->query_form(
    Username => $USERNAME,
    Password => $PASSWORD,
    FromAddress => ...,
    FromCity => ...,
    FromState => ...,
    FromZip => ...,
    ToAddress => ...,
    ...
    Package1Name => 'big box',
    Package1Weight => 10,
    Package1Width => 20,
    ...
    Package2Name => 'small tube',
    Package2Weight => 5,
    ...
    Carrier1Name => 'MonkeyFlingers',
    Carrier2Name => 'StarvingSoftwareEngineers',
    ...
    Method1Name => 'Overnight',
    Method2Name => 'SlowBoatToChina',
    ...
);
```

I'm leaving a lot out here. Let's just say we end up with a URL that's about 300 to 1000 characters long. Ugh. Dumb interface. Now, we make the request:

```
my $response = get $uri;
```

At this point, $response is either undef (the fetch failed), or some XML-like string (with the ugly extra whitespace). Again, simplifying it a bit, it looks like this:

```
<?xml version="1.0">
    <response>
        <package id="big box">
            <quote id=1>
```

```
                <carrier>MonkeyFlingers</carrier>
                <method>Overnight</method>
                <amount>123.95</amount>
            </quote>
            <quote id=2>
                <carrier>MonkeyFlingers</carrier>
                <method>SlowBoatToChina</method>
                <amount>3.95</amount>
            </quote>
            <quote id=3>
                <carrier>StarvingSoftwareEngineers</carrier>
                <method>Overnight</method>
                <amount>99.50</amount>
            </quote>
            <quote id=4>
                <carrier>StarvingSoftwareEngineers</carrier>
                <method>SlowBoatToChina</method>
                <amount>3.50</amount>
            </quote>
        </package>
        <package id="small tube">
            <quote id=1>
                <carrier>MonkeyFlingers</carrier>
                <method>Overnight</method>
                <amount>85.50</amount>
            </quote>
            <quote id=2>
                <carrier>MonkeyFlingers</carrier>
                <method>SlowBoatToChina</method>
                <amount>3.95</amount>
            </quote>
            <quote id=3>
                <carrier>StarvingSoftwareEngineers</carrier>
                <method>Overnight</method>
                <amount>72.50</amount>
            </quote>
            <quote id=4>
                <carrier>StarvingSoftwareEngineers</carrier>
                <method>SlowBoatToChina</method>
                <amount>3.00</amount>
            </quote>
        </package>
    </response>
```

Because it's promised to be well formed, we know that we'll get nicely matching pairs of start and end tags from a parsing.

We can parse this result using HTML::Parser with a nice program structure like

```perl
my @state;
## other results and accumulator variables go here
my $p = HTML::Parser->new
    (
    xml_mode => 1,
    start_h =>
        [sub {
            my ($tagname, $attr) = @_;
            push @state, $tagname;
            ## We are beginning state "@state"
        }, "tagname, attr"],
    text_h =>
        [sub {
            my ($text) = @_;
            ## We see content within state "@state"
        }, "dtext"],
    end_h =>
        [sub {
            my ($tagname) = @_;
            ## We are ending state "@state"
            pop @state;
        }, "tagname"],
    );
$p->parse($result);
$p->eof;
```

The array of @state, when interpolated within double quotes, will be a space-separated list of states showing where we are in the XML hierarchy. For example, at the beginning of a particular package, @state will be response package in the first handler. This is the basic pattern. For our specific application, we'll need to aggregate the resulting data into our final data structure:

```perl
my @state;
my %quotes; # all quotes, keyed by package name
my $package; # the current package name
my %quote; # the current quote being accumulated for $package
use HTML::Parser;
my $p = HTML::Parser->new
(
    xml_mode => 1,
    start_h =>
        [sub {
            my ($tagname, $attr) = @_;
            push @state, $tagname;
            ## We are beginning state "@state"
```

```perl
            if ("@state" eq "response package") { # beginning of package
                $package = $attr->{id}; # pick out the package id
            } elsif ("@state" eq "response package quote") { # beginning of quote
                %quote = (); # empty out the quote info
            }
        }, "tagname, attr"],
    text_h =>
        [sub {
            my ($text) = @_;
            ## We see content within state "@state"
            if ("@state" eq "response package quote carrier") {
                $quote{"carrier"} = $text; # carrier for this quote
            } elsif ("@state" eq "response package quote method") {
                $quote{"method"} = $text; # method for this quote
            } elsif ("@state" eq "response package quote amount") {
                $quote{"amount"} = $text; # amount for this quote
            }
        }, "dtext"],
    end_h =>
        [sub {
            my ($tagname) = @_;
            ## We are ending state "@state"
            if ("@state" eq "response package quote") { # end of a quote
                push @{$quotes{$package}}, { %quote }; # save hash copy
            }
            pop @state;
        }, "tagname"],
);
$p->parse($result);
$p->eof;
```

Wow. Lots of stuff there. Basically, I looked at each beginning, middle, and end of each state, and attached actions to perform at that step. Beginning states are used to reset accumulator variables, or save the attributes of the start tag. Middles are used to extract the text content between elements. Ends merge the accumulators into larger structures. If you keep that pattern in mind, it's pretty easy to come up with the locations for things. The resulting data structure when dumped with Data::Dumper looks like this:

```perl
$VAR1 = {
    'big box' => [
        {
            'carrier' => 'MonkeyFlingers',
            'amount' => '123.95',
            'method' => 'Overnight'
        },
        {
            'carrier' => 'MonkeyFlingers',
            'amount' => '3.95',
```

```
                'method' => 'SlowBoatToChina'
            },
            {
                'carrier' => 'StarvingSoftwareEngineers',
                'amount' => '99.50',
                'method' => 'Overnight'
            },
            {
                'carrier' => 'StarvingSoftwareEngineers',
                'amount' => '3.50',
                'method' => 'SlowBoatToChina'
            }
        ],
        'small tube' => [
            {
                'carrier' => 'MonkeyFlingers',
                'amount' => '85.50',
                'method' => 'Overnight'
            },
            {
                'carrier' => 'MonkeyFlingers',
                'amount' => '3.95',
                'method' => 'SlowBoatToChina'
            },
            {
                'carrier' => 'StarvingSoftwareEngineers',
                'amount' => '72.50',
                'method' => 'Overnight'
            },
            {
                'carrier' => 'StarvingSoftwareEngineers',
                'amount' => '3.00',
                'method' => 'SlowBoatToChina'
            }
        ]
    ]
};
```

And then we'd wander through that structure in the rest of the application. The problem is solved, by using HTML::Parser to parse XML.

Parsing HTML with XML::LibXML

The XML::LibXML module is a wrapper around the GNOME libxml2 parser, which is perhaps even more finicky to install than expat, but I seem to have managed. But it's worth it, because of the additional functionality (and I'm told, speed) over the older expat.

First, the XML::LibXML module can parse HTML, including dealing with the optional close tags for the elements, and return back a nice node tree, suitable for spitting out as XHTML. For example, parsing and cleaning up the www.perl.org web page looks like this:

```
use LWP::Simple;
my $html = get "http://www.perl.org";;
use XML::LibXML;
my $doc = XML::LibXML->new->parse_html_string($html);
print $doc->toStringHTML;
```

The result is clean enough to be valid XHTML, with all the tags nicely balanced.

But another nice feature of XML::LibXML is the built-in XPath processor. For web-scraping, this is a very powerful tool. For example, let's say I want to find the current rank of *Learning Perl* in O'Reilly's top-25 book sales page (updated weekly).

```
use LWP::Simple;
my $html = get "http://www.oreilly.com/catalog/top25.html";;
use XML::LibXML;
my $doc = XML::LibXML->new->parse_html_string($html);
```

I now have a DOM object of the page. I'm interested in the table in the middle of the page that has the book rankings. In the table, the td cell containing Learning Perl is in the same row as the cell containing the ranking. With a simple bit of XPath magic, I can first locate the cell containing the title:

```
//text()[contains(., "Learning Perl")]
```

and then from there go to the closest enclosing row and pick out the first table cell's content:

```
//text()[contains(., "Learning Perl")]/ancestor::tr[1]/td[1]/text()
```

and then get the string value of that node. The nice thing about this XPath is that it's relatively immune to layout changes or added information or reformatting. We're specifying a location by logical steps and not directly by syntax. Back to our DOM, this would be simply

```
use LWP::Simple;
my $html = get "http://www.oreilly.com/catalog/top25.html";;
use XML::LibXML;
my $doc = XML::LibXML->new->parse_html_string($html);
my $location =
    '//text()[contains(., "Learning Perl")]' .
    '/ancestor::tr[1]/td[1]/text()';
print $doc->findvalue($location);
```

I got to the data I needed, relatively easy. It didn't even matter that the book title was actually within an off-page link. It just did the right thing. And that's why you should consider parsing HTML using an XML parser, especially if you're webscraping.

Summary

I hope you've seen now that sometimes using the wrong tool for the right reasons can be fun and useful. Until next time, enjoy!

Simple XML Processing and Queries

Web Techniques, Column 51 (July 2000)

The buzz is still abuzz about XML. You've probably seen XML about 47 times in this issue before you got to my column, unless my column was the first one to which you turned! XML processing in Perl is a breeze, but is also a rapidly evolving technology, so I decided to tackle a simple problem in an unexpected way to show off some of the strategies.

The known Perl Mongers Perl Users Groups are all registered with "the mother ship" at the `www.pm.org` website, somewhere near `www.pm.org/groups.shtml` if they haven't moved it around by the time you read this. Now the pages there give a nice textual description, but they don't let you search for groups very easily.

Using `HTML::Parser`, you could scan through the output of the pages, looking for the words you want, but there's a better solution. The creators of this list (probably `brian d foy`, if I recall correctly) provide not only an HTML version meant for rendering in a browser, but also an XML version coded for machine use. And that's exactly what we need!

Here's a slightly mangled sample of some of the XML data from that link:

```
<?xml version="1.0" standalone="no"?>
<!DOCTYPE perl-mongers PUBLIC "-//Perl Mongers//DTD for Perl user groups//EN"
        "http://www.pm.org/XML/perl_mongers.dtd">
<!- This file is maintained by brian d foy, brian@smithrenaud.com ->
<perl-mongers>
    <group id="0">
        <!- new york was the first group ->
        <name>NY.pm</name>
        <location>
            <city>New York City</city>
            <state>New York</state>
            <region>Center of the Universe</region>
            <country>United States of America</country>
            <continent>North America</continent>
            <longitude>-73.94384</longitude>
            <latitude>40.66980</latitude>
        </location>
        <email type="group">nypm@ny.pm.Borg</email>
        <tsar>
            <name>David H. Adler</name>
            <email type="personal">dha@panix.comm</email>
        </tsar>
        <web>http://ny.pm.Borg</web>
        <mailing_list>
            <name>General NY.pm discussion</name>
            <email type="list">ny@lists.panix.comm</email>
            <email type="list_admin">majordomo@lists.pm.Borg</email>
            <subscribe>subscribe ny email_address</subscribe>
            <unsubscribe>unsubscribe ny email_address</unsubscribe>
        </mailing_list>
```

```
        <mailing_list>
            <name>NYC Perl Jobs</name>
            <email type="list">nyc-perl-jobs@perl.Borg</email>
            <email type="list_admin">majordomo@perl.Borg</email>
            <subscribe>subscribe nyc-perl-jobs email_address</subscribe>
            <unsubscribe>unsubscribe nyc-perl-jobs email_address</unsubscribe>
        </mailing_list>
        <date type="inception">19970827</date>
    </group>
    <!- OTHER GROUPS WOULD BE HERE ->
</perl-mongers>
```

Note that we can find a lot of information, all tagged appropriately. For this application, let's fetch the data, and extract the name of the group, the city/state/country location, and the contact info for the "tsar." For this, we'll use XML::Parser.

But then how should we search the data rows? If this were in a traditional relational database, we'd use a DBI interface to spew SQL queries at the database, with various wildcards and AND and OR options to make things interesting. But we don't have a database.

Well, we *can* have a "lightweight" database using the new DBD::RAM module. This module makes an "in-core" database that interfaces directly with DBI, including supporting full SQL queries!

So, the basic strategy is to put up a form asking for SQL search patterns for each of the columns, then when the form is submitted, use LWP to fetch the data, and XML::Parser to parse the data and insert it into a DBD::RAM database via DBI, then use SQL queries constructed from the form fields to generate a response. And that's pretty much what the program does in Listing 3-3.

Line 1 turns on taint checking, and warnings. Taint checking is my mandatory switch for all CGI-deployed programs, to keep me from shooting myself in the foot accidentally. (I've gotta want to shoot myself in the foot deliberately, apparently.) And warnings are handy to catch other stupid stuff, although once I deploy this script into production, I'll turn the warnings off.

Line 2 enables the compiler restrictions, preventing accidental use of mistyped variable names, soft references, and barewords. I turn this on when a program meets my "ten-ten" rule: if the program is longer than 10 lines, or I'm going to use it for more than 10 minutes.

Line 3 enables immediate output flushing on each print, handy for CGI scripts that intermingle print-style output with calls to system. I'm not doing that here, but I habitually put this in every CGI program anyway, just in case I add that stuff later.

Line 5 brings in Lincoln Stein's wonderful CGI module, along with all the form-accessing and HTML-generation shortcuts. Again, don't reinvent the wheel, when Lincoln has done such a good job (err, but not at *reinventing* the wheel, I mean).

Lines 7 through 24 set up some configuration variables. I needed some common values for both the form generation and handling the form response, so I put those here. This program is not one of my better designed programs (I threw it together in about an hour), so perhaps some of this could have been factored out a bit, but that's the way it is.

Lines 10 through 18 create a mapping from an SQL column name to a hierarchical place in the XML data tree. The first word on each line is the SQL column name (also used as the descriptive name for the form and the response). The remaining words represent the "path" to the interesting data item. The top-level on each item must be perl-monger, because that's the name of the outermost element. Again, I could probably have factored that out, but it would have made the code harder. Note that name and Tsar_name are both a name element in the XML data, so only by relative tree position could we have distinguished the two. More on this table later. The code parses the here-string into an array of arrayrefs, such that $column_def[3] will be an array reference to an array containing Country and perl-mongers group location country.

Lines 21 and 22 create derived data from @column_def: the column names, and a hash mapping the XML location to a column name.

Lines 26 to 42 dump out the CGI script response, both on the initial invocation, and the subsequent handling of the filled-out form. Because I'm illustrating back-end technology here, I've made the form very simple and structural. In a real live program, I'd have gone to some work to design a nice user interface.

The form consists primarily of the table generated in lines 32 through 38. For each SQL column name, we'll get a table row with the name on the left and a textfield input field on the right with the same name. The default value for each input field is %, which will mean "anything goes" to SQL on the response unless altered. This is needed because we are AND-ing together the various conditions, and we want unneeded conditions to be effectively ignored.

Line 44 calls the (big!) handle_form subroutine if we have been given any form-response parameters. And line 46 wraps up the main output.

The rest of the program, beginning in line 48, takes care of the response. Up to this point, it's just been a boring CGI script, so let's get some real action.

Lines 49 through 51 pull in the modules that we need. Note the use of a require rather than a use, because we don't want to load these modules if we're just printing out the form. These all come from the CPAN: XML::Parser to parse the XML (duh!), DBI to handle the SQL query, and LWP::Simple (part of the LWP massive distribution) to fetch the XML page from the Perl Monger's site.

Line 53 creates a DBD::RAM object: essentially, a nearly full-featured database living entirely in memory, compliant with the DBI specification. The RaiseError option is set, letting me get away with not putting any error checking on the rest of the calls.

Lines 54 through 56 create the data table. The columns are all of SQL type TEXT, general enough for what we're doing. If there had been any errors here, DBI would have die'd, so no need to check anything. The name table1 is arbitrary, but needs to be consistent throughout this program.

Lines 57 through 60 set up a "DBI statement handle," precompiling an SQL line that inserts a row into the table. The SQL contains placeholders (a question mark) that will be "bound" to the data when actually used.

Line 62 fetches the current XML data from the www.pm.org website. Note that if this were a real application instead of a toy, I'd provide a first level of caching right here. There's no point in refetching the data on every hit when it changes probably only once every few weeks. Look into the LWP::Simple::mirror subroutine, for example. Note that we have to use the full path to the get subroutine because we pulled LWP::Simple in with require and not use, so no importing was done.

Line 63 parses the data using an XML::Parser. The subroutine is defined in line 86, which we'll see in a moment. The result is that the database for which $insert was prepared now has many rows populated with the appropriate data. So it's time to query that data.

Lines 65 to 70 prepare an SQL query on the database, looking for all the columns that meet the conditions. Again, placeholders are used to stand in for the actual data. In this way, we don't have to worry about SQL-quoting the data, because DBI takes care of that for us.

Line 72 executes the query, binding the query parameters to the actual form values. The unchanging order of @columns ensures that everything lines up. If a parameter is not provided, we'll treat it like the "anything goes" wildcard of %, as before. This lets someone create a link like

```
http://www.stonehenge.comm/cgi/perlmonger_search?City=New+York
```

without having to specify all the other entries as %.

And finally, the output, generated as a table in lines 74 to 77. The column names are used as table headers, with the fetchall_arrayref method returning an arrayref to an array of arrayrefs to the data (essentially a two-dimensional table, but in the typical Perl fashion). Note here that we're using the cool feature (thanks Lincoln!) of CGI.pm to generate multiple td cells when given an arrayref instead of a simple scalar. That saves me one level of map-ing that would have otherwise been required.

Beginning in line 79, we have a set of related subroutines to enable the proper interface to XML::Parser. Line 80 puts us into a separate package (MyParser) so that the subroutine callback names are distinct from the rest of the program.

Lines 82 through 84 define data that is needed by all the subroutines in this section. This data will be private to the subroutines. The @state variable is a list of which XML element we are "in" during the parse, all the way back to the root. %one_group_data is the information for a particular PerlMonger group. And $insert_handle is the DBI insert statement, passed in during the initial invocation.

The initial access into this collection of subroutines is via the doParse subroutine beginning in line 86. The XML data ends up in $data in line 87, and the DBI insert statement handle is extracted in line 88.

Line 89 sets up and calls an XML::Parser object, configured to execute subroutines in the same package as this call with particular names (the "callbacks"). And this object is told immediately to get to work, parsing the XML provided in $data. This results in a number of calls to StartTag, EndTag, and Text, defined in the following lines.

Lines 93 to 99 define StartTag, which will be called with (at least) two parameters each time the XML parser object detects the beginning of an element. The $type parameter is the most important to us: it's the name of the element. Line 95 pushes this element name onto the stack.

Lines 96 to 98 check the current state by concatenating all the array elements into a double-quoted string, which automatically adds spaces between the elements. Because a space cannot appear within an element name, this is a quick way to get our unique place in the parse. If this happens to be at the beginning of a particular PerlMonger group, we reinitialize the data for this new group to empty.

Similarly, lines 101 to 107 are called for the end of each element. Again, if we're at the end of a particular PerlMonger group, then we execute the statement handle, binding the parameters to the hash values we've seen. If the value has not been defined, it's passed as undef, which looks like a NULL in the SQL table. Although the $type name is passed to this subroutine, we can be assured that we're always popping the element that we pushed before, because the XML parser would abort rather than continue to call the callbacks if the XML was invalidly nested.

Lines 109 to 114 define Text, called whenever content is detected. Line 110 computes the SQL column for this particular XML element nesting state, and if it's something we've declared interest in, we append the data to what we've accumulated for that column so far.

And that's it! You can drop this program into your CGI bin as-is and play with it, but beware, it's a CPU hog because we're not caching the fetch of the XML page from the website, nor are we saving the results of having parsed that data anywhere.

In a real application, the two phases of fetching and parsing into the database, and executing a query against that database, would probably be separated into two programs. Or, this program can be placed into a "mini-web server" using the strategies I detailed in this column in March and April of 1998, allowing the results of creating the database to be used across many hits until the hits are no longer frequent.

But as you can see, with a minimal fuss, I've got a way to scan through the data, perhaps in ways the original authors did not intend. So, until next time, enjoy!

Listing 3-3

```
=1=     #!/usr/bin/perl -Tw
=2=     use strict;
=3=     $|++;
=4=
=5=     use CGI qw(:all);
=6=
=7=     ### globals
=8=
=9=     ## mapping from SQL column name to XML state
=10=    my @column_def = map [ m{^(\S+)\s+(.*)} ], <<'END_DEFINITION' =~ /(.+)/g;
=11=    Name        perl-mongers group name
=12=    City        perl-mongers group location city
=13=    State       perl-mongers group location state
=14=    Country     perl-mongers group location country
=15=    Tsar_name   perl-mongers group tsar name
=16=    Tsar_email  perl-mongers group tsar email
=17=    Web         perl-mongers group web
=18=    END_DEFINITION
=19=
=20=    ## reductions of data above
=21=    my @columns = map $_->[0], @column_def;
=22=    my %column_mapping = map { $_->[1] => $_->[0] } @column_def;
=23=
=24=    ## end globals
=25=
=26=    print
=27=      header,
=28=      start_html("Search the mongers info"),
=29=      h1("Search the mongers info"),
=30=      hr,
=31=      start_form,
=32=      table({ Border => 1, Cellspacing => 0, Cellpadding => 2 },
=33=            (map {
=34=              Tr(th($_), td(textfield(-Name => $_, -Default => '%')))
```

```
=35=                 } @columns),
=36=                 Tr(td({ Colspan => 2},
=37=                     p("Use % for any chars, and ? for a single char"))),
=38=             ),
=39=         reset,
=40=         submit,
=41=         end_form,
=42=         hr;
=43=
=44=     &handle_form() if param();
=45=
=46=     print end_html;
=47=
=48=     sub handle_form {
=49=         require XML::Parser;
=50=         require DBI;
=51=         require LWP::Simple;
=52=
=53=         my $dbh = DBI->connect('dbi:RAM:', undef, undef, {RaiseError => 1});
=54=         $dbh->do("CREATE TABLE table1 (".
=55=                 (join ", ", map "$_ TEXT", @columns).
=56=                 ")");
=57=         my $insert = $dbh->prepare("INSERT INTO table1 (".
=58=                                 (join ", ", @columns).
=59=                                 ") VALUES (".
=60=                                 (join ",", ("?") x @columns).")");
=61=
=62=         my $data = LWP::Simple::get("http://www.pm.org/XML/perl_mongers.xml";);
=63=         MyParser::doParse($data, $insert);
=64=
=65=         my $extract = $dbh->prepare("SELECT ".
=66=                                 (join ", ", @columns).
=67=                                 " FROM table1".
=68=                                 " WHERE ".
=69=                                 (join " AND ", map "$_ LIKE ?", @columns).
=70=                                 " ORDER BY Name");
=71=
=72=         $extract->execute(map {defined param($_) ? param($_) : "%"} @columns);
=73=
=74=         print table({Border => 1, Cellspacing => 0, Cellpadding => 2},
=75=                     Tr(th(\@columns)),
=76=                     map Tr(td($_)), @{$extract->fetchall_arrayref});
=77=     }
=78=
=79=     BEGIN {
=80=         package MyParser;
=81=
```

```
=82=      my @state;
=83=      my %one_group_data;
=84=      my $insert_handle;
=85=
=86=      sub doParse {
=87=        my $data = shift;
=88=        $insert_handle = shift;      ## outer scope
=89=
=90=        XML::Parser->new(Style => 'Stream')->parse($data);
=91=      }
=92=
=93=      sub StartTag {
=94=        my ($parser, $type) = @_;
=95=        push @state, $type;
=96=        if ("@state" eq "perl-mongers group") {
=97=          %one_group_data = ();
=98=        }
=99=      }
=100=
=101=     sub EndTag {
=102=       my ($parser, $type) = @_;
=103=       if ("@state" eq "perl-mongers group") {
=104=         $insert_handle->execute(@one_group_data{@columns});
=105=       }
=106=       pop @state;
=107=     }
=108=
=109=     sub Text {
=110=       my $place = $column_mapping{"@state"};
=111=       if (defined $place) {
=112=         $one_group_data{$place} .= $_;
=113=       }
=114=     }
=115=   }
```

■ ■ ■

CGI Programming

Capturing Those CGI Errors As Email

Linux Magazine, Column 14 (July 2000)

■**Randal's Note**   Someday, I'll submit this as a module to the CPAN. Not yet.

More and more web hosting services and ISPs are providing CGI space in addition to customer web pages, as either a free add-on or an extra-cost service. And there are even a few *free* CGI servers out there on the net.

The problem with these services is that the (shared) web error log is often inaccessible or at an unknown location. That's fine if your CGI program never commits an error, or if you are using the PSI::ESP module to determine the error text. But most of us will write "blah blah or die blah" in our CGI scripts, expecting to somehow be told what's wrong when it goes wrong.

Some have resorted to dumping the error message to the browser. In fact, during development, there's nothing wrong with adding

```
use CGI::Carp qw(fatalsToBrowser)
```

to your program, and doing the debugging right in your browser window. (For details, see the CGI::Carp documentation.)

But this is a *huge* security hole if left in production code. While surfing the world wild web, I often see error messages that reveal *far* too much information. I've seen program names, user IDs, languages used, pathnames to key files, and even the exact SQL query attempted dumped out in these errors. I have no right (or need) to know that, and a bad guy can use such valuable information to assist him in breaking into the system.

So, if we can't put it into the browser, and we can't get to the error log, where else can we put the errors? Why, in email of course!

All we need is a module (let's call it FatalsToEmail.pm) that we'll stick somewhere on the system (like /home/merlyn/lib) and pull in at the top of our CGI script, like so:

```
use lib "/home/merlyn/lib";
use FatalsToEmail qw(Address merlyn@stonehenge.comm);
```

And then when the CGI script dies, the text of the error message gets sent to us, while the user is told that "something went wrong." Too cool? Yup, so read on.

The module source is in Listing 4-1. Line 1 sets up the package—important because we don't want any symbols to collide with the user of this module. Line 2 enables my favorite compiler restrictions, including requiring me to declare my variables, discouraging the use of symbolic references, and preventing barewords from being treated as quoted strings.

Lines 4 through 10 set up the four configuration variables for the module. The Address variable provides the email address to which the messages should go, here defaulting to webmaster at the mail host. Speaking of which, Mailhost sets up the mail delivery host. This doesn't have to be the final machine on which the mail ends up, but we'll need a friendly SMTP server somewhere that can handle mail from the script. The localhost default should be fine for most machines, except those that don't run a mail server on the web server.

The Cache and Seconds parameters interact to limit the amount of mail delivered. The default Cache value of undef gives the script the right to deliver a single separate piece of email for each fatal error. This is great for testing or for low-volume sites. But it'd be a potential "denial of service" attack for high-volume sites or malicious users.

So instead, we bunch up the rapidly appearing messages into a cache, guaranteed to be sent no more often than the indicated number of seconds. To get the bunching up, Cache must be set to a filename path that is writeable by the user ID executing the CGI program. A typical value might be something like /tmp/merlyn.weberrors.cache. (The actual caching strategy is defined later.) Several programs can share the same cache: the error messages within the cache are prefixed by the filename and line number from which they sprouted.

Lines 12 though 20 handle the configuration of the module. If the use line appears like

```
use FatalsToEmail qw(
  Address merlyn@stonehenge.comm
  Cache /tmp/merlyn.weberrors.cache
);
```

then we save Address and Cache to override the default values. The logic in line 15 ensures that someone can use cache or CACHE or even cAcHe for the identifier tag, and we'll still store it into the right hash slot.

Line 22 establishes the subroutine in this module as the die handler. From here on out, we're the ones who will get called on a fatal error.

Lines 24 through 44 define this handler. The text message for the fatal error shows up in $message in line 25. Line 26 gets the current local time of day to label the message consistently. Line 27 extracts information about the filename and line number from which the error message was triggered.

Lines 29 through 31 prefix each line in the message with a unique identifier, consisting of the filename, line number, time of day, and process ID number. This is helpful to group error messages in cache-dumping email, as well as provide the necessary locators to fix the problem.

Lines 33 to 39 dump a CGI response. Note that minimal information is provided.

If the CGI program has already sent an HTTP header, the header we print in line 34 will show up as content. There's nothing much I can do about that from this module, at least not in a CGI environment.

Then there's the cleanup. Line 41 triggers the email (or caching, if needed). And line 43 executes a die within the die handler. This step is needed so that Perl knows to finish aborting the program. The message shows up on STDERR, which will typically be the real web error log.

Lines 46 to 89 attempt to phone home with the error message. (Perhaps I should have called this subroutine "e_t"?) Nearly everything is inside a large eval block so that any mistakes will still set up a graceful exit from this program. The message is captured and delivered in lines 86 to 88, including both the original message that wanted to be mailed and the error that kept it from being mailed.

Lines 50 to 75 handle the cache, if needed, as determined by line 51. If we're caching, then line 52 attempts to open the cache file for both reading and writing. If that succeeds, it's time to operate.

Line 53 blocks the process until only we are using the file in this manner. We'll want to keep the time to a bare minimum from here until we close the filehandle, because we've just entered a zone where only one process at a time can be within.

Lines 55 to 62 handle the case where the cache is old enough for us to send. If the file modification time (mtime) is more than some number of seconds ago (determined by the Seconds configuration variable), then it's been a while since we wanted to send some email, and there may in fact be previous contents that we deferred. So lines 57 and 58 grab that. If there's more than 8K in the cache, we send only the first 8K and a warning. This keeps the mail message from becoming yet another denial of service attack filling up our mail spool. At most, we'll get roughly 8K every 60 seconds (or whatever Seconds is configured as). The old cached messages are prepended in front of the current message in line 59.

Lines 60 and 61 remove the cached material, so that we have an empty file that has been modified just now, regardless of whether any prior content was in the file. This is important, because we want the *next* hit within the cache window to be deferred, repeatedly, until we have another idle period. And finally, line 62 closes the cache, also releasing the lock, since we now have the information we need.

Lines 64 to 67 handle the hits within the cache window, no more than Seconds number of seconds since the previous hit. In this case, we just seek to the end of the file, and dump the message there. We are guaranteed that the message will end in a newline, but we're not sure, we would add a \n here somewhere, to ensure that each error message has lines that start with the prefix identifier computed earlier. The return in line 68 skips over all the email handling code below, since we won't be sending any mail on this trip.

Lines 71 to 73 create an initial empty cache file if it doesn't exist. We'll treat a nonexisting file as if it was an empty old file, which means it still needs to have a timestamp updated to "right now." Note the use of the "append" open operation: since we don't have a lock, we may be trying to create a file when there's already someone else in the meantime who has created the file, gotten a lock, and started writing in the file (it could happen!), so the best we can do is ask the kernel to "make the file if it doesn't exist, or be ready to append to it if it does." Which works here just as we needed it.

Now for the fun part. Lines 77 to 84 send the email message. First, we try to suck in the Net::SMTP module in line 77. This may not be possible, because the CPAN module may not be installed (it's part of the libnet bundle from Graham Barr, not part of the core installation). However, the require directive might fail, so it's inside an eval. If the require succeeds, the value of 1 is returned, stopping our inner die operation, otherwise we'll abort. The die here is being caught by the outer eval. Wheeee.

Lines 78 and 79 set up a Net::SMTP connection object to the requested Mailhost. If there are any errors, I'm told the error will be in $@, not <$!>, so I include that here in the die message. Again, this die will be caught by the outer eval block.

Lines 80 and 81 tell the SMTP server what our sender name is and what the recipient name is. The sender name will be used for error messages from the various mailers along the way, and the recipient name is the ultimate destination. Here, we're using the configured email address for both. This could get weird if the address is undeliverable: the final mail host will attempt to bounce the message *back* to the same address to which it is attempting delivery. Hmm. Not a good idea. But it's better than any alternative I could think of today.

Lines 82 and 83 provide a subject line and a body for the message. The subject line has nice bright shiny capital letters in it, including the name of the program that triggered the error for easy mail filtering by smart email readers. Note that most mail servers will also construct a Date and From and To header for us automatically, so I can lean on it to do the job.

And finally, line 84 tells the mail server we're done for this round and shuts down the connection.

That's it. Put FatalsToEmail.pm someplace accessible to your CGI script, add the appropriate use lib line to point at the directory, and you can start getting your errors via a timely email message instead of having to wade through the old shared web error log. Until next time, enjoy!

Listing 4-1

```
=1=      package FatalsToEmail;
=2=      use strict;
=3=
=4=      my %config =
=5=        (
=6=         Address => "webmaster",      # email address
=7=         Mailhost => "localhost",     # mail server
=8=         Cache => undef,              # undef means don't use
=9=         Seconds => 60,
=10=       );
=11=
=12=     sub import {
=13=       my $package = shift;
=14=       while (@_) {
=15=         my $key = ucfirst lc shift;
=16=         die "missing argument to $key" unless @_;
=17=         die "unknown argument $key" unless exists $config{$key};
=18=         $config{$key} = shift;
=19=       }
=20=     }
=21=
=22=     $SIG{__DIE__} = \&trapper;
=23=
=24=     sub trapper {
=25=       my $message = shift;
=26=       my $time = localtime;
=27=       my ($pack, $file, $line) = caller;
=28=
```

```
=29=       my $prefix = localtime;
=30=       $prefix .= ":$$:$file:$line: ";
=31=       $message =~ s/^/$prefix/mig;
=32=
=33=       print STDOUT <<END;
=34=    Content-Type: text/html
=35=
=36=    <h1>Sorry!</h1>
=37=    <p>An error has occurred; details have been logged.
=38=    Please try your request again later.
=39=    END
=40=
=41=       send_mail($message);
=42=
=43=       die "${prefix}died - email sent to $config{Address} via ⤶
                $config{Mailhost}\n";
=44=    }
=45=
=46=    sub send_mail {
=47=       my $message = shift;
=48=
=49=       eval {
=50=         ## do I need to cache this?
=51=         if (defined (my $cache = $config{Cache})) {
=52=           if (open CACHE, "+<$cache") {
=53=             flock CACHE, 2;
=54=             ## it's mine, see if it's old enough
=55=             if (time - (stat(CACHE))[9] > $config{Seconds}) {
=56=               ## yes, suck any content, and zero the file
=57=               my $buf;
=58=               $buf .= "\n...[truncated]...\n" ⤶
                      if read(CACHE, $buf, 8192) >= 8192;
=59=               $message = $buf . $message;
=60=               seek CACHE, 0, 0;
=61=               truncate CACHE, 0;
=62=               close CACHE;
=63=             } else {
=64=               ## no, so just drop the stuff at the end
=65=               seek CACHE, 0, 2;
=66=               print CACHE $message;
=67=               close CACHE;
=68=               return;
=69=             }
=70=           } else {
=71=             ## it doesn't exist, so create an empty file for stamping, ⤶
                      and email
=72=             open CACHE, ">>$cache" or die "Cannot create $cache: $!";
```

```
=73=              close CACHE;
=74=            }
=75=          }
=76=
=77=          eval { require Net::SMTP; 1 } or die "no Net::SMTP";
=78=          my $mail = Net::SMTP->new($config{Mailhost})
=79=            or die "Net::SMTP->new returned $@";
=80=          $mail->mail($config{Address}) or die "from: $@";
=81=          $mail->to($config{Address}) or die "to: $@";
=82=          $mail->data("Subject: CGI FATAL ERROR in $0\n\n", $message)
=83=            or die "data: $@";
=84=          $mail->quit or die "quit: $@";
=85=        };
=86=        if ($@) {
=87=          die "$message(send_mail saw $@)\n";
=88=        }
=89=      }
```

Implementing a Non-Visitor Counter Using SSI and the CPAN GD Module

Web Techniques, Column 13 (May 1997)

▓**Randal's Note** The non-visitor counter is no longer on display at my home page. Restoring it is on that ever-increasing list of things to do that won't get done this century unless I win the lottery or something. Also, the GD module has been stripped of its ability to generate GIF files (thanks to a scary enforcement of a software patent), although that ability will likely be re-established soon (thanks to the patent now expiring).

I'm not a real big fan of visitor counts. For one, they aren't really accurate—because of proxies and reloads, you could have an artificially high or low value. Also, what do they really communicate to the person browsing the site? Obviously, if I'm coming there, I'm either interested in the information or not. I'm not about to hit a web page, notice that the visitor counter is over 22,435, and then leave because too many people have been there!

So, in response, I created a *non-visitor counter* (NVC). Every time someone reloads my home page (at www.stonehenge.com/merlyn/), a random new number from 1 to 99,999 is generated, and then the appropriate image (or text) is displayed. And, even though this demonstration is pointless (except for its humor value), some of the tricks I use are applicable in other areas, so stay with me here.

To get the NVC into the page in the first place, I use *server-side includes* (SSIs). This means that the server (Apache here) scans through the document, looking for items like

```
<!--# ... -->
```

and replaces them with other text as the server delivers the document to the requesting client (like a browser). The client never sees these lines, and because of this, it's a little hard to look for examples on the net, because you won't see them when you view the source.

In particular, what you'll never see is what I see when I edit the file—stuff like the following:

```
<p>You are not likely to be the
<!--#include virtual="/cgi/random_visitor_th" -->
visitor to my page.
```

Here, a specific SSI directive `include virtual` (not the real name, but let that one slide) causes the CGI script `random_visitor_th` to be executed and its output to be inserted in place of the SSI directive. One sample output of this script is

```
Content-type: text/html
<img src="/cgi/bigword?29412th" alt="29412th">
```

Now, the body of that message is then inserted, replacing the SSI directive, so the user finally sees this:

```
<p>You are not likely to be the
<img src="/cgi/bigword?29412th" alt="29412th">
visitor to my page.
```

Let's see how `random_visitor_th` looks, in Listing 4-2.

Line 1 is the standard "shebang" line. No options this time. Didn't care much for them, apparently. Line 2 scrambles the random number generator, seeding it with a bitwise exclusive OR between the current process ID number ($$) and the result of the `time` operator.

Line 3 computes a random visitor number, by invoking the `rand` operator with a parameter of 100,000. This will generate a floating value somewhere between 0 and 99999.9999, which when truncated with the `int` operator is exactly what we need.

The next step is to transform this random visitor number into its ordinal form. The normal English rules apply here, as implemented in the block extending from line 4 to line 10. Each line works similarly: if the substitute is completed, the block gets exited. (Who keeps saying we need a `case` statement?) The comments indicate the cases handled.

So, after the block is complete in line 10, $VISITOR is a good ordinal word. Next, it's time to generate the output for the SSI processor, handled in lines 11 through 15.

Line 11 is a print operator, with its sole argument being a "here" string, extending from line 12 to line 14. This is often easier than typing a series of `print` operations, although here it would have been a close draw.

Line 12 declares the MIME type of the output. The output type *must* be text/html, because we are including it into an HTML document. The only other valid header might have been a `location:` redirect, which would cause the server to go fetch that item instead.

Notice that the final output text (on line 14) includes both an `img src=` and an `alt` tag. Having both of those is very important. On browsers that aren't displaying graphics (such as lynx, w3-mode, or any of the graphical browsers with image loading turned off), the alt text provides exactly the right information to read the line.

On browsers that *do* have image loading turned on, the browser turns around and does one more fetch back to the server. This time, it asks for /cgi/bigword?29412th, invoking my second script, `bigword`. This script takes its one argument and returns a GIF of the argument displayed as a word in large type. Not only that, but each letter is randomly jiggled up and down a little bit, just like those stupid "odometer" visitor counters I've stumbled across.

The bigword script now does its drawing matching using the GD module. I'm no expert on GD; in fact, this is my first little toy program with it. However, I was able to get the program up and going in about 15 minutes, which tells me that it works the way I would expect it to work, and that's a good thing.

The GD module is really just a wrapper around the industrial-strength GD library (included in the GD module distribution) written by Thomas Boutell (www.boutell.com). Thomas is probably best known as the author of the comp.infosystems.www.authoring.cgi newsgroup FAQ. With the library, you can read and write images (generally GIFs), and then scribble on them or make up new ones from scratch. The scribbling can include lines, polygons, round-ish things, and (most important for my program) text in four sizes.

Now, even though the GD library comes with the GD module, the GD module does not come with the Perl distribution. So if you don't already have GD.pm (and friends) in your @INC path, you'll need to fetch it from the CPAN (www.perl.com/CPAN/ or www.perl.org/CPAN/) under modules/by-module/GD/. Get the latest one.

Let's see how that works in Listing 4-3.

Lines 1 through 4 here precede all of my "bigger than a screenful" CGI programs (which this one clearly is).

Line 6 pulls in the GD.pm module, which in turn causes a "dynamic load" of the GD library. This means that the running Perl binary now has additional C-based code, not just additional Perl code.

Line 8 spins the dials for the random number generator. Here, I thought it simple enough just to use the default argument to srand.

Line 10 declares a file-lexical variable named $num, the word to be printed ($num is just an artifact; it had only been a number in other versions of this program).

Lines 12 through 15 make this program easier to debug. If the $< variable is equal to 60001 (the user nobody on my machine), then the script is being run under a web server. If not, then I'm probably running this script interactively. If I'm running it interactively, I don't want to output the MIME header (image/gif here), and there's no point in killing off STDERR. So I don't.

Lines 17 to 21 grab the only parameter to this CGI script by scanning the QUERY_STRING environment variable for up to 30 alphanumeric characters. This value will be equal to whatever is found after the ? in the URL. If a bad format is detected, the word "bogus" is used; otherwise, we run with it.

Lines 23 to 25 define the font of my output. gdLargeFont is a constant value defined in the GD library, and it returns back a font object, for which I also get its width and height for reference.

Line 27 defines a "jiggle" constant, which controls how far up and down each letter can randomly be placed. I define it here, because I need it to figure out the overall GIF size, computed in lines 28 and 29. The * 1 was just for symmetry, and actually an early errant version of this program had * length($num) there before I realized I was ending up with a square instead of a rectangle. Duh.

Line 31 creates the "image object." The call to GD::Image->new creates an empty canvas of the indicated size. Line 32 declares a color of value RGB = (127,127,127) (out of 255), which is kind of an ugly medium gray. Now, users don't actually see this, unless their browser doesn't support transparent GIFs, so the color really doesn't matter. Line 33 makes this color the transparent color (there can be only one transparent color in an image). (I commented this out during testing to make sure I was allocating a big enough image space.)

Line 34 enables interlacing, pretty pointless for a tiny GIF like this, but in case I reuse this code on a bigger thing, I'm already home free. Line 35 declares a red color with RGB = (255,0,0). I'll use this to write the actual text.

Lines 37 to 43 perform the actual image creation. Line 37 starts a "left edge" value at an x-value of 1 (1 pixel in from the edge, so we'll always have at least a 1-pixel border). Line 38 breaks up the string into a list of strings, one character per element in the list.

Lines 39 through 43 are performed once for each character in the original string. Now line 39 is best read as "while there are things in @chars," because that's essentially what happens. To use a loop like this, I must be very careful to shorten the size of @chars somewhere in the loop, or else I'm gonna have a pretty long wait (like forever).

Line 40 takes care of shortening @chars, by taking its first element and shifting it off into $char. Of course, now looking at this, I could have also written this as a foreach loop. Yes, as the Perl motto goes, "There's more than one way to do it."

Line 41 is where the good stuff happens. A character is placed into the image, in the indicated font $font, at the computed x and y position, using the indicated text and color. The y position is 1 (for the border) plus a jiggling amount, causing the letter to move up a random amount. Then, line 42 advances the x position an appropriate amount for the next pass.

Finally, line 45 dumps the image as a GIF. In this case, it'll be a GIF89a, because I requested transparency and interlace. And that's all there is to it!

Now, obviously, bigword can be used for more things than just the random visitor count, although you'd probably want to make the size and color user-selectable, as well as turn off that jiggle somehow. Sounds like it could be a nice general-purpose program. (Hmm. Maybe in a future column?) See you next time.

Listing 4-2

```
=0=     ### LISTING ONE [random_visitor_th]
=1=     #!/usr/bin/perl
=2=     srand ($$ ^ time);
=3=     $VISITOR = int rand 100_000;
=4=     {
=5=       next if $VISITOR =~ s/1\d$/$&th/; # 10-19
=6=       next if $VISITOR =~ s/1$/1st/; # 1
=7=       next if $VISITOR =~ s/2$/2nd/; # 2
=8=       next if $VISITOR =~ s/3$/3rd/; # 3
=9=       next if $VISITOR =~ s/\d$/$&th/; # everything else
=10=    }
=11=    print <<"EOT";
=12=    Content-type: text/html
=13=
=14=    <img src="/cgi/bigword?$VISITOR" alt="$VISITOR">
=15=    EOT
```

Listing 4-3

```
=0=     ### LISTING TWO [bigword]
=1=     #!/home/merlyn/bin/perl -wT
=2=     use strict;
=3=     $|++;
=4=     $ENV{PATH} = "/usr/bin:/usr/ucb";
=5=
=6=     use GD;
=7=
=8=     srand;
=9=
=10=    my $num;
=11=
=12=    if ($< == 60001) {
=13=      open STDERR, ">/dev/null";
=14=      print "Content-type: image/gif\n\n";
=15=    }
=16=
=17=    if ($ENV{'QUERY_STRING'} =~ /^(\w{1,30})$/) {
=18=        $num = $1;
=19=    } else {
=20=        $num = "bogus";
=21=    }
=22=
=23=    my $font = gdLargeFont;
=24=    my $char_x = $font->width;
=25=    my $char_y = $font->height;
=26=
=27=    my $jiggle = 4;
=28=    my $picture_x = (1 + $char_x) * length($num) + 1;
=29=    my $picture_y = (1 + $char_y) * 1 + $jiggle;
=30=
=31=    my $image = new GD::Image($picture_x, $picture_y);
=32=    my $background = $image->colorAllocate(127,127,127);
=33=    $image->transparent($background);
=34=    $image->interlaced('true');
=35=    my $red = $image->colorAllocate(255,0,0);
=36=
=37=    my $x = 1;
=38=    my @chars = split //, $num;
=39=    while (@chars) {
=40=      my $char = shift @chars;
=41=      $image->string($font,$x,int(1+rand($jiggle)),$char,$red);
=42=      $x += $char_x + 1;
=43=    }
=44=
=45=    print $image->gif;
```

Handling Partially Filled Query Forms with Placeholders

Linux Magazine, Column 40 (September 2002)

▓Randal's Note A lot of the code to create the actual query string and placeholders can now be replaced by `SQL::Abstract`.

CGI applications often are used for searching through some database. For example, a catalog might let you look for a particular item within a certain cost range or in a particular color. A phone book might let you search for people based on their names or addresses. An online dating service might let you pick people based on their gender, location, age, and interests.

When the CGI application is in Perl, the database query is frequently performed using the DBI interface. This amazing product of years of effort put in by several dedicated people (coordinated by Tim Bunce) allows a Perl program to interact nearly identically to over a few dozen types of databases, including both commercial and open-source databases, and even "nondatabase" databases like a comma-separated-values (CSV) file. The interaction is primarily in the form of a series of industry-standard SQL statements.

But I frequently see the transition from a CGI form element to a database SQL statement in a way that scares me from a security perspective. For example, let's say that the field `firstname` contained an SQL `LIKE` pattern for the first name of a person I'm searching for in my department. The code might go something like this:

```
my $department = 123; # determined by some login process
my $firstname = param('firstname'); # from the field
my $sql = "SELECT id FROM employees WHERE department = $department" .
  " AND firstname LIKE \"$firstname\"";
```

And at first glance, this would appear to be fine, restricting the output to people in my department. For example, if I enter `FR%` for the SQL pattern, I get the following SQL:

```
SELECT id FROM employees WHERE department = 123
  AND firstname LIKE "FR%"
```

However, suppose I know, or can guess, the syntax of this generated statement, and I enter

```
%" OR "X" = "X
```

as the first name. Yes, that's odd-looking in the query box, but notice how that expands:

```
SELECT id FROM employees WHERE department = 123
  AND firstname LIKE "%" OR "X" = "X"
```

Yes. What have I done? I've got the ANDed condition certainly, but I've introduced an OR condition that is true for every employee, and I can now dump out far more than the application originally intended!

Of course, when this happens, someone usually screams, "How do I make sure that the field doesn't contain anything that'll let the bad guys do this?" This is the wrong approach. Instead, the DBI interface includes this nice tool called *placeholders*. The query *should* have been written like this:

```
my $department = 123; # determined by some login process
my $firstname = param('firstname'); # from the field
my $sql = "SELECT id FROM employees WHERE department = ?" .
  " AND firstname LIKE ?";
my $sth = $dbh->prepare($sql);
$sth->execute($department, $firstname);
```

For every question mark in the SQL, the DBI interface will take the corresponding value from the execute method and place it into the SQL in such a way that the value is properly quoted and protected. And that solves the security problem!

Of course, a search form also might have form fields that are left blank, meaning "any value is good enough here." What's an easy way to generate the corresponding SQL and get the execute list correct? Well, you just need a little method to your madness, as illustrated in Listing 4-4, a simple application showing a phone book lookup form.

Lines 1 through 3 start nearly every CGI program I write. The -T switch turns on "taint mode," so that input values are not accidentally used to alter the external behavior of the program. The -w switch enables warnings. use strict turns on the three common compiler restrictions for larger programs: disabling symbolic references, demanding that variables be properly introduced, and disabling barewords as subroutine invocations. And finally, standard output is unbuffered—not strictly necessary for this application, but handy if we ever fork a child that might need to include things into the output stream.

Lines 6 through 9 establish a list of abbreviations for the states. I'll use this in a pop-up box definition.

Lines 11 to 25 define the query fields of my form, including the SQL snippets that should be used if they are present in the response. Each element of @QUERY_FIELDS is an arrayref. The first element is the form field name. The second element is an SQL snippet, using the question-mark placeholder. And a third element, if present, is a coderef for the routine to validate the data and alter it if necessary. We'll see precisely how these fields are used later.

Line 28 pulls in the standard CGI module, along with importing all the form access and HTML generation shortcuts.

Line 30 prints the HTTP/CGI header, the beginnings of the HTML header, and a first-order head of Query. As this is not a complete application, I didn't spend much time adorning the output.

Line 32 prints the tag for a horizontal rule and the beginning of the form. The form action parameter defaults to the same URL, bringing a form submission right back to this same program, so this CGI script both generates the original form and processes the results. This is a typical strategy for CGI.pm-based programs.

Lines 34 to 42 print the form itself, with the layout aided by a simple table. A light yellow background color defines the area of the form, designated in line 34. The first row picks up the first and last names, with their appropriate labels. The second row similarly holds the street address and the city.

The third row contains a pop-up field named state. The list of states comes from the array defined earlier. An additional item of n/a is added to the front of the list, and is also selected as the initial default. To keep this type of searching form easy to use, all fields should default to their "insignificant" state. The third row also contains a zip code field. Of course, a zip code would also uniquely define a city and state, but that's beyond the scope of this example, so we'll pretend these are all independent fields. The third row also contains the submit button.

For all three rows, the individual table cells are enclosed in a td HTML shortcut, defined by CGI.pm. And each of these cells is further nested into a table row shortcut, defined as tr. This shortcut has an unusual name because as an entirely lowercase word, it would collide with the built-in tr operator. Finally, the three rows are enclosed inside a table shortcut, with an additional hashref parameter that becomes the attributes of the table tag for the output.

And finally, line 44 closes out the form with a horizontal rule.

When the form is initially displayed in the browser, I have a chance to fill out one or more of the fields of my choice and click submit. The same program is re-invoked, but with access to the form parameters using the param function. The code beginning in line 46 handles this response.

Lines 47 and 48 hold the pieces of SQL and their corresponding values. Initially, they'll start out empty. If they're still empty after we've processed all the known fields, then we didn't get a valid query, and there's nothing further to do.

Lines 50 to 61 process each of the known form fields. $_ holds the arrayref of each field in turn. Line 51 pulls out the value for that particular parameter into the scalar $val. (Note that this won't work very well for a multivalue parameter, but it's a minor change to handle that instead.) If the parameter is not present, we skip on to the next item.

Lines 52 to 58 clean up the data from that form element. If there's a value in the third arrayref element, it's a coderef, which we call, passing the form value as its first argument. We expect the called subroutine to return either the cleaned-up data or undef, again indicating that this field is "not present." If there's no special handling subroutine, a simple editing pass is performed instead; line 55 deletes any leading whitespace, while line 56 deletes any trailing whitespace.

Looking back at lines 18 to 23, we can see that the cleanup routine for the pop-up menu takes that value and returns undef unless it contains a non-whitespace character but is not our default value of n/a.

Now, if we've made it to line 59, we have a good value in $val and the corresponding SQL as the second element of the arrayref. So, we'll push each one onto the end of its corresponding arrays to be gathered and processed later.

Once the individual form elements have been examined, it's time to determine if we have a valid query. Line 62 examines the size of the @sqls array. If this is nonempty, then we have to proceed to building an SQL statement, in line 63.

Each snippet in @sqls is a clause expected to be AND-ed with the other clauses. So we'll take the snippets and join them with an AND keyword in line 63. In front of that, we'll select the id field from the resulting record for further processing.

In a real program, we'd then execute code similar to that presented in lines 69 to 71. The SQL statement would be prepared from the joined snippets, then the placeholders would be bound to their corresponding values, and finally we'd get the matched records by their ids.

However, since this is just a demo harness, we'll dump out the SQL in line 65 and the list of values for the binding in line 66.

So, we've seen how to walk through a form, picking out the fields and constructing the corresponding SQL for them, and we've also seen the importance of using placeholders. And with no more worries about broken or malicious input values messing up your day, until next time, enjoy!

Listing 4-4

```
=1=     #!/usr/bin/perl -Tw
=2=     use strict;
=3=     $|++;
=4=
=5=     ## constants
=6=     my @STATES = qw(
=7=       AK AL AR AZ CA CO CT DE FL GA HI IA↵
                    ID IL IN KS KY LA MA MD ME MI MN MO MS
=8=       MT NC ND NE NH NJ NM NV NY OH OK OR↵
                    PA RI SC SD TN TX UT VA VT WA WI WV WY
=9=     );
=10=    ## configuration
=11=    my @QUERY_FIELDS =
=12=      (
=13=      ['firstname', 'person.firstname is ?'],
=14=      ['lastname', 'person.lastname is ?'],
=15=      ['street', 'person.street is ?'],
=16=      ['city', 'person.city is ?'],
=17=      ['state', 'person.state is ?',
=18=        sub {
=19=          my $v = shift;
=20=          return undef unless $v =~ /\S/;
=21=          return undef if $v eq "n/a";
=22=          $v;
=23=        }],
=24=      ['zip', 'person.zip is ?'],
=25=        );
=26=    ## end configuration
=27=
=28=    use CGI qw(:all);
=29=
=30=    print header, start_html, h1('Query');
=31=
=32=    print hr, start_form;
```

```
=33=
=34=   print table({-bgcolor => '#ffff88'},
=35=              Tr(td("First:"), td(textfield('firstname')),
=36=                 td("Last:"), td(textfield('lastname'))),
=37=              Tr(td("Street:"), td(textfield('street')),
=38=                 td("City:"), td(textfield('city'))),
=39=              Tr(td("State:"),
=40=                 td(popup_menu('state', ['n/a', @STATES], 'n/a')),
=41=                 td("Zip:"), td(textfield('zip', '', 10)),
=42=                 td(submit)));
=43=
=44=   print end_form, hr;
=45=
=46=   {
=47=     my @sqls;
=48=     my @vals;
=49=
=50=     for (@QUERY_FIELDS) {
=51=       next unless defined(my $val = param($_->[0]));
=52=       if ($_->[2]) {
=53=         next unless defined($val = $_->[2]->($val));
=54=       } else {
=55=         $val =~ s/^\s+//;
=56=         $val =~ s/\s+$//;
=57=         next unless length $val;
=58=       }
=59=       push @sqls, $_->[1];
=60=       push @vals, $val;
=61=     }
=62=     if (@sqls) {
=63=       my $sql = "select id from person where ".join(" and ", @sqls);
=64=       print h2("Resulting query");
=65=       print pre(escapeHTML($sql));
=66=       print pre(escapeHTML(join ", ", map { qq{"$_"} } @vals));
=67=
=68=       ## typical use:
=69=       ## my $sth = $dbh->prepare($sql);
=70=       ## $sth->execute(@vals);
=71=       ## while (my ($id) = $sth->fetchrow_array) { ... }
=72=     }
=73=   }
=74=
=75=   print end_html;
```

Rainy Day Template Fun

Unix Review, Column 31 (April 2000)

■**Randal's Note** This is one of the few columns that triggered a *negative* piece of response email, as opposed to the hundreds of letters of thanks that I've gotten over the years. Both the editor and I presumed that the guy was just having a bad day.

I grew up (and still reside) in Oregon, which is well known for having rain nearly all times of the year. However, the spring months seem to have been particularly wet, and as a child, I'd often end up doing "indoor" activities during the days with the heaviest rain.

One of the things I remember doing was a game whose name I won't mention so as not to infringe on any trademark, but that consisted of two people taking turns asking each other for various terms, like "a noun" or "a verb ending in -ed." Besides teaching us the parts of speech, it also delighted us to know that we had constructed a story by filling in the blanks of an incomplete version in an unexpected way. Of course, as we got more creative with the answers, we got better stories.

Now, what does this have to do with Perl? Well, I often see questions like this online: "How do I create a fill-in-the-blank template?" For general applications, the answer is "Go see one of the templating solutions in the CPAN." That is, go to http://search.cpan.org and enter **template** in the search box on the left. You'll see a dozen or so different ways to take advantage of existing code.

For simple problems, though, an ad-hoc approach may be best. Our story creator software is simple enough that we can code it from scratch, also to show there's nothing magic about the approach. Let's start with a simple template:

```
The [person] went to the [place].
```

How do we turn [person] into the directive "Give me a person" and put the response back in the string? Well, something like this will work:

```
$_ = "The [person] went to the [place].";
s/\[(.*?)\]/&process($1)/eg;
sub process {
  print "give me a $_[0]: ";
  chomp(my $response = <STDIN>);
  $response;
}
print;
```

What we're doing here is going through the value of $_ with the global substitution. Each time a bracketed item is found, we'll evaluate the right side of the substitution *as Perl code*. In this case, it'll be an invocation of the process subroutine, passing $1 as the parameter. The subroutine takes the input parameter to create a prompt, and then reads my response from the result. The return value of the subroutine becomes the replacement value for the bracketed item. Note the /eg on the end of the substitution—for this, we get the right side as *evaluated* code, with the substitution executed *globally*.

To get a little more flexible, we might also allow multiple words, including newlines, inside the brackets. That'd look like this:

```
{ local $/; $_ = <DATA> }
s/\[(.*?)\]/&process($1)/egs;
sub process {
  my $prompt = shift;
  $prompt =~ s/\s+/ /g;
  print "give me a $prompt: ";
  chomp(my $response = <STDIN>);
  $response;
}
print;
__END__
The [sad person] went to the [fun
place to go].
```

Now, we'll get the prompts like so:

```
give me a sad person: ____
give me a fun place to go: ____
```

And the right values will be filled in appropriately.

The addition of the s suffix to the substitution operator enables . to match an embedded newline. Inside the subroutine, we crunch all embedded newlines into single spaces. Also note that we're fetching the template from the DATA filehandle, which begins at the end of the program immediately after the __END__ marker.

Now, let's look at a further complication. Suppose I want to ask the questions in an order different from how they'll be used in the story. That makes it more fun, because having an unexpected response to the ordering is often an interesting surprise.

To do this, I'll need a way of prompting for an answer, but storing the value instead of immediately substituting it. Let's introduce a variable syntax, like so:

```
[person=person]
[place1=nearby place]
[place2=far away place]
[$person] went to [$place1], and then to [$place2].
[$person] was [emotion after a long trip].
```

Here, I'm expecting that we'll ask for a person and two places, then do some substitution, and then ask for an emotion and substitute that directly. Note that the person is used twice.

We'll say that a variable has to be a Perl identifier (alphas, numerics, and underscores), conveniently matched by \w in a regular expression. So, brackets can now contain three things, and the processing subroutine has to distinguish three cases:

- A simple prompt to be substituted

- A variable to be prompted for and remembered

- A reference to a previously established variable

We'll hold the variable values in a hash called %value. So, process will look like this:

```
sub process {
  my $thing = shift;
  if ($thing =~ /^\$(\w+)$/) { # variable reference
    return $value{$1};
  }
```

So far, we'll take the value between the brackets (coming in as $thing), and if it's a dollar sign followed by a variable name, then we'll return its current value. Next, we fix the embedded newlines, in case the starting bracket is on a different line from the ending bracket:

```
$thing =~ s/\s+/ /g;   # handle wrapping
```

And then we'll handle the "defining" case:

```
my $variable;
$variable = $1 if $thing =~ s/^(\w+)=//; # may be undef
```

At this point, $variable is either undef or the name of a variable to define and remember. What's left in $thing is now the prompt to issue, and that comes next:

```
print "Give me a", $thing =~ /^[aeiou]/i ? "n " : " ", $thing, ": ";
```

Note the extra logic here to make it "an apple" or "a carrot" when given "apple" or "carrot." Finally, let's finish up the prompting:

```
chomp(my $response = <STDIN>);
if (defined $variable) {
  $value{$variable} = $response;
  return "";
}
return $response;
}
```

Note that if it's a bracketed item defining a variable, no value is returned. If you'd rather make a definition also be an invocation automatically, you can leave out the return "". Either way, it's nice.

So, we've now got some nice code, and it works against our example earlier. If you run this code, however, you may notice that there are some extra newlines in the output. Why is this so? Well, the definition lines

```
[person=person]
[place1=nearby place]
[place2=far away place]
```

are in fact replaced with "nothing" followed by newline, three times. (If you've hacked m4 before, you may recall this as the need for frequent dnl() constructs in your input.) That's a bit messy, so let's special-case that. If a line consists entirely of a bracketed item, the trailing newline is automatically swallowed up. Not tough, but we have to get a bit messy:

```
s<^\[([^]]+)\]\s*\n|\[([^]]+)\]>
  {&process(defined $1 ? $1 : $2)}meg;
```

Here, I again have effectively an s/old/new/eg operation, split over two lines, using alternate delimiters. Note that the pattern to be matched consists of two separate regular expressions joined by the vertical bar:

```
^\[([^]]+)\]\s*\n
```

and

```
\[([^]]+)\]
```

The latter should be familiar—it's similar to what we've been using all along. The first one is a match for an entire line consisting only of the bracketed item, so that we can also scarf down the newline.

The right-side replacement text, as code, becomes slightly more complicated, because we need to use either $1 or $2, depending on which item on the left matched. The defined() took care of that. And finally, the substitution uses the additional suffix of m, meaning that ^ in the regular expression matches any embedded newline, and coincidentally spells meg, because I watched a Meg Ryan movie last night on DVD.

One final nicety: we have no way to include a literal left or right bracket in the text, so let's let [LEFT] and [RIGHT] stand for those. That'll work by including these lines early in process:

```
return "[" if $thing eq "LEFT";
return "]" if $thing eq "RIGHT";
```

Let's put it all together. And as way of demonstrating how easy it is to get stories to feed into this, I found an archive with several fill-in-the-blank stories at www.mit.edu/storyfun/ and stole the following story to tack onto the end of the program:

```
{ local $/; $_ = <DATA> }
s/^\[([^]]+)\]\s*\n|\[([^]]+)\]/&process(defined $1 ? $1 : $2)/meg;
sub process {
  my $thing = shift;
  return "[" if $thing eq "LEFT";
  return "]" if $thing eq "RIGHT";
  if ($thing =~ /^\$(\w+)$/) { # variable reference
    return $value{$1};
  }
  $thing =~ s/\s+/ /g;  # handle wrapping
  my $variable;
  $variable = $1 if $thing =~ s/^(\w+)=//; # may be undef
  print "Give me a", $thing =~ /^[aeiou]/i ? "n " : " ", $thing, ": ";
  chomp(my $response = <STDIN>);
  if (defined $variable) {
    $value{$variable} = $response;
    return "";
  }
  return $response;
```

```
}
print;
__END__
[LEFT]... from http://www.mit.edu/storyfun/I_went_for_a_walk[RIGHT]
[adj1=adjective]
[place=place]
[verbed=verb (ending in -ed)]
[adj2=adjective]
[nouns=plural noun]
[plants=plural plant]
[adj3=adjective]
[adj4=adjective]
[adj5=adjective]
[noun=noun]
[verbing=verb (ending in -ing)]
[verb_past=verb (past tense)]
[animals=plural animal]
[your name] went for a walk
Yesterday, I went out walking, and somehow ended up in [$place]. I saw
[$plants] and [$animals] -- it was [$adj2]! But I started getting
[$adj5] hungry, and needed to find my way home. But no matter where I
[$verb_past], I couldn't see the path. I decided to go around the
[$adj1] [$noun] up ahead, and discovered that it led back home! I was
[$verbed]. At dinner, when I told my [$adj3] story, my [$nouns] looked
at me with [$adj4] expressions. Then they forbade me from ever
[$verbing] again.
```

So, never again will you need to worry about those rainy days or whenever you need to have fill-in-the-blank templates. Perl can help you pass the time away and do those tasks more efficiently. Until next time, enjoy!

Using the CGI Module's save Method to Save Data into a Text File

Web Techniques, Column 16 (August 1997)

▓Randal's Note I got email saying, "This isn't a chat, it's a guestbook." Yeah, in retrospect, I agree. The live version of this code on my website got a few interesting comments over the months it was enabled, as I recall.

I've been wanting to write about the save method of the all-singing, all-dancing, gotta-have-it CGI.pm module for quite some time, as a way of saving structured data into a flat text file to be processed later. Well, I finally stumbled on to a nice little idea that works pretty well, and also provides yet another example of `flock()`-ing a data file and generating HTML on the fly.

The idea is not a new one: it's a "web chat" script. This is the kind of thing where you and others go to a particular URL at the same time, and you start typing your messages into a form field, click submit, and then get to see what the others just said at the same time as you. Kind of like the too-huge-for-its-own-good Internet Relay Chat, but with a lot fewer bells and whistles. Or a really fast-moving guestbook that keeps only the 32 most recent entries.

So I decided to hack out an under-100-line web chat script. No bells, no whistles, no frills. Stick it somewhere, and you can talk with a friend, or make friends.

Of course, writing a column like this particular one makes me a "newbie magnet," as in "someone who is likely to get a lot of uninteresting questions from people who won't do research for themselves." I can imagine the number of email requests I'll now be getting from people who are not actually programmers, but think they would be a R3AL K00L D00D to have a chat area on their website. So, they copy scripts like mine into some likely (or unlikely!) web server area, without even bothering to configure anything, and then write *me* when it breaks. (I get lots of email with a first line of "Why doesn't [*this program*] work?" and then a spew of 50 to 500 lines of code . . . joy.)

So let me state this up front, as a paragraph that I can point them to later: this script is *not* meant to be used as-is. In fact, it's not meant to be used at all. It's merely an illustration of some technology around the `CGI.pm` module, and saving and restoring queries, and yet another demonstration of `flock()`-ing. The fact that the application is a simple web chat script that actually *works* (for a very small, narrow definition of "works") is irrelevant. OK, end of disclaimer.

But, in any event, I hereby present my little toy web chat script in Listing 4-5.

Lines 1 and 2 begin nearly every lengthy program I write, enabling taint checks, warnings, and appropriate compiler and runtime restrictions.

Line 4 pulls in the `CGI.pm` module and defines the standard useful set of form-access methods and HTML-generation methods.

Lines 7 and 8 define constants, using the new `constant` module. This module is part of the 5.004 (and later, I presume) Perl distributions and was created by my associate Perl trainer, Tom Phoenix (`rootbeer@teleport.com`). However, if you don't have `constant` (or cannot get it for some ludicrous, pointy-haired-manager reason), you can replace those lines with something like

```
sub CHATFILE { "/home/merlyn/Web/chatfile" }
sub MAXENTRIES { 32 }
```

and it'll work approximately the same. These two constants define the location of the chat information and the number of prior messages to retain.

Lines 10 through 14 define a subroutine to encode the required HTML entities into their HTML-safe counterparts. Quotes, less-thans, greater-thans, and ampersands are all handled nicely.

Line 16 prints an HTTP header, the beginning of the HTML page, and an H1 header, using routines from the CGI module. Line 17 executes the `main` routine (defined later) in an `eval` block, protecting it from any dangerous `die` operations.

Should a `die` occur, the $@ variable is set to the death message; otherwise, the $@ is blank. Lines 18 through 21 detect the error, sending out the error message (properly escaped using `ent` defined previously).

Lines 23 through 38 define the main routine. I did it this way so that the eval block above is very small and easy to see. Of course, I could have just put the entire definition for main into the eval block.

Line 24 fetches the prior chat entries from the data file, including updating the file with the submitted form if necessary. More on that later when I discuss the get_old_entries subroutine.

Lines 25 through 30 print the input form to be submitted. Line 25 takes care of the horizontal line (via hr) and start-of-form information. The form will be made a POST form that is self-referential by default, meaning that a submit button in this form will cause this same script to be re-invoked.

Lines 26 through 28 create the three form fields: name, email, and message. Note here that message has a default value of the empty string, but it also has an override parameter (the final 1) set to true. This means that any prior value of message will be ignored, and the requested default (empty string) will have precedence. Because the other two fields do not have override set to true, any prior value for those fields will carry forward from one invocation to the next as a default.

Line 29 puts a submit button at the end of the form, along with a note about submitting an empty message to listen. Line 30 closes off the form.

Lines 31 through 36 display the prior messages, kept in the @entries variable. The syntax here (with for my $var ...) is new to Perl version 5.004, so again if you don't have the latest version of Perl, you'll have to make some slight adjustments. Each element of @entries goes into the lexical local variable $entry, which is then examined in the body of the loop.

Line 32 fetches the name field from a particular entry and prints it. Similarly, line 33 handles the email field. Line 34 is a little strange, because as you'll see later, we're saving the current time of day as a Unix timestamp value into the entries. Luckily, in one swift move, we can convert this to a human-readable string (using scalar localtime). Finally, line 35 takes care of the message parameter (what the user actually ended up saying).

Line 37 closes out the output of the HTML page and is the last output normally done.

Lines 40 through 74 define the subroutine that handles the interaction with the chat file. This subroutine was called from above in line 24 and is expected to return a list of the current chat entries. Line 43 creates an empty array that we'll use as the return value.

Lines 44 and 45 set up a temporary filehandle using the IO::File class. (Again, if your Perl version is not at least 5.004, you might need to upgrade to use this particular part as is.) The filehandle is opened as read/write (indicated by the +< opening mode). This filehandle allows the program to access the history of messages posted to this chat.

Line 47 ensures that only one invocation of this program at any particular time is reading, modifying, or writing the chat history file. The flock() operator will block the program until we can get an exclusive lock.

Now, from here on down to the point where we release the lock (line 71), we are the *only* script operating, so it's important to keep this amount of time short, especially on a busy system. I usually flag these moments with comments such as the ones on lines 46 and 72, which tell me rather visually how many steps are being hacked during this time.

Line 48 rewinds the file, which is not completely necessary here, but is mostly a safety precaution, because the next operation really wants to process the entire file. (I generally seek right after obtaining a flock, because the file size might have changed from the last time I looked.)

Lines 49 through 51 pull in all the historical chat messages. Each time through the loop (as long as we haven't hit end of file, detected with eof()), the CGI module's new routine is called, passing it the filehandle. This triggers the routine to read a standardized save-and-restore form data format from the file, creating an independent query record. The push() takes this and shoves it onto the ever-increasing @entries array. When we're done, @entries is a list of CGI "objects," each one containing a separate submitted chat message, along with all of its identifying information.

Lines 52 and 53 check if this particular script invocation came from a form submission containing a valid message to post, or from just a message consisting of whitespace (something to be ignored), or even if it's absent (such as the *first* time this script's URL gets called up). Note the explicit check for defined(), and then a further check for that defined element containing any non-whitespace character with /\S/.

Lines 55 through 62 transfer the user's "query" as one of the posted messages. However, we must be careful about what gets transferred across, to prevent resource hogging from a malicious and slightly clever user. So, I have to ensure that only the selected fields get added to the history file, and that those fields are limited in size.

Here, I've chosen to accept three user-returned fields (the same as in my generated form above) and limit those to 1,024 characters each. By doing so, the worst that mad user can do is fill up each slot with about 10K (1K times three items times 3 bytes per hex-escaped character, plus a little overhead). Because we limit the posts to 32 slots, we're always gonna be under 320K for the file size, then—not a big deal. Yes, there are other resource starvation issues, but at least filling up the disk is not going to be one of them.

To transfer just a limited about of information into the history file, I create a brand-new CGI object in line 55, empty except for a timestamp (using the Unix internal time value). Lines 56 to 61 then add the other three parameters from the user's input query, being careful to truncate the data to 1,024 characters without prejudice.

Lines 62 through 64 put the user's query in front of the data (so new messages are automatically visible at the top) and then ensure that only the 32 most recent messages are saved into the file.

Lines 65 through 69 rewrite the output data, using the save method. This method causes the data to be scribbled out into the history file in such a way that they can be loaded up by the code in line 50 on the next script invocation. So we've essentially got a flat text file acting as a structured data repository, thanks to the save/restore code built into CGI.pm. Cool.

And there's not much left but to close the filehandle (line 71) and return the entries (line 73). Actually, the filehandle would have been automatically closed when the subroutine exited, because the IO::File reference is a lexically local variable. Sometimes, I even therefore leave the close() out.

So, to use this script, I'd plop it into a CGI directory somewhere, create the file designated by CHATFILE, and make it writeable to the user ID of the CGI process. How you do that is pretty much site dependent, so ask your webmaster. (If you *are* your webmaster and don't know, that's gonna be a tough one.) See you next time!

Listing 4-5

```
=1=    #!/home/merlyn/bin/perl -Tw
=2=    use strict;
=3=
```

```
=4=     use CGI ":standard";
=5=
=6=     ## following must be writable by CGI user:
=7=     use constant CHATFILE => "/home/merlyn/Web/chatfile";
=8=     use constant MAXENTRIES => 32;
=9=
=10=    sub ent {                       # translate to entity
=11=      local $_ = shift;
=12=      s/["<&>"]/"&#".ord($&).";"/ge; # entity escape
=13=      $_;
=14=    }
=15=
=16=    print header, start_html("Chat!"), h1("Chat!");
=17=    eval { &main };
=18=    if ($@) {
=19=      print hr, "ERROR: ", ent($@), hr;
=20=      exit 0;
=21=    }
=22=
=23=    sub main {
=24=      my @entries = get_old_entries();
=25=      print hr, start_form;
=26=      print p, "name: ", textfield("name","", 40);
=27=      print "  email: ", textfield("email", "", 30), br;
=28=      print "message: ", textarea("message", "", 4, 40, 1);
=29=      print br, p, "(Submit an empty message to listen)", submit;
=30=      print end_form, hr;
=31=      for my $entry (@entries) {
=32=        print p(), ent($entry->param("name"));
=33=        print " (", ent($entry->param("email")), ") at ";
=34=        print ent(scalar localtime $entry->param("time")), " said: ";
=35=        print p(), ent($entry->param("message"));
=36=      }
=37=      print end_html;
=38=    }
=39=
=40=    sub get_old_entries {
=41=      use IO::File;
=42=
=43=      my @entries = ();
=44=      my $chatfh = new IO::File "+<".CHATFILE
=45=        or die "Cannot open ".CHATFILE.": $!";
=46=      ## begin critical region (keep short)
=47=      flock $chatfh, 2;
=48=      seek $chatfh, 0, 0;
=49=      while (not eof $chatfh) {
=50=        push @entries, new CGI $chatfh;
```

```
=51=      }
=52=      my $message = param("message");
=53=      if (defined $message and $message =~ /\S/) {
=54=        ## must transfer limited query to file
=55=        my $saver = new CGI {"time" => time};
=56=        for (qw(name email message)) {
=57=          my $val = param($_);
=58=          $val = "" unless defined $val;
=59=          substr($val, 1024) = "" if length $val > 1024;
=60=          $saver->param($_, $val);
=61=        }
=62=        unshift @entries, $saver;
=63=        splice @entries, MAXENTRIES
=64=          if @entries > MAXENTRIES;
=65=        seek $chatfh, 0, 0;
=66=        truncate $chatfh, 0;
=67=        for my $entry (@entries) {
=68=          $entry->save($chatfh);
=69=        }
=70=      }
=71=      close $chatfh;
=72=      ## end critical region
=73=      @entries;
=74=    }
```

Searching a Large Number of Text Files for a String and Displaying the Results on a Web Page

Web Techniques, Column 12 (April 1997)

■**Randal's Note** The bug mentioned near the beginning of this article has, of course, been fixed.

I often read "How do I make my web pages searchable?" in newsgroups. While there are many fancy packages available to WAIS-index or GLIMPSE-index or "excite" your web server, what if you just have a dozen or so scripts that have, say, come from past *Web Techniques* columns, and you want to make them available and searchable?

Well, I had that problem the other day when someone asked me, "Which of your columns talked about flock()?" I couldn't recall. So, I solved this problem once and for all with a script (talk about overkill!).

The idea for this script comes in part from a similar script written by my associate Joseph Hall (joseph@5sigma.com) as part of our CGI course training materials. (At one point, we were discussing making all the matched characters bold, which his script did not do, and he said that would take some thought, and I said I could do it in a few lines, but ended up discovering a bug in Perl that won't be fixed until 5.004, so now I have to do something that takes a few more lines as a workaround.)

The resulting web search CGI program can be seen in Listing 4-6.

Line 1 starts most of the programs I write these days, enabling taint mode with -T (to prevent outside data from unknowingly being used to my disadvantage) and -w to tell me what I've done stupidly.

Line 2 also forces me to produce all my variables as lexical variables (declared with my) rather than package variables. This is a good practice, and it speeds up the program slightly, because lexical variables have a slightly faster access rate than package variables.

Line 3 disables output buffering, which is not strictly necessary in this program, but handy nonetheless.

Line 6 takes care of the PATH. I need to set this in order to perform the glob later in the program, and it also handles any other child-process execs.

Line 8 is a flag that I'm using in the "death" handler. Initially, its value is 0, but it will be set to 1 as soon as the program has sent out an HTTP header. (Sending out the header twice is messy, although not completely painful.)

Lines 11 through 15 are my lightweight entity encoder, stolen from the last few programs I've written for this column. Line 12 puts the argument into a local $_. Line 13 replaces all HTML-nasty characters with their entity-ized equivalents. Line 14 returns this hacked string as the result.

Lines 18 through 25 define a death handler, somewhat like the ones from the past few columns, but with yet another twist. This time, the printing of the HTTP header (Content-type:...) depends on whether or not $header_printed is set. Walking slowing through this, lines 19 and 20 fetch the argument, line 21 converts the HTML-dangerous characters to their HTML-safe equivalents, and lines 22 and 23 print the message, optionally preceded by the HTTP header. Line 24 exits the program.

Line 27 creates a CGI object, and imports enough methods directly as callable functions so that I can finish the code with minimal hassle.

The next three lines (29 to 31) define path locations for this script to search. $DIR is the Unix path to the directory in question. $URL is its equivalent URL location. It's not trivial for the script to go from one to the other; hence, we need to tell it explicitly. The third line sets $FILEPAT, which is going to be used as input to a glob operator. This string therefore can contain file glob characters (such as * in this example).

Now it's time to get to some good stuff. Line 33 prints the HTTP header and lets the death handler know that the header has been printed by incrementing the $header_printed scalar variable to a nonzero value. Lines 34 through 36 print a common top of the page.

The next few lines display the actual search form. I made the design decision that the search form appears even after the result of a successful search. This way, the surfer can try a different query while looking at the results of the old query.

Line 38 displays a horizontal line and the beginning of the form. The start_form doesn't have any visual component to it—it's just for the user to know what fields belong to this form for transmitting.

Line 39 shows a textfield named search. As a nifty feature, CGI.pm will initially load this as an empty string, but on subsequent executions of the same form, the previous search string is automatically used.

Line 40 creates a checkbox named regex. This box will be initially unchecked, indicating that the string in search is to be taken literally. However, if the user checks this box (or leaves it checked from a previous invocation), then the "search" string will be interpreted as a Perl regular expression. I'll explain this further in a moment. Line 41 similarly looks for "case sensitive" versus "case ignore." Initially, the search is case sensitive.

Line 42 displays the submit button. (Well, technically, it invokes a subroutine to invoke a method to create HTML that is then printed to standard out, retransmitted by the web server to the client's browser, which then displays the submit button. But isn't it much easier to say the first?)

Line 43 marks the end of the form (not visible to the user) and a horizontal line (very visible to the user).

Line 45 looks for the existence of a parameter called search, storing it into a lexical variable named $searchstring. The first time this script is called, this string will be empty. Subsequent invocations will probably have something here. This is in fact tested in line 46. Notice we test either undefined (undef value) or empty string. The former is tested because it means this is the first time the script has been invoked; the latter is tested because it doesn't make sense to search for nothing, no matter how much the user wants to do it.

If this is a valid search (second or later time around, and something to search for), then we need to set up for the search. Line 47 puts us in the right directory, and line 48 looks for all the proper files. The filenames are stored into the @ARGV array, just right for scanning with the diamond operator (<>).

Lines 49 through 51 handle the steps of turning a string into a regular expression, or rather, making a string act like a string and a regular expression act like a regular expression. If the user wanted regular expressions, these statements are skipped, leaving $searchstring exactly the way it was. If the user did not select a regular expression interpretation, then $searchstring is hacked to put backslashes in front of all nonalphanumeric characters. Specifically, if the search string is [box], Perl will treat this as a character class looking for any single *b*, *o*, and *x* characters. After quotemeta() (a built-in function), the string becomes \[box\], which will look for a literal left bracket, a box, and then a right bracket—closer to what the user wanted for a literal string match.

Line 52 further adjusts things by creating a $ignore variable, set to either an empty string or the string (?i). It just so happens that inserting **(?i)** into a regular expression causes that regular expression to be computed as case insensitive. That's too easy.

Lines 53 and 54 spit out some HTML ahead of the search results. Note that I'm jumping into preformatted mode here, causing multiple spaces to retain their spaceness, and linefeeds to feed more lines. On most browsers, this also switches to a constant-width font, making some of the lines even line up.

Line 55 creates a $per_file counter, allowing me to keep track of how many hits I've seen in a particular file. Through micro-months of painstaking research, Stonehenge Laboratories has determined that there's no need to show more than five hits in a particular file. So I have to keep track of this.

Lines 56 to 80 form a standard sort of diamond loop, reading a line at a time from the file named by $ARGV into the $_ variable. Lines 57 to 60 handle the necessary bookkeeping at the end of each file to keep $. set correctly (this comes directly from the manpages for Perl). Line 61 tosses that mostly useless newline at the end of the line away from $_.

Lines 62 through 71 track the hits in a particular line. First, a per-line hit counter is reset to zero. Then, line 63 attempts to replace the regular expression with an empty string. This replacement is either successful or a failure. If it's successful, we have a valid occurrence of the regular expression consisting of $searchstring and $ignore, and it has now been removed from the string. Now, recall that $searchstring is either the raw search string entered by the user or one that has been hacked to have all special characters preceded by a backslash, causing it to act like an ordinary string. And $ignore is either an empty string or (?i).

What's that /o for on the end of the replacement? Well, try leaving it off, and you'll see. It causes the regular expression to be compiled once the first time we hit this statement, never again dependent on the values of $searchstring and $ignore (perfectly OK because they have only one final value per invocation of this program). Leaving that off causes the regular expression to be re-interpreted every time around this loop. Bad. Very bad. And noticeably slower if you are parsing more than five lines.

OK, back to the body. If the replacement is successful, we need to tell the user. If this is the first hit, lines 64 through 67 print a prefix for the line that consists of the name of the file as a link, followed by the name of the file as a human-readable string, and then the line number. Line 68 prints the part of the string ahead of the regular expression match as regular text, followed by the part that matched as a bold string (using the b function from CGI.pm).

Line 69 causes the left part of the string to be discarded by setting the whole string to be the part of the string after the regular expression match. This is a good way to walk a string looking for matches.

Line 70 ensures that we process only the first five matches. This keeps the program from working hard, but it also prevents infinite loops if the regular expression can match a null string. Consider what happens when someone asks to match [a-z]*, and you'll see what I mean. No forward progress when we finally bump up against a nonletter.

Outside the loop, we need to finish off the line if we have started on the line, by printing the remaining $_ followed by a newline (important, because we're in PRE-/PRE territory). If the per-file hit count exceeds five, we bail out of this particular file by closing the ARGV handle, just like above.

Line 81 closes down the search output, and line 84 prints the end of the HTML data. That's it!

As you can see, a simple program gives my users a chance to search the listings for the keywords they want, pointing them directly at the file. Pretty cool. And it even does it rather efficiently. See ya next time, and I hope you find what you are looking for. . . .

Listing 4-6

```
=1=     #!/home/merlyn/bin/perl -Tw
=2=     use strict;
=3=     $| = 1;
=4=
=5=     ## set the path
=6=     $ENV{"PATH"} = "/usr/local/bin:/usr/ucb:/bin:/usr/bin";
=7=
=8=     my $header_printed = 0;          # so the death handler knows
=9=
=10=    ## return $_[0] encoded for HTML entities
=11=    sub ent {
=12=      local $_ = shift;
```

```
=13=      $_ =~ s/["<&>"]/"&#".ord($&).";"/ge;  # entity escape
=14=      $_;
=15=   }
=16=
=17=   ## death handler
=18=   $SIG{"__DIE__"} = $SIG{"__WARN__"} = sub {
=19=     my $why = shift;
=20=     chomp $why;
=21=     $why = ent $why;
=22=     print "Content-type: text/html\n\n" unless $header_printed++;
=23=     print "ERROR: $why\n";
=24=     exit 0;
=25=   };
=26=
=27=   use CGI qw/:standard/;
=28=
=29=   my $DIR = "/home/merlyn/Html/merlyn/WebTechniques";
=30=   my $URL = "http://www.stonehenge.com/merlyn/WebTechniques";;
=31=   my $FILEPAT = "*.listing.txt";
=32=
=33=   print header; $header_printed++;
=34=   print start_html("-title" => "Search WebTechniques Perl Scripts");
=35=   print h1("Search WebTechniques Perl Scripts");
=36=   print "Search the <A HREF=\"$URL/\">⤶
              Perl WebTechniques programs</A>",
=37=     " by submitting this form:\n";
=38=   print hr, start_form;
=39=   print p, "Search for: ", textfield("-name" => "search");
=40=   print p, checkbox("-name" => "regex",⤶
              "-label" => "Use Regular Expressions");
=41=   print p, checkbox("-name" => "ignore", "-label" => "Ignore case");
=42=   print p, submit;
=43=   print end_form, hr;
=44=
=45=   my $searchstring = param("search"); # the search item
=46=   if (defined $searchstring and length $searchstring) {
=47=     chdir $DIR or die "Cannot chdir $DIR: $!";
=48=     @ARGV = glob $FILEPAT;        # get matching filenames for <>
=49=     unless (param("regex")) {     # if ordinary string...
=50=       $searchstring = quotemeta $searchstring; # make ordinary.
=51=     }
=52=     my $ignore = param("ignore") ? "(?i)" : "";⤶
                # make case insensitive
=53=     print "<P>Follow the link to get the full listing:\n";
=54=     print "<PRE>\n";
=55=     my $per_file = 0;             # how many hits this file?
=56=     while (<>) {
```

```
=57=       if (eof) {
=58=         close ARGV;              # resets $.
=59=         $per_file = 0;
=60=       }
=61=       chomp;
=62=       my $per_line = 0;          # how many hits this line?
=63=       while (s/$ignore$searchstring//o) {
=64=         print
=65=           '<A HREF="',ent("$URL/$ARGV"),'">',
=66=           ent($ARGV),"</A>:$.: "
=67=             unless $per_line++;   # first time, print prefix
=68=         print ent($`), b(ent $&);
=69=         $_ = $';
=70=         last if $per_line >= 5;  # only five hits max per line
=71=       }
=72=       if ($per_line) {           # at least one hit?
=73=         print ent($_),"\n";      # finish line off
=74=         if (++$per_file >= 5) {  # only five lines max per file
=75=           print "[skipping to next file]\n";
=76=           close ARGV;            # force EOF
=77=           $per_file = 0;
=78=         }
=79=       }
=80=     }
=81=     print "</PRE>\n";
=82=   }
=83=
=84=   print end_html;
```

Creating a CGI Form and Connecting It to a Shared Database

Web Techniques, Column 5 (August 1996)

■**Randal's Note** The new version of CGI.pm as of this article introduced the ability to use p for a paragraph. However, standard was replaced by :standard (or :all) in later releases. Oh well.

In the previous column, I showed how to use the "flock" operation to ensure that only one CGI script was touching a particular file for writing at a time. However, in that script, there was essentially no interaction with user-entered data. This time, I'm going to look at a CGI-generated form that connects to a shared tiny database.

The particular CGI script discussed here handles a common problem: allowing users to "register" themselves to access a controlled directory. Here, a URL hierarchy cannot be accessed until the user provides a valid email address that will be recorded for statistical purposes (or perhaps to generate a mailing list—ugh). The registration is validated by having the script generate a random password, which is sent to the selected email address. If the user gave a bad email address, he will never get the email, so the random password will never be known, thus blocking access from that user.

A user is allowed to select his own "login" name. A more fascist script might auto-generate both the login name and the random password.

Once the password has been received, the user may immediately return to the protected URL, because the htpasswd database has already been updated with this information. No work is required on the part of the webmaster or pagemaster (nice).

While I was finalizing the work on this month's column, Lincoln Stein sent out an email message with a brand-new alpha release of CGI.pm (version 2.20a). This new release supports something similar to the HTML::AsSubs from the full-scale LWP module. I immediately rushed off to use it, because makes the embedded HTML code sooooo much easier to read and type. However, as it was an alpha release, the version you end up using will almost certainly be different, and there may be slight interface changes. Please keep this in mind if something doesn't work.

As always, the latest CGI.pm can be found in the nearest CPAN (using Tom Christiansen's handy "nearest CPAN" locator) in the directory of

```
http://www.perl.com/CPAN/id/LDS/
```

The program (which I call "subscribe") can be found in Listing 4-7.

Lines 1 through 3 start nearly every program I write. Line 1 selects the Perl interpreter for this file, with the taint flag (-T) turned on to try to stop me from shooting myself in the foot by using external user-supplied data directly in a semi-dangerous operation. Line 2 turns on some compile-time restrictions to help me be a sane programmer, and line 3 causes STDOUT to become unbuffered, so I can ensure proper sequencing of "print" output intermingled with child-process output.

Lines 4 and 5 pull in that "new CGI.pm" module I described previously. I stuck it into a directory below my home directory, so the use lib compile-time directive in line 4 causes that directory to be searched. Line 5 pulls in the new CGI module, passing it an import parameter of standard. This causes the CGI module to create a number of subroutines directly in the current package (package main), including subroutines to generate HTML. (Remember, this was an alpha release of the new CGI module, and already one of the comments was that this name should be :standard instead of standard. Only time will tell if this change was made.)

Line 5 also creates an implicit CGI object, causing the STDIN, environment, and command-line args to be parsed for further access. You can refer to this object explicitly with $CGI::CGI, but that seems redundant now.

Lines 7 through 9 define a few configuration constants: the Unix path to the protected directory, the URL path to the same directory, and the name of the .htpasswd file within that directory. (Actually, this skeleton version of subscribe doesn't use the URL, but later versions would have, I bet.)

Line 10 defines a handy $N newline constant, used frequently later.

Lines 12 through 14 print the first (common) part of the HTML output page to STDOUT. header is actually a call to &CGI::header, which is in turn an implicit invocation of

`$CGI::CGI->header`, causing the proper CGI/HTTP header fields to be sent back to the server. Similarly, `start_html` also comes from the CGI package, printing the proper `title` directive and nearby friends. The `$N` values create newlines in the output—not necessary for HTML interpretation, but somewhat easier to read while debugging the output.

Lines 16 through 29 represent the original form input, when we're called for the first time. If this is the case, then the `param` routine (actually, `&CGI::param`) returns a false value in a scalar context. Later, when the form is submitted, it will re-invoke this script with some parameters, and thus `param` will return a true value instead of a false value, causing this portion to be skipped.

Lines 17 through 27 print the body of the HTML form. The functions `h1`, `hr`, `submit`, and `p` generate same-named HTML constructs. The functions `start_form`, `textfield`, `url`, `end_form`, and `end_html` have additional intelligence to access CGI parameters and generate more complicated HTML constructs. But as you can see, the HTML form is very clean and easy to write directly. If you do enough this way, writing the form directly starts seeming like a lot of extra work (why type `<P>` when you can type `p`, for example). Again, the `$N` values are just to make the output line-oriented for humans to look at the HTML—they serve no real function otherwise.

Line 28 exits the program if we were just printing out the initial form.

Lines 32 through 72 form an `eval` block that I can use to trap errors—both "expected" errors that I know will happen and errors that I'm not sure about. Within this block, any fatal error or `die` operator will cause an immediate jump out of the block, setting `$@` to the error text. I test this later outside the block.

Lines 33 through 43 capture and validate the three input fields. The names given in the `param` invocations here must match up with the names in the form above. For convenience, I cache these into three local variables with roughly the same names. In a serious script, I'd probably perform a little more validation than a simple regular expression, but hopefully you'll see the point here.

Note that the `die` messages here all begin with `BACK:`. I'm using this string prefix as a special value in the abnormal-exit catcher outside the `eval` block. More on that later.

Lines 46 through 48 open the `.htpasswd` database and grab it exclusively. Only one subscribe script (or other cooperating script) is allowed to have an exclusive lock on this file.

Lines 52 through 57 examine the existing `.htpasswd` database to see if the requested username has already been taken. If so, the `die` operator bails out of the loop. If not, we make it all the way through, and fall through to the next chunk of Perl.

Lines 59 to 65 add the new username to the password database, along with an encrypted, randomly chosen password. First, line 59 seeks to the end of the file (we'll probably already be there, but I like double-checking). Next, line 60 selects a random password by calling a subroutine (defined later).

Lines 61 and 62 write the username and encrypted password to the database. Note that a `salt` of `aa` is used every time—in a secure system, I'd make this a random salt by selecting any two characters from the password character set.

Line 63 sends email to the user, giving them their new (hopefully temporary) password. Line 64 similarly records the username, the real name, and the designated email address into some database for record keeping.

Line 65 closes the file, thus freeing up the `.htpasswd` file for possible alteration by another invocation of `subscribe`.

Lines 67 through 70 display an acknowledgment message because everything finally worked. Line 71 exits the program in a normal way.

Lines 73 through 92 handle all the abnormal exits from the eval block. If the error message begins with BACK:, then it's one of our early-exit "expected" errors. The remainder of the error message line is a message of some kind that needs to be displayed to the user, along with a "Please go back and try again" warning. This is handled in line 75 through 77.

If the error message didn't begin with BACK:, it's an unexpected error. Because the error might contain HTML-significant characters (ampersand, less-than, or greater-than), these need to be encoded in such a way that they'll come out properly on the displayed page. Lines 80 through 82 handle that encoding. The print at lines 83 through 86 display the properly encoded message inside a pre code block, so it'll look pretty close to the original text.

Whether the error was internal or expected, lines 88 through 90 display a standard "Go back" message. It is presumed that the user will understand how to go back to the previous page. If they don't, they probably don't need access to my protected directory.

Lines 94 through 104 define the three routines implementing some of the functions called from above. In this demonstration program, the selected random password is always "password" (very, very, very unwise in anything but a demo program like this). The user information is not actually recorded (although the parameters are at least named), and the selected password is not emailed (oh well, it's "password" every time anyway). Obviously, for the program to be useful, I'd replace these with real functions.

And that does it for the program. I'd stick it somewhere in some CGI-BIN area, and then invoke it with no parameters to get the original form.

I'd also have to create an .htaccess file for the "protected" directory, which would look something like this:

```
AuthName Protected Directory
AuthType Basic
AuthUserFile /home/merlyn/public_html/protected/.htpasswd
<limit GET POST>
require valid-user
</limit>
```

I hope you enjoyed this demonstration of using a flocked (tiny) database with a CGI form. If you'd like to see a specific Perl-and-web-related topic covered in a future column, please feel free to email me.

Listing 4-7

```
=1=     #!/usr/bin/perl -T
=2=     use strict;
=3=     $|++;
=4=     use lib "/home/merlyn/CGIA";
=5=     use CGI qw(standard);
=6=
=7=     my $target_dir = "/home/merlyn/public_html/protected";
=8=     my $target_url = "http://www.teleport.com/~merlyn/protected";;
=9=     my $target_htpasswd = "$target_dir/.htpasswd";
=10=    my $N = "\n";                      # two chars instead of 4 :-)
=11=
=12=    print
```

```
=13=      header, $N,
=14=      start_html('subscribe to protected', 'merlyn@stonehenge.com'), $N;
=15=
=16=   unless (param) {                 # generate initial form
=17=     print +
=18=       h1 ('Subscribe to "protected"'), $N,
=19=       hr, $N,
=20=       start_form('POST',url), $N,
=21=       p, 'Your desired username: ', textfield('username','',20), $N,
=22=       p, 'Your e-mail address: ', textfield('email','',60), $N,
=23=       p, 'Your real name: ', textfield('real','',60), $N,
=24=       p, submit, $N,
=25=       end_form, $N,
=26=       hr, $N,
=27=       end_html, $N;
=28=     exit 0;
=29=   }
=30=
=31=   ## main toplevel:
=32=   eval {
=33=     my $field_username = param('username');
=34=     die "BACK: Username must be lowercase alphabetic!\n"
=35=       unless $field_username =~ /^[a-z]+$/;
=36=
=37=     my $field_email = param('email');
=38=     die "BACK: Your email address must be non-empty!\n"
=39=       unless $field_email =~ /\S/;
=40=
=41=     my $field_real = param('real');
=42=     die "BACK: Your real name must be non-empty!\n"
=43=       unless $field_real =~ /\S/;
=44=
=45=     ## fields are authenticated, so now lets try to add...
=46=     open PW, "+>>$target_htpasswd" or
=47=       die "Cannot attach to $target_htpasswd: $!";
=48=     flock PW, 2;                    # wait for exclusive lock
=49=     ## begin critical region (only one proc at a time gets past here)
=50=
=51=     ## first, ensure that we don't have a duplicate username
=52=     seek PW, 0, 0;                  # beginning of file
=53=     while (<PW>) {
=54=       my ($user) = split ":";
=55=       die "BACK: sorry, that username is already taken\n"
=56=         if $user eq $field_username;
=57=     }
=58=     ## good name, so add it
=59=     seek PW, 0, 2;                  # end of file
```

```
=60=        my $password = &random_password;
=61=        print PW
=62=          join (":", $field_username, crypt($password,"aa")), "\n";
=63=        &send_password($field_email, $field_username, $password);
=64=        &record_user($field_email, $field_username, $field_real);
=65=        close PW;
=66=        ## end critical region
=67=        print +
=68=          h1("You've been added!"), $N,
=69=          p, "You've been added! Your password is arriving in email!", $N,
=70=          end_html;
=71=        exit 0;
=72=    };
=73=    if ($@) {                        # somebody died
=74=      if ($@ =~ /^BACK: (.*)/) {    # one of our BACK errors?
=75=        print +
=76=          h1('Form entry error'), $N,
=77=          p, $1, $N;
=78=      } else {                      # nope, an internal error
=79=        $_ = $@;
=80=        s/&/&amp;/g;
=81=        s/</&lt;/g;
=82=        s/>/&gt;/g;
=83=        print +
=84=          h1('Form entry INTERNAL error'), $N,
=85=          p, 'The error message was ', $N,
=86=          code(pre($_)), $N;
=87=      }
=88=      print
=89=        p, 'Go back and try again!', $N,
=90=        end_html, $N;
=91=      exit 0;
=92=    }
=93=
=94=    sub random_password {
=95=      "password";
=96=    }
=97=
=98=    sub send_password {
=99=      my ($email, $user, $pass) = @_;
=100=   }
=101=
=102=   sub record_user {
=103=     my ($email, $user, $real) = @_;
=104=   }
```

Creating a "What's New?" Table to Direct Visitors to the Most Recently Modified Files on a Site

Web Techniques, Column 6 (September 1996)

■**Randal's Note** And yes, the first few paragraphs confirm what I said in the sidebar of the last chapter. The www.perl.com/CPAN/ URL is now replaced by www.perl.org for most people, since www.perl.com is only one of many dozens of CPAN mirrors. And, of course, Teleport is long gone, having been absorbed by a company that was then absorbed by EarthLink. The "what's new" page is no longer on my home page, also relegated to the ever-increasing list of things to do.

Well, I knew it. In my last column, I wrote about fellow columnist Lincoln Stein's new CGI.pm, version 2.20a, which added a nifty feature of writing HTML within a CGI script with minimal effort. I wrote

> *However, as it was an alpha release, the version you end up using will almost certainly be different, and there may be slight interface changes.*

Well, sure enough, it did. The keyword standard became :standard, less than 48 hours after I sent the column to bed. If you had trouble making it work, go back and fix it now, especially if you are using the current rev (2.21) or later.

This time, I'm looking at a different problem that doesn't involve HTTP at all (unlike nearly all of my previous columns). But nevertheless it's a common problem facing website administrators. Specifically, how do you keep visitors coming back once they've been there?

One of the ways to keep them coming back is by changing the content of the site. But then, a new problem arises. How do you both inform the visitors that things *do* change, and where those changes are?

Well, the simplest, most mechanical way is to create a "what's new" list by examining the timestamps on your HTML files. For this month's column, I wrote a simple script to do just that. (This month's idea comes from fellow Perl hacker Joseph Hall [joseph@5sigma.com], by the way.)

The script is presented here in Listing 4-8.

Line 3 enables the compile-time restrictions, as in nearly all the scripts I write. This helps me catch typo-ed variable names and poetry-mode barewords.

Line 4 pulls in the standard File::Find module. This module is provided with the Perl distribution. If this line fails when you try to run this script, your installer made a mistake.

Line 5 adds a directory in my home directory to the standard search list for modules. I recently reorganized everything I'm getting from the CPAN (www.perl.com/CPAN/) into a nice hierarchy, so all my scripts that use CPAN modules are now looking roughly the same. I even created a methodology for installation that works really well. (Hmm. Maybe that'll be described in a future column. :-)

Line 6 pulls in the HTML::Entities module from the now-famous LWP library. This library is located in the CPAN if you don't have it; just browse to www.perl.com/CPAN/authors/id/GAAS

for the latest version. I'm using the recently released version 5. This particular module provides the encode_entities function, which I need to properly escape text into HTML.

I tried to make this script somewhat adaptable for your use, so lines 8 through 34 form a "configuration" section. You should be able to merely change the values of these variables to get the script to work for you.

Lines 9 and 10 define a full path to the top-level directory or directories that will be scanned for new files. This is similar to the first argument (or arguments) to the Unix find command.

In my configuration, I'm examining my top-level HTML directory on Teleport.

Lines 11 through 14 define a subroutine called PRUNE. This subroutine will be called repeatedly while the file tree is being walked. PRUNE will be given two parameters: the basename of the file or directory being examined, and the full path of that same file or directory. If you don't want this program to wander into private areas, just return a true value (such as 1), and the find routine will wander away from that directory. This is similar to the -prune switch of the Unix find command.

In my particular configuration, I'm avoiding any directory that contains the string private in its basename.

Similarly, lines 15 to 18 define a subroutine called IGNORE, which selects which files are not of interest or are private. IGNORE is called for each file, with parameters like those of PRUNE. If the routine returns true, then that particular file will not be considered for final output.

In my configuration, I don't want dot-files showing up (like .htaccess), nor GNU Emacs backup files (ending in ~), nor standard-named GIFs or JPEGs.

Lines 19 and 20 define how many of the newest URLs to retain. For my example, I've just got the David Letterman–style "top ten."

Lines 21 to 25 define a TRANSFORM subroutine. This subroutine is a little tricky and is needed to translate the Unix file paths into valid URLs. I'm showing the transformation for Teleport's web server, in which the file /home/merlyn/public_html/fred.html is visible via the URL www.teleport.com/~merlyn/fred.html. The filename will be given to TRANSFORM as the first parameter. The return value must reflect its proper URL form.

Note that I'm returning back just something like /~merlyn/fred.html here, because I'm expecting to use the output of this script as an include file already within the right server and protocol.

Lines 26 and 27 define a string that will precede the output list. I'm creating an unnumbered list here, so I need <UL>.

Lines 28 and 29 similarly define a string that will precede each output list element. I need <LI> for this.

Lines 30 through 33 similarly define the ending item and list strings.

If you are adapting this to your website, you should not need to make any changes below line 34.

Line 36 declares a hash (associative array) called %when. The keys to this array will be full Unix pathnames, and the corresponding values will be their mtime value in Unix internal time values. This reflects the most recent modified time in a nice, numeric, easily sortable value.

Lines 38 to 44 invoke the find routine, imported when we said "use File::Find." The first parameter has to be a subroutine reference. This subroutine will be called for each directory and file as the find routine wanders the hierarchy. Here, I'm using an anonymous subroutine directly as the first parameter, described in a moment.

The remaining arguments to the `find` routine declare the top-level directories that will be used as the initial starting points. That's gotta be `@TOP` for us, passed in line 44.

The anonymous subroutine body is defined in lines 39 through 43. Lines 39 and 40 handle the pruning of unwanted directories. We pass the basename of the current candidate (`$_`) and the full pathname (`$File::Find::name`) as two parameters to `PRUNE` (defined above). If the subroutine returns true, then not only is this guy history, but so are all of his kids and grandkids. We indicate that by setting the variable `$File::Find::prune` to 1 and returning. (This interface is described in reasonable detail in the documentation for `File::Find`.)

Line 44 ensures that we consider only plain files for the rest of the subroutine; if it's not a file, we return quickly.

Line 45 sees if the file is a potential candidate by calling the `IGNORE` routine (defined above). Again, the subroutine gets the basename and full pathname as its two arguments. If the return value is true, we bail out of this subroutine, thus ignoring the file.

If we made it through all of those hoops, then it's a file worth checking the timestamp for. Wow. Line 43 records the timestamp (computed as the tenth parameter of the return value of `stat`) into the `%when` hash, using a key of the full pathname.

When the invocation of `find` has completed, we will have gathered the timestamps of all "interesting" files. The next step is to sort these files by their timestamps, and save only the most recently changed.

Line 46 sorts the keys of the `%when` hash using a sort block, which compares the corresponding values numerically. Note that `$b` and `$a` are reversed from their traditional order, which will cause this resulting list to have those elements with the largest `%when` values first, indicating that those are the most recently updated.

Line 47 tosses everything from the `@names` array after the `$HOWMANY` element. If there are not enough elements, all of them will be retained.

Line 49 declares `$name` to be lexically local, so that the foreach loop that declares yet another local `$name` will be successful. (Sometimes strict seems to be a bit too strict. :-)

Line 50 displays the list prefix string on standard output.

Lines 51 through 58 are executed for each element of the `@names` array, putting each name into `$name`.

Line 52 creates a URL string from the full Unix path. First, the path is passed to the `TRANSFORM` routine (defined above). Next, the result of that routine is passed to the `encode_entities` routine, imported from `HTML::Entities` above. This routine escapes > as `&gt;` and so on, so that they read properly in HTML. Without this, some of the characters would break the HTML output.

Lines 53 through 57 display a particular item from the list. First, the prefix is printed, followed by the beginning of an HTML `<A>` tag, with an `HREF` attribute of the URL. This is followed by the URL again (to make it visible), and then the timestamp. Note that the timestamp is converted from Unix internal time into human-readable time using the `localtime` operator. Lastly, this is followed by the item suffix.

Line 59 finishes up the output list.

I run this script nightly from cron, sending its output to a file called `whatsnew.txt` in my top-level directory. I then include the output directly into my home page using a server-side include directive:

```
<!--#include file="whatsnew.txt" -->
```

To see the results, look at my home page, near the top:

```
http://www.teleport.com/~merlyn/
```

If you want to have the script generate an entire HTML page (say you can't use server-side includes), then you can adjust $LIST_PRE and $LIST_POST to be the complete HTML header and footer.

I hope you've enjoyed finding out "what's new." I'm toying around with web-crawling scripts for the next column, so unless I get distracted by something niftier, that's what it'll be about.

Listing 4-8

```
=1=     #!/usr/bin/perl
=2=
=3=     use strict;
=4=     use File::Find;
=5=     use lib "/home/merlyn/CPAN/lib";
=6=     use HTML::Entities;
=7=
=8=     ## begin config
=9=     my (@TOP) =                      # top level directories
=10=      qw(/home/merlyn/public_html);
=11=    sub PRUNE {                      # don't search these dirs
=12=      ## $_[0] is basename, $_[1] is full path
=13=      $_[0] =~ /private/;
=14=    }
=15=    sub IGNORE {                     # don't notice these files
=16=      ## $_[0] is basename, $_[1] is full path
=17=      $_[0] =~ /^\.|~$|\.(gif|jpe?g)$/;
=18=    }
=19=    my ($HOWMANY) =                  # keep this many new files
=20=      10;
=21=    sub TRANSFORM ($;) {             # turn path into URL
=22=      local($_) = @_;
=23=      s!/home/merlyn/public_html/!/~merlyn/!;
=24=      $_;
=25=    }
=26=    my ($LIST_PRE) =                 # prefix list
=27=      "<UL>\n";
=28=    my ($ITEM_PRE) =                 # prefix item
=29=      "<LI>";
=30=    my ($ITEM_POST) =                # suffix item
=31=      "\n";
=32=    my ($LIST_POST) =                # suffix list
=33=      "</UL>\n";
=34=    ## end config
=35=
=36=    my (%when);                      # record of stamps
=37=
=38=    find (sub {
```

```
=39=              return $File::Find::prune = 1
=40=                if PRUNE $_, $File::Find::name;
=41=              return unless -f;       # only files
=42=              return if IGNORE $_, $File::Find::name;
=43=              $when{$File::Find::name} = (stat _)[9];
=44=          }, @TOP);
=45=
=46=      my @names = sort { $when{$b} <=> $when{$a} } keys %when;
=47=      splice(@names, $HOWMANY);        # discard older stuff
=48=
=49=      my $name;                        # shuddup $name
=50=      print $LIST_PRE;
=51=      for $name (@names) {
=52=        my $url = encode_entities TRANSFORM $name;
=53=        print
=54=          $ITEM_PRE,
=55=          "<A HREF=\"$url\">$url</a> on ",
=56=          scalar localtime $when{$name},
=57=          $ITEM_POST;
=58=      }
=59=      print $LIST_POST;
```

Making Random Selections for Maximum Web Page "Freshness"

Web Techniques, Column 9 (December 1996)

■**Randal's Note** All that GNUmakefile stuff is better replaced with the proper templating solution, although at the time there wasn't a lot of cool stuff around.

Yeah, sure, there are random link scripts, and random "quote of the day" scripts out there. But I wanted to tackle the subject as well. And I wanted to give it a twist . . . some "memory."

The random program I describe here "knows" what random items have been given out recently, and biases older items with a higher probability of being selected. And it does it in a way that allows a large number of entries to run in parallel, not tying up a central database while making a decision. Cool, you say? Read on!

Not only that, it could be equally easily used for random links, random ads (bleh, but they pay the bills for the coolest free sites), or even just random graphics. Now, how much would you pay? It's free, and it can be found in Listing 4-9. Much of it is commented, but let me hit the high points here.

Lines 1 and 2 begin nearly every program I write these days. Line 1 enables taint checks and warnings, while line 2 forces me to think about the variables I am using and why.

Line 3 brings in a neat utility module that I use to get the directory part (dirname) and file part (basename) of some of the Unix paths and URLs. Line 16 forces a particular PATH, necessary if I invoke any child processes.

Lines 19 to 23 create a subroutine called ent. This routine takes an arbitrary string and HTML-encodes it so that <, &, and > appear correctly. Of course, in past columns, I simply brought in HTML::Entities, but I wanted to show you a lightweight solution that doesn't require loading the LWP into place. Line 21 is where the hard work takes place. Each character in the target class is replaced with &#, followed by the ordinal value of the character and then a semicolon.

Lines 26 through 32 define a "death handler," causing the error message to come out in a nice format. In past columns, I relied on an eval block to handle this, but once again, I am trying a different method to compare its relative difficulty, and give you "more than one way to do it" (the Perl creed).

Line 26 assigns the special signals __DIE__ and __WARN__ the value of an anonymous sub, created inline. Sure, you could have stuck this into a normal named sub, but this is cooler.

Line 27 takes the death reason (what would have gone into $@ on an eval block), and shoves it into a local $why variable. Line 28 takes off the possible newline on the end of the string. Line 29 converts the string to its HTML-safe version, using the ent routine defined above.

Lines 35 through 37 fetch some CGI/SSI interface environment variables. $DOCUMENT_URI is the invoking document's URL. I'll be using this later to validate the selected "random" directory.

$PATH_INFO is the trailing part of the URL invoking this script. For example, if this script was invoked as /cgi/random/some/path/fred.random, then $PATH_INFO is /some/path/fred.random.

$PATH_TRANSLATED is a Unix file path corresponding to the document that would have been served if we had asked the web-server for the URL found in $PATH_INFO. I'll be using this later to access the random directory and its contents. The nice thing about this particular solution is that I don't have to know what the rules are for the server to perform this translation (from URL to directory name), unlike some of the programs I've written for previous columns. The server here is performing the translation for me.

Lines 40 and 41 get the basename (everything but the filename) of both the invoking document URL and the requested random directory. Lines 47 and 48 ensure that the invoking document's URL is pointing at the same directory as the requested "random" document's URL. This is an important security check: without it, a nefarious user could quite possibly ask for someone else's random directory.

If you are customizing this script, you may also choose a standard set of "random" directories that everyone can share on your web server. For example, you may consider /random/WHATEVER.random to be legal automatically. In that case, a simple comparison of $doc_dir equal to /random would do it.

Lines 51 through 54 check the translated path to ensure that the path ends in .random and represents a valid directory. This further verifies that this directory was deliberately intended to be a random deal, and not just some directory an evil person wanted to scan and mangle.

Next, I need a list of .log files in that directory. Lines 58 through 60 take care of this. Line 59 performs a complex series of interesting things and is best read from right to left. The readdir operator in a list context returns an unsorted list of names from the directory. The grep operator keeps only those names that end in .log. The map operator glues the PATH_TRANSLATED pathname in front of each name, yielding an absolute pathname.

Lines 63 through 70 compute a weighted random selection of the candidates in a one-pass algorithm. It's a bit tricky, but at the same time nicely elegant, so let me spend a moment to describe it.

Lines 63 and 64 initialize and create two variables. $total_weight keeps track of the "weight" of all elements we've seen so far. This starts out at zero. $winner will ultimately be the chosen element of @files. Initially, it's undef. Line 65 spins the random dial so that we get a different initial starting point for each invocation of the program.

Lines 66 to 70 loop through once for each element of @files, sticking a candidate in $_. Remember, at this point, @files has a list of absolute Unix paths to filenames ending in .log in the selected random directory.

Line 67 computes a "weight" for a particular candidate. In this case, I chose to select a weight consisting of the square of the age in seconds of the particular log file. This means that an item selected 20 seconds ago (with a weight of 400) is four times as likely to be selected as an item selected 10 seconds ago (with a weight of 100). This seemed fairest to me, and in some ad-hoc tests, it caused a fairly even distribution of selections. To be fairer, I could have based something on the size of the log files, or maybe some ratios read from a file, or something. Line 68 updates the total weight (so far) to include the weight computed for this particular item.

Line 69 is where the cool stuff happens. If a random number between zero and the total weight is less than the weight of this particular item, then this particular item is a potential winner. Put another way, this item will be chosen (this weight)/(total weight) times. Now, even if this element is chosen, a later element may override it, but again, it'll be in proportion to the weights of that item. Note that on the first pass, the two weight values are identical, meaning that $winner is definitely assigned $_ the first time around. For example, if the total weight is 10 from the previous pass, and this item has a weight of 3, then it has a 3/13 chance of being picked.

When the loop is finished, $winner is a .log file (or possibly undef). However, since it came from the result of a readdir, it's still considered tainted. Since I already know that it's a pretty safe filename, I untaint the entire value using a straightforward cheat in line 75. Lines 76 and 77 attempt to open this log file for appending.

Lines 79 through 85 form a standard "flock and wait," as described in a few of my previous columns. I want to write a timestamp and host address to the log file, but I need to have this script be the only one doing it at the time. So, I stole the example directly from the perlfunc manpage at the flock entry (once again). Note that because I'm writing to the .log file, the timestamp gets updated, making this particular entry the least likely to be reused on the next pass. This is exactly what we want—a fairly fair dealing of items.

Line 89 computes a URL for the selected item. This will be the PATH_INFO (not PATH_TRANSLATED) name, appended with the basename of the selected candidate, minus the .log name.

Line 93 sends a location directive to the web server. This will cause the web server to pick the selected URL, and then insert that into the server-side include (SSI) document.

So, how to use this thing? Best illustrated by an example. Let's work it from the top down.

I have a document in the URL http://www.myserver.com/some/path/thisdoc.html, containing the SSI invocation snippet of

```
<P>And here's the random picture of the day:
<!--#include virtual="/cgi-bin/random/some/path/picture.random"-->
```

Note that the /some/path here in the invocation has to be the same as the document in which it gets included. This document also has to be enabled for SSI processing. You'll have to figure out how this is done. On my server, I just make the file executable (Apache XBitHack is turned on).

I then need a subdirectory, picture.random, containing three different things for each picture to be randomly dealt:

- The picture itself (I'm using whatever.jpg here).

- An HTML snippet that, when included, creates the proper <IMG SRC="..."> to select that picture. We'll call that whatever.html, corresponding to whatever.jpg.

- A log file, writable by the web server, that selects that particular HTML snippet. That'd be whatever.html.log here.

Luckily, I have a nice GNU Makefile that does all that:

```
J = $(wildcard *.jpg)
H = $(J:.jpg=.html)
L = $(J:.jpg=.html.log)
D = $(shell basename `pwd`)

all: $H $L
        rm -f $(filter-out $H, $(wildcard *.html))
        rm -f $(filter-out $L, $(wildcard *.log))

$H $L: GNUmakefile

%.html.log: %.html
        echo -n >$@
        chmod 646 $@

%.html: %.jpg
        echo "<table><tr><th>$<<tr><td>⤸
          <IMG SRC='$D/$<' ALT='$<'></table>" >$@
```

This Makefile is nice because I can add and delete whatever.jpg files at will, and it automatically creates or destroys the log files and HTML snippets.

When someone selects thisdoc.html, the SSI invokes my random CGI script, which looks at the .log files in the picture.random directory and picks one of them, being biased toward the ones that haven't been selected recently.

Let's say it picks whatever.html.log. That means that the script will then add the date and time and IP source address to that particular log file, and then issue a redirect to cause the server to go fetch whatever.html. That file contains

```
<table><tr><th>whatever.jpg<tr><td>
<IMG SRC='random.picture/whatever.jpg" ALT="whatever.jpg'>
</table>
```

Notice the table markup enclosing the picture reference, which gives a cute label above the picture. If I had wanted to keep it simple, I'd have just used the `<IMG SRC="...">` part.

The server then includes this snippet into `thisdoc.html`, and the user's browser finally sees this:

```
<P>And here's the random picture of the day:
<table><tr><th>whatever.jpg<tr><td>
<IMG SRC='random.picture/whatever.jpg" ALT="whatever.jpg'>
</table>
```

which will be different (probably) on each reload!

Wow. Lots of work, but hopefully, I've illustrated a couple of interesting techniques. See ya next time.

Listing 4-9

```
=1=    #!/usr/bin/perl -Tw
=2=    use strict;
=3=    use File::Basename;
=4=
=5=    ## random dealer SSI-CGI, by Randal L. Schwartz (c) 1996
=6=
=7=    ## <!--#include virtual="/cgi-bin/random/DOC-PATH/SUBDIR.random"-->
=8=
=9=    ## where DOC-PATH has to be the *same* as the path to the including
=10=   ## doc and SUBDIR.random has to exist below that directory.
=11=   ## SUBDIR.random contains *.log files which must be httpd-writeable.
=12=   ## Random fairly-dealt *.log will cause return of corresponding *
=13=   ## (sans .log) inline.  Of course, these notes are cryptic. :-)
=14=
=15=   ## set the path
=16=   $ENV{"PATH"} = "/usr/local/bin:/usr/ucb:/bin:/usr/bin";
=17=
=18=   ## return $_[0] encoded for HTML entities
=19=   sub ent {
=20=     local $_ = shift;
=21=     $_ =~ s/[<&>]/"&#".ord($&).";"/ge;  # entity escape
=22=     $_;
=23=   }
=24=
=25=   ## death handler, presumes no output yet
=26=   $SIG{"__DIE__"} = $SIG{"__WARN__"} = sub {
=27=     my $why = shift;
=28=     chomp $why;
=29=     $why = ent $why;
=30=     print "Content-type: text/html\n\n[$why]\n";
=31=     exit 0;
=32=   };
```

```
=33=
=34=      ## get CGI/SSI variables
=35=      my $DOCUMENT_URI = $ENV{"DOCUMENT_URI"};
=36=      my $PATH_INFO = $ENV{"PATH_INFO"};
=37=      my $PATH_TRANSLATED = $ENV{"PATH_TRANSLATED"};
=38=
=39=      ## compute directory names of requested path and document path
=40=      my $doc_dir = dirname $DOCUMENT_URI;
=41=      my $info_dir = dirname $PATH_INFO;
=42=
=43=      ## security checks:
=44=
=45=      ## is user asking for immediate subdir of the doc from which we're
=46=      ## being included?
=47=      $doc_dir eq $info_dir
=48=            or die "security error: $doc_dir ne $info_dir";
=49=
=50=      ## is user asking for directory ending in ".random"?
=51=      $PATH_TRANSLATED =~ /\.random$/
=52=        or die "security error: $PATH_TRANSLATED does not end in .random";
=53=      -d $PATH_TRANSLATED
=54=        or die "security error: $PATH_TRANSLATED is not a directory";
=55=
=56=      ## everything's validated, so go for it.
=57=      ## get the candidate log files:
=58=      opendir PT, $PATH_TRANSLATED or die "opendir: $!";
=59=      my @files = map "$PATH_TRANSLATED/$_", grep /\.log$/, readdir PT;
=60=      closedir PT;
=61=
=62=      ## select a weighted random candidate:
=63=      my $total_weight = 0;
=64=      my $winner;
=65=      srand;
=66=      for (@files) {
=67=        my $this_weight = (86400 * -M) ** 2; # age in seconds, squared
=68=        $total_weight += $this_weight;
=69=        $winner = $_ if rand($total_weight) < $this_weight;
=70=      }
=71=      ## $winner might still be undef at this point, ⤶
                 in which case we'll die
=72=      ## on the following...
=73=
=74=      ## untaint and open log:
=75=      $winner =~ /(.*)/s;
=76=      open LOG, ">>$1"
=77=        or die "Cannot append to $1: $!";
=78=
```

```
=79=    ## wait for it to be ours:
=80=    flock LOG, 2;
=81=
=82=    ## record this hit:
=83=    seek LOG, 0, 2;
=84=    print LOG scalar localtime, " to $ENV{'REMOTE_ADDR'}\n";
=85=    close LOG;
=86=
=87=    ## compute URL for redirect
=88=    ## (original request path and basename of winner, without log):
=89=    my ($winner_url) =↵
                ("$PATH_INFO/" . basename $winner) =~ /(.*)\.log$/s;
=90=
=91=    ## trigger an SSI redirect so that the server↵
                will fetch the data (and log it)
=92=    ## (It had better make sense inside text/html :-)
=93=    print "Location: $winner_url\n\n";
=94=
=95=    ## done!
```

Watching Long Processes Through CGI

Linux Magazine, Column 39 (August 2002)

The CGI protocol is wonderful for the remote execution of short tasks. But how do you execute a longer task? You can't just have the task slowly executing without giving some kind of feedback to the user, and eventually Apache will get bored and have the connection time out anyway.

I've seen (and written) some solutions that depend on the browser understanding *server push*, but that's not a universal feature. And then there are the solutions that involve writing simple enough HTML that the page being incrementally rendered shows some signs of activity. Again, you can't count on that across the browser spectrum.

But one solution that minimizes server overhead and client browser dependence is the use of *client pull*, also called *meta refresh*. The initial request sets up a forked process to perform the real work, and redirects the browser to a new URL, which will "pull" the results obtained so far. If the results are incomplete, an additional header instructs the browser to "refresh" the data after some number of seconds.

Now, this sounds like it might be messy, at least in terms of managing the interprocess communication. How will the new CGI invocations know which data to display? This is handled by creating a unique *session key*, which should be hard to guess but easy to hand around. For my sample implementation, I'm using the MD5 hash of some mostly unpredictable data. And where will this data be? Sure, I could use temporary files, which will then require some sort of cleaner to zap out the old, stale files, but an easier solution is to use the Cache::Cache module from the CPAN, for which I've sung the praises here in the past.

So, the basic strategy is this: the browser hits the form, and the user fills out that form. Then the browser submits the form, and after verifying good information, the response forks to run the task and redirects the browser back with a session key. The forked process runs the task, taking output as it arrives and updates a cache value, flagging when it is complete. The CGI script pulls from the cache, and displays it, sending a refresh as long as the data is not complete.

For purposes of demonstration, we'll use a typical system administration task: running a *traceroute*. Obviously, this consumes system and network resources, so you should not set this up exactly as I've written it in Listing 4-10 in a public place, unless you want angry glares from your net neighbors.

Lines 1 through 3 begin nearly every CGI program I write. I enable taint checking and compiler restrictions, and disable the buffering of standard output.

Line 5 sets the shell execution path. Because we're tainted, any use of a child command will be flagged unless the PATH itself is also untainted, and the simplest way to do that is to set it directly.

Line 7 pulls in the CGI shortcuts, including a couple of unusual entries that don't get pulled in with :all for reasons I don't fathom.

Lines 9 to 57 form the three-way switch to have this CGI program decide what its personality will be for this particular invocation. Since they are actually listed in the reverse order of their normal invocation sequence, I'll start at the bottom and work backward.

Line 56 shows a web form to accept the single parameter: the host to which we are tracerouting. This comes from a subroutine defined in lines 61 to 66. Simply put, we print the HTTP (actually CGI) header, the beginning of the HTML, titling the page as Traceroute, and then a first-level head of the same. The form comes next (with an action that defaults to the same script again), with a single submit button and a textfield. The fieldname is host, which we note for the next part of the description. Then the form is closed and the HTML completed. This is your standard trivial form.

When the user submits this form, we come back to the same script, and end up in the code starting in line 24. And here's where it get interesting.

First, lines 25 and 26 validate the input parameter and untaint it by extracting a good known narrow regex. Note that I limit the size of the hostname to 100 characters to prevent a denial of service or buffer overflow attack, and the range of characters to prevent other messiness. Be very conservative when accepting web form parameters. If the validation fails, we redisplay the form in line 53.

Line 27 fetches a unique session ID. This will be 32 hex characters that are reasonably hard to predict. The subroutine in lines 80 through 84 pulls in the Digest::MD5 module (found in the CPAN) to take some random and unpredictable data to generate such a hash. I stole the routine from Apache::Session, so if it's good enough for them, it's good enough for me.

Line 28 gets a Cache::Cache object to hold the information for the interprocess communication. The subroutine beginning in line 68 defines this object: we'll cache in the filespace, naming the application tracerouter. The data will be good for 30 minutes before purging, and a purging run will be executed automatically on the first hit after 4 hours has passed. Look ma, no maintenance run. If you decide you want to use shared memory, a simple change to this subroutine will create it in shared memory instead.

Line 29 puts the initial load into the cache. The cache is always a two-element arrayref. The first element is a flag that is true if the output is complete. The second element is the data so far.

And now the fun part. We're going to fork starting in line 31. This permits the parent process to tell Apache that we're done responding to this request, while letting the child go off to perform the long *traceroute*. If we're the parent, we need to construct a URL that points back to us, but with just the session ID. So, we clear all the stored CGI parameters (line 32); set the session ID (line 33); and then print a CGI redirect of "ourselves" (as modified), which becomes an external redirect to the browser (line 34), and we're done.

The child goes on, but it must first close STDOUT, because otherwise Apache will think there might still be some output coming for the browser and won't respond to the browser or release the connection until this is all resolved. Next, we have to launch a child process of the child to execute the *traceroute*.

We'll do this with a pipe open, which includes an implicit fork, in line 37. The grandchild process merges STDERR to STDOUT and then executes *traceroute*, passing it the validated host parameter from before. If line 40 is executed, we get a single line of output in our response with the die message.

The child (that is, the parent of the *traceroute*) reads from the filehandle opened from the STDOUT (and STDERR) of the *traceroute* starting in line 42. We declare a buffer ($buf), and as each line is read (line 43), the line is added to the buffer (line 44) and shoved into the cache storage (line 45). When the command is complete, we get end-of-file, drop out of the loop, and store the entire buffer again with an "I'm done" flag (line 46) and exit (line 47).

In short, the child process scurries off to execute the command. And the parent has told the server to tell the browser to "Please revisit me with this session key." So the browser comes back on its own volition, and ends up starting in line 9, for the third and final part of this program.

Line 10 gets the cache handle, opening to the same cache to which the forked child is writing. Line 11 gets the cache data for that session key. Now if the data is missing, either the data has expired or someone is trying to jimmy up a session key to hijack someone else's session. In either case, we show the form (again) and stop.

Line 16 generates the CGI header. Lines 17 to 19 follow that with the HTML header. If the "data complete" flag is not set, then we need to keep going after this display, so we'll add a meta-refresh tag to the head info. This instructs the browser to poll the same URL in some number of seconds (here, 5 seconds).

Line 20 labels the output with a first-level header and dumps the data (nicely HTML-escaped and wrapped in a PRE element) that we have so far. If the data is incomplete, an italicized "continuing" paragraph is appended, to let the user know that we're still working on the answer. And that's it!

So, that's a basic strategy to watching a long-running program do its job, remotely through CGI invocations. Again, be aware of the resources this web script would let your remote visitors consume and of the range of actions you'd really want to permit. Also, the child process has no awareness if the parent is finally disinterested, and it continues merrily chugging away to produce a result that no one will see. Perhaps that can be fixed in another revision of the program. But until next time, enjoy!

Listing 4-10

```
=1=     #!/usr/bin/perl -T
=2=     use strict;
=3=     $|++;
=4=
=5=     $ENV{PATH} = ↵
            "/bin:/sbin:/usr/bin:/usr/sbin:/usr/local/bin:/usr/local/sbin";
=6=
=7=     use CGI qw(:all delete_all escapeHTML);
=8=
=9=     if (my $session = param('session')) { ↵
            # returning to pick up session data
=10=      my $cache = get_cache_handle();
=11=      my $data = $cache->get($session);
=12=      unless ($data and ref $data eq "ARRAY") { # something is wrong
=13=        show_form();
=14=        exit 0;
=15=      }
=16=      print header;
=17=      print start_html(-title => "Traceroute Results",
=18=                        ($data->[0] ? () :
=19=              (-head => ["<meta http-equiv=refresh content=5>"]))));
=20=      print h1("Traceroute Results");
=21=      print pre(escapeHTML($data->[1]));
=22=      print p(i("... continuing ...")) unless $data->[0];
=23=      print end_html;
=24=    } elsif (my $host = param('host')) { # returning to select host
=25=      if ($host =~ /^([a-zA-Z0-9.\-]{1,100})\z/) { # create a session
=26=        $host = $1;                # untainted now
=27=        my $session = get_session_id();
=28=        my $cache = get_cache_handle();
=29=        $cache->set($session, [0, ""]); # no data yet
=30=
=31=        if (my $pid = fork) {      # parent does
=32=          delete_all();            # clear parameters
=33=          param('session', $session);
=34=          print redirect(self_url());
=35=        } elsif (defined $pid) {   # child does
=36=          close STDOUT;            # so parent can go on
=37=          unless (open F, "-|") {
=38=            open STDERR, ">&=1";
=39=            exec "/usr/sbin/traceroute", $host;
=40=            die "Cannot execute traceroute: $!";
```

```
=41=          }
=42=          my $buf = "";
=43=          while (<F>) {
=44=            $buf .= $_;
=45=            $cache->set($session, [0, $buf]);
=46=          }
=47=          $cache->set($session, [1, $buf]);
=48=          exit 0;
=49=        } else {
=50=          die "Cannot fork: $!";
=51=        }
=52=      } else {
=53=        show_form();
=54=      }
=55=    } else {                        # display form
=56=      show_form();
=57=    }
=58=
=59=    exit 0;
=60=
=61=    sub show_form {
=62=      print header, start_html("Traceroute"), h1("Traceroute");
=63=      print start_form;
=64=      print submit('traceroute to this host:'), " ", textfield('host');
=65=      print end_form, end_html;
=66=    }
=67=
=68=    sub get_cache_handle {
=69=      require Cache::FileCache;
=70=
=71=      Cache::FileCache->new
=72=          ({
=73=            namespace => 'tracerouter',
=74=            username => 'nobody',
=75=            default_expires_in => '30 minutes',
=76=            auto_purge_interval => '4 hours',
=77=          });
=78=    }
=79=
=80=    sub get_session_id {
=81=      require Digest::MD5;
=82=
=83=      Digest::MD5::md5_hex(Digest::MD5::md5_hex(time().{}.rand().$$));
=84=    }
```

Maintaining a Stateful "Conversation" via One Child Process per "Conversation"

Web Techniques, Column 23 (March 1998)

■**Randal's Note** This was the first of many "mini web server" columns I wrote, thanks to HTTP::Daemon. And, I even tickled a bug in Chatbot::Eliza while writing the column. These days, I tend to write mini server programs using POE instead, simply because I can multiplex other tasks while waiting for the next client connection.

One of the interesting challenges in a connectionless protocol like the web is maintaining "session" or "state" information to allow multiple interactions as part of a larger "conversation."

In past columns, I've talked about doing this with external files, with mangled URLs, and with hidden information in forms. While these are all good solutions, they still require each new CGI invocation to somehow "come up to speed" about which conversation this particular transaction is a part. In this column, let's take a different tactic.

Instead of trying to "leap" the information from one program to another, let's keep a process alive during an entire conversation, letting it die when the conversation is over. That way, the information can stay in the dataspace of that process, and all we have to do is keep reconnecting to that same process somehow.

This sounds perhaps complicated, but it is actually very simple using the HTTP::Daemon module in the LWP library that I first used in a column last year to create a web proxy server. In this case, we'll be launching a tiny web server from a CGI script that will hold the state of the conversation, and then tell the browser to go talk to this mini web server instead of the main server.

For each ongoing conversation, this will then require an additional process, so this method works nicely when you have only a small number of "conversations" going on at the same time. In part two (next month), I'll revisit this to show how to do it with just one additional process.

As I was looking for something interesting to demonstrate a stateful conversation, I was pleasantly greeted by a new addition to the CPAN: a Perl implementation of Eliza! From the manpage for Chatbot::Eliza:

This module implements the classic Eliza algorithm. The original Eliza program was written by Joseph Weizenbaum and described in the Communications of the ACM in 1967. Eliza is a mock Rogerian psychotherapist. It prompts for user input, and uses a simple transformation algorithm to change user input into a follow-up question. The program is designed to give the appearance of understanding.

This program is a faithful implementation of the program described by Weizenbaum. It uses a simplified script language (devised by Charles Hayden). The content of the script is the same as Weizenbaum's.

So, I quickly grabbed Chatbot::Eliza and used it as the basis for an interactive session with "the doctor," using a standard browser interface. And the result is in Listing 4-11.

Lines 1 through 4 start nearly every program I write, turning on taint checking and warnings, disabling buffered output, and enabling all compiler restrictions.

Line 5 pulls in the CGI module, importing the normal convenience subroutines, as well as parsing the CGI information into accessible data structures. (The CGI modules are in the standard library beginning with Perl version 5.004. If you have an older version of Perl, you should upgrade for security reasons.)

Lines 6 and 7 pull in the HTTP::Daemon and HTTP::Status modules, found in the LWP library. LWP is found in the CPAN (www.perl.com/CPAN/ or www.perl.org/CPAN/), but you probably already have it if you've been doing *any* web programming with Perl.

Line 8 pulls in the Eliza module described above. You'll almost certainly need to get this one from the CPAN (unless you're like me and daily install everything you can from the CPAN just to play with it).

Lines 10 and 11 are the only configuration constants for this program. The $HOST variable defines the name of this host for HTTP::Daemon to use. This was supposed to work automatically, but didn't for me (and thus might not for you). So, define it here.

$TIMEOUT is the number of seconds a particular "doctor" will hang out waiting for further dialogue from a particular "patient." If no further requests come within this time, the doctor vanishes. So, this is a number that's worth tuning with some thought. You'll need a separate process for each doctor, so you don't want a lot of idle doctors filling up the office. On the other hand, the doc needs to wait around long enough for the patient to come up with a meaningful response. I found two minutes (120 seconds) to be about right in some quick testing with my net friends. (Obviously, that number would be much too low in a shopping cart environment.)

Every invocation of this CGI program creates a separate mini web server. This happens by creating a new HTTP::Daemon object (in line 13), saved in $d. A nonpredictable, nonprivileged port number gets assigned automatically and recycles after some 60,000 ports, so we're pretty safe for a while.

Line 14 creates a unique identifier that the CGI script and the mini web server share secretly. This is used in later connections to the mini web server to ensure that we don't have someone trying to hijack a particular doctor session. I'm not being very secure here, since the value of rand() can be predicted given the other two parts of this URL, but this should scare off the newbies from trying anything.

Line 15 constructs the URL to which we will send the browser. It'll look something like this:

```
http://www.stonehenge.com:61714/881337239.25550.567
```

Note here the mini web server address at my web address, but port 61714, and then the unique key following of the time, PID, and a random one-to-three-digit number. All further interaction from the browser will be to this URL, triggering the mini web server. Bookmarking this URL is pointless, because the server responding to it dies after two minutes of inactivity.

Lines 17 through 22 fork off the mini web server using fairly standard forking code. Line 19 causes the parent code (acting as the CGI handler) to redirect the browser to the mini web server. Line 22 closing STDOUT is essential. Without it, the real web server won't know that we're done sending information to the browser.

The remaining lines of the program are strictly for the mini web server. Line 24 creates the Eliza object, which has stateful information about our current session.

Lines 26 through 58 form an infinite loop, processing one request at a time from a browser. This loop is exited via the `alarm()` setting on line 27. After 120 seconds of idleness waiting at line 28 for a new connection, a `SIGALRM` signal will come along. Since we're not doing anything to catch that signal, the program will hastily exit. When we get back up to the top of the loop after handling a single transaction, the alarm is reset once again to 120 seconds. (There's only one alarm to be activated, so any new setting erases the prior setting.)

Line 28 waits for a connection from a browser and captures information about the connection into an `HTTP::Daemon::ClientConn` object (described on the manpage for `HTTP::Daemon`), here saved into `$c`.

Line 29 gets the request information into an `HTTP::Request` object, saved into `$r`. This will have the `POST`ed data content in it, as we'll see shortly.

Lines 30 through 34 are the security check to make sure that it isn't just some random connection or even a bookmarked prior connection from *long* ago. The value of `$r->url->epath` is the "path" requested of this "web server." Since the URL we redirected the browser toward has our magic unique identifier out there, this better be the same.

If it's not, lines 31 and 32 trigger an HTTP error (the 403 message), including a cute text phrase. If you're experimenting and want to see this message, alter the URL slightly after you've invoked the program in the normal way.

If we've made it to line 35, we're doing normal stuff now, so it's time to send back a normal "here's your file" status.

Line 36 is a bit odd. I want to use the cool HTML-writer features of the CGI module, but this code isn't being called from a real web server, and so the CGI environment variables aren't set up properly. Luckily, the CGI module allows me to fake up a transaction, passing it the input data. *But*, in order to use the function calls instead of the method invocations for the HTML writer features, the current CGI object has to be installed in `$CGI::Q`. And that's exactly what I've done. Yes, I cheated—by looking at the source of `CGI.pm` to figure out how to do this, but it works. Here, `$r->content` is the POST data from the previous form. If it's empty, it was a GET request, but that doesn't matter here.

Line 37 is the response that the doctor speaks. I'm defaulting it to an initial greeting, which will be used if we didn't get any valid prior response.

Lines 38 to 42 handle the replies from prior invocations. The `param` method/function fetches the `message` parameter from the form data. Unless it's empty or missing, we pass it into the Eliza object, whose response comes back into `$eliza_says`. Also, we clear out the parameter, so that it won't be the default in the form below. (Forms created with the CGI module are "sticky" by default.)

Lines 43 to 55 return the content of the response back to the user. Normally, this is handled by printing to `STDOUT` in a CGI script, but we're not quite in full CGI mode here. In fact, it's sorta "no-G-I." Luckily, the `$c` connection object can act like a filehandle, so we use it as an indirect filehandle to print the return information.

Line 44 generates the HTTP header (everything after the HTTP status line printed above). Line 45 provides the initial HTML content. Line 46 generates an `H1` header, and line 47 an `HR` horizontal rule.

Lines 48 through 53 generate the response form. Note that we force a POST to our magic unique URL as the action for this form. By HTTP standards, this *must* be a POST and not a GET, because submitting this form *changes* the state of the server (in this case, our mini web server). Also, by forcing a POST, the response ends up accessible to the `->content` method above. (To get the form data of a GET method, see the `HTTP::Daemon` manpage for an example.)

Line 49 formats the doctor's response immediately above the textfield generated in line 50. Line 51 creates a submit button (with a text message in place of SUBMIT), and line 52 tells the patients that the meter is running.

After the content has been sent down the $c pipe, line 56 closes the connection, letting the browser know we are done. And then we're ready for another interaction, so we jump back in line 57 to do it all over again.

And that's all there is to it. Install it into a CGI area, tell people that the doctor is in at a URL like

```
http://www.stonehenge.com/cgi/eliza
```

and then you'll be wishing you'd implemented that credit card charge system so you could get paid for this.

Note that only the initial fetch of the CGI script will show up in your web logs, because all subsequent HTTP transactions are being performed to the mini web servers. Enjoy!

Listing 4-11

```
=1=     #!/home/merlyn/bin/perl -Tw
=2=
=3=     $|++;
=4=     use strict;
=5=     use CGI ":standard";
=6=     use HTTP::Daemon;
=7=     use HTTP::Status;
=8=     use Chatbot::Eliza;
=9=
=10=    my $HOST = "www.stonehenge.com"; # where are we?
=11=    my $TIMEOUT = 120;     # number of seconds until this doc dies
=12=
=13=    my $d = new HTTP::Daemon (LocalAddr => $HOST);
=14=    my $unique = join ".", time, $$, int(rand 1000);
=15=    my $url = $d->url.$unique;
=16=
=17=    defined(my $pid = fork) or die "Cannot fork: $!";
=18=    if ($pid) {                    # I am, apparently, the parent
=19=      print redirect($url);
=20=      exit 0;
=21=    }
=22=    close(STDOUT);                 # to let the kid live on
=23=
=24=    my $eliza = new Chatbot::Eliza;
=25=
=26=    {
=27=      alarm($TIMEOUT);             # (re-)set the deadman timer
=28=      my $c = $d->accept;          # $c is a connection
=29=      my $r = $c->get_request;     # $r is a request
=30=      if ($r->url->epath ne "/$unique") {
```

```
=31=        $c->send_error(RC_FORBIDDEN, ⏎
                    "I don't think we've made an appointment!");
=32=        close $c;
=33=        redo;
=34=      }
=35=      $c->send_basic_header;
=36=      $CGI::Q = new CGI $r->content;
=37=      my $eliza_says = "How do you do?  Please tell me your problem.";
=38=      my $message = param("message") || "";
=39=      if ($message) {
=40=        param("message","");
=41=        $eliza_says = $eliza->transform($message);
=42=      }
=43=      print $c
=44=        header,
=45=        start_html("The doctor is in!"),
=46=        h1("The doctor is in!"),
=47=        hr,
=48=        startform("POST", $url),
=49=        p($eliza_says),
=50=        p, textfield(-name => "message", -size => 60),
=51=        p, submit("What do you say, doc?"),
=52=        p("Note: the doctor is patient, but waits⏎
                    only $TIMEOUT seconds, so hurry!"),
=53=        endform,
=54=        hr,
=55=        end_html;
=56=      close $c;
=57=      redo;
=58=    }
```

Creating Thumbnails

Web Techniques, Column 29 (September 1998)

▨**Randal's Note** The "Flaming Camel" drink referenced here was an actual drink I created at the bar I owned in La Grande, Oregon. Alas, the code listed here is no longer in use, because I created a better way of generating thumbnails, indexes, and dynamic HTML for image galleries.

I recently found myself with a handful of photographs that I wanted to add to the personal section of my website. I thought to myself, "No problem. Just scan them in, upload them, add some links, and I'm done." Of course, I then remembered that I had wanted to create thumbnails of these pictures. Ugh. This made matters more complicated.

Thumbnails, which are miniature versions of original pictures, help website visitors decide whether they want to take the time to download the entire picture. (Please don't confuse this with what one of my friends calls *dumbnails*, which are full-sized downloads that are scaled *in the browser* to be small. Lame.) There's nothing worse than spending two to five minutes downloading a typical JPEG file, only to discover that you've already got it, or it looks, well, useless.

Now, all modern photo-manipulation programs have tools to scale pictures down to a small size, but the thought of doing this over and over again for each picture just didn't make sense to me. And even then, I'd have twice as many pictures to upload.

Then I remembered that I had previously installed the NETPBM tools on my website machine. This freely available package can perform many manipulations on pictures programmatically (from a command line). The NETPBM package is available from

```
ftp://ftp.x.org/contrib/utilities/netpbm-1mar1994.p1.tar.gz
```

Be sure to comply with the extremely liberal licensing agreement for this package.

So, after poring over the docs for PBM, I came up with the following command lines to make a thumbnail. For a JPEG, I type

```
djpeg infile | \
        pnmscale -xy 100 100 | \
        cjpeg -smoo 10 -qual 50 >infile.thumb.jpg
```

and for a GIF, I enter

```
giftopnm infile | \
        pnmscale -xy 100 100 | \
        cjpeg -smoo 10 -qual 50 >infile.thumb.jpg
```

Notice that only the first is different, because the remaining steps take the PNM-format data and manipulate it. This is typical when using NETPBM.

Ahh. All that was left was to wrap this up into a program. Then, as long as I was making the thumbnails with a program, I might as well generate the right HTML into my index.html directly! I wanted each picture to end up something like this:

```
<tr><td><a href="FlamingCamel.jpg">
<img
        src="FlamingCamel.jpg.thumb.jpg"
        alt="[thumbnail of FlamingCamel.jpg]"
></a></td>
<td>136K</td>
<td>
        This is me with the ingredients of a
        <em>Flaming Camel</em> drink:
        one shot Aftershock, one shot Buttershotz.
</td></tr>
```

This would then be the row of a table, so that all the thumbnails, byte sizes (in K), and descriptions ended up lined up. The thumbnails themselves are also the links to the actual pictures. Once again, Perl can do all the hard work, leaving me to come up with the creative captions.

So, first, let's take a look at the program, presented in Listing 4-12, and then we'll see how I used it.

Lines 1 through 3 begin nearly every program I write, enabling compiler time restrictions for large programs.

Line 5 defines a tag that will be placed at the head of the table in which the new entries will be inserted. It's important that you don't delete this tag from the table, or the program will create a new one! Lines 6 and 7 pull in two modules from the LWP library to help translate Unix pathnames into things we can put in HTML. Line 8 sets the Unix umask to a value that is compatible with my web server reading the files.

Lines 10 through 36 form the main portion of the code. I enclosed this section in a block and ended it with an exit 0 for emphasis. Any local variables declared within this block are useful only to the main routine, and not to the subroutines.

Line 11 determines which files will be examined as potential pictures needing thumbnails. If command-line arguments are present (as given in @ARGV), then we use them. Otherwise, we'll look at all of the binary files in the current directory.

Lines 13 and 14 set us up for an *inplace edit* of the index.html file in the current directory. The file to edit is placed in @ARGV, and the backup suffix (here, the GNU Emacs edited-file suffix of a single tilde) is placed in $^I. This is a convenient way to read a file and generate an updated version of that file without a lot of hassle.

Line 16 opens the index.html file for reading, generating a new file for output. Each line ends up in $_.

Lines 17 to 24 trigger if we've made it all the way through the index file without seeing the ADD HERE tag. In this case, we need to generate the entire table ourselves, at the end of the file.

Line 18 prints the last line that got us here. Line 19 follows that with an HTML comment to give us some direction about what to do with the following table. Line 20 dumps a simple table header along with our ADD HERE tag. Line 21 calls the &scan_pictures subroutine to create the thumbnails and dump the HTML in the right place, and line 22 finishes up the closing of the table. Line 23 breaks us out of the loop.

Lines 25 to 32 handle the case where we are now looking at the ADD HERE tag. Note that this is triggered by a regular expression that matches $TAG, but that we're automatically backslashing any characters that might be special to a regular expression. There weren't any in this particular value of $TAG, but you never know.

Line 26 copies through the line that contains the tag. Line 27 creates the thumbnails and HTML in the right place. Lines 28 through 30 copy the remainder of the index from the previous version to the new version. Line 31 breaks the outer loop.

If we haven't seen the tag, and we're not at end-of-file yet, we need to copy all the rest of the lines, and that's handled by line 33.

Lines 40 through 62 define the &scan_pictures routine. The parameter passed in is a list of filenames to scan as picture files, in a loop from lines 41 through 61.

Line 42 skips over the thumbnails. Don't make thumbnails of thumbnails, as I did on one of the first versions of this program.

Line 43 makes the name of the thumbnail file for this file, and line 44 sees if this file already exists. If it does, we presume it's up to date, so we skip over it. (A possible refinement of this program would be to regenerate the thumbnail if it's older than the source file, but I didn't need that for my application.)

Line 45 attempts to convert either a GIF or JPEG into the PNM portable format by calling the subroutine &get_pnm, defined later. If this succeeds, we have a good picture (in $pnm), and if not, we'll skip the name entirely.

Lines 46 through 48 convert this $pnm data into a JPEG thumbnail, using a filehandle opened to a shell pipe. The STDIN of pnmscale will be the PNM data. The output is sent to the file named $thumb.

If all that worked, it's time to generate the HTML for the table, handled in lines 50 through 60. Note that a filename used as a URL must be both URI escaped (using uri_escape from the URI::Escape module) and "entity-ized" (using encode_entities from the HTML::Entities module), but a filename appearing as text (in the alt text) merely needs to be "entity-ized." Whew.

The final battle here is the creation of the PNM data, in the subroutine defined in lines 64 through 71. Line 65 takes the sole argument and puts it into a temporary $_ variable.

Lines 66 through 69 try different methods of creating the PNM file. You can add other methods in this list (like TIFF or PNG) as long as the command spits out PNM on the output and exits with a zero exit status if everything worked OK.

Each command in $cmd is tried inside backquotes in line 67. If the exit status is 0, the value is returned as being good. If we make it through the list of commands without success, we'll return an undef value in line 70.

So that's all there is to the program. To use it, create a template index.html file in a directory, and then place all your GIFs and JPEGs in that same directory. With that as your current directory, invoke the program.

This program will generate all the thumbnails and add an HTML table to the *end* of your index.html file. You'll need to edit the file, moving the table up to wherever you want it. The hardest part is adding the appropriate descriptions, but at least the links, the thumbnails, and the file sizes are added for you. Don't delete the ADD HERE tag, or the next invocation won't find it.

Speaking of that, once you've got your file all set, and people are viewing your data, you can insert additional files at any time. Just place the additional JPEG or GIF files into the directory, rerun the program, and only the added files will have new thumbnails created. The HTML table entries for just those files will be added to the ADD HERE location, and you can then add descriptions and move them to where you want them (if necessary).

As you can see, thumbnails are nothing to be scared of when you can use a nice tool like Perl to take out the boring parts. Now if we could just get a way to come up with those descriptions automatically . . . hmm. Enjoy!

Listing 4-12

```
=1=     #!/usr/local/bin/perl
=2=
=3=     use strict;
=4=
=5=     my $TAG = "<!-- ADD HERE -->";
=6=     use HTML::Entities;
=7=     use URI::Escape;
=8=     umask 0022;
=9=
=10=    {
=11=        my @names = @ARGV ? @ARGV : grep { -f and -B } <*>;
```

```
=12=
=13=       local @ARGV = "index.html";
=14=       local $^I = "~";
=15=
=16=       while (<>) {
=17=         if (eof) {
=18=           print;                          # last line
=19=           print "<!-- move the following table⤶
                      to the proper location -->\n";
=20=           print "<table border=2> $TAG\n";
=21=           &scan_pictures(@names);
=22=           print "</table>\n";
=23=           last;
=24=         }
=25=         if (/\Q$TAG/o) {
=26=           print;                          # tag line
=27=           &scan_pictures(@names);
=28=           while (<>) {                    # dump remaining lines
=29=             print;
=30=           }
=31=           last;
=32=         }
=33=         print;                            # default
=34=       }
=35=     }
=36=     exit 0;
=37=
=38=     ## subroutines
=39=
=40=     sub scan_pictures {
=41=       for (@_) {
=42=         next if /\.thumb\.jpg$/;
=43=         my $thumb = "$_.thumb.jpg";
=44=         next if -e $thumb;
=45=         my $pnm = &get_pnm($_) or next;
=46=         open PNMTOTHUMB,"| pnmscale -xy 100 100 | ⤶
                   cjpeg -smoo 10 -qual 50 >$thumb"
=47=           or next;
=48=         print PNMTOTHUMB $pnm;
=49=         close PNMTOTHUMB;
=50=         print
=51=           "<tr><td><a href=\"",
=52=           encode_entities(uri_escape($_)),
=53=           "\"><img src=\"",
=54=           encode_entities(uri_escape($thumb)),
=55=           "\" alt=\"[thumbnail of ",
=56=           encode_entities($_),
```

```
=57=            "]\"></a></td><td>",
=58=            int((1023 + -s)/1024),
=59=            "K</td><td>\n  Description not provided\n</td>",
=60=            "</tr>\n";
=61=        }
=62=    }
=63=
=64=    sub get_pnm {
=65=        local $_ = shift;
=66=        for my $cmd ("djpeg $_", "giftopnm $_") {
=67=          my $pnm = `$cmd 2>/dev/null`;
=68=          return $pnm unless $?;
=69=        }
=70=        return;
=71=    }
```

Selectable Downloads via Generated tar-gz Files

Web Techniques, Column 52 (August 2000)

Randal's Note After I published this column, people kept asking, "What about content disposition?" But the trick is that "content disposition" isn't necessarily supported by every browser, but every browser I could play with took the name to save the file from the tail end of the URL. So, this solution is more portable, even if it takes a tiny bit more work.

The "Tom Phoenix" referenced here is, of course, my co-author for my other popular books and senior instructor for Stonehenge.

There are probably tens of thousands of compressed tar archives out there on the wild wild web to download. I can't imagine how much time, even on a high-speed connection, it would take to download them all. But even if the publisher of the information carefully segregated the information into a reasonable bundle, sometimes I really want only part of the data. However, I'm forced to download the entire thing (perhaps over a slow connection in a hotel room, as I often am), just to discard the parts I don't want.

That is, unless the publisher of the data provided a way to build a custom compressed archive, with only the files or directories that I choose. And that's what we have for this month: a CGI program that lets a user choose first a distribution, and then individual files from that distribution, on an item-by-item basis. Once the choice is made, a specific .tar.gz file is made just for that user. And my creation is in Listing 4-13.

This month's column idea was suggested by fellow Stonehenge Perl trainer and Usenet poster extraordinaire, the one and only Tom Phoenix (rootbeer@redcat.com), based on similar code he wrote for me to handle the downloads of exercise data and answers for our on-site training classes. I wrote this code from scratch, though, so if it isn't exactly what he was suggesting, that's my fault.

Line 1 would have had the preferred -Tw flags after the path to Perl, but I ran into unavoidable problems with both taint mode and warnings. First, the standard File::Find module in the distribution is not "taint-safe," so that's a loser. (I think this was corrected in Perl 5.6, but I haven't started using that version on my production site yet.) Second, I'm using two variables from File::Find, and with warnings enabled, I get the ugly "used only once" warning—annoying at best.

Line 2 turns on compiler restrictions, forcing me to declare my variables (no use of a default package), disabling barewords (no "Perl poetry mode") and symbolic references (no variables that contain other variable names).

Line 3 unbuffers STDOUT, ensuring that any CGI header I've generated appears before any program I fork, needed here for the *tar* launch.

Line 5 pulls in the standard CGI::Pretty module, which has the same parameters as CGI.pm, but generates nicely indented HTML. It's a little slower to run, but the HTML was fairly small from this program, and I wanted to be able to read it more easily. The :standard parameter generates the function shortcuts, rather than requiring us to use the object-oriented interface, which seems to involve a lot more typing for not a lot of real gain.

Line 6 pulls in one of my favorite modules, CGI::Carp (also found in any recent standard Perl distribution). Here, I'm redirecting any fatal runtime errors to the browser, rather than having to hunt around for them in the web error log. *Please note* that this is a potential security hole, as it reveals sensitive information to any random user out there on the net. So, don't use this in production code (but you aren't supposed to be using my programs as-is for production anyway).

Line 7 sets the PATH environment variable to something that doesn't trip up tainting or permit additional security holes. Note that *tar* needs to be found in one of these directories.

Line 11 forms the only configurable part of this code. Here, I'm specifying the directory in which I'm storing the distributions. Subdirectories of this directory define particular distributions and must not begin with a dot or a dash. (So a directory named with Morse code would definitely be forbidden.) As a security precaution, symbolic links will not be listed, for either directories or files, so the data must really live below this directory.

Line 15 sets our current directory to the top-level directory. Although we die if something breaks, this will merely trigger CGI::Carp to spit the error message out to the browser. In production code, this death should send a simple, innocuous "something broke" message to the browser, and a detailed message either logged or perhaps emailed to the webmaster.

Now, the rest of the program is "upside down," so I'll describe it from back to front.

Lines 58 to 70 get executed on the first call to this script. Here, we generate the list of distributions.

Lines 60 generates the HTTP header and the HTML header (including the message for the title bar, used when a bookmark is made). Line 61 gives the first text inside the browser window.

Lines 63 through 65 locate the distributions. We read the "dot" directory (our current directory), looking for names that don't begin with a dot or dash and are a directory but not by being a symlink to the directory. For consistency, they'll be sorted, regardless of the unpredictable order in which they're returned from readdir.

Lines 66 to 69 generate a selection form, in the layout of a radio_group. Line 66 generates the FORM tag, with an action equal to the URL of this script (defaulting the method to POST). Line 67 generates a single-column table with one or more radio buttons in a group. The group uses the same name for each form element name, but a different value. The user will select one of these items, sent to us in the dist parameter upon clicking the submit button created in line 68.

One fun feature of CGI.pm is that the list of values used in line 67 for the @names will automatically be HTML-entity-escaped, meaning that < will already be escaped to <, and so on. And, of course, the browser will re-escape the information as we come back the other way, which will be redecoded by CGI.pm on the reply. So it doesn't matter what the directory names are! For testing, I used a name that contained both less-thans and spaces, and it worked just fine. Thanks, Lincoln!

So, once a distribution has been selected, we return back to the script, and the stuff in the second pass (lines 26 to 56) gets invoked. This is detected by a nonfalse value in $dist created in line 28.

Line 29 examines the value of $dist to ensure that it is a sane distribution. Even though we give the user a choice of valid directory names, we must distrust the value returned because it is trivial to fake *any* return value, possibly giving the user access to formerly restricted files. So, the first check is to ensure that it's a name that doesn't start with dash or dot, and does not consist of any slashes. Next, it has to be a directory, and finally, it has to not be a symlink to a directory, but an actual directory.

If that's all OK, we copy $1 into $dist, to untaint it. I did this before I had to turn off taint checking because of File::Find's displeasing behavior.

Speaking of which, we pull in File::Find in line 32. I do this as a require so that I don't load all that unneeded code on the first and third passes. The downside of this is that File::Find::find is not imported, so I have to call it explicitly in line 34. Line 33 sets up the @names array, stuffed with appropriate names in line 37. (Sorry for the forward/backward references there, but that's how they match up.)

So, find is called in lines 34 though 38, looking at all the pathnames below $dist, which is in turn below the current directory. Line 36 forces any names that begin with a dash or a dot to be ignored, and further to ensure that any subdirectories that begin with a dash or a dot are not examined. This is achieved by setting the $prune variable to true, notifying File::Find::find that we don't want to descend into here. Line 37 puts the full pathname (relative to the top-level directory) into @names if it is a file and not a symlink.

Once we have the names, we start dumping the CGI response back in line 39. Line 42 begins the form, generating a self-referencing URL with a slight twist. If the CGI script is invoked as /cgi/getdist, we set the action URL to /cgi/getdist/nnnnnnnnn.tar.gz, where nnnnnnnnn is a numeric value based on the epoch time (increasing by one each second, nine digits as I write this, rolling over to ten digits in early September 2001).

The trailing name will be ignored by the script, but when the invocation generates the compressed tar archive, the browser will likely download the file to this name (or at least default to it). This will uniquely identify this download, making it unlikely to conflict with any other file in the user's download directory.

Next, lines 44 to 52 display a table (used for layout), headed up by (often bolded) column titles for the name, size, and last modification date and time. Each name from @names is passed through the map to generate one row. Similar checkbox items with identical parameter names, but differing return values, are generated. The checkbox defaults to "on," defined by the 1 in line 49. Line 50 computes the file size using -s, and line 51 gets the modification time converted as a human-readable string.

And when the submit button generated in line 53 is clicked, we come back to this same script in final pass, handled in lines 19 through 24. This is by far the easiest, as we merely need to extract the @names from the response checkboxes that had been selected, then dump out an appropriate MIME header (line 20), verify the names aren't trying to select /etc/passwd or anything else scary (line 21), and then let *tar* do all the hard work. I'm presuming a GNU tar here that can take a z flag to handle the compression. If you have to use a *gzip* in front of a non-GNU tar, this step gets slightly more complicated, or you can just forgo the compression.

Or if you're feeling quite adventurous, you can use the Archive::Tar and Compress::Zlib (both found in the CPAN) to generate the compressed archive without using an external program. (Perhaps I'll do that in a future column.)

And that's all there is to it! To start making your custom-selected compressed tar archives, stick your distributions below the configured top-level directory, and link to the CGI URL from some convenient page.

The technique of generating a compressed tar archive on the fly can also be applied to a "shopping cart" strategy. You can have many pages with different filenames on them, selected or omitted by the user, and maintain the list either as hidden fields in the forms on the client side or via some session ID technique on the server side. Then, when you're ready to generate the archive, be sure to invoke the downloading CGI URL with appropriate extra path information so that the download name is set appropriately. Be sure to revalidate all the requested names; don't let bad guys grab arbitrary files this way.

Tom Phoenix got famous (again) by suggesting this month's column idea. If you have some snippet of an idea that can be handled by 30 to 300 lines of Perl, drop me a note. If I use your idea, you'll be famous! Until next time, enjoy!

Listing 4-13

```
=1=     #!/usr/bin/perl
=2=     use strict;
=3=     $|++;
=4=
=5=     use CGI::Pretty ":standard";
=6=     use CGI::Carp qw(fatalsToBrowser); # only for debugging
=7=     $ENV{PATH} = "/bin:/usr/bin:/usr/local/bin";
=8=
=9=     ## CONFIG
=10=
=11=    my $topdir = "/home/merlyn/Web/Bundle";
=12=
=13=    ## END CONFIG
=14=
=15=    chdir $topdir or die "Cannot chdir: $!";
=16=
=17=    ## final pass
=18=
=19=    if (my @names = param('names')) {
=20=      print header("application/x-tar-gzip");
=21=      @names = grep !(/^\// or grep /^[-.]/, split /\//), @names;
```

```
=22=        exec "tar", "cfz", "-", @names if @names;
=23=        die "cannot exec tar: $!";
=24=      }
=25=
=26=      ## second pass
=27=
=28=      if (my $dist = param('dist')) {
=29=        $dist =~ / ^ (?! [-.]) ([^\/]+) $ /x and -d $dist and not -l↵
                    $dist or die "bad dist";
=30=        $dist = $1;                  # now untainted
=31=
=32=        require File::Find;
=33=        my @names;
=34=        File::Find::find
=35=            (sub {
=36=                return $File::Find::prune = 1 if /^(-|\..)/s;
=37=                push @names, $File::Find::name if -f and not -l;
=38=            }, $dist);
=39=        print header, start_html("Download a distribution");
=40=        print h1("Select your items within this distribution");
=41=
=42=        print start_form(-action => url()."/".time().".tar.gz");
=43=        print p("Select your items:");
=44=        print
=45=          table({cellspacing => 0, cellpadding => 2, border => 0},
=46=                Tr(th(["Filename",
=47=                       "Size",
=48=                       "Last modified"])),
=49=                map Tr(td([checkbox("names", 1, $_, $_),
=50=                           sprintf("%dK", (1023 + -s)/1024),
=51=                           scalar(localtime +(stat)[9])])),
=52=                @names);
=53=        print submit;
=54=        print end_form, end_html;
=55=        exit 0;
=56=      }
=57=
=58=      ## first pass
=59=
=60=      print header, start_html("Download a distribution");
=61=      print h1("Select your distribution");
=62=
=63=      opendir DOT, "." or die "Cannot opendir: $!";
=64=      my @names = sort grep !/^[-.]/ && -d && ! -l, readdir DOT;
=65=      closedir DOT;
=66=      print start_form, p("Select your distribution:");
=67=      print radio_group(-name => "dist", -values =>↵
```

```
                \@names, -columns => 1);
=68=    print submit;
=69=    print end_form, end_html;
=70=    exit 0;
```

Getting One-Click Processing

Web Techniques, Column 64 (August 2001)

■**Randal's Note**   I *still* haven't seen anything better to do this than my proposed solution in the many years since I wrote and published this.

One thing that seems to plague many web programmers is how to get "one-click" processing. No, I'm not talking about Amazon's patented technology. I'm talking about that annoyance when a user clicks the submit button two or three times before the response begins to change the browser, and you end up with a form that's been submitted multiple times.

This is no big deal if the request is idempotent—that is, a repeated request generates a consistent result and doesn't change the state of the world incrementally. However, many form submissions do indeed intend to change the state of the world somehow. For example, a shopping cart will have a "buy this item" button, and multiple clicks might end up filling up the cart with many copies of an item of which a user wants only one. Or a survey form ends up voting multiple times for a particular choice. Or a guestbook or chat room gets multiple copies of a message.

The solution often given in the communities I participate in often includes some mention of JavaScript. I'm not a big fan of having any mandatory functionality in JavaScript; in fact, I'm a rather vocal opponent. No offense to the JavaScript people, but more people these days than ever before are turning JavaScript off, thanks to the repeated CERT warnings and security holes, not to mention those evil sites that pop up windows with advertising. And because of the security concerns, more companies are installing firewalls that *strip* the JavaScript at the corporate gateway as a protection against malice, so it isn't even a choice of the user to "please enable your JavaScript" in many cases.

But luckily, there's a simple server-side solution that works with standard HTML. Simply include a unique serial number as you generate the form, and note that serial number in a lightweight server-side database. When the form is submitted, verify that the serial number is still in the database and, if so, process the form and remove the serial number. If the serial number is absent, redirect the user back to the form fill-out page, or on to the next step if needed, since you've already processed the form.

Although this technique requires a bit of work, it's actually rather painless to implement, adding maybe 25 lines of Perl code to your application.

But I also decided to take this a bit further. Sometimes when a script that both processes a form and handles its response is updated, a new field might be added or the meaning for an existing field might be altered. But if there's a form out there already being filled out, you'll end up with parameter names that don't quite fit, but you don't know it.

So as long as we're remembering via a hidden field that this form was generated recently, let's also remember the modification time of the script itself, and reject any invocations originally generated by an older version of the script! Sure, it's a bit annoying to the users, but much better than the annoyance of subtle (or dangerous) mismatches of parameter data.

In particular, we'll be noting three things from `stat`: the device number, the inode number, and the `ctime` value. A script cannot change without altering at least the last item (unless it changes twice within one second), so this is pretty robust.

And the program that does all of this is presented in Listing 4-14.

Lines 1 through 3 start nearly every CGI program I write, turning on taint checking, warnings, and compiler restrictions, and unbuffering standard output.

Line 5 pulls in the `CGI.pm` module, with all of the functions imported into the current (main) namespace.

Lines 7 though 19 set up the lightweight database. I'm using the very slick `File::Cache` module found in the CPAN, which stores temporary information with expiration times into `/tmp` in a nice controlled way. The author is updating this module to a generic architecture called `Cache::Cache`, but unfortunately a stable version of that module isn't ready as I'm writing this column.

Lines 10 through 14 connect up with the "database." By default, the serial numbers will expire in one hour, which should be enough time for an unprocessed form to be filled out and still considered valid. Note that this time is significant only for forms that are presented to the user but never submitted, thus accumulating entries in the database. Forms that are properly submitted clear the serial number from the database immediately.

Lines 16 through 19 handle the occasional purging of the old entries. Once an hour, some lucky dog gets to paw through the entries to find the ones that have gone past their expiry. We don't do this on every open or every cache update (the default modes provided by `File::Cache`), because it's really more work than it needs to be. I've asked the author of `File::Cache` to add this feature, and he's added this to `Cache::Cache` for me as a configuration option, rather than my having to code this explicitly. Joy.

Line 21 computes a "script ID": the string that will change only when the script is edited. Calling `stat` on Perl's `$0` gets the info for the current script, from which we select the device, inode, and ctime numbers, which are then joined into a single string.

Line 23 prints the HTTP/CGI header, the HTML header, and an `H1` header.

Lines 25 to 48 handle the invocation of the script when parameters are present, like in response to a form action. Since that's second, I'll come back to these in a moment.

Lines 50 to 68 handle the initial invocation of the script, where we generate the form with a nice unique serial number.

First, we get a serial number (which I'm calling `session` here because I cut and pasted this code from another program where it was the session) in lines 53 to 55. I'll shove it in as a parameter so that we can generate the hidden parameter easily as a "sticky" field. I'm using the MD5 algorithm from `Apache::Session`, which is apparently good enough for them, so it's good enough for me, although if you're really paranoid you should check out `Math::TrulyRandom` in the CPAN.

Line 58 updates the database (cache) by creating an entry keyed by the session (serial) ID. The value is set to the script ID, which we'll verify when the form is submitted to ensure that the same script that generated the form also is processing the form.

Lines 61 to 68 are your standard boring form stuff. In fact, I just copied this from the first few lines of CGI.pm's documentation. The only interesting thing I'm doing here is that I wanted a pop-up menu to also have an "other" entry, and I read about this trick recently. Simply make a textfield with the same name as the pop-up menu, and then process them together as a multi-valued field. We'll see how that works in a moment.

Note that the hidden field is included as part of the form in line 67. We'll be looking for that on the response to accept the form. And as long as we're looking down here, line 72 prints the end of the HTML whether we're printing out the form or responding to it.

OK, back up to the form response part, starting in line 26. First, line 30 fetches that hidden serial number in the session parameter.

If that's defined, lines 31 to 34 look for the session number in the database (cache). If it's found, we remove it, thus preventing any other submission with the same session key. There's a small race condition here, but I've tried to keep these pretty close together to minimize the window. If you're concerned about that, replace the File::Cache database with a database that can handle atomic test and update.

Further, the value of that database entry must also match the script ID of the current script. If not, we've updated the script after the form was generated, and we thus will reject the form data as well.

But if that all matches up (first invocation of valid session and script IDs match), then it's time to really process the data, starting in line 37.

Lines 39 and 40 grab the name, setting it to (Unspecified) if it wasn't there or was empty.

Line 41 grabs the color. Now recall that there are actually two fields called color in the form: the pop-up menu and the text field following it. The result from param('color') will most likely be a two-element list. Using the grep, we remove -other- if it's present. Thus, if a color was selected on the pop-up, we now have that color plus perhaps whatever was typed in the box, but if -other- was selected, then we have just the value of the other box. We'll save the first element of that result into $color. And thus, with a bit of magic, we've got the pop-up color, unless it's -other-, in which case we've got the text field.

This all presumes that browsers return the values in the order specified on the form. That's merely a recommendation, if I recall, and a convention, so things could get messed up. (Please write me if you know otherwise, and I'll follow up in a future column!)

And once we've got the values, we "process" the data simply by sending it back out to the screen in a nice way in lines 43 and 44. Of course, in a real application, this is where the real meat would be. The HTML of the values are escaped, because a user might have less-thans or ampersands in their name or color, and we wouldn't want that to mess up the output.

Lines 46 and 47 are reached when a form is submitted without the proper session ID. So this means that either someone doubled up on the submit button quickly, or clicked reload on the form data, or the form was from more than an hour ago, or the form was generated by a prior version of this script or just faked up as a URL somewhere. In this case, we inform the user and provide a link to start over.

And there you have it. "One-click" (no trademark here) processing, along with solving a couple of other interesting issues about pop-up forms and script maintenance. Until next time, enjoy!

Listing 4-14

```perl
=1=     #!/usr/bin/perl -Tw
=2=     use strict;
=3=     $|++;
=4=
=5=     use CGI qw(:all);
=6=
=7=     ## set up the cache
=8=
=9=     use File::Cache;
=10=    my $cache = File::Cache->new({namespace => 'surveyonce',
=11=                                  username => 'nobody',
=12=                                  filemode => 0666,
=13=                                  expires_in => 3600, # one hour
=14=                                 });
=15=
=16=    unless ($cache->get(" _purge_ ")) { # cleanup?
=17=      $cache->purge;
=18=      $cache->set(" _purge_ ", 1);
=19=    }
=20=
=21=    my $SCRIPT_ID = join ".", (stat $0)[0,1,10];
=22=
=23=    print header, start_html("Survey"), h1("Survey");
=24=
=25=    if (param) {
=26=      ## returning with form data
=27=
=28=      ## verify first submit of this form data,
=29=      ## and from the form generated by this particular script only
=30=      my $session = param('session');
=31=      if (defined $session and do {
=32=        my $id = $cache->get($session);
=33=        $cache->remove($session);   # let this be the only one
=34=        $id and $id eq $SCRIPT_ID;
=35=      }) {
=36=        ## good session, process form data
=37=        print h2("Thank you");
=38=        print "Your information has been processed.";
=39=        my $name = param('name');
=40=        $name = "(Unspecified)" unless defined $name and length $name;
=41=        my ($color) = grep $_ ne '-other-', param('color');
=42=        $color = "(Unspecified)" unless defined⏎
                   $color and length $color;
=43=        print p, "Your name is ", b(escapeHTML($name));
=44=        print " and your favorite color is ",⏎
```

```
           b(escapeHTML($color)), ".";
=45=       } else {
=46=         print h2("Error"), "Hmm, I can't process your input.  Please ";
=47=         print a({href => script_name()}, "start over"),".";
=48=       }
=49=     } else {
=50=       ## initial invocation -- print form
=51=
=52=       ## get unique non-guessable stamp for this form
=53=       require MD5;
=54=       param('session',
=55=             my $session = MD5->hexhash(MD5-↩
                      >hexhash(time.{}.rand().$$)));
=56=
=57=       ## store session key in cache
=58=       $cache->set($session, $SCRIPT_ID);
=59=
=60=       ## print form
=61=       print hr, start_form;
=62=       print "What's your name? ",textfield('name'), br;
=63=       print "What's your favorite color? ";
=64=       print popup_menu(-name=>'color',
=65=         -values=>[qw(-other- red orange yellow green blue purple)]);
=66=       print " if -other-: ", textfield('color'), br;
=67=       print hidden('session');
=68=       print submit, end_form, hr;
=69=
=70=     }
=71=
=72=     print end_html;
```

Customer Surveys and Writing XML

Web Techniques, Column 67 (November 2001)

Within the realm of good customer service, getting feedback and responding to it in a timely manner is important. A web form is a simple way to do this, but there's all that nagging stuff about validating the form fields and writing the data in a nice clean way for later processing.

Well, I gave that task a little thought, and decided that I could use a table-driven survey form generator, similar to the approach I took in this column in the past. (See "Programming in Perl," August 1999.) But that approach didn't go far enough, because it didn't permit me to validate the form responses, so I thought about how to add some hooks to handle that when needed.

Also, I started by thinking that I was going to write the survey forms by appending to a flat file (properly flocked so that we get clean writes). But as I pondered the format in which to save the form fields, it dawned on me that a simple XML structure would provide the right clues as to which field went with which value and the ability to escape special appropriate characters. As I kept working on that, I realized that this would also mean that standard XML tools could be used for data transformation and reduction, and I was quickly convinced that I'd hit pay dirt. Conveniently, the XML::Simple module in the CPAN permits me to construct a typical hash/arrayref tree, and worry about the XML conversion at the last minute (if ever).

And the result is in Listing 4-15.

Lines 1 through 3 begin nearly every CGI program I write, turning on taint checking, warnings, and compiler restrictions, and disabling the buffering of standard output.

Line 5 pulls in Lincoln Stein's CGI.pm module, along with all of the included shortcuts. Line 6 enables CGI errors to be shown on the browser—very handy while debugging, but *a security leak* if enabled in production, so remember to remove something like this before deploying this code. Line 7 defines the constants needed for file locking.

The configurable parts begin in line 9. Line 11 is the location of the ever-growing output file. This file needs to be writable by the web userid, unless this script is running set-uid.

Line 13 begins the questions for this survey. Each element of @QUESTIONS is an arrayref, pointing at an array containing (in order): the human-readable label for the question, the param name, the CGI.pm shortcut to create the form field, an arrayref containing any optional parameters for that shortcut (other than name, which is supplied automatically), and option-ally a coderef of a subroutine to run to validate this field and a flag indicating that multiple response elements for this field are permitted. These fields are discussed in detail when we look at the code that examines them.

Line 62 displays the CGI/HTTP header and the beginning of the HTML, including a page title, as well as a first-order header indicating the same within the window.

Lines 64 to 95 handle any potential response, inside an eval block so that we can use a die within to abort this part of the operation early and cleanly. If the code executes to its com-pletion, there's nothing to say but "thank you," handled in lines 108 to 110.

Otherwise, we display the form, annotated as indicated by the die return value (captured in line 96) in lines 97 to 107. Let's look at that first. Line 98 extracts a prefix from the error mes-sage that has been coded to contain the field name (if any) that has been found to be in error, into the $flag variable. We'll use this to turn that row pink in the output.

The remaining error message is displayed in line 99, above the form, which also begins this line.

Lines 100 to 106 print a table to position the elements of the form. Each row consists of two cells: the label on the left and the form field on the right. The rows are constructed by scanning through the elements of @QUESTIONS, extracting the label, param name, shortcut function, and any additional arguments (in line 102). The row is turned pink if the param name is equal to the flagged line (line 103). The left cell (label) is generated as a TH element in line 104, with an appropriate alignment.

But the real fun comes in line 105, which looks deceptively simple. The $func variable contains a coderef for a CGI.pm form field shortcut, such as textfield or popup_menu. Since all of these shortcuts take a named argument list including the name of the param as name, we can call them all the same way, passing the param name for this field, followed by any addi-tional arguments obtained by dereferencing the $opts variable. These additional arguments can be used to override default values for width and height, or provide the items for a radio button group. Simple but extremely powerful. (I actually danced a little happy jig for a few moments when I got this part of it figured out.)

The form is displayed on the very first invocation of this program, and on any subsequent invocations when $error was set. The form response comes back to this script, but now we go back to line 65 to see where it goes from there.

Line 65 creates a hash of arrayrefs, keyed by a param name, and values of all the param values for that param name. If there are no params provided (such as on the first invocation of this script), the die in line 66 aborts this upper block and defines the introductory message to show above the empty form as described earlier.

If we have at least some form data, then lines 68 to 77 process that data, one field at a time. Each form question arrayref is expanded into its fields: the label, param name, shortcut function, shortcut additional options, and the most important parts for this step, the coderef of the validator, and a multivalue-permitted flag.

Line 70 pulls out the param values for the param name given in $name. Lines 71 and 72 reject any multivalued parameter that has not been permitted to be multivalued. This is probably as a result of someone faking up a form submission, and not as a result of a normal operation.

After determining that a single-valued parameter is not somehow multivalued, the next step is to verify the presence of a specific validator in line 73. If this validator is not present, then the field is presumed valid no matter what value has been provided (useful with optional fields, for example).

Line 74 sets up a temporary value for $_ to either a scalar containing the field value or a reference to the list of field values if a multivalued parameter is permitted. I found this easier for the validators to execute regular expressions against a "regional" $_ value rather than always having to shift @_ or access $_[0]. Line 75 executes the validator, passing it a reference to the %results hash for those rare times when the validity of one field depends on the state of another.

If the validator runs to completion, then the $@ is noticed as being unset in line 76, and we go on to the next field. However, if the validator dies, the error string is prepended with the name of the current field, bracketed by newlines, which are then noticed by the form-printing routine as the field name of the line to be flagged in pink. See, it all fits together!

If we run all the validators, and everything looks good, we continue on down to line 81, which begins another inner eval block, this time just to catch errors that we don't expect. It'd be bad to have an unexpected error now show up as a message above an empty form! This block of code dumps the data as XML to a log file.

Line 83 pulls in the XML::Simple module (found in the CPAN). We don't do this on every hit, because there's a bit of unneeded expense on the invocations that won't even be thinking about XML.

Line 84 converts the %results hash into a valid XML textstream, reflecting the responses in a way that we can extract needed information using any of the popular XML processors. Lines 85 through 88 append this textstream to the $DATAFILE file, locking the file for exclusive access during the write.

For debugging purposes, I also took the XML in line 91 and encoded it for HTML display, wrapped it in a pre shortcut, and put it in a nice boxed single-cell table. This was great while I was testing, to ensure that the resulting XML for a particular form was valid as well as being parseable (and it showed off the XML for the people helping me test the script). Obviously a real program wouldn't do this.

Line 93 takes any (unexpected) error resulting from the eval block in lines 81 to 92 and dumps it to STDERR, just as if the eval block were not there.

And that wraps up the description of the main logic of the program, but a lot of this program lives in the @QUESTIONS data structure, so let's go back and examine that in more detail now.

The first field in line 15 is a simple text field, named name, with an appropriate label, and optional parameters specifying an onscreen size of 60. The resulting construct acts as if we had directly invoked

```
textfield(-name => 'name', size => 60);
```

to generate the text field. Perfect.

Lines 16 to 19 set up the second field (called email), also a text field with a size of 60. However, I've also included a validation subroutine. When the form is submitted, the value of the form field appears in $_ (which can never be an arrayref, because we haven't enabled this as a multivalue field). Thus, the two regular expressions in line 18 that examine $_ are testing the proper data. (For simplicity, I decided that a nonblank email field that didn't contain an @ is not a valid email address.) If the test fails, the die aborts this check, as well as the overall validation pass, causing this form row to be highlighted in pink upon resubmission.

Lines 20 to 23 create a pop-up menu. The values are given in line 21, which will also set the default to the first item. On form submission, we ensure that this is *not* the chosen one, and kick it back to the user if so.

Line 24 is another simple text field, with a different width just to show some variety. Lines 25 to 28 similarly are another pop-up menu.

Lines 29 to 42 form two related fields. First, we have a checkbox group that may return multiple values selected simultaneously (flagged as the 1 in line 34). These are organized in a single column (line 33). Next, if the checkbox item for Other is selected, we have a textarea for the customer to fill out as to the precise nature of "other."

There's no validation for the checkbox group; however, we need ensure that there's some data in the "other" description if Other is picked, and this is handled in lines 38 to 41. We use the first (and only) parameter passed into the subroutine, which is a reference to the entire %results hash. Digging down through there, if we see that Other is picked for the checkbox group above, then we need to also have a nonempty value for this textarea, and fail otherwise. Most fields won't have such a strong coupling: this is the exception, not the rule, and I'm comfortable with just letting the one subroutine paw through the master data to ensure that the world is sane. If you have ideas for a cleaner and yet flexible interface, let me know.

Just to show a variety of widgets, I include a radio group for the field defined in lines 43 to 48, and a scrolling list in lines 49 to 56. The scrolling list defaults to the first item, including the word Choose. The validation subroutine in line 54 ensures that this is *not* one of the actual chosen items, meaning the customer had not even looked at this field (or else had reset it, but I can't see why someone would have done that). And finally, line 57 defines a plain textarea.

And there you have it. A fairly generic survey form, validating the various form fields in a table-driven manner, along with an XML output module so we can transform or summarize the data using a wide array of XML processing tools. Now there's no excuse for you not to get customer feedback. Until next time, enjoy!

Listing 4-15

```
=1=     #!/usr/bin/perl -Tw
=2=     use strict;
=3=     $|++;
=4=
=5=     use CGI qw(:all);
=6=     use CGI::Carp qw(fatalsToBrowser);
=7=     use Fcntl ':flock'; # import LOCK_* constants
=8=
=9=     ## CONFIG
=10=
=11=    my $DATAFILE = "/home/merlyn/Web/customer_survey-data";
=12=
=13=    my @QUESTIONS =
=14=      (
=15=        ['Name (optional)', 'name', \&textfield, [qw(size 60)]],
=16=        ['Email (optional)', 'email', \&textfield, [qw(size 60)],
=17=         sub { die "Please include a full email address!\n"
=18=                 if /\S/ and not /\@/ },
=19=        ],
=20=        ['Product', 'product', \&popup_menu,
=21=         [values => ['Please Choose One', 'thx-1138', 'hal 9000']],
=22=         sub { die "Please choose a product!\n" if /choose/i },
=23=        ],
=24=        ['Model (if applicable)', 'model', \&textfield, [qw(size 30)]],
=25=        ['Overall impression', 'overall', \&popup_menu,
=26=         [values => [''Please Choose One', qw(Excellent Good Fair
                 Poor)]],
=27=         sub { die "Please choose an impression!\n" if /choose/i },
=28=        ],
=29=        [''Reason for product choice (choose all that are applicable)',
=30=         ''chose_because',                # referenced below
=31=         \&checkbox_group,
=32=         [values => [qw(Price Salesman Quality↵
                 Performance Reliability Other)],
=33=          cols => 1],
=34=         undef, 1
=35=        ],
=36=        [''Other reason for product choice (if applicable)',↵
                 ''chose_because_other',
=37=         \&textarea, [qw(rows 2 columns 60)],
=38=         sub {
=39=           die "Please give your other reason...\n" if not /\S/
=40=             and grep /other/i, @{shift->{chose_because}};
=41=         },
=42=        ],
```

```
=43=        ['Quality', 'quality', \&radio_group,
=44=         [values => ['Please Choose One', qw(Excellent Good Fair Poor)],
=45=          cols => 1,
=46=         ],
=47=         sub { die "Please choose a quality!\n" if /choose/i },
=48=        ],
=49=        ['Area of use (choose all that apply)', 'area', \&scrolling_list,
=50=         [values => ['Please Choose One Or More',⏎
                   qw(Home School Office)],
=51=          size => 4,
=52=          multiple => 'true',
=53=         ],
=54=         sub { die "Please choose an area!\n" unless
             grep !/choose/i, @$_ },
=55=         1,
=56=        ],
=57=        ['Comments', 'comments', \&textarea, [qw(rows 10 columns 50)]],
=58=       );
=59=
=60=   ## END CONFIG
=61=
=62=   print header, start_html("Customer Survey"), h1("Customer Survey");
=63=
=64=   eval {
=65=     my %results = map { $_ => [param($_)] } param;
=66=     die "Please fill out this form...\n" unless %results;
=67=
=68=     for (@QUESTIONS) {
=69=       my ($label, $name, $func, $opts, $validator, $multi) = @$_;
=70=       my @values = @{$results{$name} || []};
=71=       die "\n$name\nToo many values, try again...\n"
=72=         if @values > 1 and not $multi;
=73=       next unless $validator and ref $validator eq "CODE";
=74=       local $_ = $multi ? \@values : $values[0];
=75=       eval { $validator->(\%results) };
=76=       die "\n$name\n$@" if $@;
=77=     }
=78=
=79=     ## made it past the errors, so save it
=80=
=81=     eval {
=82=       ## so that these don't trigger outer error
=83=       require XML::Simple;
=84=       my $out = XML::Simple::XMLout(\%results);
=85=       open OUT, ">>$DATAFILE" or die "Cannot append to $DATAFILE: $!";
=86=       flock OUT, LOCK_EX;
=87=       print OUT $out;
```

```
=88=        close OUT;                      # and release lock
=89=
=90=        ## DEBUG
=91=        print table({border => 1}, Tr(td(pre(escapeHTML($out)))));
=92=      };
=93=    print STDERR $@ if $@;           # if that last thing errored
=94=
=95=  };
=96=  my $error = $@;
=97=  if ($error) {
=98=    my $flag = ($error =~ s/^\n(\S+)\n//) ? $1 : "";
=99=    print p($error), start_form;
=100=   print table({border => 0, colspacing => 0, colpadding => 2},
=101=              map {
=102=                  my($label, $name, $func, $opts) = @$_;
=103=                  Tr({$name eq $flag ? (bgcolor => '#ffcccc') : ()},
=104=                      th({align => 'right', valign => 'top'}, $label),
=105=                      td($func->(-name => $name, @$opts)));
=106=              } @QUESTIONS);
=107=   print submit, end_form;
=108= } else {
=109=   print p("Thank you!");
=110= }
=111= print end_html;
```

## CHAPTER 5

The Webmaster's Toolkit

Reducing Log Files to Summary Reports

Unix Review, Column 15 (July 1997)

Randal's Note I used a program similar to this in the rewrite of our PROM course, which became the basis of the Alpaca book, *Learning Perl Objects, References & Modules* (O'Reilly, 2003).

The acronym *Perl* was originally coined to represent *Practical Extraction and Report Language*. Although Perl has expanded in application areas and grown in capability wildly in the nearly ten years of its life, the basics of getting a report constructed from extracted data are still the basis for many Perl programming problems.

Let's take a look at a typical problem: analyzing a log file. Log files get created all over the place these days. For example, login/logout records, command invocations, file transfers, mail daemons, gopher servers, and yes, the ever-increasing use of web servers all generate lines and lines and pages of seemingly unending streams of data. Each individual transaction is probably not worth examining (unless you've had a security violation recently), but the reduction of this data to somewhat meaningful summary reports is an increasingly common task.

Let's look at a hypothetical "file transfer log" that looks like so:

```
fred wilma 08:50 730
barney betty 06:15 190
betty barney 22:27 993
barney wilma 23:47 504
fred wilma 04:29 836
betty betty 14:37 738
wilma barney 18:47 825
```

and consists of four space-separated columns containing the source host, destination host, 24-hour clock time, and number of bytes transferred.

I generated some sample data with a little test program:

```
my @hosts = qw(fred barney betty wilma);
srand;
sub randhost { $hosts[rand @hosts]; }
```

```
for (my $n = 0; $n <= 999; $n++) {
    printf
        "%s %s %02d:%02d %d\n",
        randhost, randhost, rand(24), rand(60), rand(1000);
}
```

which will spit out the proper fields. Adjust the 999 to adjust the size of the output. (This program uses the 5.004 syntax with very flexible placement of my().... If you get errors on older versions of Perl version 5, remove the my() keywords.)

So, now we have some relatively boring data. Let's see how to generate some typical reports. All reports will require that the data be parsed into columns, common for each of the parsing programs. So, let's get that out of the way first.

A skeleton parsing program looks like this:

```
while (<>) {
    my ($from, $to, $hh, $mm, $bytes) =
        /^(\S+) (\S+) (\d+):(\d+) (\d+)$/
            or (warn "bad format on line $.: $_"), next;
        # accumulate
}
# print the result here
```

If there were multiple formats in the file, the failed regular expression match could go on to try other combinations. This is useful when there are variations of field data.

So far, the program parses the data, but doesn't accumulate the numbers or print the results. Let's start with something simple: count the total bytes transferred and the number of transfer jobs

```
# for accumulate:
$total_bytes += $bytes;
$jobs++;
```

which goes inside the loop, and then to print it out, outside the loop

```
# for print:
print "total bytes = $total_bytes, jobs = $jobs\n";
```

Well, that wasn't tough. Let's try something a little more interesting. Let's see how many bytes came from each host. We'll do it with a hash, in which the key is the name of the host, and the corresponding value is the total count (and keep track of the job count in a separate hash):

```
# for accumulate:
$from_bytes{$from} += $bytes;
$from_jobs{$from}++;
```

Now to print this, we have to walk a hash to dump it:

```
# for print:
for my $from (sort keys %from_bytes) {
    my $bytes = $from_bytes{$from};
```

```
    my $jobs = $from_jobs{$from};
    print "$from sent $bytes bytes on $jobs jobs\n";
}
```

Here, the keys of %from_bytes are examined, sorted, and then used one at a time to pull out the corresponding values from the two hashes created in parallel. Hey, now we're getting somewhere.

What if we wanted the total bytes transferred, and didn't care whether it was flowing in or out overall? To do this, I use a slick trick of adding the number into two different places in the hash:

```
# for accumulate:
$total_bytes{$from} += $bytes;
$total_bytes{$to} += $bytes;
```

and then we'd walk the %total_bytes hash similar to the previous code:

```
# for print:
for my $host (sort keys %total_bytes) {
    my $bytes = $total_bytes{$host};
    print "$host did $bytes\n";
}
```

Note that if we were computing a "grand total" of bytes, the value would be double here, so be careful when you are doing this. If you wanted to be able to "grand total" this number, one step might be to allocate half of each byte-count to each host, as in:

```
# for accumulate:
$bytes /= 2; # allocation correction
$total_bytes{$from} += $bytes;
$total_bytes{$to} += $bytes;
```

There. Now a grand total of this table will show the same as the grand total of the other table. "How to lie with statistics," I guess.

So far, we have accumulations based on zero data items (the grand total) and based on one data item (like the source host). Can we do accumulations based on two or more data items? Surely, thanks to Perl's ability to have (apparently) nested hashes. Let's look at a two-way table, summarizing all transfers on both the source host and the destination host. That'd look like this:

```
# for accumulate:
$from_to_bytes{$from}{$to} += $bytes;
```

Yeah. That's it! We're now tracking the source and destination hosts. Dumping this data is a little trickier, though. Here's a line-by-line dump for all the combinations of "from" and "to":

```
# for print:
for my $from (sort keys %from_to_bytes) {
    my $second = $from_to_bytes{$from};
    for my $to (sort keys %$second) {
        my $bytes = $second->{$to};
```

```
            print "$from to $to did $bytes\n";
        }
    }
```

Yeah, a little more complicated, because we have to go through the entire matrix. The outer loop walks through all source hosts, grabbing the inner nested hash reference in $second. This inner hash is then walked via the inner loop, yielding the nested data.

The output of this program is a little ugly:

```
[...]
barney to fred did 2792
barney to wilma did 4683
betty to barney did 2333
betty to betty did 2568
[...]
```

so let's clean it up a bit, creating an actual square table. First, we have to compute all possible destination hosts for the column headings:

```
my %to_hosts = ();
for my $from (sort keys %from_to_bytes) {
    my $second = $from_to_bytes{$from};
    my @keys = keys %$second;
    @to_hosts{@keys} = ();
}
my @to_hosts = sort keys %to_hosts;
```

Here, I create a temporary hash called %to_hosts, which serves as a "set." For each of the source hosts, I pull out all the destination hosts into @keys (inside the loop), and then add those members into the "set." The final statement extracts the members of that set into an ordinary array, @to_hosts, which I'll then use for the column headers and keys. The column headers are printed with

```
printf "%10s:", "bytes to";
for (@to_hosts) {
    printf " %10s", $_;
}
print "\n";
```

and then the walk through the matrix actually is a bit simpler than the previous example:

```
for my $from (sort keys %from_to_bytes) {
    printf "%10s:", $from;
    for my $to (@to_hosts) {
        my $bytes = $from_to_bytes{$from}{$to} || "- none -";
        printf " %10s", $bytes;
    }
    print "\n";
}
```

because we don't need to get the keys of the second hash—it's already some part of @to_hosts. The output of this program looks like this:

```
bytes to:    barney    betty     fred    wilma
   barney:     3303     4429     2792     4683
    betty:     2333     2568     3928     1813
     fred:     2416     3542      226     5293
    wilma:     5267     1196     2706     4580
```

There you have it—some sample data-reduction program snippets. Have fun reducing data!

Web Access Logs with DBI

Web Techniques, Column 48 (April 2000)

▉**Randal's Note** Most of this functionality was also available in C<Apache::DBILogger>, but I rolled my own to get the CPU times, which have proved invaluable for finding expensive dynamic page hits.

A few months back, I was flipping through the wonderful *Writing Apache Modules with Perl and C* by Doug MacEachern and fellow *Web Techniques* columnist Lincoln Stein while trying to think of more bells and whistles to throw at my mod_perl-enabled web server for http://PerlTraining.Stonehenge.com. I stumbled across the section that talks about using a database instead of a flat file for the access log. Now, I had just recently upgraded and cleaned up the MySQL database for my ISP, and thought it would be nice to have more advanced statistics and reporting. So, I jumped in.

Now this was quite a jump, because I hadn't even used any of Apache's custom log features. I had a simple NCSA-compatible access log and a few specialized logs in a few directories via SSI loggers. So, I decided to go whole hog the other way. Not only am I logging the usual things (host, user agent, bytes sent, and so on), but I even log the CPU times for each transaction! This lets me see which of my URLs are burning up more CPU so I can figure out ways to cache them better, which is especially important on a machine that is shared with other users.

And the log is being written immediately to a DBI-based MySQL database. The power here is that I can use SQL queries to generate ad-hoc reports on an up-to-the-minute basis, as well as get the general reports canned up into a Perl data structure with relative ease. No more parsing flat files (not that this was much trouble with Perl anyway). The downside is that I'm now burning 1 megabyte per day for storage inside the MySQL database, but my sysadmin said just to let them burn, since disk is cheap.

Part 0: What I Needed to Have Already in Place

First, I needed to have an Apache server with mod_perl installed, including handling of all the phases. This means I said something like EVERYTHING=1 during the configuration (see the mod_perl documentation for details).

Then, I needed to have access to a live MySQL database, with a valid user and password. That's documented somewhat fuzzily in the MySQL documentation and a little clearer in the *MySQL & mSQL* book from O'Reilly and Associates.

Third, I needed to have the DBI modules installed, along with Apache::DBI adaptor. The CPAN holds these, and they're relatively painless to install.

Finally, I had to have the DBD::mysql modules installed, again from the CPAN. This was somewhat painless to install, although the installation asks a lot of questions and wants a live MySQL database to do testing, and doesn't listen to the username and password that I gave it for all the testing steps.

Part 1: Gathering the Statistics

In order to have statistics to analyze, we have to have Apache generate them. Based on the code I saw in Doug and Lincoln's book, I wrote my DBI logger, presented in Listing 5-1.

Line 1 sets up the unique package for this handler. I prefix all my local packages with Stonehenge:: (my company name) to completely distinguish them from any distribution. Line 2 enables the normal compiler restrictions. Line 4 is a comment to remind me that this handler is meant to be a PerlInitHandler, the first possible phase under which we can take control for each request.

Lines 8 through 10 pull in some useful modules for this handler. Apache::Constants gives us useful values for OK and DECLINED, used at the end of a handler to inform the server of the outcome of our work. DBI gets pulled in as well, although not importing anything. And Apache::Util gives us the ht_time function, a very fast way to convert a Unix timestamp into a variably formatted string.

Lines 12 through 14 give the DBI-specific information, including the DBI database specifier, the table being used, and the database username and password. Obviously, I've put some fake stuff in here for the heck of it, but you can hopefully see the format.

Lines 16 through 18 define the order in which the fields to be stored are generated, and the names of the columns for those fields.

Lines 19 through 24 define an SQL INSERT command to store a new record. The question-mark placeholder will let us not have to worry about quoting.

Lines 26 to 45 are actually a giant comment as far as Perl is concerned. I'm using a Perl POD directive to store an SQL statement inside the Perl program. This statement is meant to be cut and pasted into the mysql interactive command to create the table needed for this log. Otherwise, it's ignored.

Lines 47 to 102 define the handler. This subroutine will be invoked at each request, very early in the request handling phases. The first parameter (picked off in line 48) is the Apache::Request object. Line 49 ensures that we are processing only the initial request (one that should be logged), and not the later redirects or subrequests that happen in include files.

Line 51 starts the counter ticking for wall-clock time and CPU time. This variable is not referenced further in the main subroutine, but is held as a "closure" variable for the subroutine reference created in the lines starting at line 56. The five elements are wall-clock timestamp, user CPU, system CPU, child user CPU, and child system CPU.

Lines 53 through 99 form a log handler. This log handler is not installed using the normal PerlLogHandler directive, but simply by having been "pushed" here. The nice thing about doing it this way is that this log handler can now share the closure variables created above. So, the outer handler runs before anything of interest has happened for a request, and the inner pushed handler happens as just about the last possible thing in a request. That's how we are sure to get the right resources spent on this request as accurately as possible.

Lines 58 to 64 ensure that any child processes are reaped, so that the child CPU times are properly updated. Without this, the child processes don't get reaped until the cleanup phase (after the logging phase), and the child CPU values are almost always zero.

Line 67 cleverly replaces the values in `@times` with their delta values.

Lines 69 and 70 grab the two interesting `Apache::Request` objects. If a request has been redirected internally, the "original" request is not necessarily the request to which all the loggable activity has been charged, so we need to know both.

Lines 72 to 85 construct the new record to be added to the database. The values must be in the same order as the `@FIELDS` were given earlier. Most of the elements are just straight extractions from the appropriate `Apache::Request` objects, with two exceptions. The request time is a MySQL-compatible date-time value, created with the assistance of the `ht_time` function. And the request URL comes from the request string, not the `uri` value, because the request string contains the parameter items as well.

Lines 87 to 93 connect to the database and store the data. Now, this looks expensive to do on each request, but there's some caching going on here. First, I'm using `Apache::DBI` (described in a moment), which caches the connect requests, so that this happens only once per Apache server process. Second, the `prepare_cached` method enables the prepared SQL to be reused on subsequent hits. (Thanks to Tim Bunce for pointing that out to me while reviewing the code.) And the disconnect doesn't actually happen, but I include it for consistency if I ever choose not to use `Apache::DBI`.

If there's a would-be fatal error of any kind in lines 88 to 92, lines 94 to 96 catch that and throw the error in the log. For example, if the database could not connect, or the database was full, we'd see that in the error log.

So, I stuck this module somewhere in the `@INC` path for my embedded `mod_perl` interpreter, and then added the following lines to my main configuration file for Apache:

```
## DBI logging
PerlModule Apache::DBI
PerlModule DBI
PerlInitHandler Stonehenge::DBILog
```

The `Apache::DBI` module ensures a mostly transparent caching of all DBI objects created in the server. The current design requires that `Apache::DBI` be loaded before the DBI module, but I understand discussion is underway to remove this restriction. In any event, the DBI module is also pulled in, and finally a `PerlInitHandler` is established with our logging module as the handler definition.

After restarting the server, our database begins to fill up. At this point, we can use the `mysql` command to perform simple ad-hoc requests, but it's more interesting to let Perl do the canned reports.

Part 2: Analyzing the Results

So, now that I have more than a week's worth of data, I want to see just how crazy my server has been working over the past week. I'll do this by making a single HTML page that has some of the most interesting statistics. This is just a demo, so it doesn't have to be comprehensive. In real life, I'd probably have a series of pages with different views and time periods.

To grab the statistics, I'll run a Perl program periodically to update an HTML file. I do this with cron on this Linux box, with an entry that looks like this:

```
52 0-23/3 * * * /home/merlyn/bin/AnalogDB
```

And cron interprets this as "Run this command every 3 hours between midnight and 11 p.m., at 52 minutes past the hour." So it runs at 00:52, 03:52, 06:52, and so on up to 21:52. Running it more often would make it more fresh, but at some point, you'll be burning more CPU talking about how you burn CPU than you actually burned doing the real work.

The contents of AnalogDB are present in Listing 5-2. I'll point out just the highlights, since it's basically a preamble, four different reports, and a postamble.

The preamble in lines 1 to 44 set up this program to generate an HTML file on STDOUT. STDOUT has been redirected to a temporary file defined in line 32, which lives in the same directory as the ultimate output file named in line 12. The purpose of the temporary file is so that we don't confuse any existing readers until we have a complete HTML file to show, since this execution will probably take 30 seconds or so.

Lines 14 through 27 are also worth noting, as they define the subset of the records that I'm willing to describe in public. For various reasons, I have private areas of my web server, and private accesses to the web server for testing, and this SQL helps remove those from the public statistics.

Also note the SQL control in line 37. This MySQL-specific operation permits some queries to succeed where they might previously have failed, at the expense of having all queries be temporarily saved to disk on the server. Seems like a fine tradeoff to me, but it's not the default.

And finally note that the HTML is being generated with the CGI.pm shortcuts. I like that much better than I like typing less-than and greater-than.

A typical report is shown in lines 45 through 70. Lines 45 through 47 show the description of the report. Lines 49 through 63 dump an HTML table with the result contents. The table header gets created by lines 51 through 55, while the body is the result of the map beginning in line 56.

To read this, we go to the data source in line 63, which generates a query to the database and results in an arrayref of rows, each of which is an arrayref of the fields in the row. This arrayref is dereferenced in line 63 (the outer @{...}) and then spoon-fed into map. Each $_ inside the map is therefore an arrayref for one row, which gets dereferenced and stored into named variables in line 57. Since two of the three columns are URLs, I wrap the data cell in a call to show_link (defined later) to turn it into a clickable link.

The postamble in lines 176 to 181 finishes up the HTML file and renames it over the top of the previous HTML file, meaning that users will now see the updated statistics. Lines 183 to 188 define the show_link routine, returning an appropriately escaped HTML string for a link to the given URL.

And that's all there is to it! If you want, you can use PNGgraph or GNUplot to make pictures from the data. I may even show that in a future column if I get ambitious. But until next month, enjoy!

Listing 5-1

```
=1=    package Stonehenge::DBILog;
=2=    use strict;
=3=
```

```
=4=     ## usage: PerlInitHandler Stonehenge::DBILog
=5=
=6=
=7=
=8=     use Apache::Constants qw(OK DECLINED);
=9=     use DBI ();
=10=    use Apache::Util qw(ht_time);
=11=
=12=    my $DSN = 'dbi:mysql:stonehenge_httpd';
=13=    my $DB_TABLE = 'requests';
=14=    my $DB_AUTH = 'sekretuser:sekretpassword';
=15=
=16=    my @FIELDS =
=17=      qw(when host method url user referer browser status bytes
=18=         wall cpuuser cpusys cpucuser cpucsys);
=19=    my $INSERT =
=20=      "INSERT INTO $DB_TABLE (".
=21=      (join ",", @FIELDS).
=22=      ") VALUES(".
=23=      (join ",", ("?") x @FIELDS).
=24=      ")";
=25=
=26=    =for SQL
=27=
=28=    create table requests (
=29=      when datetime not null,
=30=      host varchar(255) not null,
=31=      method varchar(8) not null,
=32=      url varchar(255) not null,
=33=      user varchar(50),
=34=      referer varchar(255),
=35=      browser varchar(255),
=36=      status smallint(3) default 0,
=37=      bytes int(8),
=38=      wall smallint(5),
=39=      cpuuser float(8),
=40=      cpusys float(8),
=41=      cpucuser float(8),
=42=      cpucsys float(8)
=43=    );
=44=
=45=    =cut
=46=
=47=    sub handler {
=48=      my $r = shift;
=49=      return DECLINED unless $r->is_initial_req;
=50=
```

```
=51=      my @times = (time, times);    # closure
=52=
=53=      $r->push_handlers
=54=        (
=55=          PerlLogHandler =>
=56=          sub {
=57=            ## first, reap any zombies so child CPU is proper:
=58=            {
=59=              my $kid = waitpid(-1, 1);
=60=              if ($kid > 0) {
=61=                # $r->log->warn("found kid $kid"); # DEBUG
=62=                redo;
=63=              }
=64=            }
=65=
=66=            ## delta these times:
=67=            @times = map { $_ - shift @times } time, times;
=68=
=69=            my $orig = shift;
=70=            my $r = $orig->last;
=71=
=72=            my @data =
=73=              (
=74=                ht_time($orig->request_time, '%Y-%m-%d %H:%M:%S', 0),
=75=                $r->get_remote_host,
=76=                $r->method,
=77=                # $orig->uri,
=78=                ($r->the_request =~ /^\S+\s+(\S+)/)[0],
=79=                $r->connection->user,
=80=                $r->header_in('Referer'),
=81=                $r->header_in('User-agent'),
=82=                $orig->status,
=83=                $r->bytes_sent,
=84=                @times,
=85=              );
=86=
=87=            eval {
=88=              my $dbh = DBI->connect($DSN, (split ':', $DB_AUTH),
=89=                                { RaiseError => 1 });
=90=              my $sth = $dbh->prepare_cached($INSERT);
=91=              $sth->execute(@data);
=92=              $dbh->disconnect;
=93=            };
=94=            if ($@) {
=95=              $r->log->error("dbi: $@");
=96=            }
=97=
```

```
=98=              return DECLINED;
=99=          });
=100=
=101=    return DECLINED;
=102=   }
=103=
=104=   1;
```

Listing 5-2

```
=1=      #!/usr/bin/perl
=2=      use strict;
=3=      $|++;
=4=
=5=      use DBI ();
=6=      use CGI::Pretty qw(:all -no_debug);
=7=
=8=      ## BEGIN CONFIG ##
=9=
=10=     my $DSN = 'dbi:mysql:stonehenge_httpd';
=11=     my $DB_AUTH = 'sekretuser:sekretpassword';
=12=     my $OUTPUT = "/home/merlyn/Html/stats.html";
=13=     my $DAY = 7;
=14=     my $COMMON = <<END_COMMON;
=15=     (
=16=       (
=17=         Url not like '/%/%'
=18=         or Url like '/perltraining/%'
=19=         or Url like '/merlyn/%'
=20=         or Url like '/cgi/%'
=21=         or Url like '/perl/%'
=22=         or Url like '/icons/%'
=23=         or Url like '/books/%'
=24=       )
=25=       and Host not like '%.stonehenge.%'
=26=       and When > date_sub(now(), interval $DAY day)
=27=     )
=28=     END_COMMON
=29=
=30=     ## END CONFIG ##
=31=
=32=     my $TMP = "$OUTPUT~NEW~";
=33=     open STDOUT, ">$TMP" or die "Cannot create $TMP: $!";
=34=     chmod 0644, $TMP or warn "Cannot chmod $TMP: $!";
=35=
=36=     my $dbh = DBI->connect($DSN, (split ':', $DB_AUTH), { RaiseError => 1 });
```

```
=37=    $dbh->do("SET OPTION SQL_BIG_TABLES = 1");
=38=
=39=    print
=40=      start_html("Web server activity"),
=41=      h1("Web server activity at ".localtime),
=42=      p("This page gives web server activity viewed in various ways,",
=43=        "updated frequently for information over the prior seven days.");
=44=
=45=    print
=46=      h2("Incoming links"),
=47=      p("The following links were the most frequent ways⤵
                that people found to this site.");
=48=
=49=    print
=50=      table({Cellspacing => 0, Cellpadding => 2, Border => 1},
=51=            Tr(
=52=              th("Hits in<br>past $DAY days"),
=53=              th("Source of link"),
=54=              th("Target of link"),
=55=              ),
=56=            map {
=57=              my ($hits, $referer, $url) = @$_;
=58=              Tr(
=59=                td($hits),
=60=                td(show_link($referer)),
=61=                td(show_link($url)),
=62=                );
=63=            } @{$dbh->selectall_arrayref(<<END)});
=64=    select count(*) as Hits, Referer, Url
=65=    from requests
=66=    where $COMMON and Referer not like '%.stonehenge.%'
=67=    group by Referer, Url
=68=    order by Hits desc
=69=    limit 30
=70=    END
=71=
=72=    print
=73=      h2("Outgoing links"),
=74=      p("The following links were the most frequent ways⤵
                that people left this site.");
=75=
=76=    print
=77=      table({Cellspacing => 0, Cellpadding => 2, Border => 1},
=78=            Tr(
=79=              th("Hits in<br>past $DAY days"),
=80=              th("Source of link"),
=81=              th("Target of link"),
```

```
=82=                    ),
=83=              map {
=84=                my ($hits, $referer, $url) = @$_;
=85=                $url =~ s#^/cgi/go/##;
=86=                Tr(
=87=                    td($hits),
=88=                    td(show_link($referer)),
=89=                    td(show_link($url)),
=90=                  );
=91=              } @{$dbh->selectall_arrayref(<<END)});
=92=    select count(*) as Hits, Referer, Url
=93=    from requests
=94=    where $COMMON and Url like '/cgi/go/%'
=95=    group by Referer, Url
=96=    order by Hits desc
=97=    limit 30
=98=    END
=99=
=100=   print
=101=     h2("CPU Burning"),
=102=     p("The following hosts burnt the most cumulative CPU on the server.");
=103=
=104=   print
=105=     table({Cellspacing => 0, Cellpadding => 2, Border => 1},
=106=           Tr(
=107=               th("Total CPU seconds<br>in past $DAY days"),
=108=               th("Host making the request"),
=109=             ),
=110=           map {
=111=             my ($cpu, $host) = @$_;
=112=             Tr(
=113=                 td($cpu),
=114=                 td($host),
=115=               );
=116=           } @{$dbh->selectall_arrayref(<<END)});
=117=   select sum(cpuuser+cpusys+cpucuser+cpucsys) as Cpu, Host
=118=   from requests
=119=   where $COMMON
=120=   group by Host
=121=   order by Cpu desc
=122=   limit 30
=123=   END
=124=
=125=   print
=126=     h2("CPU Hogging"),
=127=     p("The following periods were the busiest in terms of total CPU used.");
=128=
```

```
=129=    print
=130=      table({Cellspacing => 0, Cellpadding => 2, Border => 1},
=131=          Tr(
=132=             th("15-minute period beginning<br>(localtime)"),
=133=             th("Total CPU seconds<br>burnt in the period"),
=134=            ),
=135=          map {
=136=            my ($period, $cpu) = @$_;
=137=            Tr(
=138=              td($period),
=139=              td($cpu),
=140=             );
=141=          } @{$dbh->selectall_arrayref(<<END)});
=142=    select
=143=      from_unixtime(15*60*floor(unix_timestamp(when)/(15*60))) as Period,
=144=      sum(cpuuser+cpusys+cpucuser+cpucsys) as Cpu
=145=    from requests
=146=    where $COMMON group by Period
=147=    order by Cpu desc
=148=    limit 30
=149=    END
=150=
=151=    print
=152=      h2("User Agent Bytesucking"),
=153=      p("The following User Agents sucked the most cumulative
             bytes on the server.");
=154=
=155=    print
=156=      table({Cellspacing => 0, Cellpadding => 2, Border => 1},
=157=          Tr(
=158=             th("Total Bytes<br>in past $DAY days"),
=159=             th("User Agent making the request"),
=160=            ),
=161=          map {
=162=            my ($sent, $agent) = @$_;
=163=            Tr(
=164=              td($sent),
=165=              td($agent),
=166=             );
=167=          } @{$dbh->selectall_arrayref(<<END)});
=168=    select sum(Bytes) as Sent, Browser
=169=    from requests
=170=    where $COMMON
=171=    group by Browser
=172=    order by Sent desc
=173=    limit 30
=174=    END
=175=
```

```
=176=    print end_html;
=177=
=178=    $dbh->disconnect;
=179=
=180=    close STDOUT;
=181=    rename $TMP, $OUTPUT or die "Cannot rename $TMP to $OUTPUT: $!";
=182=
=183=    sub show_link {
=184=      use HTML::Entities ();
=185=      my $url = shift;
=186=      my $html_escaped_url = HTML::Entities::encode_entities($url);
=187=      a({Href => $html_escaped_url}, $html_escaped_url);
=188=    }
```

Forcing Users Through the Front Door

Web Techniques, Column 18 (October 1997)

▓**Randal's Note** Through the years, this column has generated about half a dozen requests for me to consult to install the code on readers' sites. Who would have known that this would be an important topic, enough so that people would pay to have me implement it over and over again? I guess the idea of an "unbookmarkable bookmark" is useful.

Sometimes, people come in through the back door. No, I don't mean at your house. But suppose you set up a nice website with a great front-page graphic, and then people browse away, looking at all the stuff, and they start bookmarking some of the later pages. No big deal, you say, but then they start handing out those URLs to their friends, or worse yet, put their hotlist directly on the web.

Now, people from all over are coming into your site, never having seen your wonderful front page. OK, so only vanity requires you to have them see that graphic. But there are more real-world situations as well.

Suppose the front page contains a legal disclaimer that applies to the entire site. Sure, you can copy that same note to each page, but that'll just aggravate people.

Or suppose the entire site is sponsored (for which the sponsor expects or requires some credit) or made possible from others' work? Surely, those sponsor notices must be seen. In particular, suppose you have ads of some sort (ugh) that need to be acknowledged in some way.

Well, then you must make sure that these URLs that don't point at the front door are never used, so that people don't "come in through the back door."

How? Well, one technique is to mangle the URLs slightly, so that each URL points at a place in the tree for a limited amount of time. After that time has passed, the URL "expires" and cannot be used again. This is possible if you don't serve the URLs directly, but instead are willing to let *every* document served be handled through a CGI script. Where might you find such a script? Read on.

Put simply, every unexpired URL ends up looking like this:

```
http://www.stonehenge.com/cgi/WT/1234567/col01.html
```

where `1234567` will be the Unix time of day at which this URL was generated. The script at `/cgi/WT` gets invoked, and the rest of the URL is made available to it as data. This gives the script a chance to make a policy decision about the URL. If the URL is recent enough, the CGI script tickles the server into handing the client a page from a secret tree, like this:

```
http://www.stonehenge.com/merlyn/WebTechniques/col01.html
```

If the URL isn't recent enough, the extra path is ignored, and the script generates an error message coaxing the user back to the top page. If the script is invoked without any extra path, the top page is shown anyway, so that gives us a place to link to from other parts of the site.

The details of this script are given in Listing 5-3.

Lines 1 through 3 start nearly every nontrivial program I write, enabling warnings and taint checks, and turning on compiler restrictions.

Line 4 pulls in the `URI::URL` module, so that I can compute relative and absolute URLs relatively easily.

Lines 6 through 9 provide a few constants that I might want to change if I put this script in different environments. Nothing below this should require customization.

Line 7 defines a base URL (that must end in slash) where the documents are actually kept. Note that this URL must be permitted to the ultimate readers, but not publicized. In fact, if it ever leaks out, the users can go to this URL directly.

For the purposes of testing my program, I pointed this particular script at my own online article archive on my server.

Line 8 defines the number of seconds that a valid URL can be used as is. From this period to double this period, a URL goes through a *soft failure*—that is, a new URL is generated that points at the same place, but has been made "up to date." After that time, the URL is simply invalid and will merely bring up an error document that points the user to the top of the tree again.

Lines 11 to 16 define an entity-encoding algorithm that turns an arbitrary string into something that is safe to send to a web-browser. The &ent routine encodes double quotes, less-thans, ampersands, and greater-thans. (The two double quotes in the search string are merely to make it symmetric—a subtle touch of aesthetics.)

Lines 18 through 20 create `$info`, which contains a clean path of the particular desired document within the secret tree. This variable initially comes from the `PATH_INFO` environment variable, which will be everything after the script name (if any). If the extra path stuff is missing, `/` is substituted, and the name is adjusted to always begin with dot-slash.

Lines 22 through 26 construct a URL from the invocation parameters for this particular CGI. This is needed to perform an external redirect back to this script to add or update the timestamp part of the URL. If I had used `CGI.pm`, I could have simply referred to `$query-GTself_url`, but I wanted to avoid the overhead of pulling that entire library in just for this one operation.

Line 22 creates a `URI::URL` object using the `url` function, and each of the following lines just adds something to that object. Finally, in line 26, the `URI::URL` object is converted into a string, restoring it to a canonical form, which is then concatenated with a slash.

So far, we have the address of ourselves (`$self_url`) and a path to a particular virtual document (`$info`). If we glued those two strings back together, it'd look a lot like the original query. But that's not the point of this CGI. Instead, we'll look at $info as a pointer into the real document tree (beginning relative to $BASE), and do the right thing with it.

First, we need to see if it's a current URL or an expired URL. That's done by stripping out the leading digits from $info, putting them into $when in lines 28 and 29. If there were no leading digits, then $when remains 0.

Next, lines 33 through 52 determine if we have an expired URL, using the expression in lines 34 through 36. There are two ways for a URL to be considered expired. If the URL has illegal pathname components (backing up could reveal the pathname of the $BASE tree), we treat it as expired to get the right error message. If the URL is *not* the "top-of-tree" URL (here, ./), and the URL timestamp is more than double the expiration period, then it's definitely expired as well. Note that a $when containing 0 falls into this category, so random URL pointers into the tree are automatically expired pointers.

If the URL is expired, we need to tell the user what to do. Lines 37 and 38 construct HTML-safe strings from the requested URL and the "self" URL, and lines 40 through 49 print a response text based on that information. Note that the entry in line 47 both displays the proper URL to return to and generates it as a link so the user can go directly there without retyping. Nice touch.

Line 50 exits the program if the response text was generated. (This would be a bad thing if this script was used with Apache's mod_perl, but if you're using that, you're probably clever enough to look for stuff like this anyway.)

If we make it to line 52, it's time to deliver some document via redirection. If the requested URL is "fresh enough," line 56 provides an initial prefix in front of $info (line 53) to perform an *internal redirect*. In this case, the web server fetches and returns the URL as if that was the originally requested URL. If the requested URL is "stale" (but not expired, which was handled above), then we want to freshen up the URL by sending an *external redirect*. In this case, we need to refer to this script, together with a correct timestamp (the current time) inserted in the middle. The result is a URI::URL in $location that reflects the appropriate prefix and suffix based on the freshness of the original requested URL.

And finally, lines 59 and 60 print the redirection header.

So, presuming I've installed this at a URL like www.stonehenge.com/cgi/WT, I can now invoke this URL to get to the top of the *real* tree at www.stonehenge.com/merlyn/WebTechniques/. And that would let me browse all the pages below that (presuming they use relative URLs) without any change to the existing pages.

Except for a little hitch. What if the user fakes up a URL that has the right timestamp but a bad path after it? The server will gleefully hand back an error message that reveals that oh-so-protected virtual tree! So much for security.

Well, there's a quick and easy solution with Apache: define alternate error documents. The details about this are in the Apache documentation, in the description of the core features. For this example, it suffices to add these lines to the .htaccess file at the root of the tree being served:

```
ErrorDocument 401 "That document is not available
ErrorDocument 403 "That document is not available
ErrorDocument 404 "That document is not available
```

Sure, it's not very helpful, but at least you won't see the real URL.

Because every new invocation of /cgi/WT generates a new (probably unique) time-oriented URL, I could use this to correlate a "visit" to my website by noticing all the similar timestamps in successive hits, and derive statistics like "number of hits per visit" and "number of visits per day" instead of the more meaningless "number of hits per day." Some sites do this already (I believe www.pathfinder.com does this, for example, because I can see the ugly URLs).

While I was writing this article, I took a brief survey of my friends about the technique, and nearly all of them agreed that they hate it when sites do this. But if you have a compelling reason, here's one way to make it work. Enjoy!

Listing 5-3

```
=1=     #!/home/merlyn/bin/perl -wT
=2=
=3=     use strict;
=4=     use URI::URL;
=5=
=6=     ## configuration
=7=     my $BASE = "/merlyn/WebTechniques/"; # must end in slash
=8=     my $VALID_SECONDS = 60 * 60 * 4; # four hours
=9=     ## end configuration
=10=
=11=    ## return $_[0] encoded for HTML entities
=12=    sub ent {
=13=      local $_ = shift;
=14=      $_ =~ s/["<&>"]/"&#".ord($&).";"/ge;   # entity escape
=15=      $_;
=16=    }
=17=
=18=    my $info = $ENV{PATH_INFO};
=19=    $info = "/" unless defined $info;
=20=    $info = ".$info";                   # always "./" prefix
=21=
=22=    my $self_url = url("http:";);
=23=    $self_url->host($ENV{SERVER_NAME}) if defined $ENV{SERVER_NAME};
=24=    $self_url->port($ENV{SERVER_PORT}) if defined $ENV{SERVER_PORT};
=25=    $self_url->path($ENV{SCRIPT_NAME} || "/cgi/$0");
=26=    $self_url = "$self_url/";        # note that $self_url is a string now
=27=
=28=    my $when = 0;
=29=    $when = $1 if $info =~ s!^\./(\d+)/!./!;
=30=
=31=    ## catchall if illegal url (attempt to back up over top)
=32=    ## or expired (and not one of the entries into the tree)
=33=    if (
=34=        (index("/$info/", "/../") > -1) or
=35=        $info ne "./" and
=36=        time > $when + 2 * $VALID_SECONDS) { # hard expired URL, say so
=37=      my $r_html = ent("$self_url$info");
```

```
=38=       my $s_html = ent($self_url);
=39=
=40=       print <<"EOF";
=41=    Content-type: text/html
=42=    Status: 404 Not Found
=43=
=44=    <HTML><TITLE>Expired URL</TITLE></HEAD>
=45=    <BODY><H1>Expired URL</H1>
=46=    The requested URL $r_html has expired.  Please return to
=47=    <A HREF="$s_html">$s_html</A> to start with a new unexpired URL.
=48=    </BODY>
=49=    EOF
=50=       exit 0;
=51=    }
=52=    my $location =
=53=       url($info,                   # $info is relative to...
=54=          (time > $when + $VALID_SECONDS) ? # if too old...
=55=          $self_url.time."/" :      # this script and time (external redirect)
=56=          $BASE                     # or use as-is (internal redirect)
=57=          )->abs;                   # made absolute
=58=
=59=    print "Location: $location\n";
=60=    print "\n";
=61=
```

Throttling Your Web Server

Linux Magazine, Column 17 (October 2000)

The web server for www.stonehenge.com is a nicely configured Linux box (of course) located at a nice co-location facility and maintained by my ISP. I share the box with a dozen other e-commerce clients (mostly because I've been too lazy to move the server to a new solitary box), and that keeps me and everyone else on our toes about overloading the server, because we all have to share.

I bought a digital camera many months ago and started putting nearly every picture I took up on the site. I've got a nice mod_perl picture handler to show the thumbnails, provide the navigation, and even generate half-size images on the fly using PerlMagick.

However, as I put more and more pictures online, I started to notice some pretty creepy CPU loads from time to time. Worse than that, my ISP neighbors were also starting to complain. After investigation, I determined that I was getting hit by not-so-nice *spiders*—web programs that recursively (and rapidly) fetch the contents of many pages given a few starting points. I believe most of these to be people on fast data connections (like my current cable modem, which brings the equivalent of two T-1s into my house for $40 per month, yes!) innocently asking their web browser to download a whole area.

So, rather than pull my pictures offline, I decided to implement throttling. I didn't care so much about transfer bandwidth as I did CPU, so I chose to track recent CPU activity for each visitor. Of course, HTTP has no concept of a "session," so I took a very easy shortcut: tracking by IP address. Yes, I know, I've ranted in discussion forums a lot about how an IP address is not a user. But for the purpose of throttling, it seemed the most expedient choice.

Once I put my throttler in place, no IP address is allowed to suck more than 7% of my CPU over a period of 15 seconds. Once the CPU threshold is reached, any additional request is met with a 503 error (service unavailable), which according to RFC2616 (the HTTP/1.1 specification) also allows me to give a "retry after" value of 15 seconds to advise the program that this was a temporary condition.

The throttler consists of two related mod_perl handlers: an "access" handler to note whether or not the IP address is currently permitted, and a "log" handler to track the CPU used by the transfer. Additionally, there's an external program triggered by cron to clean up the status files needed by the handlers.

So, let's take a look at the handlers in Listing 5-4.

Line 1 puts the module into Stonehenge::Throttle. I use Stonehenge as a private prefix for all my local mod_perl goodies, to keep it separate from any CPAN-installed modules. Because mod_perl shares the namespace across all modules, it's very important to have a workable naming allocation to keep things from colliding.

Line 2 selects the critically important compiler restrictions. Designing code for mod_perl handlers requires careful attention to detail, and the use strict restrictions are a good start to that.

Line 4 reminds me that this module needs to be installed as a PerlAccessHandler by giving the appropriate syntax. I have it selected at the top-level configuration file of my site, but if I had wanted it only for the pictures directory, I could have put the access handler inside a Directory or Files restriction, or even an .htaccess file in a subdirectory.

Lines 6 through 9 define some configuration constants. Line 6 is a directory that must be writable by the web userid (in my case, nobody). This directory will hold the historical information about CPU usage.

Line 8 defines the seconds in which we compute CPU history. If we make this too large, the throttling will be slow to react. If we make it too small, it'll be a knee-jerk reaction. I've tweaked this number up and down from time to time, but the current number is 15 as shown here. Line 9 defines how much CPU a particular IP address is allowed to consume, as a percentage, over the period of time given by $WINDOW. I found the 7% solution to be appropriate.

Lines 11 and 12 define a version string, which can be queried using the mod_perl maintenance tools, as well as being in the right format should I ever get around to submitting this to the CPAN. The string comes from an RCS keyword, so I just check the file out and in, and get the right version number automatically.

Lines 14 through 16 pull in some standard constants and modules from the mod_perl interface.

Line 18 begins the handler called on each requested transfer. Line 19 is commented out, but when enabled, it uses my Stonehenge::Reload module to automatically reload this module whenever it changes. Since I'm pretty happy with the stability of this module, I've commented the line out. (Stonehenge::Reload hasn't been published, even though I've now referred to it in a few of my other published works. Perhaps someday soon I should talk about it, I suppose.)

Line 21 fetches the incoming request. This will be an Apache::Request object, as defined by the mod_perl interface. Line 22 ignores any requests that are not a request generated by an external query. This keeps internal lookups (for example, to get the MIME type for a directory index) from accidentally triggering the throttler. Line 23 grabs a log object for later use.

Lines 25 to 28 get the hostname of the remote server and perform some slight massaging. If the hostname is my ISP, it means I'm performing some request directly, and I sure don't want to be throttling myself. Also, I decided that all Google fetches should be charged to the same host, even though they appear to be coming from different hosts. Yes, I throttle even Google if it gets too sucky on my pages.

Lines 30 through 33 set up a few variables that will be needed for both this handler and the "log" handler that will be set up later. We'll note the filename of the CPU history file, the flagfile indicating the host is currently blocked, and the current CPU usage for both this process and its children.

Lines 35 through 59 "push" a log handler. This technique allows one handler phase to create a handler for another phase on the fly. More important, it allows me to share the values of some of the variables into the later phase.

Line 40 subtracts the current value of the output of the `times` operator from its previous value (saved earlier in line 32). Lines 41 to 43 compute the sum total of CPU used and rounds it off to the nearest hundredth of a second. Line 44 posts a notice in the error log, which I used for debugging but have commented out now.

Lines 45 to 48 add this CPU usage as an 8-byte value to the end of a history file. The first 4 bytes define the timestamp second at which the observation is being taken, and the last 4 bytes are the CPU seconds in units of hundredths of a second. The advantage of this format is that it's very easy to go back from that to a value (no decimal conversion), and an append will always be atomic, so there's no need to flock the file!

The rest of the log handler determines whether future requests should be blocked or not. First, line 50 defines the beginning of the window of interest. If there's already a current blockfile, lines 52 through 59 note that and exit the log handler, so we don't even have to think very hard.

Lines 62 to 70 walk the history file, grabbing each 8-byte string as a separate entry, converting it back to the timestamp and CPU used. For all the entries that occur within the window, we'll figure a total CPU. Older entries are ignored.

Lines 72 to 76 determine if the CPU is below the throttling percentage and, if so, remove any blockfile that may be present, thus letting future transactions proceed unthrottled (until the CPU is overused again).

But if we make it to line 78, we've got an IP address out there that has exceeded our threshold. Lines 79 to 81 grab the load average for logging purposes only. Line 83 likewise grabs the user agent for the log. (I've used this to determine if I should categorically deny bad user agents based on name rather than action.) And line 86, well, 86es them from the establishment by creating an empty blockfile. (The presence or absence of the blockfile is all that matters to the access handler.)

So, that's it for the log handler. Back in the access handler starting in line 94, we look for the blockfile that the log handler manages. If it's there, and new enough, we're blocking. Line 97 adds a clue for the client that we do indeed want them to come back, just not right away. Line 98 triggers the 503 error and aborts any further access within this transfer.

And that's the `mod_perl` side of things. But now we have these neat little CPU history files being created in `$HISTORYDIR`, and there's nothing in either handler to clean them up. And I can't add anything there, because the only time the file should be removed is when there's nothing happening, but the only time I'm in a handler is when something is happening!

So, there's a little program invoked from `cron` on a regular basis, using a `crontab` entry similar to

```
3-59/10 * * * * /home/merlyn/lib/Apache/throttle-cleaner
```

which invokes the program I present in Listing 5-5 every ten minutes on minutes that end on three (3, 13, 23, etc.). I try to invoke my cron stuff on unlikely minutes to avoid crowding with all those lusers that use precise multiples of 5 or 15. Bleh.

Because this is a standalone program, we've got the "shebang" line, with warnings turned on in line 1. Line 2 is the normal compiler restrictions.

Line 6 defines the same directory as the $Stonehenge::Throttle::HISTORYDIR, so if I change one, I need to change the other. It won't help to delete files that aren't in the same place. Line 7 similarly needs to be at least twice as large as the throttling window.

Lines 9 through 17 skip through the directory, looking for any file that has not been accessed in at least $SECS. For blocking files, this means that we've not seen a transaction since the blocking started. (Good, they went away permanently.) For history files, it means that we've not seen a transaction recently. In either case, the information is no longer of use, so we can destroy the file (in line 16).

And there you have it: a mechanism to keep people from making your ISP neighbors mad at you. As a testimony to its value, I recently got "Slashdotted" by having my pictures archive for "YAPC 19100" mentioned on www.slashdot.org. My hits per hour went to 20 times their normal pace for about 36 hours after the mention, and yet the load average never got above 1 or 2 during the entire ordeal. So, I've now survived a Slashdot attack.

Another success story comes from one of my clients: a Very Large online toys and games e-tailer. They told me that they had seen an earlier version of my throttler mentioned on the mod_perl mailing list and had put it in place (with some modifications) during the past Christmas buying rush. And amazingly enough, it caught many attempts by people accidentally or deliberately attempting to download their *entire* online catalog for offload browsing: something that would be both useless and prohibitively expensive. Without the throttle, they might have lost literally millions of dollars. They did in fact buy me dinner for that. Thank you.

I'm interested to hear how this kind of code saved your bacon, so if you adapt it, let me know. Until next time, enjoy!

Listing 5-4

```
=1=     package Stonehenge::Throttle;
=2=     use strict;
=3=
=4=     ## usage: PerlAccessHandler Stonehenge::Throttle
=5=
=6=     my $HISTORYDIR = "/home/merlyn/lib/Apache/Throttle";
=7=
=8=     my $WINDOW = 15;                  # seconds of interest
=9=     my $DECLINE_CPU_PERCENT = 7; # CPU percent in window before we 503 error
=10=
=11=    use vars qw($VERSION);
=12=    $VERSION = (qw$Revision: 2.7 $ )[-1];
=13=
=14=    use Apache::Constants qw(OK DECLINED);
=15=    use Apache::File;
=16=    use Apache::Log;
=17=
```

```
=18=    sub handler {
=19=      ## use Stonehenge::Reload; goto &handler if Stonehenge::Reload->reload_me;
=20=
=21=      my $r = shift;                # closure var
=22=      return DECLINED unless $r->is_initial_req;
=23=      my $log = $r->server->log;    # closure var
=24=
=25=      my $host = $r->get_remote_host; # closure var
=26=      return DECLINED if $host =~ /\.(holdit|stonehenge)\.com$/;
=27=      return DECLINED if $host =~ /\.metronomicon\.com$/; # poor purl
=28=      $host = "googlebot.com" if $host =~ /\.googlebot\.com$/;
=29=
=30=      my $historyfile = "$HISTORYDIR/$host-times"; # closure var
=31=      my $blockfile = "$HISTORYDIR/$host-blocked"; # closure var
=32=      my @delta_times = times;      # closure var
=33=      my $fh = Apache::File->new;   # closure var
=34=
=35=      $r->push_handlers
=36=        (PerlLogHandler =>
=37=         sub {
=38=
=39=            ## record this CPU usage
=40=            @delta_times = map { $_ - shift @delta_times } times;
=41=            my $cpu_hundred = 0;
=42=            $cpu_hundred += $_ for @delta_times;
=43=            $cpu_hundred = int 100*($cpu_hundred + 0.005);
             ## DEBUG
=44=            ## $log->notice("throttle: $host got $cpu_hundred/100 in this slot");
=45=            open $fh, ">>$historyfile" or return DECLINED;
=46=            my $time = time;
=47=            syswrite $fh, pack "LL", $time, $cpu_hundred;
=48=            close $fh;
=49=
=50=            my $startwindow = $time - $WINDOW;
=51=
=52=            if (my @stat = stat($blockfile)) {
=53=              if ($stat[9] > $startwindow) {
                 ## DEBUG
=54=                ## $log->notice("throttle: $blockfile is already blocking");
=55=                return OK;           # nothing further to see... move along
=56=              } else {
=57=                ## $log->notice("throttle: $blockfile is old, ignoring"); # DEBUG
=58=              }
=59=            }
=60=
=61=            # figure out if we should be blocking
=62=            my $totalcpu = 0;        # scaled by 100
=63=
```

```
=64=              open $fh, $historyfile or return DECLINED;
=65=              while ((read $fh, my $buf, 8) > 0) {
=66=                my ($time, $cpu) = unpack "LL", $buf;
=67=                next if $time < $startwindow;
=68=                $totalcpu += $cpu;
=69=              }
=70=              close $fh;
=71=
=72=              if ($totalcpu < $WINDOW * $DECLINE_CPU_PERCENT) {
                    # DEBUG
=73=                ## $log->notice("throttle: $host got $totalcpu/100
                                    CPU in $WINDOW secs");
=74=                unlink $blockfile;
=75=                return OK;
=76=              }
=77=
=78=              ## about to be nasty... let's see how bad it is:
=79=              open $fh, "/proc/loadavg";
=80=              chomp(my $loadavg = <$fh>);
=81=              close $fh;
=82=
=83=              my $useragent = $r->header_in('User-Agent') || "unknown";
=84=
=85=              $log->notice("throttle: $host got $totalcpu/100 CPU in $WINDOW secs,
                                enabling block [loadavg $loadavg, agent $useragent]");
=86=              open $fh, ">$blockfile";
=87=              close $fh;
=88=
=89=              return OK;
=90=            });
=91=
=92=      ## back in the access handler:
=93=
=94=      if (my @stat = stat($blockfile)) {
=95=        if ($stat[9] > time - $WINDOW) {
=96=          $log->warn("throttle access: $blockfile is blocking");
=97=          $r->header_out("Retry-After", $WINDOW);
=98=          return 503;              # Service Unavailable
=99=        } else {
=100=         ## $log->notice("throttle access: $blockfile is old, ignoring"); ⏎
                    # DEBUG
=101=         return DECLINED;
=102=        }
=103=      }
=104=
=105=     return DECLINED;
=106=   }
=107=   1;
```

Listing 5-5

```
=1=     #!/usr/bin/perl -w
=2=     use strict;
=3=
=4=     # $Id: throttle-cleaner,v 1.1 1999/10/28 19:44:09 merlyn Exp $
=5=
=6=     my $DIR = "/home/merlyn/lib/Apache/Throttle";
=7=     my $SECS = 360;                 # more than Stonehenge::Throttle $WINDOW
=8=
=9=     chdir $DIR or die "Cannot chdir $DIR: $!";
=10=    opendir DOT, "." or die "Cannot opendir .: $!";
=11=    my $when = time - $SECS;
=12=    while (my $name = readdir DOT) {
=13=      next unless -f $name;
=14=      next if (stat($name))[8] > $when;
=15=      ## warn "unlinking $name\n";
=16=      unlink $name;
=17=    }
```

There Can Be Only One . . . More Way to Do It!

Web Techniques, Column 54 (October 2000)

▬**Randal's Note** The Highlander solution: there can be only one! The code was written no more than an hour or two before I wrote the column, and for exactly the reasons stated in the article. Many columns were written this way: I'd solve a real world task, and then write about it when a column was due.

I find it nice that with my familiarity with Perl, I can solve those little "emergency" tasks without having to flip through a bunch of manuals to spend time learning. For example, I had a problem the other day that was causing horrible response time with my web server for www.stonehenge.com, and yet within a few minutes and a couple dozen lines of Perl code, I was able to get things back in order.

My web server is on a nicely configured Linux box co-located at an ISP with 24/7 reboot service (although the box is rarely rebooted, as you'll see why). The box is actually shared with a dozen other e-commerce sites, and this is by design, because then when the box is down, it's not just me yelling at the admin, but a dozen others that are calling as well. Thus, we all have to play nice, because we're sharing the CPU and sharing the resources.

Well, one of the customers of this ISP is the regional sales office of a Very Large Company that has one of the largest market capitalizations in the world right now. (Why they don't run these applications on their corporate website, I'm not sure, but I never asked. The usual answer is "politics and local control," so there's no point.) They apparently have some sort of free email newsletter that has subscribers counted in the mid-five-digits or so. A recent email newsletter (that went out over the weekend) basically said in effect, "We are terminating all mail subscriptions before the next issue unless you visit URL such-and-so and enter your renewal information." In other words, if the subscriber didn't respond, they'd be dropped from the list.

Well, you can imagine the panic that this would generate on a Monday morning as thousands of people returned to work to discover that they might be removed from the mailing list. The given URL mapped to a CGI script, which was being invoked dozens of times simultaneously, so there were dozens of web server processes (actually, both web server and Perl process pairs). To make things worse, the first invocation of the Perl program gathered information about the subscriber, and then made a trip through DBI to a MySQL database, to present a confirmation form and opportunity to correct the subscription information. This form was then processed by a second invocation of the same CGI script, again reconnecting with MySQL, to update the information and finish the process.

I immediately began chatting with Doug, the author of the script and the manager of the box, to try to determine why the load average on a box that is typically under 0.5 had now gone to something like 15 or 20, making my site nearly useless. After determining as many of the facts that our IRC session would let us share, I quickly suggested that Doug move the script into an `Apache::Registry` area of his `mod_perl`-enabled server. At least this would prevent multiple compilations and forks, and probably could reuse the DBI handle as well. He was pretty adamant about not doing that, because he had written the code long before he knew about `mod_perl`, and thus had likely done things that were not very clean from `Apache::Registry`'s perspective. Additionally, he felt investing the time to make it `Apache::Registry` compliant would be wasted, since this script would eventually be moved to the client's machine, which did not support `mod_perl`.

So, still watching the extremely high load average, I then suggested to him that he invoke the *Highlander solution*. In the movie *Highlander*, the catchphrase is "There can be only one!" referring to the continual showdown among these immortal beings that would eventually kill all of each other off, leaving just one victor who would inherit "the Prize." Similarly, whenever exclusive access is needed to a resource, the word "Highlander" is bandied about to mean an implementation solution or structure to control that resource.

Here, I was asking him to ensure through some locking mechanism that only one CGI invocation was being processed at a time. I had in mind a simple flock at the beginning of the script, opening up a sentinel file (no, not another television reference) and then requesting an exclusive file lock on that handle. The first script in would create the file, grab the exclusive lock, and then proceed on its merry way, releasing the lock at the end of the program when the handle was automatically (or explicitly) closed.

If a second script should be started while the first was active, it would open the same file, and then attempt to lock the filehandle. At this point, the operating system would block the second process, leaving it sitting around in a suspended state until the first process completes. Third and subsequent invocations would likewise be blocked, but the operating system releases only one process at a time for the exclusive lock.

So, as I'm trying to describe this over IRC, it becomes clear that Doug is not up to the task, so I spend a few minutes whipping up the solution. It looked like five lines of Perl, until I thought about what to do when the system was *very* busy, such as right while I was trying to get this fixed.

Let's say there were 15 script invocations. The fifteenth invocation would be sitting in a queue behind one active and thirteen pending other processes. If the delay were substantial, the web server aborts the CGI processing, causing some 5*xx*-series error indicating a server malfunction with no clue about why this is happening. I didn't consider that very friendly, so I kept moving forward with the next idea.

I changed strategy to perform a *nonblocking* exclusive file lock, in a retrying loop. A normal lock is *blocking*, in that the operating system does not return from the operation until the type of lock requested is available. However, sometimes blocking isn't wanted, such as when having an alternate resource is satisfactory. Or in this case, when we want to simply see if we can get an exclusive lock, and if not, try to get it later.

So the loop I constructed tries to get an exclusive lock ten times, sleeping one second between invocations. Each try is a "this moment only" deal. If the lock is available, we nab it and move on, knowing that we're now king of the hill. If not, we wait a while or give up. Again, recall I was typing this in a hurry, trying to get something working. And this hastily written code is presented in Listing 5-6.

Recall that this is just a snippet added to a larger script, so the normal #! line won't appear. Line 1 brings in the CGI.pm module, without any of the HTML-generating shortcuts. I left my normal :all parameter off the import list because I didn't want my change to collide with any of Doug's existing code. In hindsight, I could have switched to a temporary package like so:

```
{
    package My::Highlander;
    use CGI qw/:all/;
    # rest of this snippet goes here
}
```

And that way I could have avoided the use of the CGI:::... construct later. Yeah, there's more than one way to do it, all right.

Line 2 brings in two constants needed for the flock operator later. The Fcntl module (which I have not yet found an easy pronunciation for) defines many constants relating to file operations, and this is certainly appropriate here. I've been thoroughly chastised in public discussion areas for my use of literal numbers like 2 and 4 on flock in the past, so I want to make amends by doing it right.

Line 4 opens the sentinel file on the HIGHLANDER handle in append mode. The mode is mostly unimportant, except that we want to make sure the file is created if it doesn't exist. The filename needs to be in an area that is writable by the web server userid, and /tmp is a safe bet. The CGI program was named renew.cgi, hence the name of the file relates to the name of the script. Death here will trigger a 500 error, but like I said, I was typing fast and furious to get this to work so I could get back to work.

Lines 8 through 21 form a loop, to be executed ten times. Repetitions are controlled by the variable $count defined and initialized to 0 in line 7. Because $count is defined in a block started in line 6 (and ending in line 22), it cannot conflict with any other use of $count earlier or later in the program.

Line 9 attempts to obtain an exclusive lock on the file opened on the HIGHLANDER filehandle. The or-ing of the two values LOCK_EX and LOCK_NB (to get the number 6, but I'm cheating to know that) requests an exclusive lock, but in nonblocking mode. If the flock is successful, we get a true return value, and the last operator takes us out of the block started in line 8. If the flock fails, we drop through to line 10, which pauses the process for one second.

Line 11 increments $count and ensures that it is still below 10. If so, the redo operator pops back up to line 8, retrying the flock. If not, we've tried ten times to flock or, er, actually, nine times to flock (durn fencepost off-by-one errors!), and it's time to report the error.

Line 13 grabs the REMOTE_HOST environment variable, which will help us determine who indeed we are not serving this time. Since they have reverse DNS turned on under this server, we should be getting a nice domain name here of the host attempting to access this CGI (or at least the intermediate proxy).

However, under some circumstances, the reverse DNS fails or is not available. I couldn't remember if REMOTE_HOST contains a numeric dotted quad at that point (like 10.1.2.3) or whether it was undefined. So to be defensive in my programming (remember, I'm under the gun here), I simply used REMOTE_ADDR in line 14 if REMOTE_HOST was undefined. Probably in five more minutes of poking around, I could have determined that line 14 is probably unnecessary. But hey, it worked, and again, that was the important part.

Line 15 dumps an error message to the web server error log, presenting the program name (in $0), the current time of day (from localtime), and an indication that we failed due to a "Highlander abort." I wanted the string to be distinct enough that we could easily detect how successful this Highlander code was in deterring overloadings.

Lines 16 through 19 dump back the response for an abort. We print a CGI header with a status of 503, appropriately earmarked as "service unavailable." According to the specification, we can additionally send a "retry after" header along with this status response, which compliant clients will be able to determine a later time (measured in seconds) after which the service is likely to be restored. Honestly, I don't know what the browsers on the market do with 503 errors, but I'm at least following the standard.

Note that line 18 sends out a text/plain MIME type. Again, being lazy, I didn't want to write a full HTML page, so I took the quickest way out, letting me just type a line of text in line 19 without adding a lot of angley brackety thingies.

Line 20 aborts the program, but with a nice exit status. Since we've "handled" the error, we don't want the web server to also go through its error trigger steps by exiting with a nonzero exit status.

And there it is. Whipped out in about 15 minutes and installed immediately by Doug. But did it help?

It sure did. The load average shot down from the mid-20s to just around 2 or so—very tolerable. We both watched the error log with tail -f to see how many people were getting turned away in relation to the customers being served, and found that 70% of them were getting through just fine, and because they weren't all trying to compete in parallel, they were actually getting done with minimal fuss. Perl saved the day!

So, the next time you have an expensive script burning up too much CPU, maybe you too need to utter in your best Sean Connery accent, "There can be only one!" Until next time, enjoy!

Listing 5-6

```
=1=     use CGI;
=2=     use Fcntl qw(LOCK_EX LOCK_NB);
=3=
=4=     open HIGHLANDER, ">>/tmp/renew.cgi.highlander"
            or die "Cannot open highlander: $!";
```

```
=5=
=6=     {
=7=       my $count = 0;
=8=       {
=9=         flock HIGHLANDER, LOCK_EX | LOCK_NB and last;
=10=        sleep 1;
=11=        redo if ++$count < 10;
=12=        ## couldn't get it after 10 seconds...
=13=        my $host = $ENV{REMOTE_HOST};
=14=        $host = $ENV{REMOTE_ADDR} unless defined $host;
=15=        warn "$0 @ ".(localtime).":
                highlander abort for $host after 10 seconds\n";
=16=        print CGI::header(-status => 503,
=17=              -retry_after => 30,
=18=              -type => 'text/plain'),
=19=              "Our server is overloaded.  Please try again in a few minutes.\n";
=20=        exit 0;
=21=      }
=22=    }
```

Looking for Lossage

Linux Magazine, Column 37 (June 2002)

In last month's column, I showed how to use my web server's database-driven statistics log to figure out peak and average transfer rates. Having a database for a logging engine is great, but such a log consumes more space than I can reasonably afford. So, I tend to keep only a few months of backlogs in the database, and roll the rest out to a flat file for easy minimal storage and archival. Which made the task I faced a few days ago a bit harder.

The Linux box currently hosting www.stonehenge.com is in a rented space at a co-location facility. As with a lot of the internet shakeout everywhere, the co-lo facility was bought out by a larger networking company, and we've been having network interruptions including complete loss of service from time to time. The administrator of the box came to me looking for evidence that these outages had been for some extended periods of time, so that he could take that to the new owner and get some of his money back and pass the savings along to me.

It occurred to me that I could use the web logs from my web server, and it would have been nice to use the database-driven logs as I did in last month's column, but I needed data for a year ago. I *did* have the database dumps to restore the data, but not enough disk space to do so. Fortunately, I also had the older standard Apache access_log files, broken up by day, compressed separately, going all the way back to my first hosting machine. It was from these files that I was able to glean the data.

First, let's consider the requirements. I wanted an hour-by-hour hit count, for a given range of dates. I also wanted to filter out any local hits, because I run a link checker on my web server nightly from a process on the same box, and those hits don't reflect any network connectivity issues. I also wanted to be reasonably efficient about date parsing. That completely ruled out running Date::Manip's general date-recognition routines or anything else in the inner loop of the analyzer. The output also didn't need to be very pretty: just the hit count for an hour, from which we would apply an interpretation. And a program meeting all of my administrator's requirements is presented in Listing 5-7.

Lines 1 through 3 start nearly every Perl program I write, enabling warnings for development, turning on the compiler restrictions, and unbuffering standard output.

Line 5 pulls in a few selected routines from the `Date::Calc` module (found in the CPAN). Specifically, I needed to convert a month name to a number, a timestamp to an epoch time, and a human-readable date to a month-day-year value. Line 6 pulls in the standard `File::Find` module.

Lines 10 through 12 provide a few configuration constants that I was tweaking during development. The `@DIRS` variable gives the top-level directories that contain my web logs as starting points for a "find" operation. `$START` and `$END` give the approximate range endpoints for the analysis. They aren't precisely accurate, because my log roller doesn't run precisely at midnight, and the endpoints are merely used to determine which log files to even begin parsing. The endpoints can be given in any format interpretable by `Date::Calc`'s date format, which is pretty broad.

Lines 16 to 19 convert the human-readable string into an epoch time, first by calling `Decode_Date_US`, and if that works, by turning that year-month-day value into a Unix epoch–based value. I'm using the trick here of assigning to the `foreach` loop control variable to alter the original variable being examined.

Lines 21 to 28 locate all of the log files to be parsed. If the name matches the right pattern (line 23), and it's a file (line 24), then the stat buffer's modification time value is saved (line 25). If this value is within range (line 26), we save the full pathname to `@files` (line 27).

Line 30 is the report accumulator, counting the number of hits in a given hour. The data structure within `%count` will be described shortly.

Line 32 is a cache of month name to number, as returned by `Decode_Month`. This is necessary because I don't want to call that subroutine for every single line, so I cache the results for speed.

Line 34 begins a loop that operates on ten of the files at a time, pulling them out into a "chunk." The final chunk might be less than ten files, however. The number ten is somewhat arbitrary—a compromise between firing off `zcat` for every single file and constructing a command line with roughly 365 files for the year, possibly overflowing the maximum length of a command.

Line 35 launches the `zcat` command on the chunk of files. The ordering and clustering of the files is not relevant, since we're ultimately going to process all the files and update `%count` before generating any reports.

Lines 36 to 50 process each Apache `access_log`-style line from the logs within range. They look a bit like this:

```
foo.example.com - - [14/Mar/2002:13:18:55 -0800] "GET / HTTP/1.0" 200 3340
```

Using an extended-syntax regular expression in lines 38 to 46, I locate the lines that do not begin with my web-host name (to ensure the hit is a remote hit), but contain a date stamp in the normal form. The six memory references (pulling out the day, month, year, hour, minute, and second) are returned as a list, assigned to the variables in line 37.

Lines 47 and 48 turn the month name into a number for easier sorting. First, an attempt is made to locate it in the cache hash. If it's there, that value overwrites the previous $month value. Otherwise, Decode_Month is called, and the result is padded to two digits for easy string-based sorting.

Line 49 creates a multilevel data structure. At the top level, the key is the year and month number. Next we have the day number, converted to a pure number by adding a zero, and finally the hour number, once again converted to a pure number by adding a zero. The appropriate entry is incremented to show one hit during this period of interest. Had I been interested in, say, 15 minute intervals, I could have incremented a final key of int(($hour * 60 + $minute)/4) instead.

I'm using hashes for all the levels because I believe that for at least part of the values, I'd have "sparse" data. As it turns out, nearly every hash element in sequence was being used, so a hash of arrayrefs of arrayrefs would probably have been a better choice. But this was "fast enough," so I stopped optimizing.

Finally, it's time to show the results, using three nested foreach loops. The outer loop walks through a string-sorted list of keys, representing the year/month pairs for which data has been made available. The middle loop (starting in line 54) figures out which days of that month are present and sorts them numerically. The inner loop (starting in line 55) forces a scan for every hour of that day. Since some of the hours have zero hits, we don't want to skip over them in the output, so by forcing every hour, we can see the zero-hit results. I knew the outage was never longer than a day, or I'd have already moved my hosting service to another location. Line 57 displays the data, and we're done!

With the report generated in a timely fashion, my administrator is off to the co-lo owner, hopefully resulting in some returned monies. And the task is complete. Until next time, enjoy!

Listing 5-7

```perl
=1=     #!/usr/bin/perl -w
=2=     use strict;
=3=     $|++;
=4=
=5=     use Date::Calc qw(Decode_Month Mktime Decode_Date_US);
=6=     use File::Find;
=7=
=8=     ## begin config
=9=
=10=    my @DIRS = glob "/home/merlyn/Logs/OLD.*/.";
=11=    my $START = "1/1/2001";
=12=    my $END = "1/1/2002";
=13=
=14=    ## end config
=15=
=16=    for ($START, $END) {
=17=      my @y_m_d = Decode_Date_US($_) or die "Cannot decode $_";
```

```
=18=       $_ = Mktime(@y_m_d, 12, 0, 0); # noon on that day
=19=    }
=20=
=21=    my @files;
=22=    find sub {
=23=      return unless /^access_log.*gz$/;
=24=      return unless -f;
=25=      my $mtime = (stat(_))[9];
=26=      return unless $mtime >= $START and $mtime <= $END;
=27=      push @files, $File::Find::name;
=28=    }, @DIRS;
=29=
=30=    my %count;
=31=
=32=    my %month_name_to_number;
=33=
=34=    while (my @chunk = splice @files, 0, 10) {
=35=      open IN, "zcat @chunk |" or die;
=36=      while (<IN>) {
=37=        my ($day, $month, $year, $hour, $minute, $second) =
=38=          m{
=39=            ^
=40=            (?!web\.stonehenge\.comm)
=41=            [^\[]*
=42=            \[
=43=            (\d+) \/ (\w+) \/ (\d+)
=44=            :
=45=            (\d+) : (\d+) : (\d+)
=46=          }x or next;
=47=        $month = $month_name_to_number{$month}
=48=          ||= sprintf "%02d", Decode_Month($month);
=49=        $count{"$year $month"}{0+$day}{0+$hour}++;
=50=      }
=51=    }
=52=
=53=    for my $year_month (sort keys %count) {
=54=      for my $day (sort {$a <=> $b} keys %{$count{$year_month}}) {
=55=        for my $hour (0..23) {
=56=          my $hits = $count{$year_month}{$day}{$hour} || 0;
=57=          printf "%s %02d %02d: %d\n", $year_month, $day, $hour, $hits;
=58=        }
=59=      }
=60=    }
```

Extracting Referer Search Strings from the Referer Log

Web Techniques, Column 26 (June 1998)

■Randal's Note Shortly after I released this code, a new module popped up on the CPAN called URI::Sequin, which had this very same knowledge of URLs mapped to search engine names. If I had written this program later, I'd probably have used that module.

Last month's column could have been titled "Where Did They Go?" because I explored tracking the outbound links from my site to the interesting URLs I had provided on my pages. In this month's column, I'm looking at "Where Did They Come From?"

In particular, much of the web's content is now found these days not by interesting URLs posted on other sites, but by users typing in search queries to the big indexing engines like AltaVista, Lycos, and Infoseek. If you're maintaining a referer log, you may have noticed that the query strings typed in by the user sometimes show up when that user follows a search results link to your page. This happens because the indexer's search page is often a GET form, and the parameters of the search are therefore encoded into the URL of the search results page.

And having noticed that, I decided to write a program that would go through my referer log and extract just the search strings. This is more than an idle curiosity; it tells me exactly what people are looking for that brought them to my page, and what I should be providing more of if I want to have my site be popular. Especially if I'm selling ads or wanting to be famous.

The *referer log* (available with some configuration parameters for most popular web servers) is merely a record of the HTTP Referer header (yes, it's spelled that way for historical reasons), which will frequently point to the URL from which the URL request is being made. The referer is not necessarily supported on all browsers and will be messed up on a bookmarked entry. But for the majority of hits, the referer can give valuable information (as you can see by looking at the results of this program on your site).

The program to extract the search strings from the referer log is given in Listing 5-8.

Line 1 contains the path to Perl, along with the command-line switches that enable taint mode and warnings. Taint mode doesn't make much sense here, but I turned it on in case I decide later to make this a CGI script. Warnings are useful, but they can occasionally get in the way.

Line 2 turns on the compiler restrictions useful for all programs greater than ten lines or so. This includes disabling soft references (almost always a good idea), turning off "Perl poetry mode," and (most important) requiring all nonpackage variables to be declared. Variables will thus need to be introduced with an appropriate my directive.

Line 3 unbuffers STDOUT, causing all output to happen at the time it is printed, not when the STDIO buffer fills up. This is handy because it lets me see the output nearly immediately for a large log file, rather than having to wait until program exit time for the automatic buffer flush.

Line 5 pulls in the URI::URL module from the LWP library. This library is the all-singing, all-dancing, everything-you-wanted library to handle nearly all web-ish stuff in Perl, and can be found in the CPAN. Of course, if you're doing anything with Perl and the web, you've probably already got this installed. We need this library to pull apart the referer URL.

Line 7 defines the result hash as %count, which will ultimately hold a hash of hashes of counts of how many times each query string was used from a particular search engine. Initially, it needs to be empty, so we set it to the empty list (becoming the empty hash).

Lines 8 through 53 define the *data-gathering* loop. For each line in the referer log, we'll go through this loop once, with the line in $_. The data will be taken either from standard input or from the list of files specified on the command line.

Line 9 pulls out the referer information from the line. For a standard RefererLog-style log, this'll look like

```
there -> here
```

And since we're only interested in there, it's simple enough to just pull out all the white-space-separated items, and grab the first one, here kept in $ref. If you have a different log file format, you'll have to adjust this line to pull out the field you need.

Line 10 turns the referer string in $ref into a URI::URL object, using the subroutine url defined in that module. If $ref is empty or not a valid URL, the object may be malformed, but that'll be caught in the next step.

Line 11 verifies that we have a valid http: URL. The scheme method on the URL object returns back either a string or undef. If it's not defined, the or operator (two vertical bars) selects the empty string as an alternative, to prevent the use of an undef value in a further calculation, which triggers a warning under -w. If this URL is not an HTTP URL, then we skip it.

Line 12 extracts the portion of the URL string after the ? as a query form, if it is at all possible. The eval block protects this program from an exception in the query_form method, which throws up a die if there isn't a valid form. The result of the eval creates a new hash, %form. The keys of this hash are the query field names, and the corresponding values are the field values.

Lines 13 through 39 create a value for @search_fields, specifying for a particular search engine host what we're guessing is the search query string. This list can have many kinds of values:

- If the list is empty, then we ignore this particular search engine. (Either it's not a search engine or we can't find anything useful to note as a search string.)

- If the list consists of only uppercase words, then all fields of the query will be dumped (used for the catchall entry at the end).

- In the common case, if the list consists of one or more lowercase words, these represent form fields of interest, probably with the search string that brought the client here.

To construct this list, I started with a very small list, and ran it over my referer log of a few months. For every search engine that was dumped out as an *other*, I figured out which of the fields looked like a search list and added them in. I also got a bit of help from *Teratogen* on IRC (known in "real life" as Anthony Nemmer of EdelSys Consulting), who had apparently tackled a similar problem before and identified a significantly larger portion of the list from his own data.

The list is incomplete and evolves over time, so the names here are merely a good cross section. And, there are search engines that *don't* use a GET method to go from the search page to the results, and thus their parameters won't show up in the URL. But as you can see, a good number of the popular ones (AltaVista, Excite, HotBot, Infoseek, Lycos, Search.com, and WebCrawler) do.

Line 14 extracts the hostname from the referer URL and makes it lowercase. (We could have made all the comparisons case insensitive, but this alternative was much faster.)

Lines 15 through 38 form a long if..elsif..elsif..else structure. Note that it begins with if 0, which will always be false, but permits all the remaining cases to be symmetrical. This is nice because it allows me to swap the order of the checking trivially (by exchanging lines in a text editor) or even sorting them if I wish.

The hostname is compared with each of the regular expressions in turn. Note that some of the hostnames are looking only for a particular hostname portion, while others are bounded by the complete suffix to the end of the string. In particular, I found many different hosts with AltaVista, and they all seemed to use the same query field, so writing the test for it this way made sense.

Note that they are tested in the order presented. I found some form being used in edit.my.yahoo.com that was nothing like the query form in www.yahoo.com (and friends), so I placed a special *blocking* entry ahead of the Yahoo main entry, saying "Don't bother with this one; it's not the same." Otherwise, the ordering of this list is somewhat arbitrary, and for efficiency reasons should probably be placed with the most likely one first.

The multiway if statement is within a do block, meaning that the last expression evaluated will be the return value. If you don't like the structure requiring the use of elsif chunks, you can write other switch statements enclosed in sub-blocks, like so:

```
my @search_fields = "UNKNOWN";
{
    local $_ = lc $url->host;
    (@search_fields = "q"), last if /\baltavista\b/;
    (@search_fields = qw(s search)), last if /\bnetfind\.aol\.com$/;
    ...;
    (@search_fields = "p"), last if /\byahoo\b/;
}
```

But I didn't like the number of times I'd have to say @search_fields, and went with the do block structure instead. Another alternative might be to call a subroutine, like this:

```
my @search_fields = &map_to_engine($url);
sub map_to_engine {
    local $_ = lc shift->host;
    return "q" if /\baltavista\b/;
    return qw(s search) if /\bnetfind\.aol\.com$/;
    ...;
    return "p" if /\byahoo\b/;
    return "UNKNOWN";
}
```

And in fact, to some that looks cleaner than what I wrote. Your choice, however. After all, the Perl motto is "There's more than one way to do it."

In line 40, we check the result of that multiway test. If @search_fields is empty, it's the signal that this line is noisy, and we can skip it. Otherwise, in line 41, we'll translate this list into a hash to do a fast lookup. The map operator takes the elements of the list in @search_fields, interposes a single 1 after each element, and turns that into the %wanted hash, with keys being the original elements of the list.

Line 42 scans the form fields from %form, keeping only those elements that match the keys of %wanted in a case-insensitive manner. This is accomplished through the clever use of lower-casing the value of $_ before doing the lookup. Thus, @show_fields will be a list of all the form fields of interest, if any.

If @show_fields has one or more elements, we found a valid search site along with an interesting field (hopefully a search string). In that case, we'll save the search string for later dumping. Lines 44 through 46 store the information into a hash of hashrefs, with the first level being the host and the second level being the particular search string used at that host. A count is maintained, and for the most part it will be just an increment from undef to 1. Occasionally, when the same search string is used (or repeated), we'll get multiple hits.

On the other hand, if @show_fields is empty, we were either looking at a referer URL that had a form from an unknown site, or somehow one of the known sites didn't have the proper field. In that case, we'll dump out the entire form immediately, so that you can consider it manually to locate a search string for a future run. That's handled in lines 48 through 51, which simply dump the %form variable preceded by the search host.

Lines 55 through 63 dump the search string hash-of-hashrefs. Each of the hostnames ends up in $host in line 55. (If you don't have a relatively modern version of Perl, the for my syntax will not work. Upgrade now, because it's free and less buggy than the version you're running.)

Line 56 extracts the hashref value from the top-level hash, which is then dereferenced in line 57 to get the individual searchtext items into $text. Lines 58 to 62 dump out the hostname, textstring, and number of times each item was found (if more than once).

And there you have it. To use this program, adjust the "referer field" parsing line according to the format of your referer log, and then pass the name of the log on the command line to this program. You could even wrap this up into a nightly job, and with a little work generate an HTML output file that creates links back to the search engines in question! (Sounds like an interesting additional project if I've got another hour or two.) Enjoy!

Listing 5-8

```
=1=      #!/usr/bin/perl -Tw
=2=      use strict;
=3=      $|++;
=4=
=5=      use URI::URL;
=6=
=7=      my %count = ();
=8=      while (<>) {
=9=        my ($ref) = split; ## may require adjustment
=10=       my $url = url $ref;
=11=       next unless ($url->scheme || "") eq "http";
=12=       next unless my %form = eval { $url->query_form };
```

```
=13=        my @search_fields = do {
=14=          local $_ = lc $url->host;
=15=          if (0) { () }
=16=          elsif (/\baltavista\b/) { "q" }
=17=          elsif (/\bnetfind\.aol\.com$/) { qw(s search) }
=18=          elsif (/\baskjeeves\.com$/) { "ask" }
=19=          elsif (/\bdejanews\.com$/) { () }
=20=          elsif (/\bdigiweb\.com$/) { "string" }
=21=          elsif (/\bdogpile\.com$/) { "q" }
=22=          elsif (/\bexcite\.com$/) { qw(s search) }
=23=          elsif (/\bhotbot\.com$/) { "mt" }
=24=          elsif (/\binference\.com$/) { "query" }
=25=          elsif (/\binfoseek\.com$/) { qw(oq qt) }
=26=          elsif (/\blooksmart\.com$/) { "key" }
=27=          elsif (/\blycos\b/) { "query" }
=28=          elsif (/\bmckinley\.com$/) { "search" }
=29=          elsif (/\bmetacrawler\b/) { "general" }
=30=          elsif (/\bnlsearch\.com$/) { "qr" }
=31=          elsif (/\bprodigy\.net$/) { "query" }
=32=          elsif (/\bsearch\.com$/) { qw(oldquery query) }
=33=          elsif (/\bsenrigan\.ascii\.co\.jp$/) { "word" }
=34=          elsif (/\bswitchboard\.com$/) { "sp" }
=35=          elsif (/\bwebcrawler\.com$/) { qw(search searchtext text) }
=36=          elsif (/\bedit\.my\.yahoo\.com$/) { () } ## must come before yahoo.com
=37=          elsif (/\byahoo\b/) { "p" }
=38=          else { "UNKNOWN" }
=39=        };
=40=        next unless @search_fields;
=41=        my %wanted = map { $_, 1 } @search_fields;
=42=        my @show_fields = grep { $wanted{lc $_} } keys %form;
=43=        if (@show_fields) {
=44=          for (@show_fields) {
=45=            $count{$url->host}{$form{$_}}++;
=46=          }
=47=        } else {
=48=          print $url->host, "\n";
=49=          for (sort keys %form) {
=50=            print "?? $_ => $form{$_}\n";
=51=          }
=52=        }
=53=      }
=54=
=55=      for my $host (sort keys %count) {
=56=        my $hostinfo = $count{$host};
=57=        for my $text (sort keys %$hostinfo) {
=58=          my $times = $hostinfo->{$text};
=59=          print "$host: $text";
```

```
=60=          print " ($times times)" if $times > 1;
=61=          print "\n";
=62=      }
=63=    }
```

Tracking Click-Throughs

Web Techniques, Column 25 (May 1998)

■**Randal's Note** I still use /cgi/go on my web pages, but it's no longer the CGI script from this column. Instead, I have some code with mod_rewrite that looks like

```
RewriteRule ^/cgi/go/(.*)$ $1 [redirect,last,noescape]
```

to do the same thing without a "program." Much cooler and more efficient, but the same idea.

If your website is like any of the other 40 million pages out there, you've got links to other places on your site. These are usually some places that you found relevant, or maybe you just published your bookmarks as part of your site.

So, along I come, looking at your site, and I notice this really neat link to some interesting page. I click it and move on. However, because of the way the web works, you have no indication that I found that link interesting, and you may even start wondering if *anyone* finds the links on your carefully crafted web page useful.

Wouldn't it be nice to somehow track when someone *leaves* your site and what route they took to exit? Well, it's actually pretty easy to do, provided you're willing to take a CGI hit on each followed link. Essentially, you'll need to change all outbound links to a CGI invocation.

For example, instead of providing

```
<A HREF="http://www.perltraining.com">Get trained!</A>
```

as a link, you could change this to

```
<A HREF="/cgi/go/http://www.perltraining.com">Get trained!</A>
```

Now, although it looks like a URL down toward the end, it's really just data that shows up in the PATH_INFO environment variable of the /cgi/go CGI script on the web server. (That may seem like a lot of work to change all your existing links to match this new requirement, but stay tuned—I have a programmatic solution.)

So, if someone follows this link, the CGI script is invoked, and we get the URL as a parameter. For this to work, the script must note the invocation and then redirect the browser off to the real URL.

That's not tough either. In fact, the program ended up being shorter than I had expected, and is found in Listing 5-9.

Line 1 of this program turns on taint checks (a good idea for CGI scripts), and both compile-time and runtime warnings (generally a good idea for all programs).

Line 2 turns on all the compiler restrictions, requiring all variables to be declared, disabling symbolic references, and removing "bareword" interpretation. As always, this is a good idea for all programs over a dozen lines or so.

Line 3 disables output buffering. Because this program forks later, it's important that all output happens as it is requested.

Line 5 is the only configuration parameter for this program. The $GO_LOG variable holds the full pathname to the log file that will record the date and time of the click-through, as well as the source page and destination link.

Lines 7 through 15 form an eval block. This is a block of code that is being executed for a return value (to be stored in $result). However, at various places through the block, a die will cause an immediate exit, which we can check for later. This is a handy technique to evaluate a value with potential error conditions.

Line 8 grabs the PATH_INFO environment variable and stores it into the block-local variable $res. If for some reason this environment variable isn't defined, we abort immediately via the die.

Line 9 tries to remove the initial slash from the value originally in the PATH_INFO variable. When you invoke

```
/cgi/go/http://www.perltraining.com
```

the value of PATH_INFO is "/http://www.perltraining.com". That initial slash is annoyingly in the way, so let's just get rid of it. If no PATH_INFO was provided, then this also fails, preventing a simple invocation of /cgi/go from messing things up.

Line 10 fetches the QUERY_STRING, which is the part of the original URL after the question mark, if any. For example, if we see

```
/cgi/go/http://www.altavista.digital.com?q=Randal%20Schwartz
```

then we have to capture the part beginning with q=..., and this shows up in the QUERY_STRING variable, thankfully unmodified. If there's something out there, then we'll need to tack it on to the end of the URL that we'll be redirecting with eventually.

If there's a query string, line 11 detects it, and the query string gets appended (preceded by a question mark) in line 12.

The result has been computed into $res, and this gets returned from the block in line 14. That value will end up in $result from the assignment in line 7. Presuming, of course, that there has been no die operator executed along the way.

But if either of the die operators has been executed, the $@ variable is now nonempty, and line 16 detects this. If we've hit an error, we'll just have the CGI script return an HTTP 404 error, which the browser will interpret as "I guess I'm not gonna get to go here." This is handled in lines 17 and 18.

If we make it to line 20, we have a good solid URL to redirect this client toward, so that's handled with a simple Location header. And once we have a good redirect, it's time to note that fact. Otherwise, this was just an interesting pointless exercise.

Because we want the script to return quickly, we'll fork a background process to do the actual logging. Line 21 attempts to fork a process, storing the child pid (or 0) into $pid.

If $pid is not defined, then the fork failed. In this case, we'll make the browser wait a second or two while we write to the log file in the foreground instead. It's simple enough to do this by faking a $pid of 0 for a $pid of undefined, handled in line 22.

If we're the parent process, $pid is nonzero in line 23, and it's time to bail. If we're the kid, closing down STDOUT (in line 25) permits the web server to know that we won't be talking to the client any more.

Lines 26 through 33 write the data to the log file. Line 26 opens the log file in append mode.

Line 27 waits for an exclusive lock on the log file. Only one CGI writer will be allowed to proceed past this line at any given time.

Line 28 resynchronizes the internal buffer with the actual file and positions the file pointer at the end. This is important when flocking, because if we were blocking waiting for another script to finish, the file has now changed and we'll get data overwrite unless we seek (which forces a reread).

Lines 29 through 32 write a single information record (as a line of text) to the log file. This line is tab delimited, consisting of three fields: the current local date and time, the URL to which we are redirecting the client, and the referring page (if known).

Line 33 closes the log file, releasing the lock at the same time. It's not strictly necessary to close the filehandle at this point, since we have reached the end of the program. However, if someone comes along later to maintain this code, and adds other steps later, it's a good idea to release the lock as quickly as possible.

So, installing that little puppy as /cgi/go will start logging the invocations that invoke the script. And we can write various data-reduction Perl scripts on the log file, and will probably want to rotate log files and so on.

But that's not the end of what needs to be done. For this script to be invoked, we'll have to adjust the URL in the original HTML that we serve to the client. Sure, the text is easily adjusted in your favorite text editor, but there's a simpler way, since we have Perl at our disposal. Let's just have a Perl program that wanders through the HTML documents and edits them directly! Such a program has already been written and is presented in Listing 5-10.

Lines 1 through 3 of this program have been described previously. Line 5 pulls in the File::Find library, which I'm using to recursively locate all the HTML files in my web server's directory.

If a command-line argument or even multiple arguments are provided, they're treated as the HTML files to edit. However, if no arguments are provided, lines 7 through 11 locate all the HTML files in my website's directories.

Line 8 invokes the find routine (defined by File::Find), passing it an anonymous subroutine reference as the action subroutine, and starting from the top-level directory of my website files.

Line 12 gets rid of the ending delimiter on a read. This means that each read will read the *entire* file in one fell swoop.

Line 13 turns on "in-place editing mode." When files are read from ARGV (or the empty filehandle, as seen in line 14), they are also opened for updating, such that any print operator to the default filehandle replaces the previous contents. The suffix chosen here is ~, which makes the backup files for the replaced files look like they were edited by GNU Emacs. You can chose a more appropriate string if necessary.

Lines 14 through 26 walk through each file in @ARGV. The entire file's contents ends up in the $_ variable.

Lines 15 through 24 are actually a single substitute operator. However, notice that line 24 includes the suffix letters egi. This means that case is insensitive on the match, and the match is global across all of $_ but, most important, that the replacement side of the substitute is Perl code, not a simple variable-interpolated string.

Each time the pattern in line 15 is seen throughout $_, the code block in lines 16 through 23 is executed, and the last expression evaluated in that block becomes the replacement string. Line 16 creates three local variables, assigning two of them with the values of $1 and $2 (reflecting the current match).

Line 17 notes if this URL is worth replacing, by seeing if it begins with http: and ensuring that it isn't a reference to the click-through tracker already. If it's a valid-to-replace link, then we note that by printing a message to STDOUT, and create the new replacement string from the old URL prefixed by /cgi/go/ (in lines 18 and 19).

If the URL is not worth replacing, it's important that the replacement string be the same as the original string, handled in line 21. Regardless of whether or not a replacement has been selected, line 23 returns the string that must replace the original string.

Line 25 sends the updated string to the new file, but only if we're in in-place edit mode. (While I was testing, I commented line 13 out, and thus I was treated to merely the messages from line 19 telling me what it *would* have done had I let it.)

So, there you have it. A way of tracking click-throughs, or where people are going after they get bored with your site. Actually, I just installed this on my website, and it'll be interesting to see where people actually go. Until next time, enjoy!

Listing 5-9

```
=1=     #!/home/merlyn/bin/perl -Tw
=2=     use strict;
=3=     $|++;
=4=
=5=     my $GO_LOG = "/home/merlyn/Web/golog";
=6=
=7=     my $result = eval {
=8=       die unless defined (my $res = $ENV{PATH_INFO});
=9=       die unless $res =~ s/^\///;
=10=      my $query = $ENV{QUERY_STRING};
=11=      if (defined $query and length $query) {
=12=        $res .= "?$query";
=13=      }
=14=      $res;
=15=    };
=16=    if ($@) {
=17=      print "Status: 404 Not Found\n\n";
=18=      exit 0;
=19=    }
=20=    print "Location: $result\n\n";
=21=    my $pid = fork;
=22=    $pid = 0 unless defined $pid;    # be the kid if fork failed
=23=    exit 0 if $pid;
```

```
=24=    ## child...
=25=    close(STDOUT);
=26=    open GOLOG, ">>$GO_LOG" or die "Cannot open $GO_LOG: $!";
=27=    flock(GOLOG,2);                  # wait for exclusive
=28=    seek GOLOG, 0, 2;                # seek to end, refresh buffers
=29=    print GOLOG join("\t",
=30=                    scalar localtime,
=31=                    $result,
=32=                    ($ENV{HTTP_REFERER} || "[unknown]")), "\n";
=33=    close GOLOG;
```

Listing 5-10

```
=1=     #!/home/merlyn/bin/perl -w
=2=     use strict;
=3=     $|++;
=4=
=5=     use File::Find;
=6=
=7=     unless (@ARGV) {
=8=       find sub {
=9=         push @ARGV, $File::Find::name if /\.html/;
=10=      }, "/home/merlyn/Html/";
=11=    }
=12=    undef $/;
=13=    $^I = "~";
=14=    while (<>) {
=15=      s{(href="(.*?)")}{
=16=        my ($old,$url,$new) = ($1,$2);
=17=        if ($url =~ /^http:(?!.*cgi\/go)/) {
=18=          $new = qq{href="/cgi/go/$url"};
=19=          print STDOUT "$ARGV: changing $old to $new\n";
=20=        } else {
=21=          $new = $old;
=22=        }
=23=        $new;
=24=      }egi;
=25=      print if defined $^I;
=26=    }
```

Poor Man's Load Balancer

Web Techniques, Column 55 (November 2000)

▮**Randal's Note** As simple as this was, I got a lot of good feedback about how this code kept people from having to buy multi-kilo-buck versions of the same thing from various networking vendors. Nice. Glad I could help.

I was thinking about e-commerce the other day and chatting with my buddy Steven Lembark of Knightsbridge Solutions about the typical tiny dirty tasks related to e-commerce. He suggested that he hadn't seen any of my columns address the simple task of getting incoming requests to be "load balanced," and I said, "Hey, thanks for the idea."

After chatting with him a bit, I came up with a very simple way to ensure that incoming requests are sent to the best host for processing. It's not the most elegant approach, but it's probably the fewest lines of code you'll see on this topic, so I call it the "poor man's load balancer." Simply put, we run a daemon that gathers the load averages for the interchangeable machines in the cluster (interchangeable in that they should have identical content and response for the same URL, at least for some interesting set of URLs).

This daemon then writes a small database visible to a CGI script that can take an incoming URL and redirect the invoker to the same URL on the least-loaded machine, randomly redirecting the requests in proportion to the current load average. So, from the welcome page of the application, all the outgoing links are sent through this redirect script, and boom—the user ends up on the best machine at the moment. Not rocket science, but it'll do. So, let's take a look at how this works.

The first program to report back the load average is presented in Listing 5-11. There's not much to it. And oddly enough, since this is supposed to be a column about Perl, it's a CGI program written in (gasp!) Bourne shell! And I had started to write this program in Perl when I realized that I could just put all the smarts in the invoker rather than in this program, and since we're likely invoking it on machines that might already be pretty heavily loaded, why bother?

Anyway, all it does is invoke *uptime*, with a MIME identifier of text/plain, in line 5. I also experimented with using the Linux /proc/loadavg pseudo-file, and that generated similar results, so take your pick.

So we install that on all of our monitored boxes. What next? Well, we create a file that defines the boxes and the path to the CGI script on each box (which might be different for security or admin reasons). The file looks like a series of hosts and CGI paths:

```
www1.myhost.comm /cgi/get_load
www2.myhost.comm /cgi/get_load
www3.myhost.comm /cgi_bin/get_load
```

And then we need a daemon to wander through this file, grab all the hosts, and fetch the load averages. And that'd be the program presented in Listing 5-12.

Line 1 starts the program, turning on warnings. This is not a CGI-invoked script, so I don't turn on the usual taint checking (but see later for a description of that). Line 2 invokes the normal compiler restrictions, disabling the use of symbolic references, default packages, and barewords, which is always a good thing if the program exceeds a screenful of coding. Line 3 disables the output buffering—not really needed here, but handy in testing when you're adding print operations to see where things are going astray.

Line 5 brings in the LWP::Simple module, part of the LWP distribution in the CPAN. This quick-and-dirty program doesn't need much more in the way of web-ish interface. Perhaps you'd want to configure a specific browser-user-agent string in a production version of this program for logging purposes (to exclude it from the actual hits), or maybe you wouldn't care.

Lines 7 to 11 define the things most likely to change as we reuse or refine this program. The path in $ACTIVE is the file generated by this program, listing the hosts and their respective load averages. The directory containing the file must be writable by the program and readable by the CGI script shown later. The path in $CONFIG contains the list of hostnames and CGI URLs, as shown earlier. And finally, the loop time in seconds shows how frequently we'll poll the host. It might take longer than this, but we'll sleep if it's taking shorter.

Line 13 defines a global %hosts hash to hold the various hosts we'll poll and the CGI paths on each host. We cache this information from the $CONFIG file, so we note its most recent modification time in $host_check_time in line 14, but set that to 0 initially so that we'll read the file on the first pass. Finally, line 15 defines the baseline time so that we don't run the loop too often.

Line 17 starts a "forever" loop. Well, at least until we kill the program.

Lines 18 to 24 read the configuration file if needed. First, we see if the file is newer than the last time we looked (definitely true at the beginning of the program). If so, line 20 opens the file, and line 21 parses the lines. We throw away any commented lines, and then we grab the first two non-whitespace elements remaining to be key/value pairs for the %hosts hash. Simple parsing, and yet it lets us comment out hosts that are temporarily unavailable, say during a backup operation or something. Line 23 notes the modification time so that we don't have to reread that version of the file. (In retrospect, given the relatively tiny amount of CPU I'm likely saving by keeping this cached in memory, it probably would have been easier to just reparse the file on each iteration. Another case of premature optimization!)

So, on to gather the data. A new hash gets declared in line 25. Each host is then prodded in lines 26 to 31. The URL is constructed from the hostname and the CGI URL path. Note that the hostname might include a port number here, and this would work just fine both here and in the redirection script. Line 28 tosses error results, and line 29 looks for the first floating-point number in the response. (Both uptime and the contents of /proc/loadavg have the one-minute load average as their first floating-point value.) Line 30 stores this value into the hash.

Lines 32 through 36 save these new results. To ensure that the CGI scripts don't see a partial result, we write a temporary file with the new data, and then rename it (in line 36) as an atomic operation. It's very important when designing multitasking systems to figure out what might be erroneously partially read, and then make sure that never happens.

Finally, lines 37 to 40 ensure that we don't run through the hosts any more frequently than the minimum loop time. We take the current time from the next loop time, and if there's still some time to waste, we sleep in line 38.

So, we set this program running, perhaps launched from the system startup scripts, or perhaps just the core of the loop re-invoked frequently from cron, and that will keep our $ACTIVE file updated with fairly recent load averages for the hosts in question.

Now it's time to send the incoming requests to these hosts in a way that biases them toward the least-loaded host. That's done with the CGI script in Listing 5-13.

First, lines 1 through 3 start nearly every CGI script I write. Line 1 turns on warnings *and* taint checking, keeping me from doing something stupid with unchecked input data. Lines 2 and 3 turn on compiler restrictions and disable output buffering, as described for the daemon program.

Line 6 contains the configuration value for the path to the file created by the daemon. It's important that these stay in sync. Perhaps one solution would be to have both the CGI script and the daemon require a common file, but that would just add clutter in this example.

Line 9 pulls in the CGI module, looking in particular for the redirect function. I probably could have hand-coded the redirection instead of using CGI.pm's shortcut, but again, I'm showing the proof of concept here, not necessarily the most optimized way of doing the task. In fact, since this task is probably invoked the most frequently of anything in this particular suite of programs, you'd want this to be very lean and mean. On my own site, I'd probably rewrite this as a mod_perl handler to avoid even forking a CGI script.

Line 10 pulls in CGI::Carp so that the die messages later will not give me a 500 error during debugging, but instead get displayed to the browser. *Do not* leave this hook in a production program. You will be revealing far too much information to a would-be intruder on an error.

Line 12 opens the active file, so we can start looking for a candidate host. Line 13 declares the variable that will hold the best candidate so far and the total "scale" so far (described in a moment).

Lines 14 to 20 process each line of the active file. For each host, we grab the host (possibly including a port specification) and the load average as two whitespace-separated strings.

Line 16 adjusts the low load averages to be 0.01 automatically, otherwise we'd get a divide-by-zero in the next line.

Line 17 computes a weight or "scale" by which we will likely prefer this host, as the reciprocal of the load average squared. I made this up entirely in my head, but it makes sense (to me) because I want a machine with a load average of 0.5 to be four times more likely picked than one of 1.0. If you play with this and find a better weighting algorithm, let me know and I'll report back in a future column.

Once we have the weight for this item, we need to see if this is the one to be picked. We do this with a nice, one-pass, weighted-random-selection trick like I first used in this column in December 1996. If a random number between zero and the summed likelihood of all hosts seen so far does not exceed the likelihood of this host, then this is a host we should remember, otherwise we keep whatever we picked before. Works nice, and is nicely fair.

If we didn't pick a host, something is rotten in Denmark, and so we die. In a production environment, we'd have some host to fall back on, always, and then send some alarm up to notify that we've got an unexpected meltdown about to occur.

Line 22 starts to construct the redirection URL, by taking the hostname and turning it into the beginnings of a path. Line 23 takes the PATH_INFO and tacks in on, so that if this script were invoked as

```
/cgi/redirect/cgi/getjob
```

we'd be redirecting to

```
http://www1.myhost.comm/cgi/getjob
```

And finally, we've got the query string to deal with, in line 24. If present, we'll take everything after the question mark and tack it on to our redirection URL after a question mark.

Line 25 boots the browser out into the new location, and we're done!

We'll install this as `http://www.myhost.comm/cgi/redirect`, and then make any link that should be "load balanced" to be prefixed with this name, and the script takes care of the rest.

So, there you have it: a poor man's load balancer, all in a few dozen lines of Perl. You could pay hundreds of dollars for code like this, and you'd probably get stuff that's better documented and did more, but not as fun to tinker with. Until next time, enjoy!

Listing 5-11

```
=1=     #!/bin/sh
=2=     echo content-type: text/plain
=3=     echo
=4=     # cat /proc/loadavg
=5=     uptime
```

Listing 5-12

```
=1=     #!/usr/bin/perl -w
=2=     use strict;
=3=     $|++;
=4=
=5=     use LWP::Simple;
=6=
=7=     ## BEGIN CONFIG
=8=     my $ACTIVE = "/home/merlyn/Web/Balance/active";
=9=     my $CONFIG = "/home/merlyn/Web/Balance/config";
=10=    my $MIN_LOOP_TIME = 30;
=11=    ## END CONFIG
=12=
=13=    my %hosts;
=14=    my $host_check_time = 0;
=15=    my $loop_time = time;
=16=
=17=    { # forever do:
=18=      my $stat_time = (stat $CONFIG)[9];
=19=      if ($stat_time and $stat_time > $host_check_time) {
=20=        open CONFIG, $CONFIG or die "Cannot open $CONFIG: $!";
=21=        %hosts = map /^(\S+) (\S+)/, grep !/^#/, <CONFIG>;
=22=        close CONFIG;
=23=        $host_check_time = $stat_time;
=24=      }
```

```
=25=     my %results;
=26=     for my $host (keys %hosts) {
=27=       my $result = get "http://$host$hosts{$host}";
=28=       next unless defined $result;
=29=       next unless $result =~ /(\d+\.\d+)/;
=30=       $results{$host} = $1;
=31=     }
=32=     my $output = "$ACTIVE.tmp";
=33=     open NEW, ">$output" or die "Cannot create $output: $!";
=34=     print NEW "$_ $results{$_}\n" for keys %results;
=35=     close NEW;
=36=     rename $output, $ACTIVE or warn "Cannot rename $output to $ACTIVE: $!";
=37=     my $delay = $loop_time + $MIN_LOOP_TIME - time;
=38=     sleep $delay if $delay > 0;
=39=     $loop_time = time;
=40=     redo;
=41=   }
```

Listing 5-13

```
=1=    #!/usr/bin/perl -Tw
=2=    use strict;
=3=    $|++;
=4=
=5=    ## BEGIN CONFIG
=6=    my $ACTIVE = "/home/merlyn/Web/Balance/active";
=7=    ## END CONFIG
=8=
=9=    use CGI qw(redirect);
=10=   use CGI::Carp qw(fatalsToBrowser);
=11=
=12=   open ACTIVE, $ACTIVE or die "Cannot open $ACTIVE: $!";
=13=   my($selected_host, $total_scale);
=14=   while (<ACTIVE>) {
=15=     my($host, $loadav) = split;
=16=     $loadav = 0.01 if $loadav < 0.01;
=17=     my($scale) = 1/($loadav*$loadav);
=18=     $total_scale += $scale;
=19=     $selected_host = $host if rand($total_scale) < $scale;
=20=   }
=21=   die "Cannot find a valid host" unless $selected_host;
=22=   my $redirect = "http://$selected_host";
=23=   $redirect .= "$ENV{PATH_INFO}";
=24=   $redirect .= "?$ENV{QUERY_STRING}" if length $ENV{QUERY_STRING};
=25=   print redirect($redirect);
```

Calculating Download Time

Web Techniques, Column 63 (July 2001)

■**Randal's Note** There are professional programs out there to do what this program does for free. I'm always amazed at how much people are willing to charge for freely available information or code. Of course, the baseline 28.8 modem used in this article has long disappeared, unless you're stuck at a hotel with a dialup through a PBX.

It's a simple problem, really. You click a link to a site. It starts loading. But you're on a slow modem dialup. So it keeps loading, and loading, and loading, with the little browser icon in the upper right continuing its animation as if that will distract you enough to not notice that the page still hasn't finished. But still it keeps loading. Until finally, just when you're about to click Stop, it's done.

Why are these pages so big? Why are most pages so unfriendly to slow links? I suspect it's because most pages are being designed on intranets these days, and nobody ever bothers to go home to test it out from their ISP connection. And that's unfortunate.

As a simple test, we could at least write a little program to download the entire page with all of its links, and see how many bytes would be needed to satisfy the browser. Of course, we'd have to go through all of the HTML, looking for embedded images, sounds, objects (like Flash), and frame links. Hmm, sounds like a lot of work. Unless you have the right tools, like Perl's wonderful LWP library. So I wrote such a program, and I'm presenting it in Listing 5-14.

Line 1 turns on warnings—a good thing while developing. Line 2 enables the common compiler restrictions, forcing us to declare our variables, avoid the use of barewords, and stay away from symbolic references. Line 3 enables auto-flushing on STDOUT, so each line of output will be immediately visible as it is printed.

Lines 5 through 8 pull in four modules from the LWP library. If you don't have LWP installed, you can use the CPAN module to do this without a lot of hassle as follows:

```
$ perl -MCPAN -eshell
cpan> install Bundle::LWP
```

You may have to answer some questions if this is your first time installing with CPAN.pm.

The LWP::UserAgent module provides the web client object. HTTP::Cookies handles cookie-based interactions. HTTP::Request::Common creates common web requests. And HTML::LinkExtor parses HTML to find external URL links.

If you didn't know that these were all part of the LWP CPAN bundle, you could have just asked for them explicitly, as in

```
$ perl -MCPAN -eshell
cpan> install LWP::UserAgent
cpan> install HTTP::Cookies
cpan> install HTTP::Request::Common
cpan> install HTML::LinkExtor
```

Lines 10 through 28 define the %LINKS global hash, selecting the types of tag attributes that we believe will be loaded by the browser directly. I got this list easily; I grabbed the HTML::Tagset module and copied the value of linkElements out of there into here. Then I decided which of the items was a browser load. Please don't consider this list authoritative—it's just a best guess (and I'd appreciate feedback if I erred).

Note that one of the items is the href attribute of the link tag, which often contains the CSS file loaded by the browser. However, it also often contains other URLs that are not, and this is distinguishable only by looking at other attributes in the tag, which are unfortunately not provided by HTML::LinkExtor. Maybe a future version of HTML::LinkExtor will address this need.

Also, I'm not doing anything to look within the JavaScript of a page to get dynamic rollovers. That's a hard problem. I'd probably need a full JavaScript interpreter to do that. Ugh.

Lines 30 through 33 create the "virtual browser" as the global $ua variable, by first creating a generic object (line 30), giving it the right proxy information from the environment (line 31), setting a distinct user agent (line 32), and then setting up an in-memory "cookie jar" (line 33). The cookie jar allows us to visit pages that depend on having visited the referring URL, since any cookies will be properly handled by the virtual browser.

Line 35 calls the main routine report for each URL mentioned on the command line. Line 37 ends the program when we're done (which is not strictly necessary, since it's just subroutines from here down, but I like to keep my programs maintainable).

Now for the good stuff. The report routine beginning in line 39 is given a single URL, extracted in line 40. This routine pulls down the page and examines it for all URLs that would also have been loaded in a typical frame- and image-grokking browser. To do this, we'll maintain and populate two top-level data structures: the @todo array in line 42 and the %done hash in line 43.

The @todo array is a list of items that must still be processed, in the form of two-element references to arrays. The first element is the source URL (used to properly set the referer header), and the second element is the URL to fetch. We'll initially load the URL of interest into @todo, with an empty referer string. The %done hash serves double duty, both as a way of tracking which URLs we've already done (the keys), but also the number of bytes for that URL (the value) for later analysis.

Line 45 begins the "while there's still more to do" loop. Line 46 pulls off the first arrayref from the list, and explodes it into the referer string and the URL to be fetched. Line 47 skips over the ones we've already done.

Lines 49 and 50 fetch the page, by creating a GET request with the proper referer header and fetching it with the virtual browser. The result is always an HTTP::Response object.

If the fetch is successful, line 52 detects that. We'll take the content into $content in line 53, and put its length into the value for %done as well, keyed by the URL we just fetched.

If the content was HTML, this means the browser would then have displayed the HTML and will then crawl through looking for images, sounds, subframes, and other things, so we must do likewise. Line 55 detects the presence of such HTML by noting the MIME type of the content.

Line 57 pulls out the "base" URL from the HTTP::Response object. Normally, this is the same as the original URL. However, if the HTML header contains a "base" URL, then a browser would have calculated all relative URLs from that base URL, not the fetching URL, so we must do likewise. Luckily, the base method just does the right thing and gives us what we need, regardless of whether it was specified or not.

Line 58 sets up the `HTML::LinkExtor` object, giving it no callback function, but specifying the base URL for relative links. Without a callback function, the data is merely gathered into an internal object variable, which we'll access with a `links` method later. Lines 59 and 60 hand the HTML content to the object, triggering a complete parse pass.

Lines 61 through 71 pull out the link information, item by item. Each link (in `$link`) is an arrayref. The arrayref is dereferenced in line 62 to reveal an initial tag name (ending up in `$tag`) followed by key/value pairs of attributes, which are rolled up into the `%attr` hash.

Line 63 detects the tag name being an item of interest. The `HTML::LinkExtor` module finds *all* possible outbound URLs, but we're interested only in the ones that would be loaded by the browser right away. If the tag is in `%LINKS`, then we check each of the attributes in the list to see if it's something we saw in the HTML content (line 65) *and* it's a nonempty value (line 66).

If we have a URL of interest, we push that onto the "to-do" list, as a two-element item with the `$base` URL for a referer. I was puzzled if this should be `$base` or `$url`, and settled on `$base` for no solid reason. You could probably write me to convince me I'm wrong on this and I wouldn't take it personally.

Well, that handles the typical HTML page. But we also have some other kinds of responses from a fetch. The other typical response is a *redirect*, where the remote server indicated that a different URL should be fetched. That's handled in lines 73 to 76. First, we count the length of the content (because the browser would still be fetching all of the response content),then fetch the location header (the new URL), and then queue up a fetch of this new URL. Again, I wasn't sure what referer string should be given to this fetch, so I settled on `$url`. Again, I could be easily argued out of it (and I bet it's inconsistent among browser implementations).

And if it's not a good fetch or a redirect, it's probably an error, detected in line 77. Line 78 merely dumps this information to the invoker, on the odds that this is something that won't make much sense to try to correct from, and simple information is all that's required.

When the to-do list has been completed, we drop out of the big loop, down to the reporting phase, beginning in line 83. Line 84 creates a local temporary variable, initializing it to 0. This will be the total number of bytes fetched by the browser for this URL. Line 86 shows the URL name for labeling purposes.

Lines 87 to 90 go through all the entries in the `%done` hash. Elements of the hash are sorted by descending numeric order on the values, so that we get a quick idea of the piggiest part of the page. As each URL and byte size is pulled up, the total is updated in line 88 and formatted nicely in line 89 using `printf`.

Lines 91 and 92 do what we came here for. The total downloaded bytes are shown in line 91, and line 92 computes the download time at a conservative 2,000 bytes per second on a 28.8 dialup line. (I'm painfully aware of how slow this is, as I spend much of my time bouncing around from one hotel to another, very much missing my cable modem at home.)

Let's look at a couple of typical reports, for both `www.webtechniques.com` and my own archive of columns (and listings) at `www.stonehenge.com/merlyn/WebTechniques/`:

```
$ dltime http://www.webtechniques.com/⏎
  http://www.stonehenge.com/merlyn/WebTechniques/
http://www.webtechniques.com/ =>
      29945  http://www.webtechniques.com/gifs/covers/0105cov_straight.jpg
      18548  http://www.webtechniques.com/
      10525  http://img.cmpnet.com/ads/graphics/cs/cg/heyyou.gif
       9604  http://img.cmpnet.com/ads/graphics/cs/ar/webreview_125.gif
       9342  http://img.cmpnet.com/ads/graphics/cs/ar/wiwm_120.gif
```

```
7691  http://www.webtechniques.com/gifs/subscribeto.jpg
7336  http://img.cmpnet.com/ads/graphics/cs/cg/latest.gif
5950  http://img.cmpnet.com/ads/graphics/cs/ar/develop_120x240.gif
3577  http://www.webtechniques.com/gifs/wtlogo_right.gif
2096  http://www.webtechniques.com/gifs/logo_footer_r2_c3.gif
2056  http://img.cmpnet.com/ads/graphics/cs/ar/tech_reviews_120.gif
1934  http://www.webtechniques.com/gifs/logo_footer_r2_c4.gif
1707  http://www.webtechniques.com/gifs/logo_footer_r2_c1.gif
1463  http://www.webtechniques.com/gifs/wtlogo_left.gif
1365  http://www.webtechniques.com/gifs/logo_footer_r2_c2.gif
1094  http://www.webtechniques.com/gifs/logo_footer_r1_c1.gif
 860  http://www.webtechniques.com/gifs/triangle.gif
 419  http://www.webtechniques.com/gifs/toctab.gif
 382  http://newads.cmpnet.com/js.ng/Params.richmedia=yes&↵
   site=webtechniques&pagepos=middletile&webreview_pos=wthome
 369  http://newads.cmpnet.com/js.ng/Params.richmedia=yes&↵
   site=webtechniques&pagepos=verticalbanner&webreview_pos=wthome
 363  http://newads.cmpnet.com/js.ng/Params.richmedia=yes&↵
   site=webtechniques&pagepos=topleftbutton
 346  http://newads.cmpnet.com/js.ng/Params.richmedia=yes&↵
   site=webtechniques&pagepos=bottombutton
 337  http://newads.cmpnet.com/html.ng/site=webtechniques&↵
   pagepos=middletile&webreview_pos=wthome
 335  http://newads.cmpnet.com/js.ng/Params.richmedia=yes&↵
   site=webtechniques&pagepos=tile&webreview_pos=wthome
 333  http://newads.cmpnet.com/js.ng/Params.richmedia=yes&↵
   site=webtechniques&pagepos=top&webreview_pos=wthome
 328  http://newads.cmpnet.com/html.ng/site=webtechniques&↵
   pagepos=verticalbanner&webreview_pos=wthome
 328  http://newads.cmpnet.com/js.ng/Params.richmedia=yes&↵
   site=webtechniques&pagepos=bottom
 318  http://newads.cmpnet.com/html.ng/site=webtechniques&↵
   pagepos=topleftbutton
 301  http://newads.cmpnet.com/html.ng/site=webtechniques&↵
   pagepos=bottombutton
 290  http://newads.cmpnet.com/html.ng/site=webtechniques&pagepos=tile&↵
   webreview_pos=wthome
 288  http://newads.cmpnet.com/html.ng/site=webtechniques&↵
   pagepos=top&webreview_pos=wthome
 283  http://newads.cmpnet.com/html.ng/site=webtechniques&pagepos=bottom
 261  http://www.webtechniques.com/gifs/bottom341head.gif
 252  http://www.webtechniques.com/gifs/top341head.gif
 147  http://www.webtechniques.com/gifs/bottom127head.gif
 142  http://www.webtechniques.com/gifs/top127head.gif
  69  http://www.webtechniques.com/gifs/mid4head.gif
  54  http://www.webtechniques.com/gifs/bottom4head.gif
  53  http://www.webtechniques.com/gifs/top4head.gif
```

```
           42  http://www.webtechniques.com/gifs/pixel.gif
       121133  TOTAL
           61 seconds at 28.8
   http://www.stonehenge.com/merlyn/WebTechniques/ =>
        13916  http://www.stonehenge.com/merlyn/WebTechniques/
         9102  http://s1-images.amazon.com/images/A/TP10000000000000008.0206.⤶
    04._ZAGreetings,7,2,15,108,verdenab,8,204,102,0_ZADonate%20to%20my%20⤶
Legal%20Defense%20Fund%20today%21,7,14,50,108,times,11,0,0,0_.jpg
         5684  http://www.oreilly.com/catalog/covers/lperl2.s.gif
          861  http://images.paypal.com/images/x-click-but7.gif
          172  http://www.stonehenge.com/icons/right.gif
            0  http://s1.amazon.com/exec/varzea/tipbox/A3QRJOPB8JM4E4/T18JT4Y⤶
                V6ZQDB2
            0  http://s1.amazon.com/exec/varzea/tipbox/A3QRJOPB8JM4E4/T18JT4Y⤶
                V6ZQDB2/058-6613347-7642417
        29735  TOTAL
           15 seconds at 28.8
```

Ahh . . . look at that. That's 61 seconds of download time for the *Web Techniques* site, but only 15 seconds for my site. How nice. The big bottleneck on the *Web Techniques* home page seems to be the cover JPG. Maybe they can reduce the JPEG Q factor a bit to save some time. Or maybe this is an acceptable tradeoff. But at least now we know how long it'll take me to visit the *Web Techniques* home page from a hotel room. Time enough to hum the "Final Jeopardy" theme twice while I'm waiting. So until next time, enjoy!

Listing 5-14

```
=1=     #!/usr/bin/perl -w
=2=     use strict;
=3=     $|=1;
=4=
=5=     use LWP::UserAgent;
=6=     use HTTP::Cookies;
=7=     use HTTP::Request::Common;
=8=     use HTML::LinkExtor;
=9=
=10=    my %LINKS =                    # subset of %HTML::Tagset::linkElements
=11=      (
=12=      'applet'  => ['archive', 'codebase', 'code'],
=13=      'bgsound' => ['src'],
=14=      'body'    => ['background'],
=15=      'embed'   => ['src'],
=16=      'frame'   => ['src'],
=17=      'iframe'  => ['src'],
=18=      'ilayer'  => ['background'],
=19=      'img'     => ['src', 'lowsrc'],
=20=      'input'   => ['src'],
```

```
=21=      'layer'   => ['background', 'src'],
=22=      ## 'link'    => ['href'], ## durn, some of these are stylesheets
=23=      'script'  => ['src'],
=24=      'table'   => ['background'],
=25=      'td'      => ['background'],
=26=      'th'      => ['background'],
=27=      'tr'      => ['background'],
=28=    );
=29=
=30=    my $ua = LWP::UserAgent->new;
=31=    $ua->env_proxy;
=32=    $ua->agent("dltime/1.00 ".$ua->agent); # identify ourselves
=33=    $ua->cookie_jar(HTTP::Cookies->new); # capture cookies if needed
=34=
=35=    report($_) for @ARGV;
=36=
=37=    exit 0;
=38=
=39=    sub report {
=40=      my $start = shift;
=41=
=42=      my @todo = ["", $start];
=43=      my %done;
=44=
=45=      while (@todo) {
=46=        my ($refer, $url) = @{shift @todo};
=47=        next if exists $done{$url};
=48=
=49=        my $request = GET $url, [referer => $refer];
=50=        my $response = $ua->simple_request($request);
=51=
=52=        if ($response->is_success) {
=53=          $done{$url} = length (my $content = $response->content);
=54=
=55=          next if $response->content_type ne "text/html";
=56=
=57=          my $base = $response->base; # relative URLs measured relative to here
=58=          my $p = HTML::LinkExtor->new(undef, $base) or die;
=59=          $p->parse($content);
=60=          $p->eof;
=61=          for my $link ($p->links) {
=62=            my ($tag, %attr) = @$link;
=63=            if ($LINKS{$tag}) {
=64=              for (@{$LINKS{$tag}}) {
=65=                next unless exists $attr{$_};
=66=                next unless length (my $a = $attr{$_});
=67=                ## print "$base $tag $_ => $a\n"; ## debug
```

```
=68=                    push @todo, [$base, $a];
=69=                }
=70=              }
=71=            }
=72=
=73=        } elsif ($response->is_redirect) {
=74=            $done{$url} = length $response->content; # this counts
=75=            my $location = $response->header('location') or next;
=76=            push @todo, [$url, $location]; # but get this too
=77=        } elsif ($response->is_error) {
=78=            print "$url ERROR: ", $response->status_line, "\n";
=79=        }
=80=
=81=      }                               # end of outer loop
=82=
=83=      {
=84=        my $total = 0;
=85=
=86=        print "$start =>\n";
=87=        for my $url (sort { $done{$b} <=> $done{$a} } keys %done) {
=88=            $total += $done{$url};
=89=            printf "  %10d  %s\n", $done{$url}, $url;
=90=        }
=91=        printf "  %10d TOTAL\n", $total;
=92=        printf "  %10.0f seconds at 28.8\n\n", $total/2000;
=93=      }
=94=
=95=    }
```

Checking Your Website's Health, Part 1

Linux Magazine, Column 53 (November 2003)

■**Randal's Note** I got a lot of good feedback from this article about combining `Test::Harness` with `WWW::Mechanize`. Perhaps inspired by this article, Andy released `Test::WWW::Mechanize` shortly thereafter to handle some of the common cases directly.

In last month's column, I talked about checking one aspect of a website, namely that the internal links all point to other useful pages and that the external links are still valid.

But that's not the only thing that can go wrong with a website. If we're looking at continuous operation of an e-commerce site using the high-availability tricks described elsewhere, we also must ensure that search forms really operate and that the pages we visit have reasonable content. This is especially true for dynamically generated web pages, and particularly those that generate an "everything's OK" 200 status when the content of the page contains a Java traceback from a database connection.

So, to truly have high availability, we also have to be watching the associated programs and databases, and not just that the links all go somewhere reasonable.

The trick is to run a Perl program at regular intervals that connects to our web server and performs requests as if it was a visitor's browser. While we can do this fairly directly with the LWP package (or even low-level programming with sockets directly), I find it timesaving to use the rapidly evolving WWW::Mechanize package, found in the CPAN. This package lets me express web page fetches and form fill-out in a way that mimics my behavior with a browser, using LWP and HTML::Form to handle the details.

With WWW::Mechanize, I get a virtual user agent that steers like a browser. The next step is to figure out if we're getting the right responses from the web browser. For that, I prefer the Test::More module that is installed with modern Perl versions (and can be fetched from the CPAN for older Perl versions).

The Test::More module includes a number of tests that ultimately display a series of ok and not ok messages on STDOUT. These messages are normally interpreted by Test::Harness to give an overall thumbs-up or thumbs-down to a test (as when you are installing a module or Perl itself), but the individual messages and program flow are also directly useful.

For example, let's pretend we're in charge of search.cpan.org and responsible for its health. What would we want tested at regular intervals to ensure that it is running satisfactorily?

A quick first test would be to make sure that the top-level page can be fetched. Let's do this with WWW::Mechanize:

```
use WWW::Mechanize;
my $a = WWW::Mechanize->new;
$a->get("http://search.cpan.org/";);
```

Our virtual browser is now "looking at" the top-level page. But is it really? We can check the status using some Test::More routines:

```
use Test::More no_plan;
ok($a->success, "fetched /");
```

The ok routine evaluates the boolean returned by the success method. If the value is true, we get the output

```
ok 1 - fetched /
1..1
```

The first line says that the first test passed OK, including our comment for clear identification. The second line says that our tests were numbered from 1 to 1. While the exact format of the lines is dictated by Test::Harness (and described in that manpage), it's also grokkable by humans. If the fetch had been unsuccessful, we'd get something like this:

```
not ok 1 - fetched /
#     Failed test (./healthcheck at line 6)
1..1
# Looks like you failed 1 tests of 1.
```

The hash-marked lines are `Test::Harness` comments. Only the `not ok` and `1..1` lines are significant to the harness. But this didn't tell us why we failed. If we want to know how the result differs, we can use `is` rather than `ok`, which prints the offending value. Since we expect the status to be 200, we can check for that directly:

```
is($a->status, 200, "fetched /");
```

Now when the page fetch fails (like perhaps a 404 error), we get a more detailed message:

```
not ok 1 - fetched /
#     Failed test (./healthcheck at line 6)
#          got: '404'
#     expected: '200'
1..1
# Looks like you failed 1 tests of 1.
```

Of course, a 404 error on the root page is probably a clue that nothing else is going to work either.

We should probably make sure that we ended up with a `WWW::Mechanize` object on that new call as well. That's easy with the `isa_ok` routine provided by `Test::More`:

```
isa_ok(my $a = WWW::Mechanize->new, "WWW::Mechanize");
```

and now we get

```
ok 1 - The object isa WWW::Mechanize
ok 2 - fetched /
1..2
```

Note that we now have two tests, so the final display shows that our tests are numbered 1 through 2.

The default timeout for the user agent used by LWP is 180 seconds. If part of being "healthy" is that our website responds much faster than that, we can verify that by changing the timeout on our virtual browser:

```
$a->timeout(10);
```

We might also set our user-agent string to something more recognizable for the access logs, or maybe to ensure that our tests aren't included in the official statistics:

```
$a->agent("search.cpan.org-healthcheck/0.01");
```

If we get a good page fetch, we probably want to make sure it has the right content and isn't some other error page sent with a 200 status. A quick check might be to verify the title of the page with `Test::More`'s `like` routine:

```
like($a->title, qr/The CPAN Search Site/, "/ title is good");
```

The first argument is the target string. The second argument is typically specified using a regular expression literal object, although you can use a text string that starts and ends with a slash as well, for compatibility with old Perls that don't have `qr//`. If the target string matches, we get our next successful test. If it fails, both the target string and the regular expression are displayed, along with a failure for the test.

Obviously, this test will fail if the title is changed, so if you change the website, you'll have to change the tests. If your website is managed in a change-control system, you should also update, validate, and deploy this health check in the same manner as any other component of your website.

Let's see if the links on the front page are working correctly. We can do that with follow_link. We'll look for the link that says FAQ and see if it gets us to the FAQ:

```
ok($a->follow_link( text => 'FAQ' ), "follow FAQ link");
```

The follow_link method finds a link that has FAQ as the entire text. We could also find a link based on the URL, or a regular expression match of either the text or the URL. If multiple links match a particular requirement, we can also pick links based on their ordinal position. If the link isn't found, we get a false return, which fails the test. But if the link is found, we still need to find out if the page could be fetched:

```
is($a->status, 200, "fetched FAQ page");
```

And yet, this still might be a 200-status "error" page instead, so we should ensure that the content is as expected. This time we'll use like against the page content:

```
like($a->content, qr/Frequently Asked Questions/, "FAQ content matches");
```

Once we're satisfied that the link works, we want to go back to the beginning page for some other tests. While we could simply get the page again, let's just click our virtual back button:

```
$a->back;
```

So far, our output looks like this:

```
ok 1 - The object isa WWW::Mechanize
ok 2 - fetched /
ok 3 - / title matches
ok 4 - follow FAQ link
ok 5 - fetched FAQ page
ok 6 - FAQ content matches
1..6
```

Not bad. We know that our website is up and that at least two pages have reasonable HTML.

What if the FAQ link can't be found? We'll end up with an erroneous error and an erroneous success:

```
ok 1 - The object isa WWW::Mechanize
ok 2 - fetched /
ok 3 - / title matches
not ok 4 - follow FAQ link
#     Failed test (./healthcheck at line 10)
ok 5 - fetched FAQ page
not ok 6 - FAQ content matches
#     Failed test (./healthcheck at line 12)
#
```

```
# <!DOCTYPE HTML PUBLIC "-//W3C//DTD HTML 4.01 Transitional//EN">
... lots of text here ...
# </html>
# '
#     doesn't match '(?-xism:Frequently Asked Questions)'
1..6
# Looks like you failed 2 tests of 6.
```

Test 4 is correctly reporting that we couldn't find the FAQ link. But test 5 succeeds! The problem is that we're testing the successful fetch of the *previous* page, so it's a false positive. And test 6 is really irrelevant, because we're checking the home page for the FAQ content, which wouldn't make sense, and so we're getting a false negative.

What we need to do is skip tests 5 and 6 if test 4 fails. And also skip test 6 if test 5 fails. We can do this with Test::More's skip mechanism:

```
SKIP: {
    ok($a->follow_link( text => 'FAQ' ), "follow FAQ link")
        or skip "missing FAQ link", 2;
    SKIP: {
        is($a->status, 200, "fetched FAQ page")
            or skip "bad FAQ fetch", 1;
        like($a->content, qr/Frequently Asked Questions/,
            "FAQ content matches");
        $a->back;
    }
}
```

The skip mechanism uses a block labeled with SKIP to delimit the tests to be skipped. Since the ok function returns a boolean success, we can note a failed test, and execute skip to skip the remaining tests and exit the SKIP block. The first parameter to skip is the reason for skipping, while the second parameter is the number of tests to skip. We need to ensure the accuracy of that number because we don't want later tests to be renumbered if we skip some of these tests.

If the FAQ link can't be found, we get output that looks like this:

```
not ok 4 - follow FAQ link
#     Failed test (./healthcheck at line 10)
ok 5 # skip missing FAQ link
ok 6 # skip missing FAQ link
```

Note that the skipped tests appear to be "ok", although they've been annotated with a comment. This comment is recognized by Test::Harness so that it can say 2 tests skipped.

If the inner is fails, we will again skip, but only the one content test instead. If we maintain this code to add more tests, we'll need to update all of the skip numbers properly. Note that the back button is clicked only when we've gone forward as well.

Now let's try filling out a form by searching for a particular author. We'll start by selecting the first (and only) form on the page:

```
ok($a->form_number(1), "select query form");
```

Next, we'll look for Andy Lester's CPAN handle. (Andy is the current maintainer of both `Test::Harness` and `WWW::Mechanize`.) To do this, we need to know the form's field names, which we can get with a View Source on the web page:

```
$a->set_fields(query => "PETDANCE", mode => 'author');
```

When that's done, we can submit the form:

```
$a->submit;
```

At this point, we should be looking at Andy's detailed CPAN page. First, let's make sure it fetched OK:

```
is($a->status, 200, "query returned good for 'author'");
```

We can then see if Andy's name is mentioned somewhere on the page. This verifies that the CGI response is working, that the search engine is working, and that it's returning sensible data:

```
like($a->content, qr/Andy Lester/, "found Andy Lester");
```

And, of course, we'll want to skip back when we're done, ready for another test from the home page:

```
$a->back;
```

But if we can't find the form, or we can't fetch the page, we're executing too many tests and too much other code again, so we'll want to wrap this stuff up inside some nested skips as well:

```
SKIP: {
    ok($a->form_number(1), "select query form")
        or skip "cannot select query form", 2;
    $a->set_fields(query => "PETDANCE", mode => 'author');
    $a->submit();
    SKIP: {
        is($a->status, 200, "query returned good for 'author'")
            or skip "missing author page", 1;
        like($a->content, qr/Andy Lester/, "found Andy Lester");
        $a->back;
    }
}
```

And once again, we'll be skipping over any tests that would have given us false positives or false negatives.

In under three dozen lines of code, I now know that `http://search.cpan.org` is up and running, generating reasonable pages with links to the FAQ, and that it can execute searches for authors, returning reasonable data. And while there is room for many more tests to be performed, I've run out of room to talk about any more of it here. Next month, I'll explore this subject further, including how to notify someone only when something is breaking. Until then, enjoy!

Checking Your Website's Health, Part 2

Linux Magazine, Column 54 (December 2003)

■**Randal's Note** I've been told that this one column replaced hundreds of thousands of dollars of proprietary software at one company. Wow.

In last month's column, I showed how to create a testing program based on Perl's own testing framework together with WWW::Mechanize to test the health of a website. For reference, I've reproduced all of the code developed in last month's article in Listing 5-15.

The test code is run on demand to verify the proper operation of our target website: in this case, http://search.cpan.org. The output looks something like this:

```
1..9
ok 1 - The object isa WWW::Mechanize
ok 2 - fetched /
ok 3 - / title matches
ok 4 - follow FAQ link
ok 5 - fetched FAQ page
ok 6 - FAQ content matches
ok 7 - select query form
ok 8 - query returned good for 'author'
ok 9 - found Andy Lester
```

While invoking this program directly certainly gives us immediate status, it'd be more useful to run this program automatically and frequently. For example, I could invoke this program every five minutes from cron and then mail the results to my cell phone or pager. However, because there's a lot of output even when everything is OK, I'll be getting a lot of useless interruptions just to say "everything is OK."

Running the program under the standard Test::Harness module helps a bit. This module interprets the ok and not ok values appropriately, providing a nice summary at the end, resulting in output something like this:

```
01-search-cpan....ok
All tests successful.
Files=1, Tests=9,  2 wallclock secs ( 0.53 cusr +  0.05 csys = 0.58 CPU)
```

However, it's still hard to reduce the text to just pinpoint the errors, or know whether things were successful or a partial or total failure. Also, one thing I hate is being told the same thing over and over again when a failure occurs, or not being told when something has cleared up. And, the text doesn't squish well into a nice SMS message for my phone or pager.

So, let's take this one step further. The Test::Harness module inherits its core functionality from Test::Harness::Straps, which is still in development. We can use a Test::Harness::Straps object to invoke the test script and interpret its output in a way that is consistent with the Test::Harness interpretation, and programmatically determine which tests failed.

If we have that, we can tailor the output. One strategy might be to test every five minutes (from cron), but page a message only when things are broken, and then only once every thirty minutes. This message can be cut down to just precisely the failing tests, and perhaps the associated error output and exit status of the test program. Once the error clears up, the program can page on the next round with a single "all-clear" signal so that we can turn back around and head home again instead of finishing our trek into the office in the middle of the night to fix the problem.

Of course, there's more going on than just "all OK" and "something broken." We can consider each individual combination of "something broken" to be a different thing worthy of paging. Let's ensure that only one page per unique combination of events gets sent and one all-clear signal only when everything clears up.

Sound difficult? Not at all, especially when we use Cache::FileCache as a lightweight, time-oriented database. The resulting cron-job program is shown in Listing 5-16.

Lines 1 through 3 start nearly every program I write, turning on warnings and compiler restrictions, and disabling the buffering of STDOUT.

Lines 5 to 16 define the configuration section—things I'd be likely to change and want to locate quickly. The two time constants are defined in Cache::Cache-compatible units, which understands things like "15 seconds" and "4 hours." See the documentation for details. The $ALL_CLEAR_INTERVAL defines how often a repeat page saying "everything is OK" gets sent. If you set this to 1 day, you'll get a single page a day saying everything is OK as a nice meta-check that your health-check is OK. By setting it to never, you get one page when the monitoring starts the very first time, but never again unless it's after a failure has been fixed. Similarly, $TEST_FAIL_INTERVAL defines how often a page is sent for an identical combination of failures.

Lines 10 to 14 define the callback subroutine of what to do when an event of significance occurs. If this subroutine is called with no parameters, then it's the "all-clear" signal. Otherwise, it's the current error text. For debugging, I'm simply displaying this text to STDOUT, but by reopening standard output to a pipe to sendmail, I could just as easily send this to my cell phone or pager, presuming there's a mail gateway.

Lines 18 to 21 pull in the four modules needed by the rest of the program. Three of the four modules come with all recent Perl distributions, although you might have to upgrade your Test::Harness from the CPAN if you get an error because of Test::Harness::Straps. The fourth is Cache::FileCache, part of the Cache::Cache distribution.

Lines 23 and 24 create a temporary file and associated filehandle to let me capture the STDERR output from the various test programs being run (such as the one in Listing 5-15). The error output is usually diagnostic explanations and often elaborates on the reasons for failure. We also save the current STDERR so that we can reset it after every child process, so that our own die and warn messages end up in the right place.

Line 26 sets up the Cache::FileCache object, giving us a memory between invocations.

Line 28 ensures that our current directory is the same as the running script. This permits the paging program to be called as an absolute path in cron without having to manage the location of the test scripts, as long as they're all nearby.

Line 30 creates the Test::Harness::Straps object to interpret the result of one or more testing program invocations.

Line 32 collects the failure information that will eventually decide what we report. The array will contain arrayrefs; each referenced array has two elements. The first element is an identifying (hopefully unique) key of a failing condition, and the second is its associated text. We'll see how this gets created and reported later.

Lines 34 to 46 loop over every test file in either the current directory or a subdirectory named t, similar to the normal Test::Harness module-installation operation. Each of these tests is run separately, although the results will all be gathered for a single page. Instead of limiting the location of these *.t files to the current directory and one subdirectory, I might also want to use File::Find or a configuration file to define which tests are run.

Line 35 defines %results, having the same meaning as the Test::Harness::Straps documentation gives to the variable.

Lines 36 to 40 run a specific test file, using the Test::Harness::Straps object. Because we want to capture the STDERR output from each invocation, we must first redirect our own STDERR into the temporary file, then call the testing harness, and then restore it back. It's a bit messy, but necessary. Perhaps future versions of Test::Harness::Straps will provide a hook to do this directly.

Once we have the results, we're concerned with two things. First, did any of the tests fail? And second, did the test child exit in some unusual manner?

To see if any of the tests failed, we look at $results{details}, which references an array of individual tests and their results. Within each element of the array, the ok element of the hashref will be true if the test succeeded. If that's true, we simply ignore the test. If it's false, we'll add to @failed a new arrayref that contains an identification name for the test (offset by one because element 0 of the array is test 1) and the name the test gives itself (usually the text after the comment mark). This is all handled nicely by the map in lines 41 to 44.

If the child exited badly, we'll add another element with the wait status to @failed in line 45.

Lines 48 to 52 look at the standard error output that has accumulated from running all of the tests. If any output exists, it's gathered into another @failed entry keyed by errors.

When we get to line 54 in the program, we've run all of our tests, possibly from many different test programs, and have the results in @failed. We next create a "current problems key" in $key, resulting from joining all of the error tags into a space-separated list. If this string is empty, everything went OK, otherwise we'll end up with a list like "health.t:4 health.t:wait errors" showing that test 4 failed, the wait status was bad, and we also had some text on STDERR from one or more of the children.

Based on this error key string, we now decide whether to page or not. In line 56, we'll distinguish between "everything is OK" and "something is wrong."

If something is wrong, we'll execute the code in lines 57 to 73. First, we'll remove any marker for "everything is OK" in the cache. This ensures that the next time everything is OK, we'll send a page to say so.

Line 58 sees if we have recently sent a page with this particular error combination. If so, the value returns true from the cache, and we'll do nothing further in this invocation. (I've left the commented-out debugging print at line 59 so you can see where this happens.)

Otherwise, it's time to send a page. First, in line 61, we'll ensure that we don't duplicate this particular page within the $TEST_FAIL_INTERVAL time window.

Line 63 defines a holder for the report. Lines 65 to 70 process the @failed array, extracting out each key/value pair and then prepending each line of the value with the key for careful labeling. Even if the value is empty, at least one line containing the key is generated.

Line 72 passes this report list into the SEND_REPORT callback, defined at the top of the program. This sends the appropriate report with just the broken pieces of the collective tests.

Lines 75 to 82 deal with an "everything is OK" run. First, if there's already been an "all OK" signal recently enough, there's nothing to do (again, noted in a commented-out debugging print in line 76). Otherwise, we throw away all the recently seen failure tags in line 78 by clearing out the entire cache and then setting a flag to prevent an additional "everything is OK" message until the $ALL_CLEAR_INTERVAL has passed in line 79.

Line 81 passes an empty list to SEND_REPORT, a signal that it's time to send the all-clear message.

Although this simple test reporting tool doesn't have a lot of fancy features, it illustrates how the basics are accomplished, and how the reporting can be kept to the essentials, and it would probably work fine for a single system administrator on a typical personal or small business site. If you want more, there are larger, more complex, and even commercial solutions to being notified when things go wrong. And as always, until next time, enjoy!

Listing 5-15

```perl
=1=     #!/usr/bin/perl
=2=     use Test::More tests => 9;
=3=     use WWW::Mechanize;
=4=     isa_ok(my $a = WWW::Mechanize->new, "WWW::Mechanize");
=5=
=6=     $a->timeout(1);
=7=     $a->get("http://search.cpan.org/";);
=8=     is($a->status, 200, "fetched /");
=9=     like($a->title, qr/The CPAN Search Site/, "/ title matches");
=10=    SKIP: {
-11-      ok($a->follow_link( text -> 'FAQ' ), "follow FAQ link")
=12=        or skip "missing FAQ link", 2;
=13=      SKIP: {
=14=        is($a->status, 200, "fetched FAQ page")
=15=          or skip "bad FAQ fetch", 1;
=16=        like($a->content, qr/Frequently Asked Questions/, ⤶
                    "FAQ content matches");
=17=        $a->back;
=18=      }
=19=    }
=20=    SKIP: {
=21=      ok($a->form_number(1), "select query form")
=22=        or skip "cannot select query form", 2;
=23=      $a->set_fields(query => "PETDANCE", mode => 'author');
=24=      $a->click();
=25=      SKIP: {
=26=        is($a->status, 200, "query returned good for 'author'")
=27=          or skip "missing author page", 1;
=28=        like($a->content, qr/Andy Lester/, "found Andy Lester");
=29=        $a->back;
=30=      }
=31=    }
```

Listing 5-16

```
=1=     #!/usr/bin/perl -w
=2=     use strict;
=3=     $|++;
=4=
=5=     ## CONFIG
=6=
=7=     my $ALL_CLEAR_INTERVAL = "never"; # how often to repeat "all clear" signal
=8=     my $TEST_FAIL_INTERVAL = "30 minutes"; # how often to repeat test failed
=9=
=10=    sub SEND_REPORT {                # what do I do with a report?
=11=      ## open STDOUT, "|sendmail 5035551212\@vtext.com" or die "sendmail: $!";
=12=      @_ = "ALL CLEAR\n" unless @_;
=13=      print @_;
=14=    }
=15=
=16=    ## END CONFIG
=17=
=18=    use File::Temp qw(tempfile);     # core
=19=    use File::Basename qw(dirname); # core
=20=    use Test::Harness::Straps ();    # core
=21=    use Cache::FileCache ();         # CPAN
=22=
=23=    my $errors = tempfile();
=24=    open SAVE_STDERR, ">&STDERR" or warn "dup 2 to SAVE_STDERR: $!";
=25=
=26=    my $cache = Cache::FileCache->new({namespace => 'healthcheck_reporter'});
=27=
=28=    chdir dirname($0) or warn "Cannot chdir to dirname of $0: $!";
=29=
=30=    my $strap = Test::Harness::Straps->new;
=31=
=32=    my @failed;
=33=
=34=    for my $test_file (glob "*.t t/*.t") {
=35=      my %results;
=36=      {
=37=        open STDERR, ">&", $errors or print "dup $errors to STDERR: $!";
=38=        %results = $strap->analyze_file($test_file);
=39=        open STDERR, ">&", \*SAVE_STDERR or print ↵
                "dup SAVE_STDERR TO STDERR: $!";
=40=      };
```

```
=41=      push @failed, map {
=42=        $results{details}[$_]{ok} ? () :
=43=          ["$test_file:".($_+1) => $results{details}[$_]{name}]
=44=      } 0..$#{$results{details}};
=45=      push @failed, ["$test_file:wait" => $results{wait}] if $results{wait};
=46=    }
=47=
=48=    if (-s $errors) {
=49=      seek $errors, 0, 0;
=50=      local $/;
=51=      push @failed, ["errors" => <$errors>];
=52=    }
=53=
=54=    my $key = join " ", map $_->[0], @failed;
=55=
=56=    if ($key) {                    # bad report
=57=      $cache->remove("");          # blow away good report stamp
=58=      if ($cache->get($key)) {     # seen this recently?
=59=        ## print "ignoring duplicate report for $key\n";
=60=      } else {
=61=        $cache->set($key, 1, $TEST_FAIL_INTERVAL);
=62=
=63=        my @report;
=64=
=65=        for (@failed) {
=66=          my ($key, $value) = @$_;
=67=          my @values = split /\n/, $value;
=68=          @values = ("") unless @values; # ensure at least one line
=69=          push @report, "$key = $_\n" for @values;
=70=        }
=71=
=72=        SEND_REPORT(@report);
=73=      }
=74=    } else {                       # good report
=75=      if ($cache->get("")) {       # already said good?
=76=        ## print "ignoring good report\n";
=77=      } else {
=78=        $cache->clear();           # all is forgiven
=79=        $cache->set("", 1, $ALL_CLEAR_INTERVAL);
=80=
=81=        SEND_REPORT();             # empty means good report
=82=      }
=83=    }
```

Lightweight Persistent Data

Unix Review, Column 53 (July 2004)

■**Randal's Note** After discovering and playing with DBM::Deep for this column, I started using it on a lot of different projects, including releasing Template::Plugin::DBM::Deep to the CPAN to let me get at these objects from Template Toolkit code.

Frequently, you have data with a strong will to live. That is, your data must persist between invocations of your program, and occasionally even be shared between simultaneous invocations.

At the high end of this demand, we have entire companies devoted to creating high-performance, multiuser, SQL-interfaced databases. These databases are usually accessed from Perl via the DBI package, or by some wrapper slightly above DBI, such as Class::DBI or DBIx::SQLEngine. The details of SQL might even be entirely hidden away using a higher-level package like Tangram or Alzabo.

But further down the scale, there are some new solutions popping onto the scene that invite further observation, as well as some old classic solutions. For example, since Perl version 2, we've been able to put a hash out on disk with dbmopen:

```
dbmopen(%HASH, "/path/on/disk", 0644) || die;
$HASH{"key"} = "value";
dbmclose(%HASH);
```

The effect of such code is that we now have a key/value pair stored in an external structured file. We can later come along and reopen the database as a hash again, and treat it as if it was a hash with pre-existing values:

```
dbmopen(%HASH, "/path/on/disk", 0644) || die;
foreach $key (sort keys %HASH) {
    print "$key => $HASH{$key}\n";
}
dbmclose(%HASH);
```

While the interface was relatively simple, I wrote quite a few programs before Perl 5 came around using this storage mechanism for my persistence. However, this storage suffered some limitations: the keys and values had to be under a given size, access to the structure could not handle multiuser reads and writes, and the resulting data files were not necessarily portable to other machines (because they used incompatible libraries or byte orders).

When Perl 5 came along, new problems arose. No longer were we limited to just arrays and hashes—we could now have complex data types with arbitrary structure. Luckily, the mechanism "behind" the dbmopen was made available directly at the Perl code level, through the tie operator, as described in the perltie manpage. This let others beside Larry Wall create "magical" hashes that could perform actions on every fetch and store.

One early use of the `tie` mechanism was the `MLDBM` package, which could take a complex value to be assigned for a given key and *serialize* it to a single string value, which could then be stored much like before. For example:

```
use MLDBM;
tie my %hash, 'MLDBM' or die;
$hash{my_array} = [1..5];
$hash{my_scores} = { fred => 205, barney => 195, dino => 30 };
```

As each complex data structure was stored into the hash, it got converted into a string, using `Data::Dumper`, `FreezeThaw`, or `Storable`. If a value was fetched, it would be converted back from a string to the complex data structure. However, the resulting value was no longer related to the tied hash. For example:

```
my $scores = $hash{my_scores};
$scores->{fred} = 215;
```

would no longer affect the stored data. Instead, we got warnings on the `MLDBM` manpage to "not do this." Also, we still had all the limitations of a standard `dbmopen`-style database: size limits, multiuser access, and nonportability.

One solution that I resorted to on more than one occasion was to take over the serialization myself, and to use `Storable`'s `retrieve` and `nstore` operations directly. My code would look something like this:

```
use Storable qw(nstore retrieve);
my $data = retrieve('file');
... perform operations with $data ...
nstore $data, 'file';
```

Now my `$data` value could be an arbitrarily complex data structure, and any changes I made would be completely reflected in the updated file. The result was that I simply had a Perl data structure that persisted.

It appears that the author of `Tie::Persistent` had the same idea to use `Storable` on the entire top-level structure as well, except with a `tie` wrapper instead of explicit fetch-store phases, although I can't vouch for the code. In fact, I see a number of CPAN entries that all appear to find similar mechanisms, but none of them seem to have found the holy grail of object persistence, making it as absolutely transparent as possible in a nice portable (and hopefully multiuser) manner.

That is, until I noticed `DBM::Deep`. According to the Changelog, this distribution has been around for about two years (as I write this), but only on the CPAN for a few months. From its own description:

> *A unique flat-file database module, written in pure perl. True multi-level hash/array support (unlike MLDBM, which is faked), hybrid OO/tie() interface, cross-platform FTPable files, and quite fast. Can handle millions of keys and unlimited hash levels without significant slow-down. Written from the ground-up in pure perl — this is NOT a wrapper around a C-based DBM. Out-of-the-box compatibility with Unix, Mac OS X and Windows.*

And with a promotional paragraph like that, I just had to look. It looks simple enough. I merely say

```
use DBM::Deep;
my $hash = DBM::Deep->new("foo.db");
$hash->{my_array} = [1..5];
$hash->{my_scores} = { fred => 205, barney => 195, dino => 30 };
```

And that's it. In my next program

```
use DBM::Deep;
my $hash = DBM::Deep->new("foo.db");
$hash->{my_scores}->{fred} = 215; # update score
```

And finally, retrieving it all

```
use DBM::Deep;
my $hash = DBM::Deep->new("foo.db");
print join(", ",@{$hash->{my_array}}), "\n";
for (sort keys %{$hash->{my_scores}}) {
    print "$_ => $hash->{my_scores}->{$_}\n";
}
```

which prints

```
1, 2, 3, 4, 5
barney => 195
dino => 30
fred => 215
```

And in fact, that all just plain worked. I'm impressed. We've avoided the MLDBM problem, because the update to the nested data worked. And, there's no dependency on traditional DBMs here, so there's no size limitation or byte ordering, or even the need for a C compiler to install.

I'm told, although I haven't tested it, that I can also add

```
$hash->lock;
... do some shared things ...
$hash->unlock;
```

and thereby access shared data in multiple processes.

There also seems to be some cool stuff around encrypting or compressing the data. This definitely bears further examination.

The limitations of DBM::Deep seem rather expected. Because this is a single data file, it's being locked using flock, so we can't persist data for multiple users across machines or reliably across NFS. Also, we have to clean up after ourselves from time to time by calling an optimize method; otherwise, unused space starts accumulating in the database.

One other recent addition to the CPAN also caught my eye: OOPS. Unlike DBM::Deep, OOPS uses a DBI-style database (currently only compatible with PostgreSQL, MySQL, and SQLite) for its persistent store. However, like DBM::Deep, once a connection is made, you pretty much do anything you want with the data structure, and it gets reflected into the permanent storage. The database tables are created on request and managed by the module transparently.

The basic mode of OOPS looks like

```
use OOPS;
transaction(sub {
    OOPS->initial_setup(
        dbi_dsn => 'dbi:SQLite:/tmp/oops',
        username => undef, # no matter with SQLite
        password => undef, # ditto
    ) unless -s "/tmp/oops";
    my $hash = OOPS->new(
        dbi_dsn => 'dbi:SQLite:/tmp/oops',
        username => undef, # no matter with SQLite
        password => undef, # ditto
    );
    $hash->{my_array} = [1..5];
    $hash->{my_scores} = { fred => 205, barney => 195, dino => 30 };
    $hash->{my_scores}->{fred} = 215; # update score
    $hash->commit;
});
```

The wrapper of transaction forces this update to all be within a single transaction. We fetch the data similarly:

```
use OOPS;
transaction(sub {
    my $hash = OOPS->new(
        dbi_dsn => 'dbi:SQLite:/tmp/oops',
        username => undef, # no matter with SQLite
        password => undef, # ditto
    );
    print join(", ",@{$hash->{my_array}}), "\n";
    for (sort keys %{$hash->{my_scores}}) {
        print "$_ => $hash->{my_scores}->{$_}\n";
    }
});
```

And in fact, this retrieved exactly the values I had expected. I'll be exploring these two modules in greater depth in the future, and until then, enjoy!

Using Class::DBI for a Link Checker

Linux Magazine, Column 52 (October 2003)

Website maintenance often includes the rather mundane but important task of making sure that the carefully placed page links actually go somewhere useful. Over many years as a Perl columnist, I've written many different versions, which evolve as my mastery of Perl increases and as the tools get more powerful.

I was recently inspired by a lot of buzz I've been hearing about the rapidly developing `Class::DBI` module, a simple but powerful mechanism by which objects can be mapped to SQL-based databases, and the `DBD::SQLite` module, which puts a full SQL-based transaction-supporting database into a single file of my choosing, without the complexity of running a separate server. These two modules looked like the perfect components for my next major rewrite of the ever-improving link checker.

After a dozen hours or so trying to get my head around these new modules (including debugging things at about seven layers of indirection), I have a workable alpha version of a new link checker. The technology is similar to the version I wrote for this very column some three years ago, so you might want to refer back to the September 2000 issue for comparison. The key features include the following:

- Managed parallel processes to overlap the I/O and DNS lookups

- On-disk storage of partial state, to resume after an interruption

- Proper management of `if-modified-since` so that unchanged pages are not refetched and reparsed for links

- Flexible reporting control

- Flexible mapping of known aliased URLs, such as `index.html` being replaced by merely a trailing slash

- Flexible decisions for URLs, deciding whether to descend, check for existence, merely note, or just ignore

And all this in the 422-line program provided in Listing 5-17. Because the program is fairly long, I'll be hitting only the highlights instead of my usual rambling line-by-line description.

Lines 1 through 7 provide my standard program preamble, including pulling in the expected modules and setting up constants needed for the configuration section. The `sigtrap` module is used here to provide a death handler for any signals, which is needed so that DBI shuts down properly.

Lines 9 through 61 provide all the configuration options. From here, you decide the behavior and limits of the link checking. Most of the comments indicate the specific values, but let me point out some of the more interesting parts.

If `$REPORT` is `-1`, we get a complete dump of all pages seen, and their cross-referencing information (inbound and outbound links) and status. When it's `0` as it is here, we get a dump only of all pages that didn't come through as a successful HTTP status. We can also increase this to a number of seconds (say `1 * DAYS`), in which case we'll start hearing about a bad page only when it's been bad for at least that long. This helps with intermittent server flakiness.

The `@CHECK` array provides the starting point (or points) for this web walk. If all pages we want to check are reachable from a given URL, we need only list it here, and all the others will be found. (I've obscured the real URL here—I think it'll be obvious what I was testing against.)

The `HACK_URL` subroutine takes a `URI` object and returns a possibly modified `URI` object to represent any known aliasing. Here, I'm removing `index.html` if present, so that those links will appear only as a trailing slash. Obviously, this is very server dependent and should be constructed with care. When in doubt, start by merely returning the input parameter, and if you notice the same page being fetched twice under different names, use the subroutine to rewrite one into the other.

The PARSE subroutine takes a hacked URL in a URI object and decides how far to go with it. If PARSE returns 2, the page is fetched, and if the response is HTML, the HTML is parsed for further links. (If you did this to every URL, you'd eventually see the entire web, but it would take quite a while!) If PARSE returns 1, then the URL is "pinged" by fetching just enough to figure out if it's good or not. If PARSE returns 0, then the URL is noted for the cross-reference table, but is otherwise ignored. If PARSE returns -1, then the URL is completely ignored. Be very careful writing this routine: scanning through a lot of dynamically generated content is guaranteed to upset the webmaster.

Lines 63 to 166 implement the table classes and base classes as suggested in the Class::DBI documentation. My::DBI (in lines 65 to 99) defines the database linkage itself and defines methods inherited by all table classes.

Lines 69 and 70 set the database. Here, I'm using DBD::SQLite to create a single file at $DATABASE, which is set earlier to the file .linkchecker in my home directory. I also override AutoCommit so that most transactions are executed on a statement-by-statement basis.

Lines 72 to 78 create the tables of the database if they don't already exist, by calling methods within each table class. If the tables already exist, the error is trapped and ignored. Because the table-creation methods are kept within the program, I can start this script with no advance preparation (other than installing all the necessary modules).

Lines 80 to 98 are derived from the Class::DBI documentation as a mechanism to wrap a code reference within a transaction, automatically aborting the transaction if something goes wrong. I added the ability for the subroutine to return back a response value, which simplified some of the code, as shown later.

Lines 101 to 116 define My::Link, an object class that is mapped to the link table within the database, as declared in line 105. The link table records the links between pages from the src URL to the dst URL, creating a many-to-many relationship among the pages.

The SQL to create the link table is defined in lines 106 through 112. __TABLE__ is replaced with link, but by doing it this way, we can derive from this class and inherit this constructor.

Lines 113 through 115 define the columns for Class::DBI's benefit, including the proper object type for retrieval, as well as creating accessor methods for the columns.

Lines 118 to 165 define My::Page, mapped to the page table (as defined in line 123). Most of the heavy lifting happens here.

Using the enum pragma (found in the CPAN), we get four integer constants within this package for the various states in which a page record might exist. State_todo means we need to process this page. State_working means that one of the child processes has started working on the page, but has not yet completed it. State_done means we're done. State_unseen is for a page that has been left over from the previous run, retaining its modification stamp and outbound links to minimize the work on each new run. At the end of a new run, all unseen pages are finally deleted.

Lines 124 to 133 define the SQL to create the table. Note the interpolation of the State_unseen into the double-quoted string.

Lines 134 and 135 declare the table columns to Class::DBI. The first such column is automatically recognized as the primary key.

Lines 137 and 138 define an inverse relationship, namely that link records are referencing page records. By declaring this explicitly, many joins are automatically generated for us. Additionally, deleting a particular My::Page record also has the "cascading delete" feature of deleting any inbound or outbound links automatically, minimizing the need to write explicit code for that.

Lines 140 to 149 change a page from State_todo to State_working within a transaction. This is needed because all of the children will be looking at the same to-do list and picking an item to do. Only one child can be successful at this, and because we've wrapped it in a transaction, it works nicely. The subroutine returns a true/false value to indicate whether it successfully snagged the particular My::Page object for this process to work on.

Lines 151 to 164 similarly add a page to the to-do list, again within a transaction to prevent other children from interfering. Only new records or previously unseen records (left over from a previous pass) can be set to State_todo. The new (or reused) My::Page object is returned.

Lines 167 to 175 create an LWP::UserAgent virtual browser to fetch the pages, including giving it a distinguished agent string so we can filter it out of our web hit logs.

The main code begins in line 177. Line 180 creates the tables if needed.

Lines 183 to 186 reset any working pages to to-do pages. This happens when the program is interrupted before completing a pass, and it will retrigger any requests that might have been aborted before completion.

Lines 188 to 194 "prime the pump." If there aren't any to-do or done items, then we need to start somewhere, namely at the @CHECK URLs.

Lines 196 to 213 use the kids_do subroutine (defined later) to perform the task given by the first coderef, in parallel by forking up to a maximum of the lesser of $KIDMAX or whatever number the second coderef returns. Each kid repeatedly grabs all the to-do records, picks one at random, and tries to "own" it. If the "owning" is successful, do_one_page is called (defined later). The cycle is repeated until nothing shows up in the to-do list, at which point the child exits.

Once the kids have done their work, lines 215 and 216 remove any pages that weren't seen on this pass.

Lines 218 to 248 display the report. Pages that aren't "bad enough" are rejected from being displayed in line 222. Information about the page itself gets printed in lines 223 through 230, including the status and timestamps.

Lines 232 through 246 print the cross-reference table, showing all the inbound links (useful if the page is not successful to find out where it was referenced) and outbound links (useful when we're editing a particular page to find all bad links). The links are generally relative, unless they go up two or more levels, in which case they're made absolute from / instead, which seemed to be a good compromise for display.

Lines 250 to 254 set all the State_done pages to State_unseen, for the next pass. And that's all there is for the main program.

Lines 260 to 291 set up the processing of a particular page. Most of the logic decides whether this is a "parse" or a "ping," and how much information to use (if any) from a previous pass. Note how the mapping of the $page object to the table eliminates any need for me to write SQL code: I'm simply using $page as if it was an in-memory object.

Lines 293 to 378 form the core of the actions. As this code is very similar to this column's September 2000 code, so I'll skip the detailed description. The page is fetched (using an LWP callback), content type and status are noted, links are added, and the page record is updated. The two big differences between this code and previous code are that I'm using HTML::LinkExtor to derive the links, rather than my handwritten code from before, and I'm using objects instead of hashes to store the data.

When a link is seen, add_link (lines 380 to 397) is called to record the link in the database. If a "base" is provided, it's used to make a relative link into an absolute link. The links are "hacked" to make them canonical, and any ignorable link is ignored. As the links are getting created, there might be multiple links between the same pair of pages, causing the create to throw an exception, as triggered by the SQLite's constraint on the table.

Lines 399 to 440 manage the kids, using code lifted mostly from the August 2000 column, and is better described there. The job here is greatly simplified, however, because we don't need to do anything to the kids other than start them; they figure out their own tasks directly from the database.

Although I've run up against a deadline for this issue (in both space and time), I can see that I really need to create a "count to-do" method for My::Page, as I'm doing it the hard way in more than one place. Also, I'm sure there's some fine-tuning of some of the code steps, but at least this code runs as is and runs well. Have fun keeping your website clean of all those nasty broken links. Until next time, enjoy!

Listing 5-17

```
=1=     #!/usr/bin/perl -w
=2=     use strict;
=3=     $| = 1;
=4=     use sigtrap qw(die untrapped);
=5=
=6=     use URI;
=7=     use constant DAYS => 86400;      # for specifications
=8=
=9=     ## configuration constants
=10=
=11=    my $DATABASE = (glob "~/.linkchecker")[0];
=12=
=13=    my $VERBOSE = 1;                 # 0 = quiet, 1 = noise, 2 = lots of noise
=14=
=15=    my $RECHECK = 0.1 * DAYS;        # seconds between rechecking any URL
=16=    my $RECHECK_GOOD = 1 * DAYS;     # seconds between rechecking good URLs
=17=    my $REPORT = 0 * DAYS;           # seconds before bad enough to report
=18=
=19=    my $FOLLOW_REDIRECT = 1;         # follow a redirect as if it were a link
=20=    my $TIMEOUT = 30;       # timeout on fetch (hard timeout is twice this)
=21=    my $MAXSIZE = 1048576;           # max size for fetch (undef if fetch all)
=22=
=23=    my $KIDMAX = 5;                  # how many kids to feed
=24=
=25=    my @CHECK =                      # list of initial starting points
=26=       qw(http://www.perl.borg/);
=27=
=28=    sub PARSE {
=29=       ## return 2 to parse if HTML
=30=       ## return 1 to merely verify existence
=31=       ## return 0 to not even verify existence, but still xref
=32=       ## return -1 to ignore entirely
```

```
=33=      my $url = shift;                # URI object (absolute)
=34=      for ($url->scheme) {
=35=        return 0 unless /^http$/;
=36=      }
=37=      for ($url->query) {
=38=        return -1 if /^C=[DMNS];O=[AD]/; # silly mod_index
=39=      }
=40=      for ($url->host) {
=41=        if (/www\.perl\.borg$/) {
=42=          for ($url->path) {
=43=            return 0 if /images|photos/; # boring
=44=            return 0 if /^\/(tpc|yapc)\/.*(199[89]|200[012])/; # old
=45=          }
=46=          return 2;                   # default www.perl.borg
=47=        }

=49=        return 0 if /use\.perl\.borg$/;

=51=      }
=52=      return 1;                       # ping the world
=53=    }

=55=    sub HACK_URL {
=56=      my $url = shift;                # URI object
=57=      $url->path("$1") if $url->path =~ /^(.*\/)index\.html$/s;
=58=      $url->canonical;
=59=    }

=61=    ## end configuration constants

=63=    ### internally-defined classes

=65=    {
=66=      package My::DBI;
=67=      use base 'Class::DBI';

=69=      __PACKAGE__->set_db('Main', "dbi:SQLite:dbname=$DATABASE", undef, undef,
=70=                          {AutoCommit => 1});

=72=      sub CONSTRUCT {
=73=        my $class = shift;
=74=        for (qw(My::Page My::Link)) {
=75=          eval { $_->sql_CONSTRUCT->execute };
=76=          die $@ if $@ and $@ !~ /already exists/;
=77=        }
=78=      }
=79=
```

```
=80=      sub atomically {
=81=        my $class = shift;
=82=        my $action = shift;          # coderef
=83=        local $class->db_Main->{AutoCommit};
                    # turn off AutoCommit for this block
=84=
=85=        my @result;
=86=        eval {
=87=          @result = wantarray ? $action->() : scalar($action->());
=88=          $class->dbi_commit;
=89=        };
=90=        if ($@) {
=91=          warn "atomically got error: $@";
=92=          my $commit_error = $@;
=93=          eval { $class->dbi_rollback };
=94=          die $commit_error;
=95=        }
=96=        die $@ if $@;
=97=        wantarray ? @result : $result[0];
=98=      }
=99=    }
=100=
=101=   {
=102=      package My::Link;
=103=      our @ISA = qw(My::DBI);
=104=
=105=      __PACKAGE__->table('link');
=106=      __PACKAGE__->set_sql(CONSTRUCT => <<'SQL');
=107=   CREATE TABLE __TABLE__ (
=108=     src TEXT,
=109=     dst TEXT,
=110=     PRIMARY KEY (src, dst)
=111=   )
=112=   SQL
=113=      __PACKAGE__->columns(Primary => qw(src dst));
=114=      __PACKAGE__->has_a(src => 'My::Page');
=115=      __PACKAGE__->has_a(dst => 'My::Page');
=116=   }
=117=
=118=   {
=119=      package My::Page;
=120=      our @ISA = qw(My::DBI);
=121=      use enum qw(:State_ unseen todo working done);
=122=
=123=      __PACKAGE__->table('page');
=124=      __PACKAGE__->set_sql(CONSTRUCT => <<"SQL");
=125=   CREATE TABLE __TABLE__ (
```

```
=126=      location TEXT PRIMARY KEY,
=127=      state INT DEFAULT @{[State_unseen]},
=128=      last_status TEXT,
=129=      last_checked INT,
=130=      last_good INT,
=131=      last_modified INT
=132=    )
=133=  SQL
=134=      __PACKAGE__->columns(All => qw(location state last_status
=135=                                   last_checked last_good last_modified));
=136=
=137=      __PACKAGE__->has_many(inbound => 'My::Link', 'dst', { sort => 'src' });
=138=      __PACKAGE__->has_many(outbound => 'My::Link', 'src', { sort => 'dst' });
=139=
=140=      sub make_working_atomically {
=141=        my $self = shift;
=142=
=143=        $self->atomically(sub {
=144=                          $self->state == State_todo or return undef;
=145=                          $self->state(State_working);
=146=                          $self->update;
=147=                          return 1;
=148=                        });
=149=      }
=150=
=151=      sub create_or_make_todo {
=152=        my $class = shift;
=153=        my $location = shift;
=154=
=155=        $class->atomically(sub {
=156=                    my $item = $class->find_or_create({location => $location});
=157=                          if ((not defined($item->state)
=158=                              or $item->state == State_unseen)) {
=159=                            $item->state(State_todo);
=160=                            $item->update;
=161=                          }
=162=                          $item;
=163=                        });
=164=      }
=165=    }
=166=
=167=    {
=168=      use LWP::UserAgent;
=169=      my $AGENT = LWP::UserAgent->new;
=170=      $AGENT->agent("linkchecker/0.42 " . $AGENT->agent);
=171=      $AGENT->env_proxy;
```

```
=172=    $AGENT->timeout($TIMEOUT);
=173=
=174=    sub fetch { $AGENT->simple_request(@_) }
=175=    }
=176=
=177=    ### main code begins here
=178=
=179=    ## initialize database if needed
=180=    My::DBI->CONSTRUCT;
=181=
=182=    ## reset all working to todo
=183=    for my $page (My::Page->search(state => My::Page::State_working)) {
=184=      $page->state(My::Page::State_todo);
=185=      $page->update;
=186=    }
=187=
=188=    ## unless any are todo or finished, prime the pump
=189=    unless (() = My::Page->search(state => My::Page::State_todo)
=190=          or () = My::Page->search(state => My::Page::State_done)) {
=191=      print "Starting a new run...\n";
=192=      My::Page->create_or_make_todo(HACK_URL(URI->new($_))->as_string)
=193=        for @CHECK;
=194=    }
=195=
=196=    ## main loop, done by kids:
=197=    kids_do(sub {                    # the task
=198=            srand;                   # spin random number generator uniquely
=199=        while (my @todo = My::Page->search(state => My::Page::State_todo)) {
=200=            my $page = $todo[rand @todo]; # pick one at random
=201=            unless($page->make_working_atomically) {
=202=              # someone else got it
=203=              print "$$ wanted ", $page->location, "\n" if $VERBOSE;
=204=              next;
=205=            }
=206=            ;
=207=            print "$$ doing ", $page->location, "\n" if $VERBOSE > 1;
=208=            do_one_page($page);
=209=          }
=210=          },
=211=          sub {                      # max kids needed
=212=            scalar(() = My::Page->search(state => My::Page::State_todo));
=213=          });
=214=
=215=    ## clean out any unseen at this point (no longer needed)
=216=    $_->delete for My::Page->search(state => My::Page::State_unseen);
=217=
```

```
=218=    ## display report
=219=    print "*** BEGIN REPORT ***\n";
=220=    for my $page (My::Page->search(state => My::Page::State_done,
=221=                                   {order_by => 'location'})) {
=222=      next if $page->last_checked <= $page->last_good + $REPORT;
=223=      my $url = URI->new($page->location);
=224=      print "$url:\n";
=225=      print "  Status: ", $page->last_status, "\n";
=226=      for (qw(checked good modified)) {
=227=        my $method = "last_$_";
=228=        my $value = $page->$method() or next;
=229=        print "  \u\L$_\E: ".localtime($value)."\n";
=230=      }
=231=
=232=      for my $inbound ($page->inbound) {
=233=        my $inbound_page = $inbound->src;
=234=        my $inbound_url = URI->new($inbound_page->location);
=235=        my $rel = $inbound_url->rel($url);
=236=        $rel = $inbound_url->path_query if $rel =~ /^\.\.\/\.\./;
=237=        print "  from $rel\n";
=238=      }
=239=      for my $outbound ($page->outbound) {
=240=        my $outbound_page = $outbound->dst;
=241=        my $outbound_url = URI->new($outbound_page->location);
=242=        my $rel = $outbound_url->rel($url);
=243=        $rel = $outbound_url->path_query if $rel =~ /^\.\.\/\.\./;
=244=        my $outbound_status = $outbound_page->last_status;
=245=        print "  to $rel: $outbound_status\n";
=246=      }
=247=    }
=248=    print "*** END REPORT ***\n";
=249=
=250=    ## reset for next pass
=251=    for my $page (My::Page->search(state => My::Page::State_done)) {
=252=      $page->state(My::Page::State_unseen);
=253=      $page->update;
=254=    }
=255=
=256=    exit 0;
=257=
=258=    ### subroutines
=259=
=260=    sub do_one_page {
=261=      my $page = shift;                # My::Page
=262=
=263=      my $url = URI->new($page->location);
```

```
=264=      my $parse = PARSE($url);
=265=      if ($parse >= 2) {
=266=        print "Parsing $url\n" if $VERBOSE;
=267=        if (time < ($page->last_checked || 0) + $RECHECK or
=268=            time < ($page->last_good || 0) + $RECHECK_GOOD) {
=269=          print "$url: too early to reparse\n" if $VERBOSE;
=270=          ## reuse existing links
=271=          My::Page->create_or_make_todo($_->dst->location) for $page->outbound;
=272=        } else {
=273=          parse_or_ping($page, $url, "PARSE");
=274=        }
=275=      } elsif ($parse >= 1) {
=276=        print "Pinging $url\n" if $VERBOSE;
=277=        if (time < ($page->last_checked || 0) + $RECHECK or
=278=            time < ($page->last_good || 0) + $RECHECK_GOOD) {
=279=          print "$url: too early to reping\n" if $VERBOSE;
=280=          $_->delete for $page->outbound; # delete any existing stale links
=281=        } else {
=282=          parse_or_ping($page, $url, "PING");
=283=        }
=284=      } else {
=285=        print "Skipping $url\n" if $VERBOSE;
=286=        $page->last_status("Skipped");
=287=        $page->last_checked(0);
=288=      }
=289=      $page->state(My::Page::State_done);
=290=      $page->update;
=291=    }
=292=
=293=    sub parse_or_ping {
=294=      my $page = shift;          # My::Page
=295=      my $url = shift;           # URI
=296=      my $kind = shift;          # "PARSE" or "PING"
=297=
=298=      use HTML::LinkExtor;
=299=
=300=      ## create the request
=301=      my $request = HTTP::Request->new(GET => "$url");
=302=      $request->if_modified_since($page->last_modified) if $page->last_modified;
=303=
=304=      ## fetch the response
=305=      my $content;
=306=      my $content_type;
=307=      my $res = fetch
=308=        ($request,
=309=         sub {
```

```perl
=310=            my ($data, $response, $protocol) = @_;
=311=            unless ($content_type) {
=312=              if ($content_type = $response->content_type) {
=313=                if ($kind eq "PING") {
=314=                  print "aborting $url for ping\n" if $VERBOSE > 1;
=315=                  die "ping only";
=316=                }
=317=                if ($content_type ne "text/html") {
=318=                  print "aborting $url for $content_type\n" if $VERBOSE > 1;
=319=                  die "content type is $content_type";
=320=                }
=321=              }
=322=            }
=323=            $content .= $data;
=324=            if ($MAXSIZE and length $content > $MAXSIZE) {
=325=              print "aborting $url for content length\n" if $VERBOSE > 1;
=326=              die "content length is ", length $content;
=327=            }
=328=          }, 8192);
=329=    $res->content($content);       # stuff what we got
=330=
=331=    ## analyze the results
=332=    if ($res->is_success) {
=333=      my $now = time;
=334=      $page->last_checked($now);
=335=      $page->last_good($now);
=336=      $page->last_modified($res->last_modified || $res->date);
=337=      $_->delete for $page->outbound; # delete any existing stale links
=338=
=339=      if ($content_type eq "text/html") {
=340=        if ($kind eq "PARSE") {
=341=          print "$url: parsed\n" if $VERBOSE;
=342=          $page->last_status("Verified and parsed");
=343=          my %seen;
=344=          HTML::LinkExtor->new
=345=              (sub {
=346=                 my ($tag, %attr) = @_;
=347=                 $seen{$_}++ or add_link($page, $_) for values %attr;
=348=              }, $res->base)->parse($res->content);
=349=        } else {                 # presume $kind = PING
=350=          print "$url: good ping\n" if $VERBOSE;
=351=          $page->last_status("Verified (contents not examined)");
=352=        }
=353=      } else {
=354=        print "$url: content = $content_type\n" if $VERBOSE;
=355=        $page->last_status("Verified (content = $content_type)");
```

```
=356=         }
=357=       } elsif ($res->code == 304) { # not modified
=358=         print "$url: not modified\n" if $VERBOSE;
=359=         my $now = time;
=360=         $page->last_checked($now);
=361=         $page->last_good($now);
=362=         ## reuse existing links
=363=         My::Page->create_or_make_todo($_->dst->location) for $page->outbound;
=364=       } elsif ($res->is_redirect) {
=365=         my $location = $res->header("Location");
=366=         print "$url: redirect to $location\n" if $VERBOSE;
=367=         $_->delete for $page->outbound; # delete any existing stale links
=368=         add_link($page, $location, $res->base) if $FOLLOW_REDIRECT;
=369=         $page->last_status("Redirect (status = ".$res->code.") to $location");
=370=         $page->last_checked(time);
=371=       } else {
=372=         print "$url: not verified: ", $res->code, "\n" if $VERBOSE;
=373=         $_->delete for $page->outbound; # delete any existing stale links
=374=         $page->last_status("NOT Verified (status = ".($res->code).")");
=375=         $page->last_checked(time);
=376=       }
=377=       $page->update;
=378=     }
=379=
=380=     sub add_link {
=381=       my $page = shift;             # My::Page
=382=       my $url_string = shift;       # string
=383=       my $base = shift;             # maybe undef
=384=
=385=       my $url = $base
=386=         ? URI->new_abs($url_string, URI->new($base))
=387=           : URI->new($url_string);
=388=       $url->fragment(undef);        # blow away any fragment
=389=       $url = HACK_URL($url);
=390=       return if PARSE($url) < 0;     # skip any links to non-xref pages
=391=       print "saw $url\n" if $VERBOSE > 1;
=392=
=393=       my $newpage = My::Page->create_or_make_todo("$url");
=394=       ## the following might die if there's already one link there
=395=       eval { My::Link->create({src => $page, dst => $newpage}) };
=396=       die $@ if $@ and not $@ =~ /uniqueness constraint/;
=397=     }
=398=
=399=     sub kids_do {
=400=       my $code_task = shift;
=401=       my $code_count = shift;
```

```
=402=
=403=    use POSIX qw(WNOHANG);
=404=
=405=    my %kids;
=406=
=407=    while (keys %kids or $code_count->()) {
=408=      ## reap kids
=409=      while ((my $kid = waitpid(-1, WNOHANG)) > 0) {
=410=        ## warn "$kid reaped";     # trace
=411=        delete $kids{$kid};
=412=      }
=413=      ## verify live kids
=414=      for my $kid (keys %kids) {
=415=        next if kill 0, $kid;
=416=        warn "*** $kid found missing ***"; # shouldn't happen
=417=        delete $kids{$kid};
=418=      }
=419=      ## launch kids
=420=      if (keys %kids < $KIDMAX
=421=          and keys %kids < $code_count->()) {
=422=        ## warn "forking a kid";  # trace
=423=        my $kid = fork;
=424=        if (defined $kid) {        # good parent or child
=425=          if ($kid) {             # parent
=426=            $kids{$kid} = 1;
=427=          } else {
=428=            $code_task->();        # the real task
=429=            exit 0;
=430=          }
=431=        } else {
=432=          warn "cannot fork: $!"; # hopefully temporary
=433=          sleep 1;
=434=          next;                    # outer loop
=435=        }
=436=      }
=437=      print "[", scalar keys %kids, " kids]\n" if $VERBOSE;
=438=      sleep 1;
=439=    }
=440=  }
=441=
=442=  sub URI::mailto::host { ""; }    # workaround bug in LWP
=443=  sub URI::mailto::authority { ""; } # workaround bug in LWP
```

Writing Mini Proxy Servers in Perl

Web Techniques, Column 34 (February 1999)

■**Randal's Note** The cool part about this proxy server is that you can enable the debugging flags to see the entire conversation between a browser and a remote server. I had never considered that application, but it works nicely. Also, since most modern browsers understand compression, this is a nice tool to use on a slow dialup line, such as from a hotel room (a place I frequently find myself).

Back in this column in February 1997, I wrote an anonymizing proxy server in roughly 100 lines of Perl code. You could point your web browser at it, and you'd get a different IP address from your browser, as well as all telltale identifying information removed (like cookies). The downside of this tiny proxy server was that every fetched URL caused a process to be forked.

If a real web server were to do that, it'd probably be fairly narrow in application, so most modern web servers perform *preforking*. That is, they fork a number of servers ready to respond to an incoming request. Then as the requests come in, there's no latency from the time it takes to fork and get ready to listen.

Perl has enough tools to do this as well, so I decided to rewrite that proxy server as a pre-forking server. That alone would make it cool enough for a new column here, but I went one item better.

Most modern web browsers accept compressed data (most commonly in the gzip format), automatically uncompressing it to display to the user. Because text compresses *very* well (especially large HTML pages), we can make this proxy server automatically detect a gzip-savvy browser and compress all text downloads on the fly!

That way, if I'm running this proxy server on a machine with good net connections (like a T-1 or better), I can use it as a speed-enhancing proxy on my normal modem links. And in fact, in practice, I found it to make downloading noticeably zippier—almost spooky, actually.

And this new improved proxy server code is in Listing 5-18. Please note that because of the length of the listing, I'll be a little more terse than usual in describing individual constructs, concentrating instead on the overall strategy and flow of control.

Lines 1 through 4 start most of the code I write, making the program taint-safe, enabling compile-time restrictions, and unbuffering standard output.

Lines 6 and 7 are partially automatically generated by the RCS version control software. I'm creating two globals that have the version information in them. The variable $VERSION has just the version number, handy to print out when the server starts up and to add to the LWP user-agent string when we fetch other pages.

Lines 9 through 11 are my copyright information. It's a good idea to make the licensing terms explicit, because the default these days is pretty restrictive. Here, I'm declaring that this program can be adapted and included just like the Perl source code.

Lines 14 through 18 define a little utility function that takes each line of text in possibly multiple arguments and prefixes it with the current time and the process ID number. This utility function permits the normal die and warn operators to have better logging information, as reconfigured in lines 19 and 20. Line 21 sets up the signals using a subroutine defined later.

Lines 23 through 29 define configuration constants to control logging of various events. These flags are all examined for their true/false value. At a minimum, logging the child management and the transaction management is interesting—the other items are generally for debugging (or if you're insanely curious and don't mind reams of output).

Lines 31 through 35 control other configuration constants. Line 32 defines the hostname to which this server will bind. Obviously, you won't want to use www.stonehenge.com for your binding, so change this to something appropriate. For testing, you can make this localhost, which will prevent anyone away from your system from connecting to it. Line 33 selects the port number. If you leave it at 0, the system picks a random port number, which you can determine from the startup messages. You can also force it to be a particular port number, but if that port number is held by another process, the server cannot start.

Lines 34 and 35 control the performance as a tradeoff of resources. The more servers you start, the more likely you can handle more hits effectively, but then you also use up valuable process slots and swap memory. Line 35 is mostly out of paranoia, telling each process to quit and restart after a certain number of usages. You want to keep this value fairly high, because the first hit for each child process takes about three to five times as much CPU as the remaining hits.

The first real line of output is line 38. Not much to say there. Line 40 invokes &main to do the real work, which should never return. Again, defensive programming tells me to put an exit after that, just in case.

Lines 44 through 64 define the top-level algorithm as subroutine &main. The main code needs the assistance of the HTTP::Daemon module (from LWP) and creates a local hash called %kids (described later).

Lines 48 through 50 establish the master socket. This is an instance of HTTP::Daemon. The resulting proxy URL is dumped to standard error in line 50, and will be something like http://www.stonehenge.com:44242/. This socket (and the containing object information) is inherited by all the kids.

Speaking of the kids, we create them in lines 52 through 54. A simple foreach loop (spelled f-o-r but pronounced "foreach") invokes &fork_a_slave repeatedly. The process ID number becomes the key to the hash, with a corresponding value being the word slave. We can then detect any erroneous wait values that way, since they won't be one of our slaves. Not likely, but paranoid programming is handy and scales well.

Lines 55 to 63 loop forever, waking up whenever a kid dies, and restarting it so that there's always $SLAVE_COUNT kids waiting for web connections. There's a sleep in here so that if we go belly up while trying to fork, at least we don't thrash.

Lines 66 to 75 set up a signal group so that if any individual process takes a hit with SIGHUP or SIGINT or SIGTERM, the whole group takes the same hit. This way we can kill any process to bring down the entire family without having to use some hack like killall.

Lines 77 to 84 create a particular child slave. Line 81 forks (or perhaps not if there are no remaining process slots), saving the $pid to determine the parent versus the child. If the $pid is 0, the child runs off to the &child_does routine. The parent returns the nonzero PID value so that the top-level routines can record this as a good slave.

Speaking of &child_does, this routine (defined in lines 86 through 113) handles the top-level processing in each child slave. We're handed the master socket (kept in $master), which we'll use to get the incoming requests from the web clients that are using us as a proxy. Line 89 defines a counter to make sure we don't handle more requests than necessary.

Lines 92 through 110 define a repeating loop executing for $MAX_PER_SLAVE times. Line 93 is executed in parallel by all children. The operating system lets only one of the many children have an exclusive flock on the master socket. This is needed because we can have only one child at a time execute the accept on the socket in line 95. So, in an idle moment, we've got one child waiting in line 95 and the rest waiting in line 93. When the connection comes in, the child waiting in line 95 moves on, unlocking the port in line 97. The operating system then nondeterministically selects one of the other kids waiting in line 93 to move forward. It's pretty slick.

But, let's get back to that incoming connection. In line 98, we'll save away the CPU times and wall-clock time for later statistics. And line 100 tells the log where we got a connection from. The bulk of the work is done in &handle_one_connection (described below). But then we're ready to see how much work it took, so lines 103 to 107 compute the differential CPU user and system time, child versions of the same, and the difference in wall-clock seconds. When that's all displayed, we loop back up and become one of the kids waiting in line 93 again.

By the way, there's nothing necessarily fair about the algorithm. It's quite possible that a particular child will get back up to line 93 at exactly the right moments often enough to handle many more requests than others. But that's OK, because the kids are all basically the same anyway. It *does* have a slight bearing on how often a child gets killed and restarted, though.

When the child finally dies, it logs that in line 111, and then exits with a nice error code in line 112.

Lines 115 to 129 provide the top-level code for a particular single connection to a web client. The request comes in via line 119, which should be an HTTP::Request object. If not, line 120 causes us to die. This is somewhat incomplete, though, because we could just reset and try again, or try to figure out what was wrong. But this was close enough for my testing purposes. It *does* permit a denial-of-service attack on this proxy, though, since some 3v1l d00d could connect and spit garbage at my proxy, forcing the kid to die. Oh well.

Line 122 calls down to get the actual response, and lines 123 to 126 log it if necessary. Line 127 sends the response back to the browser, and the connection gets closed down in line 128, permitting the browser to know that we're all through.

Lines 131 to 151 validate the request before performing the real action, using some basic checks. If the scheme isn't something that LWP can handle, it gets rejected in lines 139 through 141. If it's not really a proxy request (showing up as a relative URL), that's also rejected, in lines 143 through 145. Otherwise, we go fetch it via the call in line 149.

Note the comment in line 135: this proxy is promiscuous. *Any* web client can use the proxy if the client can connect to it on the net. This means the web client also inherits my IP addresses for IP-based authorization, and that could be seriously bad. If you're gonna use this program for real, either hide it well (heh) or add some code in here to notice the peer address or whatever you'd like to do.

Well, it's about time that we really fetched the request, now that we know it's good, legal, and ready to fetch. Lines 156 through 192 define the routine to handle this, along with a static global variable to hold the user agent.

Lines 159 to 165 set up the user agent (the virtual web client) once per child process. We'll give it an agent type of the LWP version number concatenated with the version number of this proxy server. Also, if there are any environment variables defining a further real proxy server, they'll be consulted in line 163.

Lines 167 to 170 handle some logging if needed. Then line 172, as simple as it looks, does 90% of the work of this program: fetching the requested URL (finally!).

Now that we've got a response, let's hack it a bit. If it's a good response (line 174) that's a text-ish file (line 175), and it's not already encoded (line 176), and the browser accepts gzip-encoded transfers (line 177), we'll replace the content with a gzip equivalent, thus reducing the transmission time at the slight expense of some CPU horsepower at both ends.

Line 178 brings in the Compress::Zlib module (found in the CPAN). This defines the memGzip routine used in line 180 to compress the content. If the routine succeeds, then we'll update the content, length, and encoding in lines 182 through 184, and log it (perhaps) in lines 185 through 187.

And that brings us to the end! Whew.

If you want to try this program out:

1. Change the $HOST value to something appropriate.

2. Fire it up in a window.

3. Note the proxy address URL dumped out after master is ... right at the startup.

4. Put that address into your proxy settings for your browser.

5. Go surfing!

You should see the proxy server as it takes each hit, along with the CPU usage for each transaction. The first hit will take a little longer than the rest, because some of the LWP code (and possibly the Compress::Zlib code) needs to be brought in.

Some possible areas of expansion are as follows:

- Make the proxy recognize banner ads, and return either no content for a response or a 1×1 GIF, or even a GIF that has the right size and shape but the word "BLOCKED" in place of the ad. You won't make any friends in the banner ad business this way, however.

- Always add Accept encoding: gzip to the proxy request, and then you can save reception time in *both* legs of the journey for those servers that attempt to encode everything just like this proxy.

- Add a cookie jar handler just like I described two months ago.

- Make this an anonymous proxy server by deliberately stripping out all the cookies and other identifying parts of the transaction.

However, these would have all made the program even longer than it is, so I'll leave those as an exercise for you (or perhaps for a future column). Enjoy!

Listing 5-18

```
=1=    #!/home/merlyn/bin/perl -Tw
=2=    use strict;
=3=    $ENV{PATH} = join ":", qw(/usr/ucb /bin /usr/bin);
=4=    $|++;
```

```
=5=
=6=      my $VERSION_ID = q$Id: proxy,v 1.21 1998/xx/xx xx:xx:xx merlyn Exp $;
=7=      my $VERSION = (qw$Revision: 1.21 $ )[-1];
=8=
=9=      ## Copyright (c) 1996, 1998 by Randal L. Schwartz
=10=     ## This program is free software; you can redistribute it
=11=     ## and/or modify it under the same terms as Perl itself.
=12=
=13=     ### debug management
=14=     sub prefix {
=15=       my $now = localtime;
=16=
=17=       join "", map { "[$now] [${$}] $_\n" } split /\n/, join "", @_;
=18=     }
=19=     $SIG{__WARN__} = sub { warn prefix @_ };
=20=     $SIG{__DIE__} = sub { die prefix @_ };
=21=     &setup_signals();
=22=
=23=     ### logging flags
=24=     my $LOG_PROC = 1;            # begin/end of processes
=25=     my $LOG_TRAN = 1;            # begin/end of each transaction
=26=     my $LOG_REQ_HEAD = 0;       # detailed header of each request
=27=     my $LOG_REQ_BODY = 0;       # header and body of each request
=28=     my $LOG_RES_HEAD = 0;       # detailed header of each response
=29=     my $LOG_RES_BODY = 0;       # header and body of each response
=30=
=31=     ### configuration
=32=     my $HOST = 'www.stonehenge.com';
=33=     my $PORT = 0;               # pick next available user-port
=34=     my $SLAVE_COUNT = 8;        # how many slaves to fork
=35=     my $MAX_PER_SLAVE = 20;     # how many transactions per slave
=36=
=37=     ### main
=38=     warn("running version ", $VERSION);
=39=
=40=     &main();
=41=     exit 0;
=42=
=43=     ### subs
=44=     sub main {                  # return void
=45=       use HTTP::Daemon;
=46=       my %kids;
=47=
=48=       my $master = HTTP::Daemon->new(LocalPort => $PORT, LocalAddr => $HOST)
=49=           or die "Cannot create master: $!";
=50=       warn("master is ", $master->url);
=51=       ## fork the right number of children
```

```
=52=        for (1..$SLAVE_COUNT) {
=53=          $kids{&fork_a_slave($master)} = "slave";
=54=        }
=55=        {                                # forever:
=56=          my $pid = wait;
=57=          my $was = delete ($kids{$pid}) || "?unknown?";
=58=          warn("child $pid ($was) terminated status $?") if $LOG_PROC;
=59=          if ($was eq "slave") {       # oops, lost a slave
=60=            sleep 1;                   # don't replace it right away (avoid thrash)
=61=            $kids{&fork_a_slave($master)} = "slave";
=62=          }
=63=        } continue { redo };          # semicolon for cperl-mode
=64=      }
=65=
=66=      sub setup_signals {             # return void
=67=
=68=        setpgrp;                      # I *am* the leader
=69=        $SIG{HUP} = $SIG{INT} = $SIG{TERM} = sub {
=70=          my $sig = shift;
=71=          $SIG{$sig} = 'IGNORE';
=72=          kill $sig, 0;               # death to all-comers
=73=          die "killed by $sig";
=74=        };
=75=      }
=76=
=77=      sub fork_a_slave {              # return int (pid)
=78=        my $master = shift;           # HTTP::Daemon
=79=
=80=        my $pid;
=81=        defined ($pid = fork) or die "Cannot fork: $!";
=82=        &child_does($master) unless $pid;
=83=        $pid;
=84=      }
=85=
=86=      sub child_does {                # return void
=87=        my $master = shift;           # HTTP::Daemon
=88=
=89=        my $did = 0;                  # processed count
=90=
=91=        warn("child started") if $LOG_PROC;
=92=        {
=93=          flock($master, 2);          # LOCK_EX
=94=          warn("child has lock") if $LOG_TRAN;
=95=          my $slave = $master->accept or die "accept: $!";
=96=          warn("child releasing lock") if $LOG_TRAN;
=97=          flock($master, 8);          # LOCK_UN
=98=          my @start_times = (times, time);
```

```
=99=          $slave->autoflush(1);
=100=         warn("connect from ", $slave->peerhost) if $LOG_TRAN;
=101=         &handle_one_connection($slave); # closes $slave at right time
=102=         if ($LOG_TRAN) {
=103=           my @finish_times = (times, time);
=104=           for (@finish_times) {
=105=             $_ -= shift @start_times; # crude, but effective
=106=           }
=107=           warn(sprintf "times: %.2f %.2f %.2f %.2f %d\n", @finish_times);
=108=         }
=109=
=110=       } continue { redo if ++$did < $MAX_PER_SLAVE };
=111=       warn("child terminating") if $LOG_PROC;
=112=       exit 0;
=113=     }
=114=
=115=     sub handle_one_connection {      # return void
=116=       use HTTP::Request;
=117=       my $handle = shift;            # HTTP::Daemon::ClientConn
=118=
=119=       my $request = $handle->get_request;
=120=       defined($request) or die "bad request"; # XXX
=121=
=122=       my $response = &fetch_request($request);
=123=       warn("response: <<<\n", $response->headers_as_string, "\n>>>")
=124=         if $LOG_RES_HEAD and not $LOG_RES_BODY;
=125=       warn("response: <<<\n", $response->as_string, "\n>>>")
=126=         if $LOG_RES_BODY;
=127=       $handle->send_response($response);
=128=       close $handle;
=129=     }
=130=
=131=     sub fetch_request {                # return HTTP::Response
=132=       use HTTP::Response;
=133=       my $request = shift;            # HTTP::Request
=134=
=135=       ## XXXX needs policy here
=136=       my $url = $request->url;
=137=
=138=       if ($url->scheme !~ /^(https?|gopher|ftp)$/) {
=139=         my $res = HTTP::Response->new(403, "Forbidden");
=140=         $res->content("bad scheme: @{[$url->scheme]}\n");
=141=         $res;
=142=       } elsif (not $url->rel->netloc) {
=143=         my $res = HTTP::Response->new(403, "Forbidden");
=144=         $res->content("relative URL not permitted\n");
=145=         $res;
```

```
=146=       } else {
=147=          ## validated request, get it!
=148=          warn("processing url is $url") if $LOG_TRAN;
=149=          &fetch_validated_request($request);
=150=       }
=151=    }
=152=
=153=    BEGIN {                          # local static block
=154=      my $agent;                     # LWP::UserAgent
=155=
=156=      sub fetch_validated_request { # return HTTP::Response
=157=        my $request = shift;              # HTTP::Request
=158=
=159=        $agent ||= do {
=160=          use LWP::UserAgent;
=161=          my $agent = LWP::UserAgent->new;
=162=          $agent->agent("proxy/$VERSION " . $agent->agent);
=163=          $agent->env_proxy;
=164=          $agent;
=165=        };
=166=
=167=        warn("fetch: <<<\n", $request->headers_as_string, "\n>>>")
=168=          if $LOG_REQ_HEAD and not $LOG_REQ_BODY;
=169=        warn("fetch: <<<\n", $request->as_string, "\n>>>")
=170=          if $LOG_REQ_BODY;
=171=
=172=        my $response = $agent->simple_request($request);
=173=
=174=        if ($response->is_success and
=175=            $response->content_type =~ /text\/(plain|html)/ and
=176=            not ($response->content_encoding || "") =~ /\S/ and
=177=            ($request->header("accept-encoding") || "") =~ /gzip/) {
=178=          require Compress::Zlib;
=179=          my $content = $response->content;
=180=          my $new_content = Compress::Zlib::memGzip($content);
=181=          if (defined $new_content) {
=182=            $response->content($new_content);
=183=            $response->content_length(length $new_content);
=184=            $response->content_encoding("gzip");
=185=            warn("gzipping content from ".
=186=                 (length $content)." to ".
=187=                 (length $new_content)) if $LOG_TRAN;
=188=          }
=189=        }
=190=
=191=        $response;
=192=      }
=193=    }
```

Building an Icon Factory

Web Techniques, Column 47 (March 2000)

■**Randal's Note** The technique of caching web data via the 404-handler mechanism was relatively unknown when I wrote this column, but has now become standard fare for many large websites. If anything, ignore the part about the icons, and concentrate on the neat 404-handler concepts.

There's no doubt about it. I'll never be mistaken for a "web designer." I'm not very good at drawing things, and I tend to spend more of my energy making sure the content gets delivered in accessible ways, without making sure it's also pretty to look at.

But I was tired of people talking about my company's site at www.stonehenge.com as "great content, but it sure looks ugly." So, I consulted some designer friends of mine and came up with a new makeover. As always, it's a work in progress, but if you compare it with the old site, you'll see that I was at least open to new ideas.

A lot of the design process involved looking at variously colored rounded corners, anchoring the corners of a box made with table elements. The designer traditionally makes these corners using some graphic tool, and then laboriously uploads the file to the server along with the edited HTML to see if everything plays correctly.

But that's because most designers aren't programmers. Since *I* didn't want to go through all that work while I was dinking around, and I was already editing the HTML directly on the server, I decided to make a smart URL that *generated* the corner images as needed.

Here's the basic strategy. Let's start with a blue box with nice rounded corners and some content in the middle. We'd put something like this into an HTML page:

```
<table bgcolor=white cellspacing=0 cellpadding=0>
<tr>
    <td><img src="/icon/16x16-nw-0000ff.gif"></td>
    <td bgcolor="#0000ff"><img src="/icon/1x1.gif"></td>
    <td><img src="/icon/16x16-ne-0000ff.gif"></td>
</tr>
<tr>
    <td bgcolor="#0000ff"><img src="/icon/1x1.gif"></td>
    <td>My content goes here</td>
    <td bgcolor="#0000ff"><img src="/icon/1x1.gif"></td>
</tr>
<tr>
    <td><img src="/icon/16x16-sw-0000ff.gif"></td>
    <td bgcolor="#0000ff"><img src="/icon/1x1.gif"></td>
    <td><img src="/icon/16x16-se-0000ff.gif"></td>
</tr>
</table>
```

Now, there are a few things to note here. I have a lot of image links that look like so:

```
/icon/WIDTHxHEIGHT-DIRECTION-COLOR.gif
```

and that means what it means. I'll need to stick a corner icon GIF there, with the appropriate pixel width and height, and hex-defined color (here 0000ff, meaning 0 red, 0 green, and maximum blue). The "direction" is a two-character compass direction, where "ne" means "northeast corner." The color is the "foreground color," presuming that the background is transparent.

There are also a few cells that have an image URL like this:

```
/icon/WIDTHxHEIGHT.gif
```

and these are for those ugly 1×1 purely transparent GIFs required because some browsers refuse to display or decorate empty TD elements. Bleh. We need this to color the sides of the box, using a table element with a controlled background color and no content except for the transparent GIF. The nice thing about this approach is that it is entirely flexible and depends only on the size of the contents.

Now for the tricky part: making those GIFs. Well, not really. You see, in the directory served for the URL /icon, I have the following .htaccess file (this is Apache with mod_perl, of course):

```
ErrorDocument 404 /perl/makeicon
```

Now, what does that mean, when someone asks for /icon/1x1.gif? Well, if there was nothing else in that directory, we normally would have gotten a 404 error directly to the browser. But the ErrorDocument directive says to handle that 404 error via an "internal redirect" to the new URL.

In this case, I have a Perl program that runs under mod_perl at that URL. The directory of /perl is set to be handled by Apache::Registry, which allows CGI-like programs to be embedded directly into the server as needed. In my /perl directory, I have this .htaccess file:

```
SetHandler perl-script
PerlHandler Apache::Registry
PerlSendHeader On
Options +ExecCGI
```

which causes a URL referencing into the directory to trigger all the Apache::Registry magic.

But now for the cool part. This /perl/makeicon program looks at the filename that wasn't found, computes the GIF needed to satisfy the specifications, then both returns that GIF *and* saves it into the /icon directory with the right name! That means that any later hit with the same URL will simply be treated as a normal fetch. Like magic, it's a self-building icon repository. So the only overhead is on the very first hit when the icon isn't found.

The program is presented here in Listing 5-19.

Line 1 begins with the path to my installed Perl. This isn't needed for an Apache::Registry script, but it helps GNU Emacs figure out that I want to go into Perl editing mode.

Lines 2 and 3 turn on compiler restrictions and turn off output buffering, common for scripts like this.

Lines 5 through 9 set up a die handler. Throughout the rest of the code, I use a die to declare that something is wrong. Most usage errors should simply result in the server returning a normal 404 error, but for unexpected things, I'll want a log entry made into the Apache error log. Thus, I use die 404 in various places where I simply want to return a 404. Any other death message (that doesn't contain a literal 404 somewhere) will be logged via the warn operator, but still yield a 404 status return to the web client.

Line 12 gets the `Apache::Request` object for the failed request. The parameter extracted with `shift` is the object for *this* request, but we want the *previous* request to find out what GIF was requested; hence the call to both `shift` and `prev`.

Lines 18 and 19 extract the Unix `$filename` of the requested URL. That is, if there'd been a file there, we wouldn't see the invocation as a 404 handler. And then we get the directory and the filename within that directory into `$dir` and `$base`, respectively.

Lines 22 through 24 extract the specification for this icon from the filename. It must end in `.gif`, and have a height and width. In addition, a color may be specified as six hex characters, making up the red, green, and blue values defined in hex pairs. If the color is absent, a completely transparent GIF of the requested size is made instead.

And then the style can be added, to define a corner. If the style is absent, we get a rectangle of the requested color. The style is one of the four compass corners, and it may be followed by an optional i to indicate inverse (or inside, I can't recall which). Thus, a style of `nw` generates a northwest outer corner of color-on-transparent, while `sei` generates a southeast inner corner of transparent-on-color.

If any part of the filename is unexpected, we punt and generate a 404 error. Similarly, line 27 detects preposterous GIF sizes and punts as well.

Line 30 brings in the (old) GD library, formerly found in the CPAN. If you didn't grab and install the one that can generate GIFs, you're out of luck now. It's no longer there, having been replaced by a legally safer one that makes only PNGs. I don't know whether to be more mad at Unisys (which is enforcing the patent that makes GIFs a licensed commodity), CompuServe (which created a popular file format that used patented processes), the U.S. Patent and Trademark Office (which permits software patents), or the big browser makers (for not having good PNG support in existing browsers). But in any event, I'm still running the GIF-making GD so that this works. Just don't tell Unisys.

Line 31 makes a blank image of the right size as an object. Again, if anything breaks, we just punt to 404 and hope that someone is watching the error log.

Lines 32 and 33 make the transparent color. It has to be a defined color, and I pick a slightly off-gray in hopes that no designer will ever want to use precisely this ugly color (because that would break everything else). If I were really paranoid, I would watch for color selections of `7e7f80` above, but I don't care enough to add that. Also, as the first color allocated, it's automatically the background for the rest of the image.

At this point, we have a completely transparent GIF of the right size, but if any color is defined, lines 35 to 51 kick in to finish the job.

Line 36 transfers the hex color specification into a real color object, saved in `$ink`. We'll use this to make a solid color, or the corner, as needed.

Lines 38 to 47 handle a rounded-corner GIF, by picking the correct center point for an oval and then painting it. I thought I would need to get clever and decide how much of each oval to draw, but as it turns out, GD does the right thing anyway, even when I'm apparently drawing "outside" the GIF. Lines 42 to 45 handle the "invert" corners by first filling the entire GIF with the requested color, and then selecting the transparent color as the ink.

Once we've finished inking the GIF, line 55 creates the actual `GIF89a` image into a string. This string now needs to go two places: out to the browser and into the file (for the next hit).

Lines 58 to 66 create the icon file. The `Apache::File` module is like `IO::File` with a lot less overhead, and it creates a scoped filehandle. We save the GIF information into a file that is near to the final location, but named uniquely. That way, the final step is a rename operation that happens "atomically," in a way that no process can ever see a partially written GIF.

Now, in order for this to work, the $dir directory must be writable by the Apache process. I set mine to permissions of 777, and that works just fine. If that isn't done, the file isn't created, although we would still dump out the GIF to the web client.

Speaking of that, lines 68 to 70 dump out the computed GIF. And we're done!

Even if you aren't using mod_perl, you can still set up an Apache error handler to trigger a CGI program that does much of what I've done here. You'll need to look at the environment variables beginning with REDIRECT_... in the CGI program to know what GIF was requested; that's a bit simpler with the mod_perl interface, as you have seen. Also, you can't use Apache::File, but changing that to IO::File would work nearly identically.

You'll probably want to purge old unused icons, so a cron job that comes along once a night purging any icons that haven't been accessed in a week or so might just do the trick. It's safe to delete too much, because even if we accidentally deleted every GIF at once, the next hit would simply trigger the 404 handler to re-create them once again!

I hope this technique inspires you to think of 404 handlers as something more than just a fancy way of saying "We don't have this." Until next month, enjoy!

Listing 5-19

```
=1=     #!/usr/bin/perl
=2=     use strict;
=3=     $|++;
=4=
=5=     $SIG{__DIE__} = sub {
=6=       my $arg = shift;
=7=       warn "makeicon died with $arg" unless $arg =~ /404/;
=8=       print "Status: 404\n\n";
=9=     };
=10=
=11=    ## we are a 404 handler, so we need to get the request⤸
                that triggered the 404:
=12=    my $r = shift->prev;
=13=
=14=    ## if the request was for a subdirectory or had args, bad news:
=15=    die 404 if not $r or $r->args or $r->path_info;
=16=
=17=    ## now extract the expected filename, which we'll need to generate:
=18=    my $filename = $r->filename;
=19=    my ($dir,$base) = $filename =~ m{(.*)/(.*)}s;
=20=
=21=    ## and ensure that it's a gif that we want to make:
=22=    my ($height, $width, $style, $color) =
=23=      $base =~ m{^(\d+)x(\d+)(?:-(?:([ns][ew]i?)?-)?([0-9a-fA-F]{6})?)?\.gif$}
=24=      or die 404;
=25=
=26=    ## don't let people burn my CPU
```

```
=27=    die 404 if $height * $width > 2000 or $height * $width < 1;
=28=
=29=    ## Time to make the gif:
=30=    require GD;
=31=    my $im = GD::Image->new($width,$height) or die 404;
=32=    my $grey = $im->colorAllocate(126,127,128); # I hope we don't collide
=33=    $im->transparent($grey);
=34=
=35=    if (defined $color) {           # if no color, make transparent spacer gif
=36=      my $ink = $im->colorAllocate(unpack "C*", pack "H*", $color);
=37=
=38=      if (defined $style) {         # it's a corner arc
=39=        my $center_x = $style =~ /^.e/i ? 0 : $width-1;
=40=        my $center_y = $style =~ /^s/i ? 0 : $height-1;
=41=
=42=        if ($style =~ /^..i/) {     # invert
=43=          $im->fill(0,0,$ink);
=44=          $ink = $grey;
=45=        }
=46=        $im->arc($center_x,$center_y,$width*2,$height*2, 0, 360, $ink);
=47=        $im->fill($center_x,$center_y,$ink);
=48=      } else {                      # it's a rectangle
=49=        $im->fill(0,0,$ink);
=50=      }
=51=    }
=52=
=53=    ## good job! time to write it out:
=54=
=55=    my $gif = $im->gif;
=56=
=57=    ## if this fails, we just generate dynamically each time, no biggy
=58=    require Apache::File;
=59=    my $tmpname = "$dir/.$$.$base";
=60=    if (my $tmp = Apache::File->new(">$tmpname")) {
=61=      print $tmp $gif;
=62=      close $tmp;
=63=      rename $tmpname, $filename or warn "cannot rename $tmpname ⏎
                to $filename: $!";
=64=    } else {
=65=      warn "couldn't create $tmpname: $!";
=66=    }
=67=
=68=    print "Status: 200\nContent-type: image/gif\n\n";
=69=    print $gif;
=70=    exit 0;
```

Basic Cookie Management

Web Techniques, Column 61 (May 2001)

■**Randal's Note**   This is probably my most frequently referenced column whenever the subject of cookies comes up. In a few lines of code, I show how to safely "brand" a browser, check for cookie acceptance, and deal with timeouts. I still haven't seen any writing since then that explains the subject with this kind of direct clarity. I also wish this particular chunk of code were available in a CPAN module. Ahh, another thing for the ever-increasing to-do list.

Ahh, cookies. One of my pet peeves is the amount of bad cookie code I see out there, including the reaction that a website gives me when I choose not to permit cookies (usually because I'm feeling rebellious).

Cookies are one of many ways to turn the stateless HTTP into a stateful session-based series of transactions. (Some of the others include using some sort of authentication, or mangling the URLs, or including hidden data in forms.) But cookies get my ire up because many web programmers presume that "one user is one browser," because that's the basic model of the cookie itself as well. That's demonstrably completely untrue. I myself have three different browsers open at the moment, and I have been known to go into an internet cafe from time to time to use the browsers supplied there. While I personally move from one browser to another, my cookies don't follow me!

The *wrong* way to use cookies, therefore, is to have a login form, and on successful login, send out a cookie that lasts until the year 2010 to that browser. That's bad. I can't log in on another browser, and if I forget to log out of a browser at an internet cafe, the next user who stumbles across the same website is (gasp!) already logged in as me!

Another wrong way to use cookies is to send out a bunch of data in a cookie, like the entire contents of the shopping cart. I say "wrong" because most people who do this seem to trust the data as it's being returned on the next hit, and nothing stops me from changing the price of that $300 item I just bought to $1 instead, if it's all coming from the cookie.

Still another wrong way to use cookies is to send dozens of cookies, like one for each graphic. Goodness knows, I've been to some sites and had to accept a baker's dozen of cookies before I even see the entire page.

And yet another wrong way is to let the cookie's expiration time serve as the security policy for timing out an active user. A browser does *not* have to respect any expiration times. Do not count on that.

And even worse, sometimes I've seen servers go into infinite loops checking for cookies to be set, and redirecting if the cookie is not set, never telling the user why things are awry.

Can you tell I've seen a lot of bad cookie code? Do you now understand why the hairs generally stand on the back of my neck when someone mentions, "I need cookies for this application"? Well, then read on.

There *is* a reasonably safe way to use cookies. Use cookies only to brand a particular browser, and only for the duration of a browser session. The cookie should be a single small cookie with a short but unguessable value (such as the MD5 hash of some cryptographically strong material). Then, this particular "branded" browser will be sending back this cookie only while it is currently open.

Next, take the brand-mark and use it to key into a database to look up a particular user for that branded browser. The database should have a timestamp of recent activity and be distrusted after the timeout period.

Finally, use the verified user value to key into *another* database for session information, like a shopping cart or personal preferences. Don't use the browser-brand value for anything other than a one-step mapping to a user, because otherwise the user cannot migrate her session over to a new browser without restarting some of the transaction, and that's annoying. (In fact, you should probably permit the same user to log in on multiple browsers simultaneously.)

Sounds hard? Nah. It's just a few dozen lines of Perl code. How do I know? I hacked it out just recently. And I present this sample reference implementation of this strategy in Listing 5-20. Please keep in mind that this is not a complete application—just the part that handles the "What user is logged into this browser?" question.

Lines 1 through 3 start nearly every program I write, turning on taint mode (good for CGI programs), warnings (good for catching stupid mistakes), and compiler restrictions (good for catching more stupid mistakes), and disabling buffering on STDOUT (good for CGI programs).

Line 5 pulls in the veritable CGI.pm module, including all the function shortcuts.

Lines 7 to 29 handle the "branding" of a particular browser with a unique cookie. Keep in mind that this has to be done before we've sent *anything* to standard output, because we may need to issue a new Set-Cookie header or perhaps a redirect to ourselves as a cookie test.

Line 8 fetches the $browser cookie, if any. If present, $browser is now a unique string (actually, an MD5 signature of some unique data). However, if it's absent, we've got some work to do to make this browser our own.

Lines 9 and 10 recognize the common case, after this program has been invoked once, namely that we've got a good browser ID. The _cookiecheck parameter is described later, but we must make sure it's out of the mix for later code.

If we had no cookie in line 9, then we have two possibilities: either the cookie had never been sent or the browser refused to send it back. In either case, we first prepare a potential new cookie using lines 12 though 15. The MD5 module (found in the CPAN) allows us to create a 32-character hex string from a given arbitrary data item. In this case, we're using the time of day, a random number, the process ID, and the stringified hashref of a newly created throwaway hash, simply as icky glue.

This is not as secure as using cryptographically strong items; there are modules in the CPAN to make it harder to guess. However, this code *was* lifted directly from Apache::Session, a well-known chunk of code to handle session management, so I feel confident knowing I can at least blame someone else.

Line 17 distinguishes if this is a first invocation rather than an invocation where we've had at least one chance to set a cookie (and was therefore refused). If _cookiecheck is defined, we've had at least one try to get it right, so we dump out an HTML page (lines 19 to 23) stating our demands. We also try setting a cookie one more time; maybe users will get tired of saying "reject this cookie," or maybe they just didn't like that particular hex string (who knows?).

The form submission in line 22 will cause us to come back to the same page, but with _cookiecheck possibly still set. (If not, then we'll get two hits to get back to here again, just as when we started.)

If this is the first visit, then _cookiecheck will not be set, so we set it in line 25 and do an external redirect to ourselves to verify the cookie is indeed present.

By the time we hit line 30, we've now branded the browser with a unique cookie identification, and that's in $browser.

The next step is to determine if this browser is "logged in" or not. We'll keep track of that with a lightweight database, made possible with the File::Cache module from the CPAN. (Late-breaking news: the author of this module has started to generalize the caching structure into a separate Cache::Cache module, so by the time you read this, things might work differently, so beware.)

Line 34 "opens" the cache by creating a cache object in $cache. We'll set the cache items to expire within an hour, meaning that no user can be logged in for longer than one hour of inactivity. You might permit this to be longer or shorter (longer for low-risk items, shorter for high-risk items), but one hour is a good starting point.

Lines 41 to 44 handle a small housekeeping chore for the cache. If a user doesn't come back but hasn't logged out, her cached user ID still exists as a file in the database directory (until the next time it is fetched). But it most likely won't be fetched, since that cookie will also expire when the browser is closed, so we've got a dead file sitting around. Every four hours, the _purge_ entry will expire, so we'll let the first lucky user who happens to invoke this program right after that go through the cleanup process. This should be very lightweight; if you're concerned about doing this at CGI time, you could instead pull this out to a separate cron job (but be sure the job runs as the web user, not as you).

Line 46 pulls out the user associated with this browser, if any. If there's an entry in the cache, but it's older than an hour, the entry is deleted, and we get back undef, the same as if the entry doesn't exist. So if there *is* a defined value here, it's current, and the user is logged in as $user. Otherwise, there's no user associated with the browser uniquely identified with $browser.

Lines 50 to 66 handle the transitions between logged in and logged out. If the user is logged in and has requested a logout, lines 52 to 55 handle that. The parameter requesting logout is deleted (for sticky forms), and the user is removed from the cache database. $user is also undefined to reflect this for the rest of the program.

Lines 57 to 65 handle logging in. First, the requested username and password are read. Next, the username is checked for well-formedness (which I've arbitrarily defined here as "looks like a Perl identifier"), and then we verify the correct password for this user by calling verify. I've defined a simple version for this down at the bottom of the program in lines 98 to 101 that simply returns true if the username is a substring of the password. Please don't use this in real life—this is just a demo. If the password's good, $user gets set; otherwise, we reject the attempt.

Lines 68 to 83 handle the actions useful within the current state.

For logged-in users, we'll do a couple of things. Each time a logged-in user returns to the page, we update the cache time in line 70, to permit her to stay logged in for another hour from now. Line 72 displays a simple "log out" form button, which re-invokes this same program including a _logout parameter. Recall that this parameter was being tested up in line 51.

For logged-out users, lines 74 to 82 display that status and present a simple login form with a submit button, using a table for layout. Please don't fault my lack of HTML design skills: I'm illustrating structure here, not my graphics aptitude, which I admit is sorely lacking.

The code from line 85 on would be where your real application goes, using the code above as a framework. The rest of the application could count on $user to be the name of an authenticated user logged into the browser of choice and active within the past hour. As a sample do-nothing application, I thought I'd leave in my testing code that I used while developing this program to see what the current cookies and parameters contained.

Lines 87 to 94 execute a loop twice: once with $title set to Cookies and a $f set to the coderef for the cookie function (provided by CGI.pm), and a second time with Params and the param function instead. I had originally written this as two separate displays, but then writhed a bit at the similarity of the code, which I then factored out and parameterized. Thank goodness for coderefs.

Line 90 prints the second-level header for the title, then follows it with a table containing the cookie or parameter keys in the first column, followed by their value in the second column. Because both cookies and parameters can be multivalued, I've added code to join multiple values by commas (line 92). Also, since both the keys and values can contain HTML-significant markup (less-thans, greater-thans, ampersands, and so on), I pass the data through escapeHTML (provided by CGI.pm) before display.

Note that line 93 invokes the function (either cookie or param) with no arguments to get a list of all things of that type, while the end of line 92 invokes that same function, passing it one item of that type to get its value. It's very nice that they have that same interface.

Lines 98 to 101 were described earlier, but this is also a part of the program you'd definitely want to rewrite for a real application.

So, in summary, cookies can be reasonable for session management, as long as the logged-in state is clear, a logout button is clearly visible, the cookie expires when the browser is closed, and the session expires after an inactivity timeout value (typically an hour) is reached. Have fun handing out cookies, and don't forget the milk. Until next time, enjoy!

Listing 5-20

```
=1=     #!/usr/bin/perl -Tw
=2=     use strict;
=3=     $|++;
=4=
=5=     use CGI qw(:all);
=6=
=7=     ## cookie check
=8=     my $browser = cookie("browser");
=9=     if (defined $browser) {        # got a good browser
=10=      Delete("_cookiecheck");      # don't let this leak further
=11=    } else {                       # no cookie? set one
=12=      require MD5;
=13=      my $cookie = cookie
=14=        (-name => 'browser',
=15=         -value => MD5->hexhash(MD5->hexhash(time.{}.rand().$$)));
=16=
=17=      if (defined param("_cookiecheck")) { # already tried!
=18=        print +(header(-cookie => $cookie),
=19=               start_html("Missing cookies"),
=20=               h1("Missing cookies"),
=21=               p("This site requires a cookie to be set. Please permit this."),
```

```
=22=                    startform, submit("OK"), endform,
=23=                    end_html);
=24=        } else {
=25=          param("_cookiecheck", 1);   # prevent infinite loop
=26=          print redirect (-cookie => $cookie, -uri => self_url());
=27=        }
=28=        exit 0;
=29=      }
=30=
=31=      ## At this point, $browser is now the unique ID of the browser
=32=
=33=      require File::Cache;
=34=      my $cache = File::Cache->new({namespace => 'cookiemaker',
=35=                                    username => 'nobody',
=36=                                    filemode => 0666,
=37=                                    expires_in => 3600, # one hour
=38=                                    });
=39=
=40=      ## first, some housekeeping
=41=      unless ($cache->get(" _purge_ ")) {
=42=        $cache->purge;                  # remove expired objects
=43=        $cache->set(" _purge_ ", 1, 3600 * 4); # purge every four hours
=44=      }
=45=
=46=      my $user = $cache->get($browser); ## either the logged-in user, or undef
=47=
=48=      print header,start_html('session demonstration'),h1↵
=48=            ('session demonstration');
=49=
=50=      ## handle requested transitions (login or logout)
=51=      if (defined $user and defined param("_logout")) {
=52=        Delete("_logout");
=53=        $cache->remove($browser);
=54=        print p("You are no longer logged in as $user.");
=55=        undef $user;
=56=      } elsif (not defined $user and defined (my $try_user = param("_user"))) {
=57=        Delete("_user");
=58=        my $try_password = param("_password");
=59=        Delete("_password");
=60=        if ($try_user =~ /\A\w+\z/ and verify($try_user, $try_password)) {
=61=          $user = $try_user;
=62=          print p("Welcome back, $user.");
=63=        } else {
=64=          print p("I'm sorry, that's not right.");
=65=        }
=66=      }
=67=
```

```
=68=    ## handle current state (possibly after transition)
=69=    if (defined $user) {
=70=      $cache->set($browser,$user);  # update cache on each hit
=71=      print p("You are logged in as $user.");
=72=      print startform, hidden("_logout", 1), submit("Log out"), endform;
=73=    } else {
=74=      print p("You are not logged in.");
=75=      print
=76=        startform,
=77=          table({-border => 1, -cellspacing => 0, -cellpadding => 2},
=78=              Tr(th("username:"),
=79=                 td(textfield("_user")),
=80=                 td({-rowspan => 2}, submit("login"))),
=81=              Tr(th("password:"), td(password_field("_password})))),
=82=              endform;
=83=    }
=84=
=85=    ## rest of page would go here, paying attention to $user
=86=
=87=    for ([Cookies => \&cookie], [Params => \&param]) {
=88=      my ($title, $f) = @$_;
=89=
=90=      print h2($title), table
=91=        ({-border => 0, -cellspacing => 0, -cellpadding => 2},
=92=          map (Tr(th(escapeHTML($_)), td(escapeHTML(join ", ", $f->($_)))),
=93=            $f->()));
=94=    }
=95=
=96=    ## sample verification
=97=
=98=    sub verify {
=99=      my($user, $password) = @_;
=100=     return index($password, $user) > -1; # require password to contain user
=101=   }
```

Index

forums.apress.com

JOIN THE APRESS FORUMS AND BE PART OF OUR COMMUNITY. You'll find discussions that cover topics of interest to IT professionals, programmers, and enthusiasts just like you. If you post a query to one of our forums, you can expect that some of the best minds in the business—especially Apress authors, who all write with *The Expert's Voice*™—will chime in to help you. Why not aim to become one of our most valuable participants (MVPs) and win cool stuff? Here's a sampling of what you'll find:

DATABASES
Data drives everything.

Share information, exchange ideas, and discuss any database programming or administration issues.

INTERNET TECHNOLOGIES AND NETWORKING
Try living without plumbing (and eventually IPv6).

Talk about networking topics including protocols, design, administration, wireless, wired, storage, backup, certifications, trends, and new technologies.

JAVA
We've come a long way from the old Oak tree.

Hang out and discuss Java in whatever flavor you choose: J2SE, J2EE, J2ME, Jakarta, and so on.

MAC OS X
All about the Zen of OS X.

OS X is both the present and the future for Mac apps. Make suggestions, offer up ideas, or boast about your new hardware.

OPEN SOURCE
Source code is good; understanding (open) source is better.

Discuss open source technologies and related topics such as PHP, MySQL, Linux, Perl, Apache, Python, and more.

PROGRAMMING/BUSINESS
Unfortunately, it is.

Talk about the Apress line of books that cover software methodology, best practices, and how programmers interact with the "suits."

WEB DEVELOPMENT/DESIGN
Ugly doesn't cut it anymore, and CGI is absurd.

Help is in sight for your site. Find design solutions for your projects and get ideas for building an interactive Web site.

SECURITY
Lots of bad guys out there—the good guys need help.

Discuss computer and network security issues here. Just don't let anyone else know the answers!

TECHNOLOGY IN ACTION
Cool things. Fun things.

It's after hours. It's time to play. Whether you're into LEGO® MINDSTORMS™ or turning an old PC into a DVR, this is where technology turns into fun.

WINDOWS
No defenestration here.

Ask questions about all aspects of Windows programming, get help on Microsoft technologies covered in Apress books, or provide feedback on any Apress Windows book.

HOW TO PARTICIPATE:
Go to the Apress Forums site at **http://forums.apress.com/**.
Click the New User link.